UNDERSTANDING PROGRAMMING

An Introduction Using C++

SECOND EDITION

Scott R. Cannon

Utah State University

BROOKS/COLE

THOMSON LEARNING™

Australia • Canada • Mexico • Singapore • Spain • United Kingdom • United States

BROOKS/COLE

THOMSON LEARNING

Acquiring Editor: *Kallie Swanson*
Marketing Team: *Christopher Kelly,*
 Samantha Cabaluna
Assistant Editor: *Grace Fujimoto*
Production Coordinator: *Kelsey McGee*
Production Service: *Matrix Productions/*
 Merrill Peterson
Manuscript Editor: *Frank Hubert*

Permissions Editor: *Sue Ewing*
Interior Design: *John Edeen*
Cover Design: *Roger Knox*
Print Buyer: *Jessica Reed*
Typesetting: *Carlisle Communications, Ltd.*
Cover Printing, Printing and Binding:
 Webcom, Ltd.

For more information about this or any other Brooks/Cole products, contact:
BROOKS/COLE
511 Forest Lodge Road
Pacific Grove, CA 93950 USA
www.brookscole.com
1-800-423-0563 (Thomson Learning Academic Resource Center)

Printed in Canada

10   9   8   7   6   5   4   3   2   1

Library of Congress Cataloging-in-Publication Data

Cannon, Scott R., (date)
  Understanding programming: an introduction using C++/Scott R. Cannon—2nd ed.
    p.   cm.
  ISBN 0 534-37975-3
  1.C++ (Computer program language) 2. Computer programming. I Title

QA76.73.C153 C35 2001   00-044458
005.13'3—dc21

Contents

Chapter 11   String Processing 256

Chapter 12   Designing with Simple Classes and Structures 272

Preface

To the Instructor

In every class, there will be students who find programming natural and intuitive. An instructor must be careful not to teach only these students. All students need and appreciate a text with a good teaching approach.

Understanding Programming: An Introduction Using C++, Second Edition, is not intended to be a definitive manual on C++. It is focused on teaching and uses two principles. First, students learn best when they first see and appreciate an immediate need. Second, students learn best by *doing* and *experiencing*.

This text attempts to get students writing meaningful programs as early as possible. In practice, students don't really begin to appreciate programming as a useful problem-solving tool until they see loops and conditions. The first few chapters take a breadth-first approach. Students are first taught *one* way to do I/O, *one* variable type, *one* way to do a condition, and *one* loop statement, and they quickly begin coding useful and interesting programs with this subset of C++. There is no need to teach all there is to know about one concept before introducing the next—it just delays meaningful experience. Later, after the student has some experience and understands the kinds of useful applications that can be addressed, the text returns to other loop variations, other condition statements, compound Boolean expressions, other data types, and so on. The breadth-first approach allows the text to postpone detail issues, such as nested combinations of `if` and `if-else` statements, mixed mode expressions, automatic casting, truncation, and so forth until after students have been given a solid start. Accordingly, *the text tries to avoid teaching mechanisms and concepts that allow errors students are not yet ready to understand.*

As you can see, the breadth-first approach is *spiral* in nature. A concept or method is first introduced in simplified form. Gradually, as the need for more capability is demonstrated, the primitive form is expanded upon until the full concept is presented. This also means that the text may be spiraling in on several topics at the same time. For example, simplified conditions, simplified loops, and functions are presented before returning to more detail on conditions. The purpose is simple—get students writing meaningful programs as soon as possible. Experience then leads to motivation and understanding when more detail is presented.

Chapters are actually *teaching* units, not *topic* units. You will not find all there is to learn about a particular topic in one chapter. While that may be ideal for a reference manual, it is not always appropriate for a teaching text. Students may not be ready to appreciate or may not even need the whole topic.

If you attempt to compare this text with other traditional approaches, you may find that a chapter-by-chapter relationship is not particularly valid. For example, you may easily identify the chapter that covers loops in another text, but looping concepts and syntax are presented here over several chapters. Although there is a chapter covering program design and problem solving, additional material on these concepts is also spread over the entire book. Methods of style, documentation, and software engineering are also presented throughout the text as the complexity of programs expands and the student is more capable of appreciating the need in larger software projects. In general, concepts attempt to build upon needs demonstrated in previous examples and assignments.

Some of the more advanced topics in C++ are presented in an introductory way, preparing students for future classes in which these topics will be studied in more detail. Some advanced topics are not even broached—too much syntax and feature study tends to weaken a good foundation.

A word of caution to instructors transitioning from C: C++ is taught here as a separate language and not just as an extension to C. You may be surprised to see that the type `int` isn't introduced for several chapters. C++ provides *internal float rounding* and allows the early use of a single data type `float` for simple loop counters and condition tests *without a significant concern for truncation errors* or other technical problems that might be found in C. It might give a C programmer heartburn to see a `float` variable used as a loop counter, but using a `float` this way is quite practical in early C++ programs. Why not just start with `int`? Once again, *my goal is to get students into programs with calculations, conditions and loops, and functions as soon as possible*. Starting with `int` would delay formula implementation. Teaching the often-confusing concepts of truncation and mixed mode expressions would take longer. The text naturally spirals back to types, mixed mode expressions, and automatic casting. That is not very traditional, but students get into meaningful programs quicker than would be otherwise possible. Later chapters explain internal representations and the trade-off between different data types.

GUI programming

Students often are a bit confused in an introductory computer course because they don't see many console programs similar to what they are writing. A simple introduction to Microsoft® Windows programming is provided in Appendix C for the commonly used Microsoft® Visual C++ 6.x system. *This discussion is careful not to swamp the student with a very complex topic*. Rather, using wizards and a couple of simple controls, students are shown how to implement a set of simple dialog graphical user interfaces (GUIs). My students have more fun with this interesting and relevant topic than with anything else. I have found this simplistic approach well within the reach of beginning students.

Strings

String variables are important. Using arrays of `char` for strings significantly postpones the use of strings until the student understands arrays and pointers. Otherwise, students will often make pointer and semantic errors that they are not ready to understand. C++ `string` variables, on the other hand, are very intuitive to students who have learned other variable types. Unfortunately, `string` variable standards are actually somewhat recent: not every teaching lab has the latest system. While most C++ systems have one or more string types, headers, implementations, and methods vary. This text teaches both `char` array and `string` approaches and leaves the decision up to the instructor. Use either approach—or both.

Second edition

This second edition is not only updated but is significantly revised from the first edition. A specific chapter on problem solving and design techniques has been added. The use of functions has been spread over more chapters. Exercises and questions at chapter ends have been expanded. Material that is traditionally considered optional in an introductory course is presented in the form of appendixes. The second edition has been updated to provide students help with current Windows 95/98/00/NT systems and Microsoft Visual C++ 6.x.

A few pedagogical features

 You'll see this icon when an incorrect approach is demonstrated.

 This icon lets you know that a program or code fragment contains an error.

- **Syntax Boxes** Syntax is presented with model forms, which are more rules of thumb than rules. This supports the spiral method of teaching. When additional syntax is presented for a construct or topic, it does not need to replace or contradict the simpler forms given earlier.
- **Examples** Few students are patient enough to wade through the study of a long and involved example. Examples are paramount, however, since few students think abstractly enough to solve new problems simply by learning rules. I have tried to provide many example programs and code segments that are straightforward and to the point.

- **Learning by Experimentation** Some exercises require experimentation and creativity. Each chapter includes a few Experiment boxes containing suggestions for simple "what if" experiments to teach an important topic. These assignments encourage trial and experimentation.

- **Creative Challenge** Each chapter includes a few problems that may not have a simple or complete solution that can be implemented using what the student has been taught to that point. The purpose is to demonstrate the need for upcoming topics and to encourage self-study. They also encourage innovation and creative thinking.

To the Student

The goal of *Understanding Programming: An Introduction Using C++* is to help you begin writing meaningful and useful programs as early as possible. As a result, the simplified models and mechanisms presented in a chapter may not completely express all the capabilities of the C++ language associated with the feature being described. They will, however, express enough of the capability of the language to significantly add to your ability to solve more and more complex and useful programs. These simplified models are gradually expanded with more detail and capability as you progress.

Program examples are simple—complete when necessary, but otherwise only code fragments. Execution diagrams showing how variables would change during execution accompany important examples. Examples of common programming mistakes and errors are marked with a road sign containing a bug figure or a Wrong Way! message.

Paragraphs that contain helpful hints, important concepts, or rules of thumb are marked with a Concept margin note. Important vocabulary terms are italicized within the text and marked with a Key Term margin note. Each chapter also includes shaded boxes containing "what if" experiments that ask you to try different tests with programs and just see what happens! The idea is that you need to learn by personal experiences as well as by study.

Each chapter has a selection of assignment projects that utilize the tools learned from the chapter. Some of these assignments also demonstrate the need for tools to be learned in the next chapter. At least one Creative Challenge problem is posed at the end of each chapter. These problems may not have a simple solution using what you have learned by that point. They can usually be solved with some *creative* or *innovative* application of previously learned tools. Some may not have complete solutions at that point in your skills. In these cases, you will need to solve as much of the problem as you can and specify or describe the limitations of your solution. The purpose of these special problems is to help you understand and appreciate the need for the tools and skills you will learn in the next chapter!

The C++ language was chosen for a number of good reasons. For one, it is a practical and commonly used language that will support you through the rest of your degree study and into the commercial world. It is also a powerful language that allows you to begin writing meaningful programs quickly without the need to first learn difficult topics. In addition, the C++ language supports models and methods that are very important to the development of large, complex software systems, which are becoming more and more common in the world.

Good luck! You will find that computer science is both challenging and a lot of fun.

Web Access

Brooks/Cole provides a Web site for this text. This site contains download files for all executable programs, notes on errata, and other useful material. To access this site, begin with the Brooks/Cole home page, www.brookscole.com.

Acknowledgments

This second edition of *Understanding Programming: An Introduction Using C++* represents not only the work of the author, but also the efforts and contributions of a number of people to whom I owe thanks, most especially Kallie Swanson, computer science editor at Brooks/Cole Publishing Company.

My thanks also to production editor Merrill Peterson of Matrix Productions, copy editor Frank Hubert, and Bev Kraus of Carlisle Communications for their contributions toward making this edition a reality.

The development of this text has greatly benefited from the contributions of numerous reviewers who offered their various perspectives. I thank each of them for their ideas and suggestions.

Anthony Aaby, *Walla Walla College*

Thomas J. Ahlborn, *West Chester University*

Bonnie Bailey, *Morehead State University*

Sara Baase, *San Diego State University*

Julius Brandstatter, *San Francisco State University*

Dale Bryson, *Umpqua Community College*

George Converse, *Southern Oregon State College*

Yonina Cooper, *University of Nevada–Las Vegas*

Mary Courtney, *Pace University*

Chuck Dierbach, *Towson State University*

H. E. Dunsmore, *Purdue University*

Larry Egbert, *Utah State University*

Rhonda Ficek, *Minnesota State University Moorhead*

Roy Fuller, *University of Arkansas*

David Herscovici, *St. Mary's College of California*

Michael Johnson, *Oregon State University*

Hang Lau, *Concordia University*

Allen Miller, *College of San Mateo*

William C. Muellner, *Elmhurst College*

Ann Marie Pagnotta, *Nassau Community College*

Brenda Parker, *Middle Tennessee State University*

Mark Pavicic, *North Dakota State University*

Lucasz Pruski, *University of San Diego*

William Root, *San Diego State University*

Sue Sampson, *Bellevue University*

Dieter Schmidt, *University of Cincinnati*

Martha Tilman, *College of San Mateo*

Richard Weinand, *Wayne State University*

Scott R. Cannon

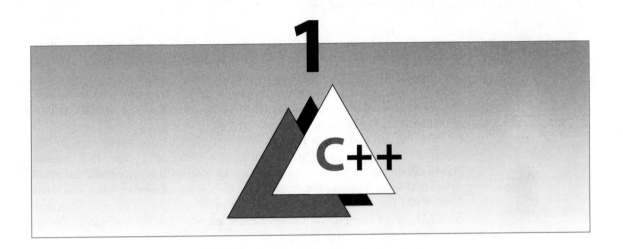

Your First C++ Program

This chapter presents the fundamentals of creating your first simple program in the C++ language. This includes a simple introduction to high-level languages, program variables, and declarations. In addition, you will learn how to do simple program input, calculations, and output. By the end of the chapter, you should be able to write and run complete C++ programs to do such tasks as calculate the area of a circle.

1.1 Programming with high-level languages

KEY TERM
central processing unit

Prior to writing your first program, let's take a quick look at what a computer actually is and what it is capable of doing. While there are many variations and types of computers, we will take as our model the personal computer (PC) that can be found in so many homes and schools (Figure 1.1). The PC in your school laboratory or home consists of six basic parts: the *central processing unit* (CPU), memory, auxiliary memory, a keyboard and mouse input device, a monitor output or display device, and perhaps a printer.

KEY TERM
volatile

Memory is used to hold two types of information: programs and data. A program is just a sequence of instructions. The keyboard is used under the control of the processor to input or place these two types of information into the computer memory. The processor is then able to read a program and data from this memory

1

and use them to produce useful results. Now, you might ask what the disk drive is! A disk is just another type of memory. Memory is classified into two simple categories: memory that loses contents stored when the power is turned off (*volatile memory*) and memory that retains values when power is removed (*nonvolatile* memory). Internal memory can be made of both volatile and nonvolatile sections; disk memory is nonvolatile.

The internal nonvolatile memory of a computer is usually read-only. In other words, it has been factory set to hold certain data. Often, this is called ROM memory (read-only memory). Those sections of internal memory that are volatile are usually called RAM (random-access memory). (Maybe a more appropriate name would have been WRM for write/read memory, but perhaps that makes a more difficult acronym.) There are some newer forms of RAM memory that are also nonvolatile, but they are not often found in PCs.

Disks are particularly useful since the internal volatile memory of a computer is erased or lost when the power is turned off. Data and programs saved on a disk remain and are available when the computer is again started up. Obviously, the monitor is used to display information from the memory, as is the printer, and thus they are output devices. A CD-ROM is a type of disk which is generally only written to once but later read many times.

KEY TERMS
assembly
instruction,
machine
language

All processing done by the PC is handled or controlled by the CPU. Unfortunately, CPUs are actually not able to perform very sophisticated operations. Even the most powerful CPUs available are limited to the basic data-handling capabilities of add, subtract, multiply, divide, compare two values, and move data or instructions to and from memory. These commands are known as the basic *assembly instruction* set of the CPU or the CPU *machine language*.

Usually, the more powerful we claim a processor is, the faster it can perform these basic functions—often on the order of many million operations per second. But if processors are actually quite simple in their operation capability, how can computers perform amazingly difficult tasks such as designing aircraft or charting weather patterns? The complexity is not in the capability of the computer but in the capability of the computer programs!

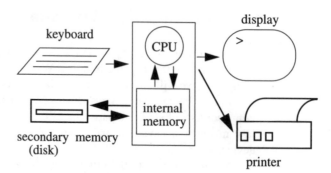

Figure 1.1   Basic components of a simple computer
system

A programmer's task is to devise a logical sequence of basic instruction-set commands which lead to the (more complex) desired result. The real power is in the mind and skill of the programmer. For example, the following set of English-like CPU commands (each representing a machine instruction) might represent a calculation for the circumference of a circle (using the formula $circ = 2\pi r$) for some hypothetical computer:

```
LOAD        radius
LOAD        pi
MULTIPLY
LOAD        two
MULTIPLY
STORE       circle
```

Here, `radius`, `pi`, `two`, and `circle` are simply names used to represent the symbolic locations or addresses of where these values are stored in memory. (We have ignored for the moment how the values needed found their way into memory in the first place.) As you might expect, if the programmer must express these instructions in basic instruction-set operations (add, subtract, multiply, divide, compare, and move data), complex programs would be very difficult to write and very prone to mistakes. This was actually the case with the first computers! It didn't take long, however, for computer scientists to decide that there had to be a better way.

Another problem was evident to the first computer scientists. Each different CPU manufacturer usually has a slightly different basic instruction set for its particular family of CPUs. The machine language for an Intel CPU may represent the same primitive capabilities as those of the Motorola CPU in a Macintosh PC, but the encoding and implementation of these capabilities are different. As a result, a machine language program written for an Intel CPU will not work in a Macintosh, and vice versa. Such a program was not portable. It could not be taken from one computer family to another and still work. The program had to be completely rewritten.

An important change in programming began when programs were written that could take a textual representation of a formula (representing many machine language operations) and translate that representation into the appropriate basic instruction-set operations for a given CPU. For example, the circumference calculation might be expressed simply as

```
circle = 2.0 * radius * pi;
```

KEY TERMS
compiler, high-level language

It is then the responsibility of this conversion program to transform the higher-level formula into the appropriate basic instruction-set operations for the desired CPU. In reality, this conversion program is translating from one language to another. Programs that can do such translations are called *compilers*. If the syntax or forms of grammar used to express formulas and other operations are sufficiently powerful, they define what we call a *high-level language*. C++ is one such language; there are many others such as Java, Ada, and Modula-2. A high-level language is in fact similar to English in many ways; there are grammar, punctuation, and syntax forms as well as semantic meaning to statements.

Now, don't confuse the compiler with the language it is designed to translate or the computer for which the translation is intended. The Microsoft C++ system contains a compiler to translate a C++ program into machine language for a PC with an Intel CPU. The Gnu C++ compiler might be used to translate the same C++ program into a different machine language for a SunSPARC CPU. If we have a C++ compiler for each different CPU, however, the original C++ program is now portable! To use a program from a Motorola CPU on an Intel PC, we can simply recompile the program using an Intel-specific compiler.

KEY TERM
standard program

This is a fairly general statement and assumes a *standard program*. A standard program does not attempt to take advantage of any specific capabilities of one system which may not be available on others. Through traditions, through market forces, and finally through specific cooperative agreements, the computer industry has agreed on a certain set of capabilities that each C++ compiler and computer system must be able to handle. If a program is written to these standards, it should be portable. In other words, each C++ compiler should be able to translate the program to the machine language of the associated target CPU. Now, many compilers provide capabilities that go beyond the standard. If you take advantage of these capabilities, your program may not be portable.

You might ask why we simply don't use English as a programming language and eliminate the need to learn C++! While that may work in science fiction movies, we will need to wait for a future star date to see it happen. It would be very difficult to implement with today's technology. For one thing, the meaning of what we say in English is often very dependent on context, inflection, and idioms. For example, saying "time passes" would imply one meaning if said during a high-school reunion and quite a different meaning if said by a head football coach to his quarterback. Programming languages all must be relatively context-free and unambiguous. The compiler must be able to translate the exact meaning of your program without any extra information about the context of your request in the larger world environment.

KEY TERMS
build, make

After writing a program in a high-level language, the compiler is invoked to translate the program statements or requests into the basic machine instruction operations the CPU is capable of executing. In addition, a program must be linked to any other programs or resources that it will use during execution. This entire process of preparing a program for execution is often called a *build* or *make* (as in "I'm finished entering my program and I'm ready to do a make").

1.2 A simple C++ program

In general, your first C++ programs will follow the form shown here:

```
#include <iostream.h>
definitions, declarations, and functions
void main()
  {  declarations and statements
  }
```

Syntax form

The italicized words represent generic placeholders; you fill in specific definitions, declarations, and statements to accomplish a specific program purpose. The italicized items are optional. For example, our initial programs will not need anything in the *definitions, declarations, and functions* section. The compiler will read this program from top to bottom and from left to right, just as we read English.

KEY TERM
format

The *format* of a program is the style we use to organize the appearance of the program (that is, the spacing, indentation, and how we organize lines). The compiler, however, doesn't care how the program looks or is formatted; it must simply read correctly from top to bottom and left to right. While the compiler might not care how you format your programs, certain standards have evolved which make a program easier to read by other humans (such as your class grader). For example, we line up the closing } directly under the opening {. Throughout the text, we will point out such standards when they become appropriate.

Let's take a look at each component of a program in turn. The first line, `#include <iostream.h>`, is an indication that the program is going to communicate with the user by doing input and output operations (I/O). For now, input means that the program is going to accept data or information from the keyboard. Output means that the program is going to display information on the screen. You will learn more about the effect of this line in later chapters. The next important line, `void main()`, simply marks the place where the program execution should begin.

Each high-level request for a calculation or other activity is called a statement. The braces { } enclose the statements of the program that must be translated into machine instructions. You might envision a statement as being similar to a sentence in English. Just as there are different categories of sentences in English (declaratory, interrogative, etc.), there are several different types of statements in C++. They can be categorized into several groups including:

- Output—a request to have the CPU display information on the screen or other output device.
- Input—a request to have the CPU accept information from the keyboard or other input device.
- Assignment—a request to have the CPU store or assign a value to a location in memory. The value may be the result of a calculation.
- Condition—a request to have the CPU choose between several different blocks of statements based on a comparison or test of memory values.
- Loop—a request to have the CPU repeat a block of statements multiple times.

Naturally, there are many variations in each group. We will start by learning some simple statements in the first three groups (input, output, and assignment) and find we can begin to write useful C++ programs.

An output statement can have a variety of forms, many of which we will see later on. One of the simplest forms, used to instruct the CPU to write information on the display monitor, looks like the following:

```
cout << value << value ... <<value;
```

Syntax form

KEY TERM
literal

The use of ellipses here (. . .) indicates that this form represents a list with a varying number of values to be output. There is a << operator or symbol for each value to be written to the monitor. Notice that the statement ends with a semicolon. This is true of all C++ instruction statements. Also, this statement may be used to write many different types of values. For example, a value to be output may be a constant. It may be a simple message placed inside of quotation marks. We call such a message a *literal*. Take a look at some possible output statements:

```
cout << "This program was written by Fred Jones";
cout << 95 << "days wasted";
```

A literal in C++ can contain any character except the backslash and the double quote. These have a special meaning. The double quote obviously indicates the end of the literal. The backslash indicates that the following character also has a special meaning. There are a couple of these special-meaning combinations that you should be aware of. A **\n** is interpreted as a Return character. A **\t** is interpreted as a tab character. You might ask: How can I print a double quote character? The backslash can also be used to disable the meaning of the double quote or the backslash itself, so they are treated as ordinary printing characters. For example:

```
cout << "hello \"my\" world!"; // displays: hello "my" world!
cout << "hello \\my\\ world!"; // displays: hello \my\ world!
```

Another value that can be output is the end-of-line marker. This value causes the display to terminate the current line and begin again on the next line, similar to the Carriage Return key on a typewriter. The predefined name **endl** is used to represent the end of line. For example, Listing 1.1 is a complete C++ program.

Listing 1.1

```
//  A simple C++ program
#include <iostream.h>
void main()
    {  cout << "Hello world!" << endl;
    }
```

KEY TERM
comment

Take a look at the first line of this program—the one which begins with the // symbol. This is known as a *comment*. Anytime a C++ compiler encounters this symbol (//), it assumes the rest of the line is for documentation, and the rest of the line is simply ignored. Comments are for human documentation—notes to yourself and other programmers to help explain the purpose or intent of program sections and make the program more human-readable. This is particularly helpful in case someone else needs to understand and perhaps modify what the original programmer did. Comments may be placed by themselves on separate lines or at the end of any statement line.

As mentioned earlier, the `#include` line indicates to the compiler that this program will be performing I/O operations. The next line marks the beginning of the instruction statements of the program, which are enclosed within the { } symbols. The program has only one statement: a request that the CPU output the literal message `Hello world!` to the display, followed by a carriage return.

KEY TERMS
program
development
environment

To enter this program into memory, perform a make, and then execute it, you need to understand the use of a *program development environment* (PDE). (These actions depend on which computer system and compiler system you are using. If you are using Microsoft Visual C++ or Gnu C++, you may refer to the appendix with that title at the end of this text.) The PDE is simply a set of programs (including the compiler) written to allow you to enter a program into memory or disk, accomplish editing changes, perform a make, and instruct the CPU to execute the translated program. In any case, when the PDE has finished a make and the program is executed, the following appears on the display:

```
Hello world!
```

This program is trivial, of course. Let's take a look at a program that can do something worthwhile. Suppose we wish to write a program that could be used to calculate the area of a circle. To do this, we need to know how to instruct the CPU to receive (or input) a number from the keyboard representing a radius, apply a formula for the appropriate calculation, and finally output the result of that formula to the display.

1.3 `float` variables and declarations

KEY TERM
declaration

Before we write an instruction or statement to do input, we must always declare a name that is associated with each memory location used to hold values being received. We reserve and label a memory location for a particular type of value through the use of *declarations*. There are several different types of values the C++ language can immediately recognize. We'll see all of the standard types in later chapters and even see how to create new ones ourselves. To begin, however, we really need only one type. We will start with real numbers—a number with a decimal point. In C++, these are called **float** values.

CONCEPT
variables are
associated with
memory

The general form of a **float** declaration is given in the following box. The italicized *variable* is a label or name for a memory location we wish to hold a value. A **float** variable is then simply a label or a name for a memory location that holds a real number. The variable name then represents the contents of the memory location with that label. Computer scientists tend to be very terse, however. Rather than say *the value at the memory location labeled "cost"*, we usually just say *the value of "cost"* or, even shorter, just *"cost."* A variable (meaning the contents of the associated memory location) may hold only one value at a time:

```
float variable, variable, ... variable;
```

Syntax form

Some possible declarations are:

```
float cost, time;
float age, weight, height, color;
```

CONCEPT
a variable holds
one value

Some students find it easy to envision computer memory as a large collection of post office boxes. Each box has a unique name associated with it and is capable of holding information. This analogy is excellent as long as we remember that a box (variable) *may only hold one piece of information at a time*. Each time a new value is placed into a variable, the old or previous value is lost or overwritten.

We may choose any name for a variable as long as three rules are followed. The name:

CONCEPT
variable name rules

1. must begin with a letter

2. may consist only of letters, digits, and the underscore (_)

3. may not be a *reserved word*

KEY TERM
reserved word

(It is actually possible to begin a variable name with an underscore, but it can lead to confusion and is not recommended.) A *reserved word* is one that has a predefined meaning for the language. For example, **main**, **float**, and **void** are the reserved words you have seen so far. We will identify more in later chapters. In addition, many compilers limit the useful length of a variable name to 31 characters, so it is prudent to keep the name reasonably short. Take a look at the following possible declarations:

```
float age, cost, weight_95, class_number;
float temperature_fahr;
float thrust1, thrust2;
float mastertime, missedclients;
```

CONCEPT
name case

Also be aware that variable names are case sensitive! In other words, the following example declares four different **float** variables:

```
float Age, age, AGE, AgE;
```

CONCEPT
descriptive names

Since a program will need to be read and understood by other humans in addition to the computer, *always give variables names that in some way describe the nature or purpose of the value stored*. The compiler doesn't care what names you use, of course, but other programmers (and your class grader) will find your program much easier to understand if the names of variables in some way describe what they are intended to hold.

1.4 Program input

A statement used to receive values from the keyboard and place those values into memory locations labeled with variable names has the form given in the following syntax form box:

```
cin >> variable >> variable >> ... variable;
```

Syntax form

Note that each variable listed is preceded by the `>>` operator. For example, the execution of the following statement would make the computer pause and accept two real numbers to be placed into the variables `age` and `cost`, respectively;

```
cin >> age >> cost;
```

CONCEPT
separate input
values with tabs,
returns, or blanks

When the user enters two real numbers via the keyboard, they should be separated with a blank, Return key, or tab to allow the computer to recognize them as separate numbers. Each number should contain a decimal point. If you leave the decimal point out, one will be assumed at the right side. It doesn't matter whether the user enters these two values on separate lines or enters them both on the same line (separated by a blank or tab). The program will read the input from left to right and top to bottom just as we humans do to find as many values as there are variables to fill. Blanks and carriage returns are simply ignored. In other words, the following could also be used to achieve the same result:

```
cin >> age;
cin >> cost;
```

1.5 Assignments and expressions

CONCEPT
the assignment
statement

We now need to learn the statement used for formula calculations: the *assignment* statement. The general form is given in the following syntax form box. The variable on the left side is where we wish the result of a calculation to be placed. The expression on the right represents the calculation. The basic operators available for real number calculations are +, -, /, *, and, of course, parentheses:

variable = expression ;   **Syntax form**

KEY TERMS
operator
precedence

Expressions may contain variables and constants. A constant is simply a real number (with a decimal point) explicitly written into the expression. The order of *operator precedence* for an expression is the same as you learned in algebra: If parentheses are not used to indicate an operator order, multiplication and division are done first, followed by addition and subtraction. If an expression has two arithmetic operators at the same precedence, they are simply done from left to right. In other words, the following assignment statement

```
cost = 2.0 + rate * 7.9 / (factor + 5.6);
```

implies that `factor+5.6` is to be calculated prior to being used in the division. In other words, the value of `factor` is to be added to `5.6`, and that intermediate result will be used in the division. Next, the two operators `*` and `/` have the same precedence, so the value of `rate*7.9` is to be calculated prior to division and these two operations are simply done from left to right. Finally, the `+` operator will be performed to add the value of `2.0` to the rest of the calculation. An expression may refer to the values currently assigned to variables or any explicit constants.

Naturally, using a variable in an expression implies that it previously was assigned a value or a value was read into it with an input statement. The foregoing assignment statement would not make much sense if the variables `rate` and `factor` did not already contain values. If the compiler detects this *might* be the case when this statement is actually executed, it will usually give you a warning.

CONCEPT
use the decimal
point

Notice that each constant contains a decimal point. You will later learn about integer constants (and variables) that do not contain decimal points, but for now, all the problems we initially need to solve can be done with **float** variables and real constants. If you forget and leave a decimal point out of a constant, you may not see the accuracy you expect in your calculations. The reason for this will be explained in Chapter 6.

Remember, the compiler (and thus, the CPU) does not consider the spacing of an expression. Adding blanks or tabs to group subexpressions would, of course, have no effect. Take a quick look at the following assignment statement. Even though the spacing may seem to indicate otherwise visually, the * operator evaluated first:

```
time = age+delay * 7.9 ; // (delay*7.9) is still calculated first!
```

Take a look at some possible assignment statements for a few simple geometry formulas:

```
area = 3.14 * radius * radius;
```
$$a = \pi r^2$$

```
fraction = (height - length) / (height + length);
```
$$f = \frac{H - L}{H + L}$$

```
coef = (volume - area) * (volume - area);
```
$$c = (v - a)^2$$

You have learned that an output value can be a literal, a constant, or the **endl**; it can also be the value of a variable. The program for circle area might now look like that found in Listing 1.2.

Listing 1.2

```
// Calculate the area of a circle given a radius value
#include <iostream.h>
void main()
{    float area, radius;
     cout << "enter a radius:";
     cin >> radius;
     area = radius * radius * 3.14;
     cout << "the area is " <<area<<endl;
}
```

When this program is executed, the statements are considered one at a time in the same order as they are written: The two float variables area and radius are first defined. Next the message enter a radius: is sent to the output device (the display monitor). The computer then pauses and waits for the user to enter a real number, which is then placed in the memory location reserved for the radius variable. Next a calculation is performed: The value of variable radius is first multiplied by itself (squared), then multiplied by 3.14 (the value used for pi), and the result is placed in variable area. The last statement outputs the message the area is followed by the value in variable area and a carriage return. The following is what the user of this program might view as the program is executed. (The user entry is underlined.)

```
enter a radius: 7.5
the area is 176.625
```

EXPERIMENT

What would happen if one of the variables in Listing 1.2 were changed to an illegal name? Change area to 2area and recompile or make and see what happens.

1.6 Program debugging

KEY TERMS
run-time, syntax,
semantic errors

Often, when programs are written, mistakes are inadvertently made. Commonly, program development proceeds in an iterative fashion until we are convinced that the program is doing what we intended and is without mistakes (Figure 1.2). There are three types of mistakes, or *bugs,* which may occur. These are *run-time* errors, *syntax* errors, and *semantic* errors.

Run-time errors occur when a program is executed with a statement that requires the CPU to do something it is not able to accomplish. One very common example of such an error is a request for division by zero:

```
temp = 0.0;
rate = 1.0 / temp;
```

Syntax bugs are errors in grammar or spelling, whereas semantic bugs are errors in logic or meaning. An example of an English syntax error might be leaving out a

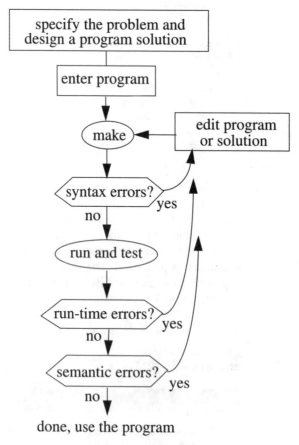

Figure 1.2 Program implementation cycle

verb in a sentence. A logic error might exist in a sentence that is grammatically correct but makes no sense:

```
The dog his paw.              ( syntax or grammar error )
A paw ate the dog.            ( good grammar, but illogical )
```

Of course, recognizing that the second sentence is illogical depends on your understanding of what the nouns "dog" and "paw" represent. If "paw" is your nickname for a tiger, it becomes reasonable.

Syntax errors are recognized by the compiler and result in error messages when a make takes place. When a syntax error is detected, the compiler makes an attempt to inform the programmer of the program line that contains the error and the nature of the error. Unfortunately, this is a very difficult task for some types of errors, and a programmer should always view error messages from the compiler as a best guess. Nevertheless, the actual error is usually at or just before the location specified. If more than one error is present, the compiler may become confused and not catch all the errors. In addition, the compiler may occasionally issue more than one error message for the same error if there is doubt as to the exact nature of the error. Consider the programming attempt to calculate the volume of a box in Listing 1.3. (Numbers have been added to the listing to help identify particular statements.)

Listing 1.3

```cpp
// Calculate a box volume given height, length, and width
1  #include <iostream.h>
2  void main()
3  {  float height, lenth, width, area, volume
4     cout << "enter height, length, width: ";
5     cin >> height >> length >> width;
6     area = height + length;
7     volume = area * width
8     cout << "volume is " << volume;
9  }
```

If you look closely, there are three syntax errors and one semantic or logic error present. First, the variable `lenth` declared in line 3 is not the same as the variable `length` used in the **cin** (pronounced "see in") and assignment statements of lines 5 and 6. Which statement is in error? The second and third errors are missing semicolons at the end of the declaration statement of line 3 and the assignment statement of line 7. The logic error is in the assignment statement of line 6 where `height` and `length` are added instead of multiplied. When a make is performed, the following messages were noted by the compiler:

```
Error, line 4: declaration syntax error
Error, line 5: undefined symbol 'length'
Error, line 7: statement missing ';'
```

While line 3 (the declaration statement) is missing a semicolon, the compiler placed the error on line 4 and misdescribed the correct nature of the mistake. The misspelling of `length` in the declaration statement was detected in line 5 (the `cin` statement) when the correctly spelled variable was determined to not have an associated declaration. The use again of the undeclared `length` in the assignment statement was not noted. The missing semicolon in the `cout` (pronounced "see out") statement was correctly identified. In general, the compiler error messages will be quite helpful in debugging your programs, but you must consider that they are simply the compiler's best effort in interpreting the cause of the bugs and not their true nature.

There is a chance that when you enter a statement incorrectly, it may simply have an interpretation different from what you intended. For example, consider the following example of what the programmer intended to enter:

```
diameter = radius * 2.0;
```

and what was actually typed:

```
diameter = radius = 2.0;
```

CONCEPT

not all errors
generate error
messages

The second statement is obviously not what was intended, but it does not generate a syntax error message! The reason is this statement has a valid interpretation (which will become apparent as you progress in the course). So, what is the bottom line with regard to syntax error messages? If a statement is incorrectly formed for your intended meaning, you have a bug. If the malformed statement has a valid interpretation in C++, you will not necessarily see an error message. If there is no valid meaning, the compiler will issue at least one error message, but the suggested cause and location of the error may occasionally be off target from the true nature of the bug. Now, suppose that using these error messages as guides, we edit the program at this point to correct these syntax errors and again perform a make.

Once the compiler verifies that no syntax errors are present, that does not imply that the program is free of bugs. Notice that the logic error was not mentioned in the error messages. Naturally, the compiler has no idea as to the purpose or intent of the program—it simply translates a syntactically correct program to do what you have told it to do. Compilers do not understand English. They cannot read your variable names and imply what they represent in nature. To the compiler, a variable name is just a sequence of characters. In addition, the compiler has no idea what the formula for the volume of a box should be in the first place.

Logic or *semantic* errors are usually found by program testing. In this particular case, we might hand-calculate the volume of a set of known boxes (or *test cases*) and compare the results with those generated by the program. For this program, the comparison would indicate a logic error since the hand and program results would definitely not match. When the syntax errors are corrected and the program executed, the following would be viewed by the user:

```
enter height, length, width: 4.0   5.5   7.8
volume is 74.18
```

Using a calculator, we expect the volume to be 171.6. The compiler is able to understand and translate the instructions we have given. They just are not the instructions that lead to a correct volume calculation. The program does what we told it to do, not what we wanted or intended it to do.

Table 1.1 Execution table for the box volume program

	Statement	Height	Length	Width	Area	Volume
4	`cout ...`	—	—	—	—	—
5	`cin >> ...`	4.0	5.5	7.8	—	—
6	`area = ...`	4.0	5.5	7.8	22	—
7	`volume = ...`	4.0	5.5	7.8	22	171.6
8	`cout << ...`	4.0	5.5	7.8	22	171.6

If it is determined that a logic error is present, an execution table can be helpful in locating the source of the error. This table simply shows the expected values of variables at the end of each program statement, as determined by hand with a calculator. Consider Table 1.1 for the box volume program (after the syntax errors have been corrected) for a box 4.0 x 5.5 x 7.8 inches.

After completing this table by hand, one can compare it with the actual values of variables during program execution using one of two means. First, if a tool called a "debugger" is available, it will allow you to step through program execution one statement at a time and display the values of selected variables at the end of each statement. In other words, a debugger can automatically generate the execution table for you. (You may wish to refer to Appendix C of the text if you are using Microsoft Visual C++.) Second, if a debugger is not available, we can simply add extra **cout** statements to the program to output the values of variables at significant locations as program execution proceeds. For example, consider Listing 1.4.

Listing 1.4

```
// Calculate the area and volume of a box given height, length,
and width
#include <iostream.h>
void main()
{    float height, length, width, area, volume;
     cout << "enter height, length, width: ";
     cin >> height >> length >> width;
     cout << height << length << width;
     area = height + length;
     cout << area;
     volume = area * width;
     cout << "volume is " << volume;
}
```

When Listing 1.4 is executed, the following is viewed by the user:

```
enter height, length, width: 4.0 5.5 7.8
45.57.89.5volume is 74.1
```

The program asked that the values of `height`, `length`, `width`, and `area` be output, but they have all been run together so that it is difficult to determine which digits are part of which variable value! Returning to the program, the intermediate `cout` statements are modified to allow spacing between variables and to add helpful annotation:

```
...
cout << "height is" << height << " length is" << length
        << " width is" << width << endl;
...
cout << "area is" << area << endl;
cout << "volume is" << volume;
```

When this corrected program is executed, the user now views the following when a new make is performed and the program is reexecuted:

```
enter height, length, width: 4.0 5.5 7.8
height is 4 length is 5.5 width is 7.8
area is 9.5
volume is 74.1
```

The values of `height`, `length`, and `width` have been correctly output, indicating that the values were correctly read in. The value of `area` is displayed as 9.5, however, and we predicted 22. This gives us a clue to reexamine how `area` is calculated, which helps to identify the semantic error. After correcting this semantic error and removing the extra `cout` statements, the final program is given in Listing 1.5.

Listing 1.5

```
// Calculate the volume of a box
#include <iostream.h>

void main()
{   float height, length, width, area, volume;
    cout << "enter height, length, width:";
    cin >> height >> length >> width;
    area = height * length;
    volume = area * width;
    cout << "volume is" << volume;
}
```

EXPERIMENT

What would happen if one of the variables in Listing 1.5 was not declared? Remove `area` from the **float** declaration and recompile.

There is much more to program debugging. In future chapters, we will not only consider more debugging concerns but also look at methods and approaches that tend to prevent us from making a variety of mistakes in the first place.

1.7 History of C++

C++ wasn't the first high-level language developed, not by a long shot. High-level languages such as FORTRAN have been around since the late 1950s. These early languages were not particularly powerful in the sense that it took a lot of programming to express the solutions to some problems. Some applications still required segments of a program to be written in machine language. In addition, these programs were prone to bugs and were often difficult to modify and maintain. Learning from these early efforts, computer scientists have proposed and developed better and better languages to address these shortcomings.

In the late 1960s, a language called BCPL (Basic Combined Programming Language) was developed at Bell Laboratories to combine the features of a high-level language and the utility of machine language. An improved version was later named B. (No, there never was an A language). The next improvement came in the early 1970s by the team of Kernighan and Ritchie, and it was named C. This language became very popular and widely accepted, particularly within universities. It still is. There is a C compiler for nearly every computer system on the market today. Programmers find it easy to express complex programming problems tersely in C using what is called procedural programming style.

While C is very powerful, programs written in this language are still notorious for being prone to difficult bugs. In addition, a C program can often be quite difficult to maintain and modify, particularly if the program was originally written by someone whose programming style was personalized and whose documentation was spotty or less than adequate.

By the 1980s, computer systems and computer programs were becoming quite large and complex. The cost of designing, implementing, debugging, and later modifying and upgrading programs became very high. Computer scientists began to examine an approach to programming that specifically addressed the problems of readability, maintainability, and reusability. The approach came to be known as object-oriented programming, or OOP for short. This way of approaching complex programs was quickly shown to reduce costs and allow complex programs to be more rapidly developed while reducing the opportunity for difficult bugs. It became apparent to the industry that this approach had some significant advantages.

While several strictly OOP programming languages were developed (most notably SMALLTALK), the popularity of C lead to some of the constructs and capabilities of OOP being added as extensions to this language. The symbol ++ in the C language means to advance (as you will learn in a later chapter), and naturally, the name for this extended C language became C++. It has become widely accepted in both industrial and academic settings. Just as with C, every general-purpose computer has an available C++ compiler system.

C++ is a true advancement of the C language in the sense that a standard C program can be compiled with a C++ compiler. All the features and capabilities of C are available. Many of the newer aspects of the OOP approach have supplanted these older C features, however. Thus, C++ is really a separate language. In this text, we will assume you wish to learn C++, and little effort will be made to differentiate the aspects of C++ that are supported by C and those that are not. The older procedural programming style most often used in C still has a few nice advantages, however, and is definitely not out of date. You will also be exposed to many of the beneficial features that were inherited from C.

1.8 Example projects

Suppose a programmer wished to print letterhead on a printer. Now, a good word processor is probably much more appropriate for this task, but a reasonable program could be written in C++ with the statements presented in this chapter. The output statements of the program would simply generate text lines. The predefined **endl** word would be used to add blank lines where appropriate. After the program is debugged, appropriate redirection commands could be used to send the output to the printer (depending on the computer system you are using). Look at Listing 1.6.

Listing 1.6

```
// Generate a company letterhead
#include <iostream.h>
void main()
{   cout <<endl<<endl<<endl<<endl<<endl<<endl;
    cout << "          World Wide Widgets" << endl;
    cout << " 123 Avarice Place        Metropolis, USA" << endl;
    cout << " ***********************************" << endl;
}
```

A more practical program might be one to convert English feet measurements into metric meters. Before attempting to write such a program, you need to find the appropriate formula:

$$meters = feet \times 0.3048$$

As we logically think about the steps to arrive at a correct solution, we might come up with the following:

1. Input the number of feet to be converted from the user.
2. Calculate the number of meters for that many feet.
3. Display the calculated number of meters.

Naturally, we first need to declare any variables used by the program. It appears there are two. The best descriptive names might be `feet` and `meters`. When the program wishes to input a value for `feet`, it is important that the user be prompted to know when to enter the correct value. When outputting the converted result in meters, it is also best to include the original number of feet for two reasons. First, it makes the output more self-documenting. Second, the user has a self-check to verify that the correct input was received. Writing the program is now simply a matter of using the appropriate C++ syntax, as shown in Listing 1.7.

Listing 1.7

```
// Convert feet to meters
#include <iostream.h>
void main()
{    float feet, meters;
     cout << "Enter the number of feet to be converted to meters: ";
     cin >> feet;
     meters = feet * .3048;
     cout << feet << " feet is " << meters << " meters" << endl;
}
```

This approach of first logically thinking about the specific steps to be accomplished before we worry about how to express them in C++ represents a peek at basic program design methods. We will return to this issue. Keep in mind for now that a program can be divided into two problems. First, what steps are needed to arrive at a correct solution? Second, how should these steps be coded into C++?

Take a look at still another example. Suppose we now have a much more complex formula to apply. For example, let's calculate the surface area of a clipped right-circular cone (illustrated in the following figure):

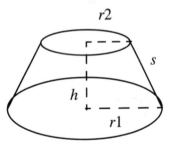

The formula we find in a good geometry text is the following:

$$area = \pi[r1^2 + r2^2 + (r1 + r2)s]$$

The steps needed for this program are similar to the previous one. In fact, having written this type of program before, the new program should be easy. We will find that solving a problem using an approach that worked for other similar problems makes many programs fairly easy to write:

1. Input the radii, side length, and height.
2. Calculate the associated area using the given formula.
3. Display the area.

It appears the program will need four variables for input, and you might choose the names `minor_radius`, `major_radius`, `height`, and `side`. The answer or result might be named `surface_area`. Rather than try to code this entire complex formula in a single assignment statement, let's break it into subexpressions. Looking inside the braces, we'll call the first `sum_of_squares` and the second `radii_product`.

Once again, the user should be adequately prompted for what the program expects for input. Since this program will be more difficult to understand and read by another, we'll use more comments (Listing 1.8).

Listing 1.8

```
// Calculate total surface area of a truncated right-circular cone
#include <iostream.h>
void main()
{    float minor_radius, major_radius;     // cone top and bottom radii
     float height, side;                   // cone height and side length
     float surface_area;                   // total cone surface area
     float sum_of_squares, radii_product;  // subexpression values in formula
// prompt user and input needed variables
     cout << "enter major and minor radii";
     cin >> major_radius >> minor_radius;
     cout << "enter cone height and side length";
     cin >> height >> side;
// calculate area formula using subexpressions
     sum_of_squares = major_radius*major_radius + minor_radius*minor_radius;
     radii_product = (major_radius + minor_radius) * side;
     surface_area = 3.14 * (sum_of_squares + radii_product);
// display results and input data
     cout << "radii:" << major_radius << ", " << minor_radius << endl;
     cout << "height and side:" << height << ", " << side << endl;
     cout << "total surface area:" << surface_area << endl;
}
```

An example execution of Listing 1.8 looks like this:

```
enter major and minor radii  4.0 5.75
enter cone height and side length  3.5 3.91
radii:  4, 5.75
height and side: 3.5, 3.91
total surface area: 273.761
```

1.9 Summary

KEY TERMS   Several terms that are important for you to understand were introduced in this chapter:

1. *central processing unit (CPU)*—the brains of a computer where actual calculation and processing take place.

2. *volatile memory*—memory (usually internal) that loses its contents when the power is turned off.

3. *nonvolatile memory*—memory (usually disk) that retains its contents even when the power is removed.

4. *assembly instruction set* or *machine language*—the primitive machine operations that a CPU is constructed to perform.

5. *compiler*—a program that is able to translate a textual source program in a high-level language into another program consisting of only the basic instruction set of the CPU.

6. *high-level language*—a programming language that allows the expression of operations and formulas for calculations in a manner closer to a human way of expressing the steps of a problem.

7. *standard program*—a program written using only standardized features of a language which are consistently recognized across different compilers.

8. *make*—to compile a high-level source program and link it with necessary system resources to prepare it for execution. Also called a *build*.

9. *format*—the visual style or layout of a program or statement.

10. *literal*—a textual message enclosed within quotation marks.

11. *comment*—a textual message preceded by the // symbol and used for human-readable documentation.

12. *program development environment (PDE)*—a set of programs containing an editor and a compiler which is used to translate, link, and execute a program written in a high-level language.

13. *declaration*—a statement specifying the name of a variable to be associated with a particular type of data. (We will later see that other things can also be declared.)

14. *variable*—a symbolic name associated with a location in memory and used to store a value.

15. *reserved word*—a word specifically reserved to have a built-in meaning to the compiler.

16. *operator precedence*—the order in which operators in an expression are evaluated when not specified by parentheses.

17. *semantic errors*—errors in logic or intent not usually detected by the compiler.

18. *syntax errors*—errors in spelling and grammar detected by a compiler.

19. *run–time errors*—statements requiring the CPU to do something it is not able to accomplish.

CONCEPTS   There were several syntax forms to remember in writing your first C++ programs. The general form of your first C++ programs will be the following:

```
#include <iostream.h>
definitions, declarations, and functions
void main()
    {  declarations and statements
    }
```

You have not yet learned about definitions—that will come later. Decimal variables used in a program must first be declared using a statement in the form: **float** *variable, variable, . . . , variable* ;

Values can be output using a statement in the form: **cout** << *value* << *value . . .* << *value* ;

A value may be a variable, a constant, or a message literal in quotes. Decimal values can be input to variables using a statement in the form: **cin** >> *variable* >> *variable . . .* >> *variable* ;

When entering multiple decimal values for input, they should be separated with blanks or tabs.

Variable names must not be reserved words and must begin with a letter or underscore. They may contain letters, digits, and the underscore. They should usually be less than 31 characters in length. Letter case is significant.

Variables may be assigned the results of calculations using a statement in the form: *variable = expression* ;

The operators *, /, +, and - are available along with parentheses. Operator precedence dictates that * and / are performed before + and - when parentheses do not indicate otherwise. When equal-precedence operators occur without overriding parentheses, they are performed from left to right. Constants may be used in assignment statement expressions. A constant is always written with a decimal point at this time in your career.

The following facts, hints, and helps are useful to remember:

■ Variables should always be named descriptively.

■ A variable may hold only one value. If a new value is stored into a variable using an assignment or input statement, the previous value is overwritten.

■ If a syntax error is present, the compiler will issue an error message, but messages may not always accurately describe the nature or location of the true mistake. A statement that represents something different from what the programmer intended to write, but that nevertheless represents some other valid C++ construct, will not usually result in an error message.

■ Semantic errors can be located with a debugger or an execution table using test data for which the programmer predicts the correct answers manually.

Table 1.2 **Example Segments**

`float age, weight;`	establish two real variables with these names
`cin >> age;`	input a value into age
`cost=5.6+4.2*3.0;`	multiply 3.0 times 4.2, add the result to 5.6, assign to cost
`cout << "the value is: << cost;"`	output the message followed by the value of cost

1.10 Exercises

1.10.a Short-answer questions

1. Memory that loses its contents when the power is removed is _____ memory.
2. Memory that retains its contents when the power is removed is _____ memory.
3. A statement that identifies a variable name to a program is known as a _____ statement.
4. The act of preparing a program for execution is called a _____.
5. Text enclosed within quotation marks is known as a _____.
6. A word that has a predefined meaning in a C++ program and cannot be used as a variable name is known as a _____ word.
7. Explain the difference between a semantic and a syntax error.
8. If a new value is assigned to a variable, the old value is _____.
9. Indicate if the following are input or output statements:
   a. `cin >> x;`
   b. `cout << y;`
   c. `cin >> a >> b;`
   d. `cout << "hello";`
10. Which of the following are valid variable names?
    a. `temperature`
    b. `cost_of_living`
    c. `$deposit`
    d. `side2`
    e. `weight_`
    f. `percent%_raise`
11. Propose valid variable names for the following information:
    a. the cost of an new car
    b. the number of yards gained in a football game
    c. the square root of the variable `distance`
    d. the average value of a list of scores
    e. the time required to pay off a loan

12. Declare appropriate variables to be used in the calculation of the number of square feet in a triangular residential lot.

13. Express the following formulas as assignment statements (or perhaps as groups of assignment statements with subexpressions):

   a. $x = \dfrac{ay^2 + 3}{(4 - a)}\pi$

   b. $val = (x + y)(x - y)$

   c. $cost = (rate)(value - 1)$

14. Based on the given values in the four variables listed here, show what values would be assigned as a result of the following statements:

value	cost	markup	price
7.5	8.1	10.0	

   a. `price = value + cost * markup;`
   b. `price = (value + cost) * markup / 2.0;`
   c. `price = value + cost * markup + value / 2.0;`

15. When prompted by a program to enter two values, should they both be entered on the same line (separated by a blank or tab) or should they be entered on separate lines?

16. Explain a possible reason why a compiler syntax error message may be associated with the line following the statement in which the error actually occurs.

17. Briefly explain why a compiler may not be able to detect semantic errors in a program.

18. Briefly explain how semantic errors are normally detected.

19. List the reserved words presented in this chapter.

20. What is the purpose of comments in a program?

1.10.b Projects

1. Write and test a complete C++ program to input the dimensions of a rectangular building lot and then calculate and output the total square footage. Be sure to use appropriate prompting messages to the user and good annotation messages to describe the output.

2. Write and test a complete C++ program to input a radius and then calculate the volume of the corresponding sphere. The formula is: $vol = \dfrac{4}{3}\pi r^3$

3. Write and test a complete C++ program to calculate the area of a general trapezoid. The formula is: $area = \dfrac{1}{2}(a + b)h$

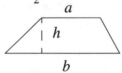

4. Write and test a complete C++ program that can be used to convert a weight in the pound system to an equivalent weight in the metric kilogram system. There are 2.2 pounds in a kilogram.

5. Write and test a C++ program to calculate and output an employee paycheck. Your program should input two numbers: the number of hours worked and the hourly rate.

6. Write and test a C++ program to convert Fahrenheit temperatures into Centigrade. The formula is: $\frac{5}{9}(f - 32) = c$.

Try $\dfrac{5.0}{9.0}$

7. Using an earth radius of 6356.912 km and the speed of sound in dry air at 0°C of 331.36 m/sec, write and test a C++ program to determine how long it would take a loud noise to travel a percentage of the earth's circumference. The input to this program should be a decimal number less than or equal to 1.0. For example, an input of .25 should produce the time it would take a loud noise to traverse 25% of the earth's circumference.

8. Write and test a C++ program to calculate an estimated mass for the earth. In other words, how many kilograms is the earth? You may assume the earth is spherical with a radius of 6356.912 km and a mean density of 5.522 gm per cm^3. Refer to project 2 for the formula for spherical volume. Notice that you will need to perform conversions to ensure that the units of the formula you use are all the same.

9. **Creative Challenge:** Modify the program of project 2 so that it calculates the volume of three different spheres, not just one. The program will of course need to prompt for three different radii and output three different volumes. You have not yet been taught an efficient way of programming a solution to this problem, but it can be done with what you already know. Be creative.

10. **Creative Challenge:** Modify project 5 to allow for overtime pay. Employee pay should be calculated as the number of hours worked times the hourly rate with time and a half for overtime (the hours worked over 40). For example, consider the following example execution:

```
enter hours worked and hourly rate: 37.5 5.75
pay is: $ 215.625
```

Since this employee worked fewer than 40 hours, the pay is just 37.5 times 5.75. Now, if the employee had worked over 40 hours, overtime would need to be considered:

```
enter hours worked and hourly rate: 47.5 5.75
pay is: $ 294.6875
```

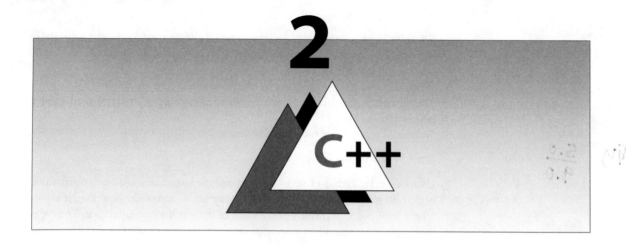

Simple Choice and Repetition

What can we do when different conditions call for different formulas in a program? This chapter presents the fundamentals of making choices in a program using alternatives. In addition, methods for repeating instructions are introduced. By the end of the chapter, you should be able to write programs that are able to process many sets of input data and test each input data value to determine which instructions need to be executed.

2.1 The conditional statement

At the end of the previous chapter, one assignment required a programmer to calculate employee paychecks (project 10). Take a minute and review that problem. The difficulty with this task is that there are two different formulas: one for employees with no overtime and one for employees with overtime. The only methods of solving this problem were (a) to write two different programs or (b) to apply both formulas blindly in one program and present the user with a correct and an incorrect answer! The user then had to examine an employee timecard and determine which program to run or which answer to accept.

KEY TERM
conditional
statement

High-level languages are, of course, perfectly capable of allowing choices to be specified. That is the purpose of the *conditional statement*. The conditional statement allows a program to examine data and choose an appropriate set of instructions for execution. The general form is as follows:

```
if ( expression )
    statement₁
else
    statement₂
```

Syntax form

KEY TERM
flow of control

The **if** and **else** are additional reserved words. The meaning of the condition is simple: If the given *expression* is true, the first *statement* is executed. If the *expression* is not true, then the second *statement* is executed. In other words, only one of the two statements is ever executed. What can these statements be? Any C++ statement is allowed; the output (using **cout**), input (using **cin**), and assignment statements from the previous chapter are of course usable, as are other **if** statements. (We shall see later that another form of the **if** statement is also available, as well as other types of conditional statements.) The flow of execution or *flow of control* through the **if** statement is represented by the diagram of Figure 2.1.

KEY TERM
relational
expression

Most commonly, the expression used in an **if** statement is a *relational expression*. This means that the relationship between two variables or constants (or perhaps simple arithmetic expressions) is tested. There are six relational or comparison operators that can be used. Four are introduced here. (We'll see the other two after we learn more about other data types.)

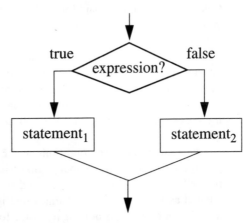

Figure 2.1 Symbolic representation of flow of control through the **if** statement

CONCEPT
relational
operators
Some relational operators are:

>	greater than
<	less than
>=	greater than or equal to
<=	less than or equal to

For example, consider the following relational expressions:

```
a < b            true if the value of a is less than that of b
x >=(y+2.0)      true if x is greater or equal to the value of (y+2)
z > 25.0         true if z is greater than 25
```

We are now ready to construct some complete **if** statements. Consider the following simple example:

```
if (a <= b)
    cout << "a is less than (or equal to) b";
else
    cout << "a is greater than b";
```

This program fragment will output the first message if the value of variable a is less than or equal to the current value of variable b. The second message would be output otherwise, when the value of variable a is greater than b.

With the conditional statement, we can revisit the employee pay problem with a much more practical solution. If you remember, an employee's pay is calculated from one of two formulas. If the employee works less than or equal to 40 hours, the pay is calculated with the formula: $pay = hours \times rate$. If the employee works overtime, time and a half is paid for the hours over 40 and the second formula is applied: $pay = (40 \times rate) + (overtime \times 1.5 \times rate)$, where overtime is the hours worked over 40. Refer to Listing 2.1.

In this listing, a comment is used to document the name of the program and provide a brief description of its purpose. In general, a good programmer will provide comments at the top of each program to state the name of the program, clarify its purpose and intent, and provide other useful information such as the name of the programmer and the date. We will discuss more about documentation later in the text.

Now, there are two conditions or **if** statements in this program. The user is first prompted to input the hours worked and the pay rate. After these values are input and stored in variables hours and rate, the number of overtime hours is calculated as hours - 40. If this value is greater than 0 (meaning the employee actually worked overtime), the overtime formula is applied to calculate pay. If not, the regular formula is applied for pay. After pay has been calculated, it is then output to the user. Finally, overtime is again tested in the second **if** statement, and one of two messages is added to the output to indicate whether the employee did or did not work overtime.

Listing 2.1

```cpp
// CALCPAY.CPP  A program to calculate paychecks
#include <iostream.h>
void main()
{   float hours, pay, rate, overtime;
    cout << "enter hours and rate: ";
    cin >> hours >> rate;
    overtime = hours - 40.0;
// employees working more than 40 hours receive overtime
    if (overtime > 0.0)
        pay = (40.0 * rate) + (overtime * 1.5 * rate);
    else
        pay = hours * rate;// no overtime paid for this employee
    cout << "pay is" << pay;

    if (overtime > 0.0)
        cout << "overtime worked" << endl;
    else
        cout << "no overtime worked" << endl;
}
```

If we run this program for an employee who did not work overtime, the output might look like this:

```
enter hours and rate: 38.0 6.25
pay is 237.5    no overtime worked
```

An employee who did work overtime might produce the following interaction:

```
enter hours and rate: 46.0 6.25
    pay is 306.25    overtime worked
```

EXPERIMENT

What would happen if the user enters integers instead of real numbers? Listing 2.1 expects the user to enter real numbers.

CONCEPT

use proper indentation

Since a program often needs to be read by more than one programmer, we are concerned with using a consistent and readable style. Just as giving variables descriptive names is considered good style, proper program indentation is very helpful in making it obvious which statements belong to the true and not true segments or clauses of a condition. Note that the two **cout** statements in Listing 2.1 are indented, and the **if** and **else** are aligned in good paragraph notation. This helps to show the human reader which statements are subordinate.

If one of the two statements is not needed in the **if**, a semicolon by itself can be used to indicate an empty or null statement. (We'll see later that there is a simpler method to solve this problem.) For example:

```
if (a < b)
   cout << "a is larger";
else
   ;
```

2.2 Statement blocks

We can combine blocks of statements by enclosing them inside **{ },** or brace symbols. This indicates we wish the entire block to be treated as a single *compound* statement. For example, all the statements of the main program are enclosed inside braces — a program consists of a single compound statement. Let's go back to the employee pay program of Listing 2.1. It might make more sense and make the program more readable if we were to test if hours are greater than 40 and then calculate using the overtime or regular formula depending on the answer. Listing 2.2 is an example of such a modified program.

Listing 2.2

```
// CALCPAY2.CPP  A program to calculate paychecks
//Contains blocked statements
#include <iostream.h>
void main()
{   float hours, pay, rate, overtime;
    cout << "enter hours and rate: ";
    cin >> hours >> rate;

    if (hours > 40.0)
    { overtime = hours - 40.0;
      pay = (40.0 * rate) + (overtime * 1.5 * rate);
      cout << " pay is " << pay << " overtime worked" << endl;
    }
    else
    { pay = hours * rate;
      cout << " pay is " << pay << " no overtime worked" << endl;
    }
}
```

EXPERIMENT

What would happen if a semicolon were added immediately after the else in Listing 2.2?

This program is somewhat easier to read since the two different ways of calculating pay and the associated output messages are clearly compartmentalized. If, for example, we wish to modify the section dealing with overtime, we would be less concerned about how that modification might affect the section concerned with regular pay. The idea here is to avoid allowing modifications in one section of a program to introduce errors in another. We will return to this concept again and again throughout this text. An example of the execution of this program would look like the following:

```
enter hours and rate: 45.0  7.25
pay is 344.375 overtime worked
```

EXPERIMENT

What would happen if you output a variable before you assign a value to it?

Now, suppose you were to inadvertently leave out the braces of the false section of the **if** statement in Listing 2.2:

```
if (hours > 40.0)
    { overtime = hours - 40.0;
      pay = (40.0 * rate) + (overtime * 1.5 * rate);
      cout << " pay is " << pay << " overtime worked";
    }
else
    pay = hours * rate;
    cout << " pay is " << pay;
```

Even though you have indented appropriately, only the pay assignment statement is considered as the false section of the **if**. In this case, the bottom output statement is executed regardless of the **if** expression since it is now outside (or after) the **if**. This is not a syntax error, but it is certainly a semantic error because that is not what was intended.

Once again, there is another form of the **if** statement, and there are more conditional statements. Rather than spend time on them here, let's get right into program looping. We'll come back to conditions.

2.3 The *while* statement

At the end of Chapter 1, an assignment was made for a program to calculate the volume of three different spheres (Creative Challenge 9). The only straightforward method of solving this problem was to duplicate the statements needed for a single sphere three times! For example, refer to Listing 2.3.

Listing 2.3

```cpp
// CALCVOL.CPP    A program to calc. the volume of 3 spheres
#include <iostream.h>
void main()
{   float volume, radius;

    cout << "enter a radius:";        // first sphere
    cin >> radius;
    volume = (4.0 / 3.0) * radius * radius * radius * 3.14;
    cout << "the volume is" << volume << endl;

    cout << "enter a radius:";        // second sphere
    cin >> radius;
    volume = (4.0 / 3.0) * radius * radius * radius * 3.14;
    cout << "the volume is" << volume << endl;
    cout << "enter a radius:";        // third sphere
    cin >> radius;
    volume = (4.0 / 3.0) * radius * radius * radius * 3.14;
    cout << "the volume is" << volume << endl;
}
```

This approach is, of course, very impractical if the number of different data to be processed is large. A simpler approach is to instruct that certain statements (or compound statement blocks) are repeated using the **while** statement:

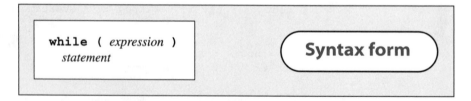

```
while ( expression )
    statement
```

Syntax form

CONCEPT

the while statement

When a **while** statement is encountered during the execution of a program, it instructs the CPU to repeatedly execute the associated *statement* as long as the *expression* is true. The same relational operators you learned to use with the **if** expression can be used in the **while** expression. The flow of execution through a **while** statement might be symbolically represented as in Figure. 2.2.

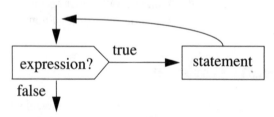

Figure 2.2 Symbolic representation of the flow of execution through a while statement

KEY TERM
loop

Note from Figure 2.2 that the *expression* is first tested. If true, the associated statement is executed. Control returns back to retest the *expression* and the cycle continues. This is called a program *loop*. Nearly all useful programs contain some type of loop, and we will return to this mechanism often in this text. For example, the following outputs the numbers 1, 2, 3, 4, 5, 6, 7, 8, 9:

```
n = 1.0;
while (n < 10.0)
{   cout << n << endl;
    n = n+1.0;
}
```

EXPERIMENT

What would happen if you use the wrong comparison operator? Change the relational operator from < to > and try the program just given.

2.4 User's manual

CONCEPT
write the user's
manual first

Let's return to the problem of finding the volume of a number of different spheres. Rather than fixing the number of radii to be entered at three, we will extend the problem and let the user instruct the program when all spheres have been calculated. We often begin the design of a program by writing the *user's manual* first. These are the instructions given to users to help them properly operate the program. After all, if we cannot describe how the program is going to interact and perform, we really don't know what to write! Writing the manual first is part of our program analysis and design. We will return to this concept later. For now, if we choose to name our program CALCVOL2, this might be our manual:

> When the CALCVOL2 program is run, it begins by prompting you to enter a radius. Respond by typing the radius value and press the Enter key. The program then displays the volume for the sphere with this radius using the formula $volume = \frac{4}{3}\pi(radius)^3$ and again prompts you for a radius for another calculation. When you have processed all radii, enter a value of –1.0 for a radius. This indicates that you are done, and the program terminates.

With this user's manual, we know just what the interaction will look like when the program is executed—something just like the following dialog (where user responses to program prompts are underlined):

```
enter a radius: 2.0
volume for radius 2 is 33.4933
```

```
enter a radius: 3.5
volume for radius 3.5 is 179.503
enter a radius: -1.0
program done.
```

2.5 Use of program loops

The **while** statement is used to generate a program loop for a variety of different reasons. In general, all program loops can be classified as *indefinite* or *counted*.

2.5.a Indefinite loops

KEY TERMS
indefinite loop, sentinel

The next job is to write a program that acts as described in the user's manual presented earlier. Consider Listing 2.4. Since you cannot predict how many times the statement block of the **while** will repeat simply by looking at the program, it is known as an *indefinite loop*. The number of repeats depends on how many radii the user wishes to process. When an indefinite loop depends on the user entering a special value to indicate that the program should stop looping, this special value is known as a *sentinel*. Obviously, a sentinel must be a value that does not normally occur in the list of values being read and processed. An indefinite loop that terminates upon reading a sentinel value has the following general model:

```
cin >> variable;
while (expression comparing variable with sentinel)
{   calculation or other use of variable;
    cin >> variable;
}
```

CONCEPT
the sentinel loop

If the variable used in the testing expression was not first input, it would not have a known value at the first test, and the behavior of the loop may be unpredictable. Similarly, if the variable was not filled with new input at the bottom of the repeated block, it could never change and cause the loop to terminate. If this loop executed once, it would execute an infinite number of times!

KEY TERM
infinite loop

There is a special term for a loop that never terminates — an *infinite loop*. Consider the following small example:

```
range = 7.0;
while (range > 5.0)
{   value = range * 2.0;
    cout << value;
}
```

WAY! WRONG

Notice that the value of variable `range` never changes inside the repeating block of statements. When executed, the CPU will continually (or infinitely) compute and output the value of `range*2` as fast as it can. When this occurs, you can usually interrupt or abort the program if the loop contains an input or output statement by pressing Ctrl-C on the computer keyboard.

Another common mistake made by beginning programmers is to place a semicolon after the parentheses as follows:

```
while (range > 5.0) ;
{   value = range * 2.0;
    cout << value;
}
```

WAY! WRONG

Remember that the semicolon by itself can be an empty or null statement. In the example, it is this empty statement that is being repeated—another infinite loop. The compiler, of course, does not consider that you properly indented the block of statements; the block will be treated as simply following the loop, not as a part of it.

Using this mechanism or model of an indefinite loop, we can now write the program to calculate sphere volumes as follows in Listing 2.4.

Listing 2.4

```
// CALCVOL2.CPP Calculate sphere volumes with a user-
// controlled indefinite loop.
#include <iostream.h>
void main()
{   float radius, volume;
    cout << "enter radius values (-1 to stop): ";
    cin >> radius;
    while (radius > 0.0)
    { volume = (4.0 / 3.0) * radius * radius * radius * 3.14;
      cout << "the volume is " << volume << endl;
      cin >> radius;
    }
}
```

EXPERIMENT

What would happen if you enter a list of five radii on the same line before pressing the Enter key? Listing 2.4 expects the user to enter one radius value at a time.

2.5.b   Counted loops

When the number of times a loop repeats can be determined by looking at the program, it is known as a definite or *counted loop*. Suppose we wish to rewrite the CALCVOL program so that it always processes five spheres. In other words, we do not expect the user to enter anything special to stop the loop; it always repeats exactly five times. Before writing this new CALCVOL program, let's consider first the following simple definite loop to output HELLO five times as shown in Listing 2.5.

Listing 2.5

```
// HELLO.CPP A program to output  "HELLO" 5 times
#include <iostream.h>
void main()
{   float count;
    count = 0.0;
    while (count < 5.0)
    { cout << "HELLO" << endl;
      count = count + 1.0;
    }
}
```

An example of the execution of this program looks like this:

```
HELLO
HELLO
HELLO
HELLO
HELLO
```

First, look at the assignment statement count = count + 1.0;. While that would give a heart attack to an algebra teacher, this is not algebra but a program assignment instruction. It indicates that 1.0 is to be added to the old value of count and this new value is to be placed back into the variable count. This is often called an accumulating or an incrementing assignment statement. (Actually, this is so common in C++ that there is a special operator for this action. We'll come back to that issue later. For now, incrementing a variable this way will help you become more aware of the difference between algebra and assignment statements.)

Let's take a look at how the loop works. The program first initializes a variable (in this case, count) to zero. Each time the bottom of the loop is reached, the program adds 1.0 to this variable, and the CPU jumps back to the top of the loop. The **while** loop tests this variable to determine whether the loop should be repeated. The execution table for this segment is given in Table 2.1.

Table 2.1   **Execution table for Listing 2.5**

Statement	Count	Expression	Output
count = 0.0	0.0		
while (count < 5.0)	0.0	true	
cout << "HELLO"	0.0		HELLO
count = count + 1.0	1.0		
while (count < 5.0)	1.0	true	
cout <<"HELLO"	1.0		HELLO
count = count + 1.0	2.0		
while (count < 5.0)	2.0	true	
cout << "HELLO"	2.0		HELLO
count = count + 1.0	3.0		
while (count < 5.0)	3.0	true	
cout <<"HELLO"	3.0		HELLO
count = count + 1.0	4.0		
while (count < 5.0)	4.0	true	
cout <<"HELLO"	4.0		HELLO
count = count + 1.0	5.0		
while (count < 5.0)	5.0	false	

In general, any block of statements could be made to repeat five times by placing it inside the foregoing loop. To change the number of iterations, one simply changes the test expression to compare against a different number limit. Take a look at the following diagram:

```
count = 0.0;
while (count < Max)
{
```

> *whatever statements are placed here will be executed exactly* Max *times*

```
    count = count + 1.0;
}
```

Let's go back now to the problem of processing exactly five different spheres. We will simply copy the statements from the original program (which processed only one sphere) and use them to replace the cout << "HELLO" statement in the definite loop segment in Listing 2.5 (see Listing 2.6).

Listing 2.6

```
// CALCVOL3.CPP Program to calc. sphere volumes using
// a definite loop for 5 iterations
#include <iostream.h>
void main()
{   float radius, volume, count;
    cout << "enter radius values: ";
// loop for 5 iterations
    count = 0.0;
    while (count < 5.0)
    { cin >> radius;
      volume = (4.0 / 3.0) * radius * radius * radius * 3.14;
      cout << "the volume is " << volume << endl;
      count = count + 1.0;
    }
}
```

EXPERIMENT

What would happen if you forgot to increment the counting variable? Remove the count=count+1.0 statement and try the program in Listing 2.6.

2.5.c Summing and counting

A common use of the loop is to sum a series or list of values. Let's use an indefinite loop to input a list of positive values. The loop should terminate when the sentinel value of −1.0 is read. Each time a new value is input, that value will be added to the sum of all the previous values (Listing 2.7). Notice that prior to adding values into the variable sum, it is first initialized to zero. In this manner, the first time the statement

```
sum = sum + number;
```

is executed, the zero in sum is replaced by the first value read. Each successive time this statement is executed, sum will be replaced by the previous sum value plus the new value just input.

Listing 2.7

```
// SUM.CPP A program to sum a list of positive values
#include <iostream.h>
void main()
{   float number, sum;
    sum=0.0;
```

```
        cout << "enter a list of positive values (ending with -1.0): ";
        cin >> number;
        while (number > 0.0)
        {sum = sum + number;
         cin >> number;
        }
        cout << " sum is " << sum << endl;
}
```

Here is an example execution of the program:

```
enter a list of positive values (ending with -1.0): 5.0 7.0 9.0 -1.0
sum is 21
```

The execution table for the program in Listing 2.7, assuming the same list, is given in Table 2.2.

CONCEPT
initialization

There is a shorthand method of declaring and initializing a variable in one statement. Instead of a declaration and an assignment statement to set sum to zero, the following is equivalent:

```
float sum = 0.0;
```

In general, any variable name in a declaration statement can be followed by an assignment symbol = and an initial value. You should remember that this initial value is stored for the variable only once—when it is set up or allocated.

Suppose, the *count* of values read is to be displayed in addition to the sum. We can add another variable called count, which is initialized to 0.0 at the top of the program. Each time a new value is read and summed, we simply add 1.0 to count.

Table 2.2 Execution table for Listing 2.7 and inputs 5.0, 7.0, 9.0, −1.0

Statement	Expression	Number	Sum
cout << "enter...		?	0.0
cin >> number		5.0	0.0
while (number > 0.0)	true	5.0	0.0
sum=sum+number		5.0	5.0
cin >> number		7.0	5.0
while (number > 0.0)	true	7.0	5.0
sum=sum+number		7.0	12.0
cin >> number		9.0	12.0
while (number>0.0)	true	9.0	12.0
sum=sum+number		9.0	21.0
cin >> number		−1.0	21.0
while (number>0.0)	false	−1.0	21.0
cout << "sum is ...			

At the end of the indefinite loop when the sentinel is read, sum contains the total of all values read and count contains the number of values read. Obviously, the average of all values can then be calculated (Listing 2.8).

Listing 2.8

```
// SUMAVE.CPP A program to sum and average a list
// of positive values
#include <iostream.h>
void main()
{   float number, sum = 0.0, count = 0.0, average;
    cout << "enter a list of positive values (ending with -1.0): ";
    cin >> number;
    while (number > 0.0)
    {   sum = sum + number;
        count = count + 1.0;
        cin >> number;
    }
    cout << " sum is " << sum << endl;
    average = sum / count;
    cout << "The average is: " << average << endl;
}
```

Notice that this program would run into problems if the very first number entered were the sentinel value of –1.0. In that case, the **while** loop would not even be entered. When the assignment statement to calculate average was reached, count would be zero and a run-time error would occur since division by zero is not possible. (What would you do to prevent this run-time error from occurring in this situation?)

KEY TERM

condition variable or flag

Sometimes the condition that should cause a loop to terminate is more complex than a single condition or comparison of values. Occasionally, a loop should be terminated when any one of a set of possible conditions becomes true. In these situations, it is often convenient to use a *condition variable* (sometimes called a *flag*). A condition variable is simply a variable that is initialized to a predetermined value. The loop is set to terminate when the condition variable changes. We will use 1.0 as the predetermined value. When the loop should stop, we will change this value to zero. Within the loop, as many **if** statements as are needed are used to test the several conditions that might cause the loop to terminate and change the condition variable if any of these conditions are true.

For example, suppose a loop is needed to sum an indefinite list of positive values until either (a) a sentinel value of a negative number is encountered or (b) the sum becomes greater than 100. This loop should terminate if either of these conditions is true. To accomplish this, we will define a condition variable called done and initialize it to 1. Each time a value is read, it will be tested as a possible sentinel. Within the loop, each new value of the running sum will be tested to check for a value greater than 100. We will assume the first value read is never the sentinel:

```
float done = 1.0;
float sum = 0.0;
float value;

cin >> value;                      // get the first value

while (done > 0.0)
{   sum = sum + value;
    if (sum > 100.0)               // check for sum limit
        done = 0.0;
    else
    {   cin >> value;              // get next input value
        if (value < 0.0)           // check for sentinel
            done = 0.0;
        else ;
    }
}
```

Keep in mind that there are other statements used in program looping, just as there are other conditional statements in addition to the **if**. Before we examine these other statements, let's first gain some experience in applying loops and conditions in relevant and practical programs.

2.6 Nested conditions and loops

What if we have a need to express more than two choices or alternatives in a program? For example, suppose there were three different formulas for calculating employee pay from the previous example:

1. If an employee works 40 hours or less: $pay = hours \times rate$

2. From 40 to 60 hours: $pay = (40 \times rate) + (overtime \times 1.5 \times rate)$

3. Over 60 hours: $pay = (40 \times rate) + (overtime \times 2.0 \times rate)$

In other words, employees are paid time and a half for overtime if they work between 40 and 60 hours, but they are paid double time for all overtime hours if they work more than 60 hours. We need to be able to express these three choices in a program. One method of using the **if** statement to make multiple choices is to *cascade* the choices. Figure 2.3 is a symbolic diagram of these three cascaded choices.

In each choice of this diagram, the number of hours worked is compared with increased limits. This same diagram might also be represented in a skeletal C++ form. In this form, we simply substitute ovals containing the symbolic English of needed operations:

```
if (hours <= 40.0)
{
}                    (  use formula 1  )
else
```

```
{   if (hours <= 60.0)
    {
    }            use formula 2
    else
    {
    }        use formula 3
}
```

Making this type of skeletal segment allows the programmer to ensure that the braces are properly placed and that the appropriate true and false sections of each choice are in the correct locations. Later, it is a simple matter to remove the ovals and fill in the specific statements associated with each symbolic English statement. This skeletal diagram can easily be converted to a C++ program, which is shown in Listing 2.9

Now, you may be thinking that some of the braces in Listing 2.9 are not really necessary, which is true. You may decide at this point to eliminate any brace pairs that enclose only a single statement. It would not be wrong, however, simply to leave them in place! Suppose that during a future modification or program upgrade, you needed to change formula 1 and replace it with several statements. If the braces are already in place, the potential for introducing an error is much less than if you now must realize they need to be inserted.

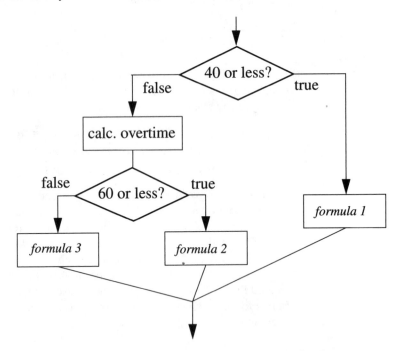

Figure 2.3 Cascading two **if** statements to make three choices.

Listing 2.9

```cpp
// CALCPAY3.CPP Program with 3 formula choices
#include <iostream.h>
void main()
{   float hours, pay, rate, overtime;
    cout << "enter hours and rate: ";
    cin >> hours >> rate;

    if (hours <= 40.0)
    {   pay = hours * rate;
    }
    else
    {   overtime = hours - 40.0;
        if (hours <= 60)
        {   pay = (40.0 * rate) + (overtime * 1.5 * rate);
        }
        else
        {   pay = (40.0 * rate) + (overtime * 2.0 * rate);
        }
    }

    cout << "pay is " << pay;
}
```

Notice that the careful indentation and placing of braces help the reader follow the logic and intention of the program. Consider how difficult it would be for another programmer (or the grader for your class!) to follow this program if no indentation was used and if the braces were not consistently placed.

Suppose a program is needed to output a table of powers for the numbers 1.0 to 10.0. For each number, the square, cube, fourth, fifth, and sixth power are to be output in a form similar to the following:

```
Table of Powers
    N       2       3       4       5       6
   1.0     1.      1.      1.      1.      1.
   2.0     4.      8.      16.     32.     64.
   3.0     9.      27.     81.     243.    729.
   4.0     16.     64.     256.    1024.   4096.
   5.0     25.     125.    625.    3125.   15625.
```

This can easily be accomplished with nested definite loops. First, of course, there must be a segment to print the table title and headings. Next we will need to output five lines, one for each value of N. Let's consider first the outer loop, which will be responsible for these five lines of the table.

```
cout << "table of powers" << endl;
cout << "   N    2    3    4    5    6" << endl;
N = 1.0;
while (N <= 5)
{
```

display a line of 6 powers of N

```
    N = N + 1.0;
}
```

Let's now consider the responsibility of the nested oval. This can be accomplished with another loop with one iteration for each power of N. Each successive power of N is just N times the previous power. The first value output is N^1, which of course is just N. The loop must output six values and then an end of line:

```
count = 0.0;
power = 1.0;
while (count < 6.0)
{   power = power * N;
    cout << "    " << power;
    count = count+1.0;
}
cout << endl;
```

This is often an effective way to approach nested loops and is known as *top-down design*. We will return to this topic in the next chapter. When using nested loops, it is often helpful to the reader if you place a comment at the end of each loop indicating which expression is controlling the loop. The completed program is written by doing a little pasting and adding declarations for the variables utilized (Listing 2.10).

Listing 2.10

```
// GENTAB.CPP Generate a table of powers of the values 1 to 5
#include <iostream.h>
void main()
{   float N, count, power;
    cout << "table of powers" << endl;
    cout << "   N    2    3    4    5    6" << endl;
    N = 1.0;
    while (N <= 5.0)
    {   count = 0.0;
        power = 1.0;
        while (count < 6.0)
        {   power = power * N;
            count = count+1.0;
            cout << "    " << power;
        }                                   // end of (count < 6) loop
```

```
      cout << endl;
      N = N + 1.0;
   }                                    // end of (N<=5) loop
}
```

2.7 Example project

Suppose a grading program is needed to calculate the average grade for 25 students. Each student has anywhere from two to ten different grades. The program is to output the average grade for each student and a summary table indicating the number of As, Bs, Cs, Ds, and Fs. We will use a flat grading scale where As are 90 and above, Bs are 80 up to less than 90, and so on.

The input data are organized so that each individual student is represented by a list of numbers on a single line. The first number is a student ID, and the rest of the numbers are grades ending with a sentinel value of –1.0. For example, here is some possible input (for the first four students):

```
2345 89.4 91.3 67.8 83.5 75.2 -1.0
3456 75.0 57.6 81.0 65.0 -1.0
4567 98.2 93.4 81.2 79.3 87.5 88.5 95.6 97.4 -1.0
7890 73.0 65.8 83.5 87.2 -1.0
...
```

The output is to list each student ID and an associated average grade. At the bottom of the output, the summary of grades is given. For example:

```
student 2345         average 81.44
student 3456         average 69.65
student 4567         average 90.14
student 7890         average 77.38
...
grade summary:  A 4, B 6, C 10, D 4, F 1
```

Let's start with the declarations for variables we think we might need for the program:

```
float A=0.0, B=0.0, C=0.0, D=0.0, F=0.0;// grade counts
float ave, sum, grade, grade_count;// grade calculation vars
float ID;                          // student ID number
float count;                       // loop counter for 25 students
```

Using the top-down approach, let's first look at a segment that could be used to process the entire list of students. The actual work of processing a single student will be left as a symbolic oval:

```
count = 0.0;
while (count < 25.0)
```

```
    {
```
> process a student to calculate "average" grade

> determine grade and increment the appropriate grade count

```
        count = count + 1.0;
    }
cout << "A " << A << ", B " << B << ", C " << C << ", D " << D
    << ", F " << F << endl;
```

Now we need to flesh out the first oval, which has the job of processing a single student. The first input number is just the student ID, and the rest of the numbers are a sentinel list of grades. We will use a summing loop to add them up and count the number of grades. The average is then just this sum divided by the grade count:

```
cin >> ID;
grade_count = 0.0;
sum = 0.0;
cin >> grade;
while (grade > 0.0)
{   sum = sum + grade;
    grade_count = grade_count + 1.0;
    cin >> grade;
}
ave = sum / grade_count;
```

Notice that we reset sum to zero at the top of the loop rather than in the declaration. That is because it needs to start over for each of the 25 students, not just the first! Now let's flesh out the second oval. We will use a sequence of nested **if** statements to test which grade category this average falls within and then simply increment that category:

```
if (ave >= 90.0)
    A = A + 1.0;
else if (ave >= 80.0)
    B = B + 1.0;
else if (ave >= 70.0)
    C = C + 1.0;
else if (ave >= 60.0)
    D  = D + 1.0;
else F = F + 1.0;
```

The final program is now written by pasting these segments in the appropriate places (Listing 2.11).

Listing 2.11

```cpp
// AVEGRADE.CPP Calculate 25 average student grades, report summary
#include <iostream.h>
void main ( )
{   float A=0.0, B=0.0, C=0.0, D=0.0, F=0.0;    // grade counts
    float ave, sum, grade, grade_count;         // grade calculation vars
    float ID;                                   // student ID number
    float count;                                // loop counter for 25 students
    count = 0.0;
    while (count < 25.0)                         // loop over 25 students
    {   cin >> ID;
        grade_count = 0.0;
        sum = 0.0;
        cin >> grade;
        while (grade > 0.0)                      // loop through list of grades
        {   sum = sum + grade;
            grade_count = grade_count + 1;
            cin >> grade;
        }                                        // end of (grade > 0.0) loop
        ave = sum / grade_count;                 // calc this student's grade

        if (ave >= 90.0)                         // add a count to appropriate
            A = A + 1.0;                         //   grade category
        else if (ave >= 80.0)
            B = B + 1.0;
        else if (ave >= 70.0)
            C = C + 1.0;
        else if (ave >= 60.0)
            D = D + 1.0;
        else F = F + 1;

        count = count + 1.0;                     // bottom of (count < 25) loop
    }
        cout << "A " << A << ", B " << B << ", C " << C << ", D " << D
        << ", F " << F << endl;
}
```

2.8 Summary

KEY TERMS   Several new terms were introduced in this chapter:

1. *conditional statement*—an expression that is either true or false, often used in an **if** statement.

2. *flow of control*—the flow of execution or the order in which statements are executed.

3. *relational expression*—a true/false condition using the relational operators.

4. *loop*—repeated execution of a statement or block of statements.

5. *indefinite loop*—a loop where the exact number of iterations or repeats cannot be predicted by examining the program code.

6. *definite loop*—a loop that will repeat a predetermined number of times.

7. *infinite loop*—a loop that never finishes or exits.

8. *sentinel*—a special input value that indicates an indefinite loop should terminate.

9. *counted loop*—a loop that uses an incrementing variable to maintain a running count of the number of loop iterations.

10. *condition variable*—a program variable used in a loop condition to represent the combination of several different relations, which is tested and changed using multiple **if** statements within the loop.

CONCEPTS   The syntax forms introduced in this chapter covered two new statements, the **if** and the **while**.

```
if ( expression )
    statement
else
    statement

while ( expression )
    statement
```

Most commonly, the expression tested for the **if** and **while** is a relational comparison. Four relational operators for comparison expressions were introduced:

```
>    greater than
<    less than
>=   greater than or equal to
<=   less than or equal to
```

A common use of the **while** is for a loop that is used to process an indefinite list of input values ending with a sentinel value. This loop has the following form:

```
cin >> variable;
while (expression comparing variable with sentinel)
{   calculations or processing;
    cin >> variable;
}
```

Another use of the **while** is for a loop that executes a counted or definite number of times. This loop has the following form:

```
count = 0.0;
while (count < number of iterations  )
{   calculations or processing;
    count = count + 1.0;
}
```

It is possible to initialize a variable as part of a declaration statement by following the variable name with an assignment operator and a value.

Two important hints to program development were given:

1. To make a program more readable, indentation of nested statements and alignment of opening and closing braces should be consistent.

2. A good first step to designing a program solution is to write the user's manual defining how the program and user will interact and what the program will produce or calculate from the input.

Table 2.3 Example segments

`if (age <= 56.0)`
`    cout << "young" << endl;`
`else`
`    cout << "old" << endl;`
	if age is less than or equal to 56, output "young"; otherwise output "old"

`sum = 0.0;`
`while (sum < 10.0)`
`    sum = sum + 1.0;`
	Start sum at 0
	While sum is less than 10, continue to add 1.0 to sum

`cin << age;`
`while (age < 25.0)`
`{   cout << "valid age" << endl;`
`    cin << age;`
`}`
	Read a value for age
	While input values are less than 25, output "valid age".
	When not less, continue . . .

2.9 Exercises

2.9.a Short-answer questions

1. A statement that a program uses to choose between two alternative formulas is called a _____ statement.

2. A true/false test of a pair of values or variables is called a _____.

3. A loop that repeats a fixed or predetermined number of times is called a _____ loop.

4. A loop where the exact number of repeats or repetitions is not known is called a _____ loop.

5. To aid in program design, the _____ is often written (before or after) the program.

6. If the user is to first enter the count for a list of values (followed by the values themselves), the programmer would use a _____ loop.

7. If the user is to enter a sentinel value at the end of an indefinite list of values, the programmer would use a _____ loop.

8. List and explain the four relational operators presented in this chapter.

9. Will the following comparisons return true or false? Assume `a=4.0` and `b=3.0`:

   a. `(a < b)`

     b. `(a >= b)`
     c. `(a > b)`
     d. `(a < 4.0)`
     e. `(a >= 4.0)`

10. Draw a symbolic diagram or flowchart of a program segment that could be used to output the message PASS or FAIL for a given test score. Assume 65 and above is a passing score.

11. Draw a symbolic diagram or flowchart of a program segment that could be used to output a letter grade for a test score. Assume 90–100 is A, 80 up to less than 90 is B, 70 up to less than 80 is C, and so on.

12. What would be a good sentinel value for the following indefinite-list input data?
    a. a list of student ages
    b. a list of mean temperature differences between consecutive days
    c. a list of daily gas mileage rates for a company car
    d. a list of daily checking account balances

13. Give a section of code that could be used to
    a. output YES if the variable `cost` is less than 0.0 (otherwise do nothing)
    b. output YES if the variable `cost` is greater than 0.0 but not greater than 100.0 (otherwise do nothing)

14. Give a section of code that could be used to output YES if the variable `cost` is greater than 100.0 or output NO if `cost` is less than or equal to 100.0.

15. Give a section of code that could be used to input and sum a list of exactly 25 values.

16. What is the output result of the following program segments?

    a.
    ```
    float n;
    n=0.0;
    while (n<10.0);
    {   cout << n << endl;
        n = n+2.0;
    }
    ```

    b.
    ```
    float n, k;
    n=0.0;   k=0.0;
    while (n<4.0)
    {    while (k<2.0)
    {    cout << n << "," << k << endl;
        k = k+1.0;
        }
        n = n+1.0;
    }
    ```

17. Describe the nature of the following syntax errors:

    a.
    ```
    if x > y   cout << "yes";
    else cout << "no";
    ```

    b.
    ```
    if (x >= y)
        {   cout << "yes";
            y = y+1.0;
    else cout << "no";
    ```

18. Give a program segment using a condition variable that could be used to sum input values until (a) the sum was greater than 100.0 or (b) a negative sentinel value was input.
19. Give a program segment of nested `if` statements that could be used to output YES if the variable `age` is (a) less than 100.0 and (b) greater than 25.0. If neither condition is true, the segment should output NO.
20. Give a program segment to input an indefinite list of positive values ending with a negative sentinel value and then output the maximum value read.

2.9.b Projects

1. Write a program to input a test score in the range 0 to 100.0 and then output the message `passing` if the score is above 65.0 or the message `failing` if the score is less than or equal to 65.0.
2. Modify the program written for project 1 so that the program will process an entire list of test scores. Assume the test scores will be entered one per line and that the list will end with a negative sentinel score.
3. Modify the program written for project 2 so that the number of test scores processed and the average of all test scores are output just before the program terminates.
4. Write and test a program to output a letter grade for a given test score using the criteria of short answer question 11.
5. Modify the program written for project 4 so that letter grades are output for a list of test scores. Assume test scores will be entered one per line and that the list will end with a negative sentinel score.
6. Modify the program written for project 4 so that letter grades are output for a list of exactly five test scores. Assume test scores will be entered one per line. After the fifth test score has been processed, the program should automatically terminate.
7. Write and test a complete program to input and sum a list of numbers until any one of the following conditions is true: (a) the sum exceeds 100.0, (b) a negative value is input, or (c) a maximum of 25 numbers have been summed. When the loop terminates, output the sum.
8. Write a program to calculate and output the minimum, maximum, and average of a list of positive test scores. Assume the scores will be entered one per line and that the list will end with a negative sentinel score.
9. **Creative Challenge:** Project 6 assumes that test scores are all positive. Suppose a program were needed for scores that could take on any value: positive, zero, or negative. Write a program to solve the general problem of finding the average of a list of values (positive, zero, or negative). Assume any value is possible and any number of values may be entered. You have not yet been taught a simple way of solving this problem, so be as creative as you can with what you know. You may need to place some extra requirements on the user or some additional constraints on the program, but get as close to the ideal solution as you can.

10. **Creative Challenge:** Write a program to calculate the square root of a number N. A square root can be approximated by making an initial guess of the root. This initial guess can, of course, be checked by squaring and comparing against the number N. Obviously, the initial guess will probably be quite wrong. A better guess can be calculated from this initial guess using the following formula:

$$nextguess = 0.5\left(lastguess + \left(\frac{N}{lastguess}\right)\right)$$

where N is the number for which a square root is to be calculated. Use 1.0 as your initial guess. This formula allows a previous guess at the root (lastguess) to be improved (nextguess). Repeat this calculation until the difference between two successive guesses is less than 0.005.

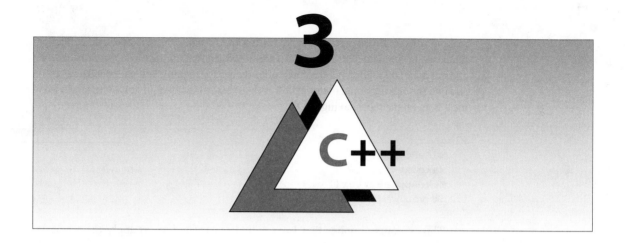

Simple Functions

As we begin to write more complex and involved programs, you will begin to find that they are harder and harder to design, implement, and manage. This chapter presents methods of modularizing complex programs into smaller and more manageable units called functions. Proper use of functions will significantly reduce your workload as a programmer.

3.1 Modular programming concepts

There are many analogies to computer programs in the world around us. Consider the following simple recipe for my wife's homemade rolls:

> Dissolve 1 cup hot water, 1/2 cup sugar, and 1/2 cup oil in large bowl.
> Add 3 well-beaten eggs, 2 teaspoons salt, 2 cups flour, and mix well.
> Add 1 Tbs yeast dissolved in 1/4 cup warm water and 2 1/2 cups additional flour.
> Mix until well blended. Let sit for 1 hour, then cover and refrigerate overnight.
> Roll onto floured board and cut into 2.5" circles. Dip into melted butter and fold.
> Let rise on ungreased baking sheet for 2 hours.
> Bake at 400 degrees for 10 minutes or until lightly browned.

The idea of the recipe is that, by carefully following the instructions step-by-step, you can make rolls. If friends have this set of instructions, we could ask them to make some rolls simply by saying, "Please make rolls," rather than going to the bother of instructing them in each individual step. In essence, we have modularized the action of making rolls and we might even give this module a name: `MakeRolls()`. The parentheses in the name are used here simply to differentiate this as a *function module* and not a variable. Now if I have a similar recipe for making jam called `MakeJam()` and one for making apple butter called `MakeAppleButter()`, my wife might leave me a note on the table saying:

```
Please:
    MakeRolls();
    MakeJam();
    MakeAppleButter();
thank you.
```

This of course implies that I am politely instructed to (a) apply the recipe instructions for making rolls, then (b) apply the recipe instructions for making jam, and finally (c) apply the recipe instructions for making apple butter. In other words, the line `MakeRolls()` implies that I am to use or execute the instructions of this module. In computer science, asking a program to execute the instructions of a function is known as calling or invoking the function. The note is a request that the instructions of the `MakeRolls()` module are to be called, followed by calling the `MakeJam()` module, followed by calling the `MakeAppleButter()` module.

The note would be rather complex and harder to understand if all the required instructions of each recipe were given. Rather, they are modularized into three distinct and independent functions. These functions also represent reusable modules. Next week, my wife might leave a note asking that only rolls be made. Rather than restate the instructions, she would just reuse the function name `MakeRolls()`.

This analogy is related to computer programs in that we can modularize a block of instructions into a distinct and independent process and give it a representative name. Each time we wish the block of instructions for a function to be executed, we can simply invoke the function by referring to it by the given function name. First, we will examine how functions are written in C++ and then how such functions can be used to simplify and better manage the creation of complex programs.

The `main()` programs we have written so far have all been functions themselves. To write functions in C++, we follow a similar format but give these additional functions new names. The name `main()` is reserved for the first function to be executed when the program is run. The first syntax form box of Chapter 1 is repeated here for convenience.

```
#include <iostream.h>
definitions, declarations, and functions
void main()
    { declarations and statements
    }
```

Syntax form

CONCEPT
placing functions

Notice that there is a location between the #include line and the void main() line where functions may be placed. In general, a function should be placed above any of the other functions (or the main program) that will need to use it. (We will see in Chapter 8 that functions may be placed in other locations, but those are concerns we do not wish to address just yet.) Formally, a function is a kind of definition. When you write or specify a function, we say you are "defining" the function.

3.2 Top-down design with functions

The general format for a function is given in the following syntax form box:

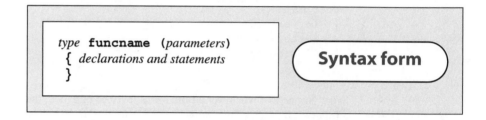

```
type funcname (parameters)
{ declarations and statements
}
```

Syntax form

As in other chapters, the items in italics are to be replaced with specific items of the programmer's choosing. We will initially use the reserved word **void** for the function type, as we have done with the main() functions or programs we have written so far.

CONCEPT
begin function names with a capital

The name given to a function (funcname) must follow the same rules as those for a variable name. We should, of course, give functions names that describe in some way what the purpose of each function is. It is usually very helpful to begin a function name with a capital letter. In that way, it is immediately obvious which program names are associated with variables and which are associated with functions. Notice also that a function name is always followed by a set of parentheses.

KEY TERM
parameters

The *parameters* item in the syntax form box is new. Parameters actually are optional and not every function will have them. For example, our previous main() programs did not. The parentheses are required, however, even if there are no parameters inside them. (We will return to parameters.)

This concept of modularization can be very helpful when designing a complex program. While writing the main() program, a programmer can refer to a module of instructions using a function name. Rather than deal with the details of how these module instructions are to be written, a programmer often simply refers to the function *abstractly* and continues with the bigger picture of writing the main() program.

In other words, a programmer may replace a pseudocode oval in a preliminary design with a function. For example, suppose a program is needed to print a company letter to a client. The programmer might begin with a general English outline of the steps this program needs to take:

1. Output the company letterhead and greeting
2. Output the letter
3. Output the standard closing

Since each of these steps probably represents many program statements (outputs), the programmer might choose to use a function for each one. In addition, the first and third also represent processes that might be useful in future letters. The main program can now be written using these function names:

```
#include <iostream.h>
```

$\left(\text{needed function definitions}\right)$

```
void main()
{   Letterhead();
    Letter();
    Closing();
}
```

Notice that whenever a function is invoked or called, the name of the function is followed by a set of parentheses. This is important and allows the compiler to know you wish a function to be invoked and that you are not simply referring to a variable.

The smaller problems associated with each function can now be worked on separately. (In fact, they could be worked on by three different programmers.) In effect, the programmer has applied a divide-and-conquer strategy by dividing a complex problem into separate modules and then attacking each module independently. The three functions might be written as follows:

```
void Letterhead()
{   cout << "      World Wide Widgets" << endl;
    cout << "      123 Easy Street" << endl;
    cout << "      New York, NY" << endl << endl;
}

void Letter()
{   cout << "Dear Sir or Madam," << endl;
    cout << "Your account is past due. We appreciate" << endl;
    cout << "prompt payment for services." << endl << endl;
}

void Closing()
{   cout << "Sincerely," << endl << endl << endl;
    cout << "Monty B. Jones, Pres." << endl;
}
```

These function bodies should be placed after the #include line and before the void main() line of the main program as in Listing 3.1.

Listing 3.1

```cpp
// LETTER.CPP  A program to generate a company letter
#include <iostream.h>

// Letterhead()  Prints the standard company letterhead
void Letterhead()
{   cout << "        World Wide Widgets" << endl;
    cout << "        123 Easy Street" << endl;
    cout << "        New York, NY" << endl;
}

// Letter()  Prints an overdue form letter
void Letter()
{   cout << "Dear Sir or Madam," << endl;
    cout << "Your account is past due. We appreciate" << endl;
    cout << "prompt payment for services." << endl;
}

// Closing()  Prints the standard company closing
void Closing()
{   cout << "Sincerely," << endl << endl << endl;
    cout << "Monty B. Jones, Pres." << endl;
}

// main program body
void main()
{   Letterhead();
    Letter();
    Closing();
}
```

EXPERIMENT

What would happen if parentheses are left off a function call?

3.3 Functions that return a value

CONCEPT
returning values

Often, a function is used to perform some task or process *and then return a result* for the main program (or other calling function) to use. This is accomplished by (a) specifying the *type* of result to be returned and (b) using the **return** statement to cause a value (of the specified type) to be handed back to the main program (or some other calling function). We will learn of several different types in a later chapter. For now, the only type you are familiar with is **float**. The **return** statement is simple—just the reserved word **return** and the single value or expression result to be returned:

```
return expression ;
```
Syntax form

The expression is commonly placed within parentheses, but that is not required. For example, suppose we need a program that can be used to calculate the monthly payments on a range of loan periods (number of months to pay off). The user is expected to provide the loan amount, the interest rate, and the range of loan periods (from 0 to 72 months). The program is to generate a table of monthly payments. A programmer might start with the following design:

> *Get the loan amount. Be sure it is a positive value.*

> *Get the loan interest rate. Be sure it is a positive value.*

> *Get the starting period. Be sure it is a positive value.*

> *Get the ending period. Be sure it is a positive value.*

> *Output the monthly payment for each loan period from start to end.*

The programmer would notice that the first four steps are very similar and might use a single function to accomplish these steps. The next step might then be to refine the outline using C++ code and to use functions for these first steps representing details that have not yet been worked out. The first four steps might simply call a function named GetPosAmount () as shown here (we'll ignore the last oval for now):

```
amount = GetPosAmount();
rate = GetPosAmount();
startperiod = GetPosAmount();
endperiod = GetPosAmount();
. . .
```

Notice that the instructions associated with the GetPosAmount () function are being reused! Instead of restating these instructions four different times, we simply call the function four times. Our program is significantly smaller than it would have been had we repeated the instructions. A possible implementation of the GetPosAmount () function is given in Listing 3.2. Notice that the type of the function is not **void**, but **float**, indicating that the function is to do a job *and return a decimal answer to the calling program*. The value to be returned is specified in the **return** statement.

Listing 3.2

```
// GetPosAmount()   Inputs and returns a positive value
float GetPosAmount()
{   float temp;
    cout << "Enter a positive value: ";
    cin >> temp;
    while (temp < 0.0)
    {   cout << "**Negative value, enter a positive value: ";
        cin >> temp;
    }
    return (temp);
}
```

This function prompts for and inputs a value from the user and then places the value into variable `temp`. If the value is less than zero, the function responds by warning the user of an entry error and reprompts for another value in a loop. This loop continues to reprompt and accept a new value until the user finally enters a positive value. This value (in variable `temp`) is then returned. An example of the execution of this function would look like this:

```
Enter a positive value:  -4.5
**Negative value, enter a positive value: -4.5
**Negative value, enter a positive value: 4.5
```

The code of this function could be copied into each of the `main()` program sections corresponding to steps 1 through 4 of the English outline, but look how much smaller and simpler the program is when the code is made general in a function that is simply reused for each of these four steps.

EXPERIMENT

What would happen if the calling program does not assign or use the returning value of a function?

3.4 Function parameters

Frequently, a function needs some additional information to complete its task. For example, suppose the statement of the problem is refined to more carefully ensure that valid input is being used: The loan amount must be between 0 and 30,000. The interest rate must be between 0 and 1.0. The starting period must be between 1 and 71. The ending period must be between the starting period and 72. The first design might be:

> *Get the loan amount. Be sure it is between 0 and 30,000.*

> *Get the loan interest rate. Be sure it is between 0 and 1.0.*

> *Get the starting period. Be sure it is between 1 and 71.*

> *Get the ending period. Be sure it is between the starting period and 72.*

> *Output the monthly payment for each loan period from start to end.*

KEY TERM

argument

The first four steps again involve getting a value from the user, but now we are interested in verifying that it lies within a known range. These four steps are still similar; they simply have different values which define a correct range. Values that are to be passed to a function for use in doing the job required are called *arguments*. Argument values are passed to a function when it is called simply by placing them inside the parentheses just after the function name. These arguments are then automatically copied into the function just before it begins execution (as will be illustrated in a moment).

What about the actual table calculation? Let's also call a function for this last design pseudocode oval. This last function will need to know the starting period and the ending period to produce a table:

```
amount = GetValueBetween (0.0, 30000.0);
rate = GetValueBetween (0.0, 1.0);
startperiod = GetValueBetween (1.0, 71.0);
endperiod = GetValueBetween (startperiod, 72.0);
CalcTable (startperiod, endperiod);
```

CONCEPT

use of function
return value

In each step, the function is called and passed values to be used in the statements of the function. The single value returned by the function is then stored into an appropriate variable. Actually, *the value returned by a function can be used in any expression just as the value of a constant might be used.* The following line would output the value returned by the function call (but fail to save it for later use):

```
cout << GetValueBetween (0.0, 30000.0) << endl;
```

The next instruction would multiply the value returned by a function call by 5.0, add 3.0, and save the result in variable demo:

```
demo = GetValueBetween (0.0, 30000.0) * 5.0 + 3.0;
```

These two instructions are just for demonstration, of course; they have no use in the loan program that is being developed.

A function is written to accept values being passed into it from a list of arguments by defining the variables which are to receive these values between the parentheses of the function heading or title. Refer back to the syntax form box for functions at the beginning of this chapter. These variables are known as *parameters* (as mentioned previously). Listing 3.3 gives the `GetValueBetween()` function needed by the programmer in the design given earlier. We'll ignore the code for the `CalcTable()` function for now—or leave it as an exercise for the student.

When the `GetValueBetween()` function is called, the first argument in the call is copied into the first parameter, the second argument is copied into the second parameter, and so on for as many parameters as are defined. The number of argument values passed to a function must match the number of corresponding parameters listed in the function definition. At this point in your career, an argument may be a constant, a variable, or even an expression. The variable name of a parameter may be the same as or different from the corresponding argument.

Listing 3.3

```
#include <iostream.h>

// GetValueBetween()  Inputs and returns a value which is between
// parameters min and max.
//IN: min -- the minimum acceptable input
//     max -- the maximum acceptable input

float GetValueBetween (float min, float max)
{   float temp, accept;
    cout << "Enter a value between " << min << " , " << max;
    cin >> temp;
    accept = 1.0;
    while (accept > 0.0)
      {   if (temp >= min)
              if (temp <= max) accept = 0.0;
              else ;
          else ;
          if (accept > 0.0)
            {   cout << "** illegal value, enter again: ";
                cin >> temp;
            }
          else ;
      }
    return (temp);
}

void CalcTable (float startperiod, float endperiod)
{   ...
}

void main ()
{   float amount, rate, startperiod, endperiod;

    amount = GetValueBetween (0.0, 30000.0);
    rate = GetValueBetween (0.0, 1.0);
```

```
        startperiod = GetValueBetween (1.0, 71.0);
        endperiod = GetValueBetween (startperiod, 72.0);
        CalcTable (startperiod, endperiod);
}
```

In Listing 3.3, the parameter variables which are to accept the argument values being passed to the function (when it is invoked) are declared inside the parentheses following the function name in the place where the function is actually written or defined. When a function is invoked or called, argument values are placed inside the parentheses to be passed to the function and used.

Thus, when a function begins, the parameters will already contain initial values—copies of the argument values passed to the function when it was invoked. When the function `GetValueBetween()` is called, there must always be two values between the parentheses. The first value will be copied into the variable `min`, and the second value will be copied into the variable `max`. Consider Figure 3.1. This figure is an attempt to diagram the action of calling the function `GetValueBetween()`. The top section diagrams what occurs when the function is called. If variable `x` is `5.5` and `y` is `7.8` when this function is called, these two values are copied into `min` and `max`, respectively. If the user enters `2.3` into `temp`, the function outputs the message `** illegal value, enter again:` and awaits another user input. If the user enters `6.5` the second time, this value falls between `min` and `max` and is accepted. The bottom section shows what occurs when the function returns the value of `temp` (`6.5`) back to the main program to be copied into the variable `z`.

Notice that the opening and closing braces of Listing 3.3 are carefully lined up one above the other. Statements that are part of the same block are indented the same amount. Subordinate statements that are part of an **if** statement are indented beyond the parent **if**. These are part of good programming style as we have previously mentioned. They definitely make the program much easier for others to read and follow.

KEY TERM

comment header

Notice also that the parameters of the function have special comments associated with them at the top of the function. In general, a good programmer is expected to place a block of comment lines at the top of each and every function. This comment block should, at a minimum, document and describe (a) what is expected to be passed into the function as parameters, (b) what the function is to accomplish, and (c) what the function is expected to return for the calling program to utilize. Naturally, the programmer may not know exactly what the values of the parameters and arguments will be when the program is executed but can still document what these parameters and the return value will represent and what the legal range of each should be. This is typically called the *comment header*.

The function parameters are labeled with the word `IN` within this comment header of Listing 3.3. This is to remind the reader that the function only receives copies of the corresponding arguments when the function is called. For example, in Figure 3.1, the values of `5.5` and `7.8` are passed from the variables `x` and `y` in the main program into the function parameters `min` and `max`. If the function were to change the value of variable `min` for some reason, this would *have no effect on the variable* `x` *in the main program*.

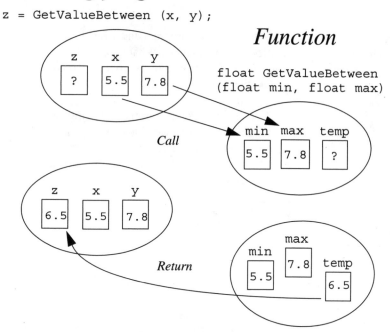

Calling program

```
z = GetValueBetween (x, y);
```

Figure 3.1 Parameter passing and function value return

3.5 Scope of variables

CONCEPT
function variables
are local

Note that in Figure 3.1 the function and main program are shown inside separate ovals. The purpose is to illustrate that these are separate functions and *each has its own separate set of variables*. Normally, the only variables that a function statement can reference are those that are declared in the same function. (There are methods of declaring variables that both can share, but that is a future topic. In addition, those methods are avoided in a well-designed program.) Remember that the main program is also a function and the same rule applies; the main program statements cannot reference any of the variables declared in any of the functions. The means of sharing values is by passing arguments into parameters and by functions returning values.

```
float SomeFunc(float x)
{   float y;
    y = z * x;              // ILLEGAL: z is not in this function!
    return (y);
}
void main()
{   float a, b;
    a = 5.9;
```

```
      y = a;          // ILLEGAL:  y is not in this function!
      b = SomeFunc(a);
      . . .
```

What if a main program and a function have variables of the same name? *They are separate and distinct.* What happens to function variables when the function returns? They are removed from program memory. In other words, *new memory space for function variables is allocated each time the function is called and deallocated when the function exits.*

Consider the example of the following section of code. Both the main program and the function have a variable named cost. The value of the main program cost is passed into the function to become the value of the function's variable cost. Even though the function changes its own value of cost, that change has no effect on the main program cost.

```
void SomeFunc (float cost)
{   cost = 7.2;
    cout << "In SomeFunc(), cost is" << cost;
}
void main ()
{   float cost;
    cost = 15.5;
    SomeFunc (cost);
    cout << "In main(), cost is" << cost;
}
```

The output of this code is:

```
In SomeFunc(), cost is 7.2
In main (), cost is 15.5
```

3.6 Constants

Often, a value used within a program or function is always a constant. For example, the numeric value of pi doesn't change. Rather than write this numeric constant into each expression calculation in a large program, it is often simpler to declare a name or identifier to be associated with each value that will not change. This is accomplished by using the qualifier **const** as is shown in the following syntax form box:

const float *identifier* = *value* ;   **Syntax form**

An identifier is just a name that follows the same rules you learned for variables names. To help you remember that this is a special identifier which will never change in value, it is a good idea to use a name in all capital letters:

```
const float PI = 3.14159;
```

The identifier PI can now be used throughout the function in which it is declared. If the function were ever to attempt to change the value associated with this name, a compile-time error message would result.

```
PI = 3.0;
```

Names that are associated with **const**ants must be initialized at declaration with the value they are intended to represent. They may never subsequently be assigned another value. Suppose a program needs to contain several summing loops, each for a list of the same number of values. This loop count could easily be defined in a const variable and referred to by each loop:

```
const float LOOPCOUNT = 25;
float count1, count2, count3 ;
. . .
while (count1 < LOOPCOUNT);
. . .
while (count2 < LOOPCOUNT);
. . .
while (count3 < LOOPCOUNT);
. . .
```

Now, if the program is ever modified to change to another size list, only the declaration and initialization for LOOPCOUNT need to be updated. Otherwise, the new programmer making the modification would need to search throughout the function looking for all situations where this value was referenced (and hope that all were identified).

In general, a good programmer will identify all the constants in a program and declare **const** identifiers for each. Throughout the program, these constants are referred to by name. Modification of the program at a later date becomes much simpler, and the program becomes much more readable and self-documenting for others. For example, suppose a program has many different loops which must all execute 25 times. The programmer wisely defines a **const** identifier LOOPCOUNT and references it in each loop condition. Now suppose the programmer needs to change all these loops to execute 50 times. Rather than edit each of the many loops, he or she can simply edit the single line that declares and initializes LOOPCOUNT.

Naturally, if a constant is declared within a function, it may only be referenced inside that function, just as with other variables. Suppose a constant is needed throughout a set of functions. Does it need to be redefined within each? The answer is no. If you reexamine the syntax form box at the beginning of this chapter, you will see that declarations may be placed after the `#include` statements and before the `main()` program (as well as functions and other definitions). Since these declarations are not within any one function, they become *global* to the rest of the file that follows—any function below the global declarations in the file can reference these identifiers. Just as with functions, a global constant name must be declared above any of the functions that wish to reference it.

In the following example file, the globally defined constant `PI` can be referenced and used in any of the file functions: `Function1()`, `Function2()`, or the main program.

```
#include <iostream.h>

const float PI = 3.14159;          // a globally defined constant

float Function1 ()
{ ...
}
float Function2 ()
{ ...
}
void main()
{ ...
}
```

CONCEPT

avoiding global variables

If **const** identifiers can be declared globally, why can't regular variables also be declared globally? Well, they can—it just isn't a good idea. It has been learned through years of experience that such globally accessible variables make a program more prone to errors and much more difficult to modify and maintain.

Look at it this way: If other programmers need to understand your work, they would expect that any values being used by a function are listed in the function parameters and documented with `IN` comments in the function heading. Any value returned by the function is given in a **return** statement and also documented in the function header. Another programmer should feel confident that a modification made to a function which does not disturb these `IN` parameters and returning value should have no other effects or impacts on the main program or functions that call it.

KEY TERM

side effect

If, however, a function also modifies a globally accessible variable used by other functions, that may be very difficult to see or recognize when reading the program. A simple modification to such a function by someone unaware of this global variable access could introduce effects with global consequences. An effect produced by a function that is not documented in the function header is called a *side effect*. Good programmers cautiously avoid allowing the potential for side effects in a function. If a programmer always tries to avoid the use of globally accessible variables, this potential for undesirable side effects is reduced.

The bottom line is this: Good programmers do not normally use global variables to ensure a style that leads to easy-to-read and easy-to-modify functions. Suppose, however, that a function needs to return more than a single result? There are more direct methods of accomplishing this than through global variables as you will see in Chapter 4.

CONCEPT

define functions below constants

Can you intermix function and constant declarations? Well yes, but it may not be a good idea. The simplest form to follow is to first declare all constants, next define all functions, and then define the main program. The reason for this suggestion is that a globally declared constant is only accessible to functions (and the main program) below the constant declaration. This concept is, of course, also true for functions as was mentioned earlier. Functions are only accessible to other functions (and the main program) below the function definition.

3.7 Example project

An interesting problem is encountered when trying to determine how many different combinations or committees of people can be chosen from a group. The formula associated with the number of ways r people can be selected from a group of n persons is the following:

$$C(n, r) = \frac{n!}{(n-r)!r!}$$

Here the ! math symbol indicates a factorial. The factorial of a number is defined as follows:

$$x! = x(x-1)(x-2)(x-3)\ldots 1$$

So, 5! is 5(4)(3)(2)(1), or 120. Now, suppose a committee of three is needed out of a group of seven people:

$$C(7, 3) = 7! / (7-3)! \, 3! = 5040 / ((24) \, 6) = 5040 / 144 = 35$$

In other words, there are 35 different committees of three that can be formed from a group of seven people. Now, a program to determine combinations would be simple to write if a function were available to perform these calculations. If such a function were available, the main program could look something like the following:

```
void main ()
{   float group_size, committee_size, combinations;
```

(*prompt user and perform inputs*)

```
    combinations = Combi (group_size, committee_size);
```

(*echo inputs and display the result*)

```
}
```

All this main program does is get input values from the user, call the `Combi ()` function for the calculation, and display the answer (along with an echo of the input data). Now, the function itself must in turn calculate three different factorials. The simple approach is to write a `Factorial ()` function and just call it three times in an expression:

```
float Combi (float group, float committee)
{   float combinations;
    combinations = Factorial (group) /
        (Factorial (group - committee) * Factorial (committee));
    return (combinations);
}
```

A factorial can be calculated with a loop that counts down until a value of 1 is reached. For each count of the loop, a running product is calculated for decreasing values of the argument n:

```
float Factorial (float n)
{   float product = 1.0;
    while (n > 1.0)
    {   product = product * n;
        n = n - 1.0;
    }
    return (product);
}
```

Since the `Combi ()` function calls the `Factorial ()` function, it should be defined below it. Since `main ()` calls `Combi ()`, the main program should be below them both. Now, let's improve the main program a bit so that it continually prompts the user for input and performs calculations until the user responds to indicate no further committee calculations are needed. We will also add an **if** statement to verify that the group size is larger than the size of the committee. The entire project with appropriate function header comments looks like Listing 3.4.

Listing 3.4

```
// Combcalc.cpp  Combinations calculations program
// Prompts the user for a group and committee size and then calculates
// number of different committees that can be formed.
#include <iostream.h>

// Factorial()  Returns the factorial of the argument n.
// IN:  n is a positive integer
float Factorial (float n)
{   float product = 1.0;
    while (n > 1.0)
    {   product = product * n;
```

```
        n = n - 1.0;
    }
    return (product);
}


// Combi ()  Returns the number of different committees
// that could be formed from group
// IN: group is a whole-number value greater than committee
//     committee is a positive whole-number value.
float Combi (float group, float committee)
{   float combinations;
    combinations = Factorial (group) /
        (Factorial (group - committee) * Factorial (committee));
    return (combinations);
}


void main()
{   float group_size, committee_size, combinations;
    float done = 1.0;
    while (done > 0.0)
    {   cout << "enter the size of the group and committee: ";
        cin >> group_size >> committee_size;
        if (group_size >= committee_size)
        {   combinations = Combi (group_size, committee_size);
            cout << "for " << group_size << " people and " <<
                committee_size << " sized committees, the ";
            cout << "number of committees is " <<
                combinations << endl;
        }
        else
            cout << " ** illegal values; group must be larger" << endl;
        cout << "Do you wish another calculation? ";
        cout << " enter 1.0 for yes, 0.0 for no: ";
        cin >> done;
    }
}
```

Now, there are three interesting "aspects" connected with this program which are not apparent in the program listing. First, if the number of committees is very large, the output value will appear in a somewhat unusual format. For example, consider the following execution using Borland C++ 4.5:

```
enter the size of the group and committee: 27 8
for 27 people and 8 sized committees,
the number of committees is 2.22008e+06
Do you wish another calculation? enter 1.0 for yes, 0.0 for no: 0.0
```

We will return to this particular format in Chapter 6. (Look ahead if you are interested—the topic is called "E-notation.") In general, **float** values that are very large or very small default to this new notation.

The second interesting aspect occurs when we use a group of people larger than about 35. The program results in a run-time error message:

```
enter the size of the group and committee: 35  8
**floating point overflow**
```

This particular error indicates that the program has attempted to calculate or store a **float** value larger than the computer is capable of representing. In other words, there are limits to the size or range of a **float** value!

The third aspect occurs when a group or committee size is entered as something other than a whole number. The program accepts this nonsensical input and dutifully outputs a nonsensical answer! The bottom line is this: We are becoming aware that **float** variables and values have limitations and may not be appropriate in all programming problems. There is a growing need for more capability in expressing data. Fortunately, there are additional variable types which address these concerns. We'll return to this problem.

EXPERIMENT

What would happen if the user enters values such as 5.5 or 9.3? The program in Listing 3.4 would be in error. How would you check the parameters of the Combi() function to verify that they were whole numbers? (Chapter 6 will examine this problem.)

3.8 Library functions

Many of the simpler functions we might need in a program have been written before. Groups of such functions can be placed into one or more system libraries and made available to program developers. All C++ development systems provide a standard library and usually also provide one or more specialized libraries of useful functions. You may think of a library as just a file containing a set of predefined functions. Rather than storing the source code version of these functions, libraries usually store only a precompiled version, but that is not particularly important to the following discussion.

3.8.a The standard library

KEY TERM
standard library

The *standard library* consists of functions that are common to all C++ development systems. These are functions with standardized names, parameters, and returning values which are provided with the software development system you are using. If you write a program under one development environment using or referencing one or more of these standard library functions (perhaps using Microsoft C++ on a personal computer), you can feel confident that your program will also compile and run correctly under another (perhaps using Gnu C++ on a workstation computer).

If your development environment has been set up correctly, you may use any of these library functions in a program simply by including the correct *header file* at the top of your program. The header file name always ends with .h, and it provides the correct interface to the needed library functions. The syntax for including an appropriate header file is the same as that used for **iostream.h**, which is itself one of these library header files. For example, to use the library function that calculates a square root, you must include the **math.h** file in addition to the **iostream.h** file as follows:

```
#include <iostream.h>
#include <math.h>
```

By referencing the appropriate header file, the development environment knows how to interface the needed functions in the library to the executable program being generated.

There are numerous library functions and they perform a variety of tasks. As we learn more of the C++ language, more of these functions will be introduced. Each development environment usually has a library manual or other such documentation to indicate how these functions are to be used, what they are intended to return, and what header files must be included. To start, some of the more common math functions are listed in Table 3.1. To use any of these functions, you need to include the math.h header file at the top of your program.

Listing 3.5 gives an example program which calculates the height of a tower and the distance from the observer to the top, given the ground distance from an observer to the tower and the angle the observer must look up to see the top. (To convert from degrees to radians, multiply by π and divide by 180.) The formulas used are:

$$ht = base \times \tan(angle)$$

$$dist = \sqrt{base^2 + ht^2}$$

Table 3.1 Some common standard library functions requiring
math.h

Name	Argument (`float`)	Returns (`float`)
cos(x)	x is an angle in radians	cosine of x
sin(x)	x is an angle in radians	sine of x
tan(x)	x is an angle in radians	tangent of x
sqrt(x)	x is any positive value	square root of arg
exp(x)	x is any value	exponential e^x
log(x)	x is any positive value	natural logarithm ln(x)
fabs(x)	x is any value	absolute value of x
pow(x, y)	x and y are any values	x raised to the y power

Note that even though both the function CalcHypot() and the main program have variables declared with names base, angle, and dist, they are separate and distinct variables.

Listing 3.5

```
// Program to calculate the height of a tower
#include <iostream.h>
#include <math.h>

// CalcHypot() A function to calc. and return the hypotenuse
// of a right triangle.
// IN:base; the base of the triangle
//     angle; an angle in degrees between the base and hypot.
float CalcHypot (float base, float angle)
{   float radians, ht, dist;
    const float pi_radians = 0.01745;       // pi / 180.0;
    radians = angle * pi_radians;
    ht = base * tan(radians);
    dist = sqrt (base*base + ht*ht);
    return (dist);
}

void main()
{   float base, angle, dist;
    cout << "enter base distance to tower:" ;
    cin >> base;
    cout << "enter angle (in degrees):" ;
    cin >> angle;
    dist = CalcHypot (base, angle);
    cout << " distance from observer to top: " << dist << endl;
}
```

3.8.b Specialized libraries

In addition to the standard library, each development system usually also provides one or more libraries of other useful functions the vendor felt customers might utilize. These extra functions are not standardized, and a program that uses them may not compile under a different development system. For example, the function clrscr() is available with the Borland C++ special console control library. This function simply clears the screen and moves the cursor to the top left corner. To gain access to this function, the **conio.h** header file must be included. The libraries of special functions associated with a particular system are usually documented in special manuals or on-line information. Be cautious in using specialized library functions because they can prevent your program from being used on other systems.

3.9 **Summary**

KEY TERMS

Terms associated with functions that were introduced in this chapter are the following:

1. *parameter*—a special function variable which is initialized with a corresponding argument value when the function is invoked.

2. *argument*—a value to be passed to a function (when the function is invoked) and represented by a corresponding parameter.

3. *comment header*—a block of documenting comments at the top of a function definition that clarifies the use of parameters and the intent of the function.

4. *side effect*—a function effect that is not documented in the function header, typically associated with a change to a global variable.

5. *standard library*—a collection of useful functions that is common to all C++ program development systems.

6. *header file*—a file referenced in an #include line which gives a program access to a set of external or library functions.

CONCEPTS

In this chapter, you learned that one method of simplifying a complex program is to modularize operations into *functions* to break a problem into more manageable pieces. Each problem piece can then be attacked separately. The general form of a function is as follows:

type funcname (*parameters*)
{ *declarations and statements*
}

Several important concepts were presented concerning the use of functions. If a function does not return a value, the type is **void**. If it returns a decimal number, the type should be **float**. The value returned by a function can be utilized in any expression similar to how a simple constant is used.

Variable values can be passed to a function as arguments. The arguments passed to a function must match the number and order of parameters a function expects. Function parameters must be declared within the parentheses following the function name in the head or top of the actual implementation.

Identifiers declared inside a function are local to that function and cannot be referenced by the main program (or other functions). Each time a function is called, its local variables are reallocated or created. When a function exits, its local variables are deallocated or destroyed.

Libraries consist of prewritten functions which are generally useful for a variety of programming problems. Including the appropriate header file at the top of a program allows access to and use of library functions.

Identifier names can be declared to hold constant values through use of the **const** declaration qualifier. Such **const** identifiers declared immediately after

#include statements become globally accessible to all functions and the main program below the declaration.

Several important hints regarding good programming practice were presented. It is important to choose descriptive names for functions to improve the readability of a program. Constants should be defined using the **const** qualifier for a declaration. This allows constants to be symbolically named in a program and makes the program more readable. In addition, later modifications to constants can be made in a central location.

While constants are often declared to be globally accessible, regular variables should not be. Make it a practice to share information with a function only through arguments/parameters and returning function values. Programmers who get into the habit of using globally accessible variables often inadvertently introduce side effects to functions which invariably cause problems when others must later make modifications to a program.

Table 3.2 Example segments

cost = CostCalc (5.4);	Call CostCalc and pass the value 5.4. The returning value is to be assigned to cost.
return (age);	The current function will return the value of age to the calling program or function.
const float FACTOR = 1.0;	FACTOR represents the constant 1.0.
#include <math.h>	This program will call math library functions.
float CostCalc (float x) { float y;	y and x are only accessible or visible within this function.

3.10 Exercises

3.10.a. Short-answer questions

1. The value to be passed to a function is known as a _____.
2. A variable that receives a copy of a value when a function is called is known as a _____.
3. Briefly explain the difference between *arguments* and *parameters*.
4. A _____ _____ is used to document the use of parameters and the intent of a function.
5. The _____ _____ is a collection of useful functions that is common to all C++ systems.
6. To access a function in the standard library, the _____ header file must be included.

7. To specify a function that returns a value, the function definition should use the word _____ prior to the function name.

8. May variables declared inside a function be referenced or used inside the `main()` program as well?

9. Explain where functions should be declared.

10. Explain where `const` identifiers are typically declared.

11. Give an example statement which could be used in a program to calculate the square root of the variable `distance`.

12. If a function does not return a value, with what *type* must the function be declared?

13. Identify and explain the syntax error in the following:

```
float SomeFunc (float cost)
{   float cost;
    ...
}
```

14. Is it possible for two distinct variables in a program to have the same name? Explain.

15. The following function is intended to calculate the payments on a car loan given the number of months to payoff and the interest rate:

```
float Payment (float num_months, float interest_rate)
   { ...
   }
```

Show how this function could be used to calculate and output the payments on a 52-month loan at 9%. Remember, 9% is actually 0.09.

16. Briefly explain what you would expect to happen if a function has two parameters declared, yet the main program attempts to call the function with only one argument.

17. If `SomefuncA()` calls or invokes `SomeFuncB()`, in what order should these two functions be defined?

18. Suppose a program used for student grading has a maximum of 50 points for each assignment and test. This constant is used throughout the program in all associated functions. Declare a globally accessible constant for this value and show how it would be initialized.

19. The following program is required to calculate the square root of a variable. What must be added for the library function `sqrt()` to be accessible?

```
void main()
{   float voltage;
    cin >> voltage;
    cout << "root is: " << sqrt (voltage);
}
```

20. Briefly explain why it is good practice to use header comments at the top of a function. Propose three different types of information that might be documented in header comments.

3.10.b. Projects

1. Write a program to input a list of numbers representing angle measurements in degrees. Output a table of sines and cosines. The input list should terminate with a negative value. The following input list

   ```
   0.0 5.0 10.0 20.0 30.0 45.0 90.0 -1.0
   ```

   should produce output similar to this table:

   ```
   angle    sine        cosine
   0.0      0           1.0
   5.0      0.08716     0.99619
   10.0     0.17365     0.98481
   20.0     0.34202     0.93969
   30.0     0.5         0.86603
   45.0     0.70711     0.70711
   90.0     1.0         0
   ```

2. Write a program that inputs a sentinel list of positive angles in degrees and outputs the corresponding angles in radians. Use a function named `Radians()` for the conversion.

3. Write a function named `SumOfWholeNums()` that accepts a whole number N as a parameter and then calculates and outputs the sum of whole numbers from 1 to N. Use this function to output the sums of whole numbers from (a) 1 to 10.0, (b) 1 to 25.0, (c) 1 to 75.0, and (d) 1 to 100.0. For example, the following main program might be used:

   ```
   void main()
   {   SumOfWholeNums (10.0);
       SumOfWholeNums (25.0);
       SumOfWholeNums (75.0);
       SumOfWholeNums (100.0);
       cout << "done";
   }
   ```

4. If a person falls from a building of height h feet, the altitude A of the unfortunate victim at any time t can be calculated with this formula:

   $$A = h - \frac{32t^2}{2}$$

   Write a function named `FallTable()` which accepts a building height as a parameter and then outputs a table of victim altitudes for every second of fall (until the victim hits the sidewalk and has a negative altitude).

5. Write a function named `ConvertTemp()` that accepts a Fahrenheit temperature and returns the equivalent temperature in Centigrade. Use this function to convert the Fahrenheit temperatures 60.5, 32.0, 0.0, and −5.0 to Centigrade. For example, the following main program might be used:

   ```
   void main()
   {   float temp;
       temp = ConvertTemp (60.5);
       cout << temp << endl;
   ```

```
        cout << " 32.0 F = " << ConvertTemp (32.0) << endl;
        cout << " 0.0 F = " << ConvertTemp(0.0) << endl
        cout << "-5.0 F = " << ConvertTemp (-5.0) << endl;
}
```

The formula for temperature conversion is: $cent = \left(\frac{5}{9}(fahr - 32)\right)$

6. Write a program to solve Creative Challenge problem 9 of Chapter 1 using a function to calculate the volume of a sphere.

7. Write a program to solve Creative Challenge problem 10 of Chapter 1 using a function that accepts pay rate and hours worked parameters and returns the appropriate paycheck value. Remember that employees working over 40 hours receive time and a half for overtime.

8. Assume student grades will be input into a program with one student per line for 20 lines. Each student line will consist of five different grades. The output of the program should consist of (a) the maximum average, (b) the minimum average, and (c) the grand or overall average of the class. Use a function named StudentAve() to input a student's information and return the average of those five grades.

9. Write a function named LoanCost() which accepts three parameters: the amount of a loan principal, the number of months a payment is to be made (period), and the interest rate. The function should calculate and return the cost of the loan (or the difference between the principal and the total amount to be paid back to the bank). The formula is

$$cost = principal - period \times payment$$

where payment is the monthly payment:

$$payment = \left[\frac{rate}{1 - (1 + rate)^{-period}}\right] \times principal$$

Use this function in a program that inputs two loans and outputs the difference in cost between the two loans.

10. **Creative Challenge:** Suppose an X,Y coordinate system is used to mark the position of a hiker on a map. This two-number position represents the number of miles east (X) and north (Y) of a central location. A hiker who walks a given distance in a particular compass direction will of course be at a new X,Y position on the map. Write a program with useful functions which accepts an initial X,Y position and then a list of compass directions and distances. The list should terminate with a negative distance as a sentinel. Output the final X,Y position of the hiker. For example, the input might be similar to the following:

```
125.7        -45.8
  5.9        270
 10.3         84
 -1
```

which would indicate that the hiker began at 125.7 miles east and –45.8 miles north (which of course is just 45.8 miles south) of the central location. The hiker then traveled 5.9 miles in a direction of 270 degrees and then 10.3 miles in a direction of 84 degrees. Remember that compass directions are in degrees which need to be converted to radians before calling any of the trigonometry library functions:

$$radians = \frac{degrees \times \pi}{180}$$

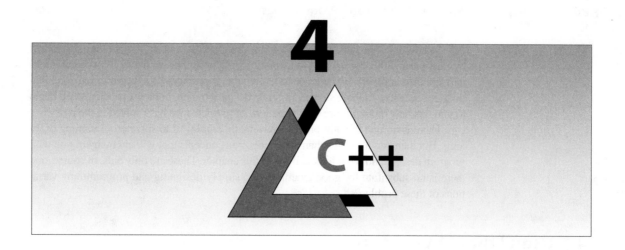

Problem Solving and Program Design

Understanding the syntax and rules of C++ is actually only a small part of programming. Problem solving or program design is a vital skill for a programmer. This chapter doesn't introduce any new C++, but rather revisits the problem-solving process and presents some modeling and conceptual aids.

4.1 Learning to solve programming problems

The problem-solving or program-design part of programming cannot (unfortunately) be expressed as a set of rules or fixed steps. It involves analytical as well as creative thinking—logic and imagination. There is no one type of person who is able to learn program design. True, program design comes easier to some, but it can be learned and applied by a fairly wide range of people.

It is not strictly a left-brain versus right-brain endeavor. Those with a more analytical nature may develop program-design ability in a somewhat different manner than those with a more creative or imaginative nature. Once learned, however, both personality or intellect types are often very effective programmers. It is not uncommon to see a computer science major with a minor in art or music. It is also common that the best students in a computer science class might be business, humanities, or social science majors.

Now, some students may initially struggle with program design. Occasionally, students will have a mind-set against "story" kinds of problems—perhaps from a bad algebra class experience. Once over this little hump, however, they do quite well and often go on to become accomplished programmers.

So how does one initially learn program-design skills? For most of us, they are learned by *example* and by *experience*. We learn the steps that can be used to solve a certain problem and then apply that experience to future similar problems. We begin to see combinations or sequences of these simpler program designs in more complex problems. We begin to find that new problems are only variations of problems we have solved in the past.

There is no one thought process universally employed to solve programming problems. But there are a few mechanisms, tools, and concepts that will aid many of you with program design, and we'll look at these in this chapter. These are only aids, of course, and there is no substitute for good examples and simply designing and programming variations of these problems.

4.2 Useful thought processes

Program problem solving is similar to working with a faulty three-burner stove: Suppose you move into a new apartment that has a three-burner stove. For lunch that day, you wish to cook tamales and chili. You place the tamales in one pot on burner 1 and place the chili in a second pot on burner 2. After turning on both burners, you go study while your lunch heats. After a while, you return to find both pots still cold—the stove is broken. You quickly check burner 3 and find that at least this burner still works.

KEY TERM
decomposition

Now you have a problem—two pots to heat, but only one burner. As an experienced computer scientist, you apply an important principle: *decomposition*. You break a complex problem into a set of simpler problems that can be solved one at a time. Concentrating on just heating the tamales, you move them from burner 1 to burner 3 and heat.

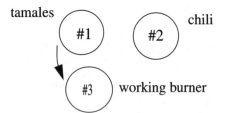

Now you are left with just half the problem: how to heat the chili. You move the chili from burner 2 to burner 1 *because that is a problem you have solved before!*

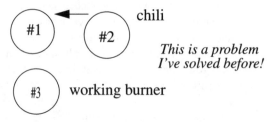

A silly example, of course, but it illustrates two useful thought processes: decomposition and using previous experience.

4.3 Basic components

Look for ways to apply your experience. Let's focus on the body of a program and ignore the boilerplate syntax at the top for a moment. Those details and the declarations of variables you have used can be added last.

CONCEPT

basic components

Here is a very important concept: *All programming problems can be solved with a sequence of only six components*. The first three are trivial:

1. input: collect information or data from the outside world

2. process: calculate or process existing information or data

3. output: display information or results to the outside world

A component is simply one or more C++ statements. Think about the program of Chapter 1 to calculate the area of a circle (Listing 1.2). The executable sections were:

```
cout << "enter a radius: ";        // output information
cin >> radius;                     // input or collect data

area = 3.14 * radius * radius;     // process or use the data

cout << "the area is " << area << endl;// output results
```

You have already mastered basic design for each of these three components! You know how to prompt the user to indicate what the program wants. You know how to input values from the user into variables. You understand how to implement a formula. You know how to output results to the user.

Suppose you must design a program to convert feet to meters (Listing 1.7). You quickly recognize that this is again a variation of your previous experience. What about a program to calculate the square of pi? This program doesn't need to input any information from the outside world—the value of pi doesn't change. You are now prepared to solve a wide variety of simple program problems based on your experience with the preceding circle program.

4.4 Compound design

Now, most programming problems are not simple sequences of the three basic components. They are compound—containing conditions and/or loops. The last three components are:

4. indefinite loop

5. definite loops

6. conditions

4.4.a Loop designs

Anytime a program needs to process more than a couple of similar inputs or values, a loop is indicated. In Chapter 2, you saw examples of two different kinds of program loops. The first was the indefinite loop. This type of loop was used when the number of repetitions depended on some value calculation or a sentinel input when the loop actually ran. You learned this type of loop was associated with a condition variable. We'll call this component 4:

```
get or calculate the first value of the variable;
while (expression comparing variable with a sentinel value)
{   components to be repeated;
    get or calculate the next value of the variable;
}
```

KEY TERM

pseudocode

  Here we used italics and conservational English to represent details to be filled in later. This is known as *pseudocode*. For example, suppose the problem is to calculate the areas of a list of circles. For each circle, the user supplies a radius. After the list of radii has been input, the user inputs a negative number as the sentinel:

```
cin >> radius;
while (radius > 0.0)
{
```
  (*calculate and output area using radius*)
```
    cin >> radius;
}
```

  If it is helpful to more profoundly separate pseudocode from the actual C++ code being designed, draw an oval around it. I didn't bother with the details of the pseudocode, which are basic component details to be left for later. I'll come back to that, and I know I've solved a problem like that in the past.

  Now suppose the problem is to calculate and output volumes for a list of boxes. The user is to input height, length, and width for each box. After the list, the user is to input a negative number as the sentinel. Okay, this is just a variation of the sentinel loop:

```
cin >> height;
if (height > 0.0)
{
```
  (*input a width and length*)

  (*calculate the volume using height, width, and length*)
```
    cin >> height;
}
```

Suppose now the problem is to calculate the squares of integers beginning with 1 as long as a square is less than 1000. Again, it's just a variation. The condition variable is calculated rather than input:

```
n = 1.0;
square = n * n;
while (square < 1000.0)
{   cout << "square of " << n << " is " << square << endl;
    n = n+1;
    square = n * n;
}
```

You might recognize that the first calculation of square when n was 1 didn't really require a multiplication, but it made my program easier to understand. We'll come back to that later. With this fourth sentinel construct (and the first three trivial basic components), you have the experience to solve an even wider variety of programming problem variations.

The second type of repetition was the *counted loop*. We'll call this component 5. This was used whenever a loop was to repeat a specific number of times. In other words, the program knows how many times to repeat a set of components before the loop began:

```
initialize or set the counter variable to 0
while (variable  <  maximum)
{   components to be repeated
    variable = variable + 1.0;
}
```

Suppose that the programming problem is to input a set of exactly five boxes and output the calculated volumes:

```
count = 0.0;
while (count < 5.0)
{
```

> *input a height, width, and length*

> *calculate a volume using height, width, and length*

> *output the volume*

```
    count = count + 1;
}
```

Summing can be done with either loop variation. This is accomplished by initializing a summing variable to zero prior to the loop. Within the loop, each new calculation or value is added to the running sum.

```
sum = 0.0
while (...
{
    sum = sum + value;
}
```

4.4.b Conditions

As you remember, a condition or `if` statement is used whenever a decision or choice must be made. This is component 6. The decision is made by comparing two values or variables using the `>`, `<`, `>=`, and `<=` operators:

```
if ( compare two values )
{   components to be executed if comparison is true
}
else
{   components to be executed if comparison is false
}
```

As you remember, either of the two sections—the true or false components—could be empty and represented with a single semicolon. Suppose we again look at the problem of calculating a paycheck. An overtime formula is used if an individual works more than 40 hours and a standard formula if not:

```
cin >> hours;
if (hours > 40.0)
{
        calculate pay using overtime formula
}
else
{
        calculate pay using regular formula
}
cout << "pay is " << pay << endl;
```

If you think about it, all other examples of conditions you have seen are variations of this solution.

4.5 Top-down design

Your study of the previous chapters has given you examples and experience with the six basic components of a programming problem solution. Some future problems you will see may require quite a large sequence of these six components—you will learn alternate ways of specifically expressing these components and the data or variables they use in more *compact* ways appropriate to more complex problems in future chapters.

The concept of the six basic components is quite fundamental. *Every programming problem can be solved with a sequence of the six components.* Notice, however, that the two loop components and the condition component contain nested components themselves, which may in turn be other sequences. It is this possibility of loops within loops or conditions within loops within conditions (etc.) that makes program problem solving nontrivial!

4.5.a Concept

Start by making sure you know how to solve the problem with paper and pencil. Make up a set of input data and work through the data to generate expected output. If you can't do this step, it doesn't make sense to proceed with program design. Save the results of this work because you'll need them later to compare against your program results.

Now you are ready to start with the program design. The approach most often used to solve these nontrivial problems is to *start with a design that ignores the details of nested components.* The beginning design is simply a sequence of the foregoing six components. Next, we continually refine the solution by replacing vague components with less vague components until the solution is in C++.

Start by looking for the overriding structure in a component or problem. First, ask yourself if a component is really a straight sequence of smaller or finer components and express these one after the other. If your pseudocode or description of the component includes words such as "next" or "then," you may have a straight sequence. Expand your component in to a sequence of components. Once you find that the sequence doesn't readily expand any further, consider each component with the following three sets of questions:

1. *Is this component processing more than one set of data?* A component must have a loop if it needs to process more than one set of data or repeatedly calculate more than one set of results. If it needs a loop, *can I determine how many times the loop must execute?* This is true if the statement of the problem indicates the number of data sets to be processed or the number of output results to be produced. It is also true if you are able to calculate this number with a paper and pencil from currently known information prior to asking this question. A positive response indicates a definite loop; a negative response an indefinite loop.

2. If it does not need a loop, *does this component have alternatives?* A component needs a condition if there are alternate components that are to be executed based on previously input or calculated data.

3. If it is not a loop or a condition, *does this component require information from the user*? If so, it is an input. *Does this component display information or prompts to the user*? If so, it is an output. *Does this component involve a formula or math calculation*? If so, it is a process component.

Based on the answers to these questions, the next design of the program can be given. Let's review the structure of the compound components for indefinite loops, definite loops, and conditions. An indefinite loop can be expressed with the following pseudocode:

```
get or calculate the first value of the variable;
while ( expression comparing variable with a sentinel value )
{   components to be repeated
    get or calculate the next value of the variable;
}
```

A definite loop has the following structure:

```
count = 0.0;
while ( count < maximum )
{   components to be repeated
    count = count + 1.0;
}
```

Naturally, there is nothing special about the variable name `count`. Another name could be used.

A condition has the following pseudocode structure;

```
if ( compare two values )
{   components to be executed if comparison is true
}
else
{   components to be executed if comparison is false
}
```

Once we have the next design, we can attack a particular pseudocode component to further refine vagaries into specifics by repeatedly considering the same three question sets—as applied to that specific component. When no further pseudocode remains, we have a final design solution. The final work of adding variable declarations and other boilerplate is usually quite mechanical and requires little imagination.

A program solution starting with a correct first design has an excellent chance of leading to a correct program. A solution starting with an incorrect first design has no chance of leading to a correct solution.

4.5.b Example

Let's do a fairly complex example (at least for this point in your career): A pharmaceutical company sells six different cold medications and needs a program to help a doctor with dose calculations. The company would like to have a doctor first input a patient weight. Next the doctor will input a list of drugs with each entry consisting of the drug number followed by the dose rate (mg per lb of body weight for a prescription). If a patient is over 120 lbs, the dose is calculated as the dose rate times the patient weight. Otherwise, the dose is 120 times the dose rate. Finally, the program should also output the average dose for the list of drugs entered.

If we cannot do this with pencil and paper, we have little chance of writing a correct program, so let's do a self-test. Suppose the doctor enters the following input:

```
115    (patient weight)
56     2.1
86     0.3
75     1.4
97     0.9
68     2.3
39     1.8
```

If you arrived at the following manually determined output for this future program, you are ready to proceed. If not, go back and study the problem description. (Remember, this patient is under 120 lb.)

```
dose for drug 56 is 252
dose for drug 86 is 36
dose for drug 75 is 168
dose for drug 97 is 108
dose for drug 68 is 276
dose for drug 39 is 216
average dose is: 176
```

We could start with a single oval;

> *Get the patient weight, then input the list; calculate and output doses, then output the average dose.*

Not very helpful. Now, start the decomposition process. First we note that this is a straight sequence of three components:

> *Get the patient weight*

> *Input the list; calculate and output the correct dose for each drug.*

> *Calculate then output the average for all drugs*

The first and last ovals look easy. Analyze the middle oval by asking these questions:

Is this component processing more than one set of data? Yes. This component is a loop since multiple drugs need to be processed. This loop will also need to do summing for calculated doses so that an average can be output.

Can I determine how many times the loop must execute? There are exactly six drugs so the loop must be definite.

Based upon these answers, the middle oval can be expanded. Using our experience from previous similar programs, we'll include the obvious details for controlling the loop. Since this is the first time we have used actual code, we'll call this our first design:

Get the patient weight

FIRST DESIGN

```
count = 0.0;
while ( count < 6 .0)
```

{ components to be executed for each drug

```
    count = count + 1.0;
}
```

Calculate then output the average for all drugs

There are still three vague pseudocode components in this design. Let's look at the one inside the loop first: What needs to be done for each drug in the input? Input the drug number and dose rate, calculate and sum the dose and output the calculated dose:

Get the patient weight

SECOND DESIGN

```
count = 0.0;
while ( count < 6.0 )
{   cin >> drug_num >> dose_rate;
```

calculate, sum, and then output the dose

```
    count = count + 1.0;
}
```

Calculate then output the average for all drugs

The middle oval again looks like a straight sequence. Outputting the dose is easy, and we can fill in that detail. The details of performing a summing operation are in our experience and can also be filled in. We remember we need to initialize a summing variable to zero above the loop and then add each calculation to this variable within the loop:

Get the patient weight

count = 0.0;
sum_dose = 0.0;
while (count < 6.0)
{ cin >> drug_num >> dose_rate;

    calculate the dose

    sum_dose = sum_dose + dose;
    cout << "dose for " << drug_number << " is: " << dose << endl;
    count = count + 1.0;
}

THIRD DESIGN

Calculate then output the average for all drugs

Again, consider the middle oval: There are two formulas for a drug dose calculation and the remaining oval is a condition based upon whether the patient weight is over 120 lb or not:

Get the patient weight

count = 0.0;
sum_dose = 0.0;
while (count < 6.0)
{ cin >> drug_num >> dose_rate;
    if (patient_weight > 120.0)
    {
        calculate dose using formula for heavy patients
    }
    else
    {
        calculate dose using formula for light patients
    }
    sum_dose = sum_dose + dose;
    cout << "dose for " << drug_number << " is: " << dose << endl;
    count = count + 1.0;

}

FOURTH DESIGN

Calculate then output the average for all drugs

The two formulas can now be implemented. Let's resolve the top pseudocode oval as well. At the top, you want to output a prompt as well as input the weight:

```
cout << "Drug dose calculations; input the patient weight: ";
cin >> patient_weight;
count = 0.0;
sum_dose = 0.0;
while ( count < 6.0 )
{   cin >> drug_num >> dose_rate;
    if (patient_weight > 120.0)
    {   dose = dose_rate * patient_weight;
    }
    else
    {   dose = dose_rate * 120.0;
    }
    sum_dose = sum_dose + dose;
    cout << "dose for " << drug_num << "is:" << dose << endl;
    count = count + 1.0;
}
```

> FIFTH DESIGN

> *Calculate and output the average for all drugs*

The last pseudocode oval is to be done after the loop. The remaining responsibility is to calculate and output the average dose. This is obviously a straight sequence. The completed design (still without the required variable declarations, boilerplate, and comments) now needs to be tested and debugged:

```
cout << "Drug dose calculations; input the patient weight: ";
cin >> patient_weight;
count = 0.0;
sum_dose = 0.0;
while ( count < 6.0 )
{   cin >> drug_num >> dose_rate;
    if ( patient_weight > 120.0 )
    {   dose = dose_rate * patient_weight;
    }
    else
    {   dose = dose_rate * 120.0;
    }
    sum_dose = sum_dose + dose;
    cout << "dose for " << drug_num << " is: " << dose << endl;
    count = count + 1.0;
}
average_dose = sum_dose / 6.0;
cout << "average dose is: " << average_dose << endl;
```

This approach to design ensures that the opening and closing braces are matched, that nested **if** statements each have appropriately placed components, and that each loop is initialized appropriately.

Now, while above example illustrates the concept of logical step-wise decomposition, do not expect that every programming problem can be mechanically designed by following a simple set of rules. This procedure and these questions will help, but some program designs also require a certain degree of flexibility and creativity. This approach will, however, get you off to a good start.

4.5.c Desk testing

Desk testing can be helpful to verify a design prior to actual coding. You need four pieces of paper: On the first sheet you have the written program design. On the second sheet, draw a box for each of the variables used in the final design and write the name of the variable above the box. On a third sheet of paper, write an example set of input data that the user might type. The fourth sheet is blank. This is where you will write output during the execution of the program. Now pretend that you are the computer and "execute" your program one step at a time.

Place a check mark beside a program line each time you execute it. When a program line indicates that data are to be input into variables, cross off the data consumed from the input sheet and copy the data value into the appropriate variable boxes. Be sure to cross off the previous variable value since a variable may only represent the last value stored there. Each time you execute an output line, write the corresponding output on the output sheet.

At each output line, go back and compare your execution answer with the paper-and-pencil solution you produced *before the program solution was designed*. Any differences will help you identify lines in the program design which do not produce the expected results.

4.5.d Debugging revisited

The final step in program problem solving is to actually test-run your program. Add declarations for all variables used, the appropriate #include statements at the top, and other necessary boilerplate. Let's review the process of debugging. As you remember from Chapter 1, when you compile or make your program to prepare for execution, the program development environment (PDE) will find syntax errors or typos.

Let's take another look at why the PDE compiler will always indicate that a syntax error exists, but may not be able to correctly determine *where* and *why*. In other words, a PDE will attempt to show you the line that contains the error and give you an explanation of why the line is in error, but the location and explanation may be incorrect. In addition, one syntax error may produce more than one error message as the PDE attempts to cover all the possibilities. Consider the following program:

```
1. void main()
2. {   cin >> a >> b;
3.       if (a > b)
4.       { cout << "a is greater" << endl;
5.       }
6.       else
```

```
7.      { cout << "b is greater or equal";
8.      cout << "program is done";
9.      cout << "thank you.";
10.}
```

The programmer forgot the closing } below the **else**. Since the PDE compiler does not consider indentation (which is strictly to make the program more readable to humans), the error isn't detected until the end of the program is reached. The last } on line 10 is matched with the opening { on line 7. At the end, the PDE still hasn't found a remaining } to match the opening { on line 2. This typo by the programmer may produce a variety of error messages (and often more than one), but none of them will accurately indicate that a missing } is needed between lines 7 and 8.

Think of syntax error messages as simply being best guesses by the PDE. All you can count on is that the error will be detected at *or after* where the actual syntax error or typo occurs.

As we discussed in Chapter 1, a program may also contain logic and semantic errors. A good PDE always comes with a debugger, which is an invaluable tool that allows you to single step through your program and watch as statements change variables or branch in a condition (among other things). Refer to the appropriate appendix at the end of the text for your system. If your system is not included, your instructor will have the information you need to use the debugger for execution testing.

KEY TERM
foot printing

The addition of helpful output statements is called *foot printing*. Extra output statements are placed in the program to notify the programmer of computer progress and perhaps the current value of important variables as execution proceeds. These output statements are not part of the problem-solution design and are just added to provide additional output to aid in debugging. Regardless of the debugger or PDE used, foot printing can be employed to aid in identifying semantic and logic errors.

4.6 The software life cycle

Let's take a look at the larger picture of how programs are developed in the commercial world. Consider for a moment that you are the manager of a software development group in a large company. Ask yourself the following question: "What is a successful program?" There are many possible answers to this question. You may claim that a good program must *run correctly* and *be efficient*. These, of course, are insufficient since a program may be completely without bugs and run very efficiently, and yet do nothing particularly useful. Okay, amend your response to include that a good program must also *perform a useful task*. But what about a correct, efficient program that does an important job, but is so difficult to use that clients quickly look for other solutions? Now you amend your answer to include that a good program must be *easy to use* (have a good user interface). In addition, you might expect to upgrade or modify a program. If a program is not *easily maintained*, initial usefulness will fade.

All five of these concepts are important to a *good* program, but insufficient for a *successful* program. The graveyards of business are full of software companies that have gone broke with program products that were good—correct, efficient, useful, as well as easy to use and maintain! On the other hand, there are some highly successful programs that still contain annoying bugs, that are disappointingly slow, or that are only moderately useful or perhaps difficult to use. Can you see where we're headed? A successful program is one that makes money! Now, not all programs are written to be sold to outside customers. Many companies employ a software staff to produce programs for the company's own use. This may include engineering, military or scientific research firms, or even government and public-service institutions. Nevertheless, the analogy is still true. These organizations operate effectively by saving money on the cost of operations (including software). If the cost of developing programs is more than the savings realized when these programs are used or implemented in company operations, the programs are not successful.

CONCEPT
a program must be cost-effective

This may seem a little hard-nosed and capitalistic, but it is the way the free-market world works. We can be a bit more specific: A successful program costs less to produce and maintain than the sales or savings it generates. Naturally, to have the best chance of generating sales or savings, a program should have the five qualifications initially proposed: be correct, efficient, useful, maintainable, and easy to use. To these five qualifications, we now add one more: *A program must be cost-effective.* It also follows that a good programmer must be cost-effective. If one programmer can produce a good program in fewer salary hours than another, his or her value to the company is greater. A good programmer who cannot produce programs in a cost-effective manner will end up flipping burgers.

The same concept is important for programming students or professionals who only program occasionally. You need to produce good programs as quickly as possible to have time for other important things in your career (and perhaps a social life). In this text, much more than just C++ language syntax and rules are presented. The goal is to teach you how to program, of course, but in a way which will lead to a successful career. Some of the concepts that are introduced are just as important now while you are still a student (and working on relatively small programs) as they will be when you are a software professional (working on much larger programs). In any case, a lot of study and experience have gone into these proven concepts. Our experience is that when correctly followed, they tend to lead to good cost-effective programs. Cost is a relative term: It might relate to a company paying your salary or might relate to your own invested time.

KEY TERM
software life cycle

Experience has shown that the following five stages of development are part of a successful commercial software product. They are appropriately named the *software life cycle.* You may find slightly different terms used in other texts, but the concepts are generally the same.

1. **Analysis**. During this stage, the purpose for the proposed program is analyzed. What are the client's needs and requirements? Does the client have a clear understanding of his or her needs? What are the expected benefits? What are the trade-offs or alternate approaches? What is the expected or potential profit or savings?

Near the end of this stage of development, a budget and schedule are generally formed. The goals and objectives of the program are specified.

2. **Design**. Formulas and algorithms are developed or decided on. A programming language is chosen. The user interface is designed and the user's manual is written. This allows both the customer or consumer and the programmer/company to agree on exactly what the program will do and how it will be used. Any misconceptions between the client's expectations and the programmer's goals should be resolved. Consider this metaphor: It is generally cheaper and faster to build a three-lane bridge than to build a two-lane bridge and add a third lane later.

3. **Coding**. During this stage, the actual program and functions are written and debugged.

4. **Testing**. The completed program is rigorously tested to verify that the program works correctly and according to the user's manual and the specifications developed during the analysis stage.

5. **Maintenance**. Features are modified, enhanced, or added to meet the evolving needs and requirements of the client.

KEY TERM
software
engineering

The effective management of these stages is called *software engineering*. All active programs are in one of these stages. Many programs cycle through the five stages repeatedly as new revisions and releases are continually being developed from earlier versions. The time and budget allocated to each stage vary with the type and complexity of the software being developed. However, it is almost universally true that the coding and maintenance stages require more time and budget than the other three combined. It is also true that the maintenance stage generally requires more than two or three times as much budget and time as the coding stage.

4.7 Summary

KEY TERMS

Several new terms are presented in this chapter on problem solving and program design.

1. *decomposition* — breaking a large problem down into a sequence of smaller and simpler problems.

2. *pseudocode* — expressing code segments in conversational English, leaving details of how these statements are to be expressed in C++ until later.

3. *desk testing* — the process of "executing" a design with paper and pencil as if you were the computer.

4. *foot printing* — adding extra output statements to a program to have the computer indicate progress and intermediate values of variables.

5. *software life cycle* — the steps or stages of commercial software development which experience has shown lead to successful programs.

6. *software engineering* — the application and effective management of methods for software development.

CONCEPTS The concepts of decomposition and applying experience from previously solved problems are very useful in producing good programs.

A simple premise can be used to help design software solutions to problems: All programs can be designed with a sequence of the six components that you have learned from previous chapters. These six design components are:

1. input statements
2. output statements
3. calculation or formula implementation statements
4. indefinite loops
5. counted loops
6. conditions

(Future chapters will demonstrate efficient variations of these components and ways of shortening long programs.) Each of these components has a basic design that you have learned from previous examples and applied in previous projects. Most of the complexity of program design comes from the fact that loops and conditions may contain nested components.

When designing a programming problem solution, it is best to start with recognizing the basic sequence of these components, leaving any details and nested components as pseudocode for a later refinement. The basic sequence can be recognized by asking the basic questions outlined in this chapter.

Pseudocode components can be refined or broken down into a more detailed sequence of the basic components by again asking the foregoing questions for that pseudocode component. Each subsequent refinement replaces pseudocode with a sequence of more refined pseudocode and explicit C++ statements. When no more pseudocode remains, the design is ready for desk testing. Finally, variable declarations, #include statements, and other boilerplate are added, and the program can be debugged.

4.8 Exercises

4.8.a. Short-answer questions

1. List the five stages of the software life cycle.
2. List and explain the six basic design components.
3. Explain what a professional programmer will attempt to accomplish during the analysis stage of the software life cycle.
4. Explain what a professional programmer will attempt to accomplish during the design stage of the software life cycle.
5. During which stage of the software life cycle will a program design actually be coded into C++?
6. Explain what a professional programmer will attempt to accomplish during the testing stage of the software life cycle.
7. Explain what a professional programmer will attempt to accomplish during the maintenance stage of the software life cycle.

8. Which stage of the software life cycle is likely to require the greatest amount of budget and time?

9. Indicate which of the six basic design components should be used in the refining of the following pseudocode components. You do not need to refine the pseudocode—just indicate which single component would be used in the next design refinement (each of the following represents a single component).

   a. Calculate the number of inches associated with the variable `feet`.

   b. Choose either formula A or formula B to calculate interest on the variable `principal`.

   c. Process six sets of mortgage data to produce monthly payment values.

   d. The user will input the number of student scores in the class. Following that number, the user will input each individual score. Process these grades to output a letter grade for each score.

   e. The user will input a list of student grades followed by a score of −1. Process these grades to output a letter grade for each score.

   f. The user will input a list of student grades followed by a score of −1. Process these grades to obtain a total score so that the average score can later be calculated.

10. Consider the program of Listing 2.1. Work backward from this program to produce a first design of the program, leaving all nested components as pseudocode.

11. Consider Listing 2.2. Work backward from this program to produce a first design of the program, leaving all nested components as pseudocode.

12. Expand the first design of problem 11 to produce a second or more refined design.

13. Consider Listing 2.8. Work backward from this program to produce a first design of the program, leaving all nested components as pseudocode.

14. Expand the first design of problem 13 to produce a second or more refined design.

15. Consider Listing 2.9. Work backward from this program to produce a first design of the program, leaving all nested components as pseudocode.

16. Expand the first design of problem 15 to produce a second or more refined design.

17. Consider Listing 2.10. Work backward from this program to produce a first design of the program, leaving all nested components as pseudocode.

18. Produce a first design for the following problem: A buyer needs a program to calculate the total cost of an apple order. The user will input the number of apple boxes and the cost per box. The program should output the total order cost.

19. Produce a first design for the following modification to problem 18: If an apple order exceeds $1000, the total cost is reduced by 5%.

20. Expand the first design for the previous problem 19 to a second refinement.

21. Produce a first design for the following problem: A contractor needs to know the total number of board feet in a stack of 15 wood planks. For each plank, the user will input the length, width, and thickness in inches. Board feet for a plank can be calculated with the following formula:

$$board\,feet = \frac{(length \times width \times thickness)}{144}$$

22. Expand the first design for problem 21 to a second refinement.
23. Produce a first design for the following problem: A bodybuilding clinic would like to know the average weight of all customers over 150 lb. The user will input a list of body weights followed by −1. The program should output the average weight of all customers over 150 lb.
24. Expand the first design for problem 23 to a second refinement.
25. Produce a first design for the following problem: A dealership needs to estimate the average amount of time for a car repair. The user will input a list of repair times measured for cars seen during the last week. The list will terminate with −1. The program should output the average repair time.
26. Expand the first design for problem 25 to a second refinement.

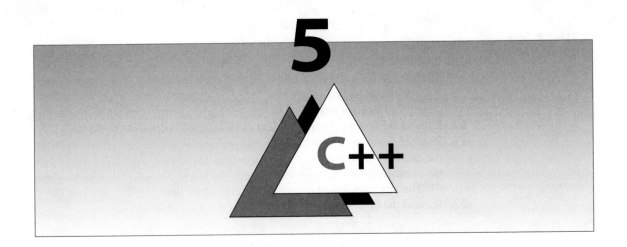

Designing with Functions

As you begin to appreciate the utility of modularizing complex programs, you will also begin to appreciate that some functions could be useful in more than one program. In this chapter, we introduce methods that facilitate the reuse of functions. Up to this point, you have learned how to write functions that return a single value or result. We now need to address the more general case of functions that must return more than one value. For example, how would you write a function to accept three arguments and then sort them into numeric order?

5.1 Designing with reusable modules

Remember our previous discussion of the software life cycle? Computer scientists have learned from experience that the more easily and efficiently a program can be written and maintained, the greater the chance that the software will be produced on time and cost under budget. This is particularly true of software that can be resold as upgraded versions. For example, my word processing program is revision 7.0. Each time a new revision is released, I pay a fee to upgrade to the latest version. If the company that produces this program can easily modify and reuse parts of the previous version, the cost of the coding and maintenance stages is greatly reduced. This means that the company can either make more money on later versions or reduce their prices to outsell competitors. In fact, it is not uncommon for a software company to expect the first several versions of a product to *lose* money, hoping to make it up on later revisions (through easy maintenance) once the product is established with a satisfied customer base.

The bottom line is that successful programmers want to rapidly produce code that can easily be reused in later versions and other programs. There are several methods and techniques to aid in this goal which are either a fundamental part of C++ or easily used within the language. Naturally, good documentation of code is important. This enables other programmers to more easily understand the purpose and methods of a section of code. The use of functions to modularize a complex problem is also an important technique. A well-written function with careful documentation can easily be reused. When a change must be made to a program, the developers can quickly identify those functions that are affected. Later revisions of a program or new program products might be substantially written by reusing functions from previous programs. In fact, functions are often designed with that thought in mind: How might this function be generally useful in a wide variety of similar programs?

Designing with reusable functions can also greatly simplify debugging. This concept is particularly important to students. You have probably learned from experience by now that the greatest amount of time spent completing a programming assignment is associated with finding the location and nature of bugs! *Designing* a solution, *writing* a program, and even *correcting* a bug can be relatively quick work. Finding and determining the nature of a bug, on the other hand, can easily eat up hours and hours of time you hoped to spend on other things. If this has not yet happened, it will! If you write programs using modular functions, you will find that your programs are significantly easier to debug.

KEY TERM
encapsulated

Remember from the previous chapter that the documentation for each function should carefully specify what parameters are being passed into a function (along with expected values or ranges) and what value or result is being returned by the function. Through using a debugger or extra output statements, one can quickly verify these conditions at the beginning and end of each function. This approach allows you to quickly localize the cause of a bug, making the actual debugging much simpler. To begin, a properly designed function is *encapsulated*, meaning that the only contact it has with the rest of the program is through the arguments being passed and the single result being passed back. It should not modify or change any other parts of the bigger program. In other words, it should have no side effects.

5.2 Reference parameters

To be more effective in designing functions that are versatile and perhaps have potential for reuse, we need to be able to write more general functions that can produce and return more than a single result. All our function parameters to this point have been IN parameters, meaning that values are being passed into a function for use. In C++, parameters can also be OUT or even IN/OUT parameters.

KEY TERM

reference
parameters

CONCEPT

declaring reference
parameters

Suppose we wish to write a function that can be used to accept two values and then exchange them. In other words, the function accepts two arguments as parameters and then swaps their values. Obviously, this function will need in some way to return two values back to the caller. To do this, we use *reference parameters*.

If the declaration of a parameter contains the **&** symbol after the parameter type, that parameter refers back to the corresponding argument. Subsequently, any changes the function makes to a reference parameter affect changes to the corresponding argument. This is best illustrated by example (Listing 5.1).

`float & ` *variable*	**Syntax form**

Listing 5.1

```
// Swap()  Accepts two values as reference parameters and exchanges
// these values.
// IN/OUT: a, b -- When the function is called, these are any values. When the
//  function returns, the values referenced by a and b have been exchanged.
void Swap ( float& a, float& b)
{   float temp;
    temp = a;
    a = b;
    b = temp;
}
```

Notice that the declaration of parameters a and b includes the **&** symbol. Let's take a look first at a *conceptual* explanation and the *actual* explanation. Remember when parameters were introduced in the previous chapter, you learned that the values of arguments were *copied into* the corresponding parameters when the function was called. Simply extend that analogy — the values of the parameters are *copied back* into the corresponding arguments when the function returns. Now, that is not actually what occurs, but thinking this way may help you initially understand reference parameters. Consider the following main() program which calls Swap():

```
void main()
{   float x, y;
    x = 5.5;
    y = 7.7;
    cout << "x is " << x << "  y is " << y << end;
    Swap (x, y);
    cout << "x is " << x << "  y is " << y << end;
}
```

Conceptually, when the Swap() function is called, the value of x is copied into the parameter a and the value of y is copied into the parameter b (Figure 5.1).

The values of a and b are swapped within the function (see Listing 5.1) and the function returns. Conceptually, the values of a and b are simply copied back into x and y for further program use (Figure 5.2).

When executed, this program produces the following output:

```
x is 5.5    y is 7.7
x is 7.7    y is 5.5
```

This conceptual model is easy to understand, and it helps you learn the use of reference parameters. But it is not actually what occurs. A reference parameter is similar to a forwarding address used by the post office. If people go on an extended trip, they might ask the post office to forward any mail addressed to them to another location. In other words, mail arriving at the home is automatically forwarded to the vacation residence. In a similar manner, any use of a reference parameter in a function is forwarded to the corresponding argument in the caller. Figure 5.3 shows the relationship between main() and Swap() when the function is called—in other words, just before the first instruction of Swap()

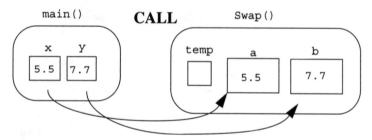

Figure 5.1 Conceptual function call

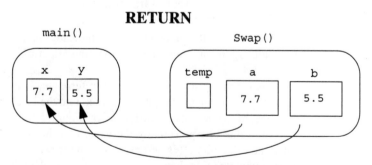

Figure 5.2 Conceptual diagram of function return

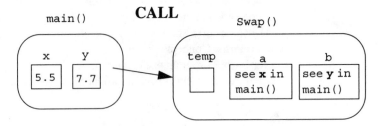

Figure 5.3   State of program just before the first instruction of Swap().

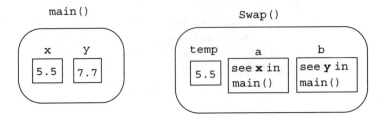

Figure 5.4   Effect of the statement: temp = a; in Swap().

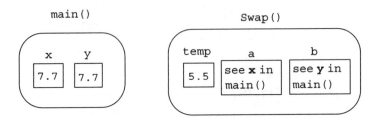

Figure 5.5   Effect of the statement a = b; in Swap().

The notes in the parameter boxes indicate this forward reference to the corresponding argument. Now let's examine the effect of the first statement: temp = a; (Figure 5.4).

The function's use of variable a is referred back to x in the main program. Subsequently, the value of x or 5.5 is copied into the local variable temp. Now look at the effect of the next statement: a = b; (Figure 5.5).

The value of b is actually the value of y in the main program. Subsequently, when the value of 7.7 is assigned to a, the forwarding address in a refers the 7.7 to be assigned to x in the main program. Now look at the effect of the last statement: b = temp; (Figure 5.6).

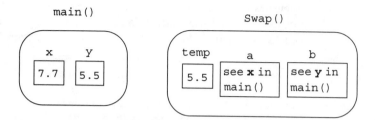

Figure 5.6 Effect of the statement b = temp; in Swap().

When Swap() ends and control is passed back to the main program, the net effect of calling Swap() has been to exchange the values in the two arguments. This of course would be true for any two arguments:

```
void main ()
{   float f1, f2, f3;
    f1 = 100.0;
    f2 = 200.0;
    f3 = 300.0;
    Swap (f1, f2);
    Swap (f2, f3);
    cout << f1 << " " << f2 << " " << f3 << endl;
}
```

This main() program will first swap the values in f1 and f2 and then the values in f2 and f3 to produce the following output:

```
200 300 100
```

EXPERIMENT

What would happen if you inadvertently left the & off the declaration of a reference parameter? Remove one of the & symbols in a parameter of Swap() and test the resulting function.

Note that it is the function declaration of parameters and not the calling program that determines whether parameters will be IN or IN/OUT. At this point, we have seen examples of IN parameters (Chapter 4) and IN/OUT parameters (this chapter). What is an OUT parameter? Anytime a function ignores or does not care about the value of a reference parameter when the function is called, we label it an OUT parameter. Consider a function with the responsibility to input a list of values and return the maximum, minimum, and average of the list to the calling program. We will specify that the list terminates with a negative sentinel value (suggesting a **while** I/O loop). Three values need to be returned. The function in Listing 5.2 uses two reference parameters to return the maximum and minimum and the function value to return the average.

Listing 5.2

```
// GetAveMaxMin()  Calculate the average, max, and min of
// a list of positive values terminating with a negative number
// ASSUMPTION: List must contain at least one positive value
//   OUT: max, min will be the list maximum & minimums
//   Returns: The average of the list

float GetAveMaxMin (float& max, float& min)
{   float sum=0.0, count=0.0, value;
    cin >> value;                         // get the first value
    max = value;
    min = value;                          // assume it is both the max and min
    while (value > 0.0)                   // check for sentinel
    {   sum = sum + value;
        count = count + 1.0;              // sum and count values in loop...
        if (value > max)                  // compare against previous
              max = value;                // assumptions for max and min...
        else ;
        if (value < min)
              min = value;                // (and change if needed)
        else ;
        cin >> value;
    }
    return (sum / count);                 // calculate and return average
}
```

KEY TERM
assumption

Notice first that the comment block at the top of the function contains an AS-SUMPTION comment. Such comments are used to qualify the assumptions or conditions that must be made if the function is expected to perform correctly. If the list does not contain at least one positive number, the function should not be expected to work correctly. In other words, the programmer is documenting that the function fails when the list is empty (contains only the negative sentinel value) because of improper use. ASSUMPTION comments should be used any time special constraints or assumptions must be made regarding the use of a function.

In this function, when a value is assigned to the reference parameter max (or min), it will actually be assigned to the corresponding argument provided by the caller. For example, consider how this function might be used:

```
void main()
{   float agemax, agemin, ageave;
    float grademax, grademin, gradeave;
    ageave = GetAveMaxMin (agemax, agemin);
    gradeave = GetAveMaxMin (grademax, grademin);
    ...
```

This `main()` program would expect to input two lists: The first should represent a list of ages and the second a list of grades. The same function is used to calculate the average, maximum, and minimum for both lists. The function is being *reused*, even within the same program.

Reference parameters themselves can be further used as arguments to other function calls. The compiler will automatically keep track of the home address to which multiple or cascaded forwarding addresses refer. This is similar to someone who has mail forwarded to a vacation condo at the beach and subsequently moves and has mail forwarded to a lodge in the mountains. Any mail sent to the individual's home address will be forwarded to the condo at the beach, which will cause it to be further forwarded to the lodge in the mountains. (This of course does not imply that computer professionals all make enough money to take vacations long enough to worry about forwarding mail.)

CONCEPT
illegal reference
parameters

Reference parameters allow changes to the corresponding arguments; thus, literals, constants, expressions, or **const** identifiers are not appropriate to use as arguments if the corresponding parameter is a reference.

```
void SomeFunc (float &cost)
{   cost = cost + 1.0;
}
void main ()
{   SomeFunc (5.0);
    ...
```

WRONG WAY!

EXPERIMENT

What would happen if you inadvertently used a constant as an argument for a reference parameter? Would you see a compile-time error message or not?

5.3 Top-down debugging with stubs

Consider now a program that must input three values and then output them in correct numeric order. Following our practice of using modular functions and a simple main program, this might be expressed as follows:

```
void main()
{   float r, s, t;
    cin >> r >> s >> t;
    Sort (r, s, t);
    cout << "in order: " << r << " " << s << " " << t << endl;
}
```

KEY TERM

function stubs

In other words, we can write the main program without having solved the problem of how to actually do the sorting. We can also then debug the main program prior to writing the `Sort3()` function using a function *stub*. A stub is nothing more than a function that doesn't yet do anything meaningful, but provides a verification of the initial parameter values and passes back fixed or known values. For example:

```
// Sort3()  Sorts the three parameters in numeric order
// IN/OUT: x, y, and z are returned in numeric order
// (currently only a stub)

void Sort3 (float& x, float& y, float& z)
{   cout << "values passed to Sort():" << end;
    cout << x << " " << y << " " << z << end;
    x = 1.0;
    y = 2.0;
    z = 3.0;
}
```

Now when the program is run, three values are read in from the user and the values of 1 2 3 are output (regardless of the input values). Nevertheless, we can test the `main()` program to verify at least that much is correctly occurring: I/O is working correctly and parameters are being correctly passed and returned. Rather than coding an entire program and then debugging it, a program is coded and debugged in little steps. This approach is part of top-down design.

Significant jobs are relegated to functions that will be written some time in the future. These functions are initially implemented as stubs and the program is tested to verify that I/O is being appropriately executed and arguments are being correctly passed. When the function stub is fleshed out with meaningful operations, any bugs are most likely localized to that small block of operations just added. This approach allows us to debug in a *stepwise* fashion. The smaller the code we are debugging, the less time it is likely to take. The total time it takes to debug two small code sections separately is nearly always much less than the time it would take to debug the code all at once. It might take a bit more time to write stubs before completing the program, but it will pay off in the long run. (So, if you have other classes during this term or have hopes for a social life outside this class, you might pay particular attention to this concept.)

As your programming assignments for this class become larger and more complex, debugging time will become a more significant issue. From my experience in teaching introductory computer programming, I'll go out on a limb here and claim that if you follow the set of principles of style I'm about to list, you will probably save at least 10 hours of time this term, which would otherwise be spent in debugging exasperation:

CONCEPT

principles of
programming style

1. Design your programming solutions by breaking them into distinct modular functions. Functions should generally be less than 10 to 20 instructions in length. Your main program should be quite simple—I/O and calls to the appropriate functions.

2. Place a comment block at the top of each function carefully documenting the purpose of the function. Specify the expected values or legal ranges of IN parameters. Specify the nature of the value being returned by the function (if any) and the relationship with the parameters.

3. Use the debugger (tracing statements while watching variables—refer to the appropriate appendix for your system). If a debugger is not available, place extra **cout** statements at the top and bottom of each function to verify that parameters and the return value are as expected. Debug first with functions implemented as stubs.

4. Run your program using a set of test data for which you have calculated the expected output by hand.

You will still spend time debugging—even the best programmers do. These steps, however, will reduce the likelihood of spending an inordinate amount of time on this stage. You will find you are usually only debugging a few lines of code rather than an entire program. Even if your bug is due to a misunderstanding of the language, you will quickly be able to localize the bug, which will make seeking help much easier.

KEY TERM
algorithm

Let's now complete or flesh out the Sort3() function. Before writing code, we need an appropriate approach or *algorithm* that will lead to the correct solution. An algorithm is simply a formal name for a sequence of steps that lead to a correct solution. This is similar to the recipe for rolls in Chapter 3. We'll start with pseudocode in English. The following algorithm will put values in the three variables 'x', 'y', and 'z' in numeric order (smallest to largest):

```
if 'x' and 'y' are out of sequence
    swap the values in variables 'x' and 'y'
if 'y' and 'z' are out of sequence
    swap the values in variables 'y' and 'z'
if 'x' and 'y' are again out of sequence
    again swap the values in variables 'x' and 'y'
```

This is a simple variation of what is commonly known as "bubble sort." We simply look at the adjacent pairs of numbers and exchange or swap those that are out of sequence until the three variables are in order. Out of sequence simply means that the first is greater than the second. (Take a moment and convince yourself that for any three variable values, this algorithm will place them into numeric order.) Since we already have a Swap() function written, we can reuse it in this application (Listing 5.3).

Listing 5.3

```
// Sort3() Place three parameters into numeric order
// IN/OUT: x, y, z are any values. Upon return, they
//   will be in numeric sequence
void Sort3 (float& x, float& y, float& z)
{   if (x > y) Swap (x, y);
```

```
        else ;
        if (y > z) Swap (y, z);
        else ;
        if (x > y) Swap (x, y);
        else ;
}
```

5.4 Header files and projects

Up to this point, the only practical method of reusing a function from another program was to copy the function lines from one program file to another. One could certainly use the program development environment editor to do this (with the appropriate cut-and-paste command), but there is a simpler mechanism which is much less prone to error. Remember the library functions of Chapter 3? A program can reference and utilize library functions such as sqrt() by including the appropriate math.h file at the beginning of the program. For example, a program to input a value and output the square root of that value could be coded as in Listing 5.4.

Listing 5.4

```
// calcroot.cpp A program to calculate the square root of an input value
#include <iostream.h>
#include <math.h>
void main()
{   float value;
    cout << "Enter a value: ";
    cin >> value;
    cout << "Square root is: " << sqrt(value) << endl;
}
```

The compiler locates and utilizes the sqrt() function in a standard library of math functions. There is no need to copy the source into the calcroot.cpp file. A similar mechanism is available for user-written functions as well and provides a useful means of making functions more reusable. Up to this point, all of our programs (and functions) have existed in a single source file. To make a function easier for other programs to reuse, however, we will place useful functions in a file separate from the main program.

Refer back to Listing 5.3. If we envision that this Sort3() function may be useful in future programs, we perform four steps:

CONCEPT

use of project files

1. Place the program lines (or source) for Sort3() in a separate file — perhaps named sort3.cpp. This file (Figure 5.8) contains the program lines for the Sort3() function and any functions that Sort3() needs to call — in this case, the Swap() function.

```
void Sort3 (float& x, float& y, float& z);
```

Figure 5.7 Source file for sort3.h

```
// Swap()  Accepts two values as reference parameters and
// exchanges the values.
// IN/OUT: a, b -- When the function is called, these are any
//    values. When the function returns, the values ref'd by
//    a and b have been exchanged.
void Swap ( float& a, float& b)
{  float temp;
   temp = a;
   a = b;
   b = temp;
}

// Sort3() Place three values in three ref. parameters
// into numeric order
// IN/OUT:x, y, z are any values. When returned, they
//    will be in numeric sequence
void Sort3 (float& x, float& y, float& z)
{   if (x > y) Swap (x, y);
   else ;
    if (y > z) Swap (y, z);
   else ;
    if (x > y) Swap (x, y);
   else ;
}
```

Figure 5.8 Source file for sort3.cpp

2. As a companion to this file containing the function definition, create a new file containing a copy of the function heading (the line containing the function type, name, and parameter declarations) followed by a semicolon (Figure 5.7). We will name this file sort3.h. The .h extension refers to the fact that this file contains a function heading and not the function implementation.

3. At the top of the program in which we wish to call the Sort3() function, we will add an appropriate **#include** statement for the header:

```
#include "sort3.h"
```

Notice that the file name is enclosed with quotes, not < > brackets.

```
sortvals.cpp
sort3.cpp
```

Figure 5.9 Project file for the `sort3` project

4. Finally, we will add the file `sort3.cpp` into our project file using our appropriate program development environment. (Refer to the appropriate appendix for information on your system. In some systems, a project file is also referred to as a *makefile*. Basically, a project file contains, among other things, a list of files which must be compiled and linked to produce the completed program.) For example, suppose the main program is in the file `sortvals.cpp`. In this case, the project file would contain two entries (Figure 5.9).

The `#include` is actually a directive to the compiler to copy the text from the named file into the file being compiled. The `< >` brackets indicate that a header file is located in a default systems directory. The `" "` quotes indicate a header file is located in the current directory. The main program file might look similar to Figure 5.10. This file would not include the `Sort3()` function source, only the appropriate `#include` to bring in the `Sort3()` function heading file.

5.4.a Function prototypes

KEY TERM

prototype

A function heading is more formally called a *prototype* (short for "function prototype declaration"). As mentioned, a function prototype declares the function type, function name, and parameter list, but not the actual instructions of the function. While the first line of a function does not normally end with a `;`, a prototype must. A prototype does not actually need to contain the names of parameters, just the list of types. For example, the following is also a valid prototype for the `Swap3()` function;

```
void Sort3 (float&, float&, float&);
```

```
// sortvals.cpp  A program to input and sort 3 values
#include <iostream.h>
#include "sort3.h"
void main()
{ float r, s, t;
  cin >> r >> s >> t;
  Sort3 (r, s, t);
  cout << "in order: " << r << " " << s << " " << t << endl;
}
```

Figure 5.10 Source file for `sortvals.cpp`

It is usually most convenient, however, simply to copy and paste the first line or heading of a function definition to make a prototype. That way, they are sure to be the same. Don't forget to add the `;`.

Refer again to Figure 5.10 and let's follow what occurs when the `#include "sort3.h"` line is used. When the contents of the `sort3.h` file are copied into the main program during compilation, it will appear to the compiler as follows:

```
. . .
void Sort3 (float& x, float& y, float& z);

void main( )
{   float r, s, t;
    cin >> r >> s >> t;
    Sort3 (r, s, t);
    cout << "in order: " << r << " " << s << " " << t << endl;
}
```

The function heading or prototype declaration at the top notifies the compiler that the `Sort3()` function will not necessarily be found within this source file, but will be found in one of the other files listed in the project. It also allows the compiler to verify that all calls to this function have the correct number and type of parameters. The main program may utilize any of the functions with headers in the `sort.h` file. In this example, that is just the `Sort3()` function. If we had also placed a prototype for the `Swap()` function into the `sort.h` file, that function would also be accessible to the main program.

All functions listed as prototypes in the `.h` file can be called in the file where the appropriate `.h` is included. A function in the corresponding `.cpp` file, which is not listed as a prototype in the `.h` file, is essentially invisible to the including file. In other words, the `main()` program cannot call `Swap()` and isn't aware that it exists. You might refer to `Swap()` as a private function. More on this later.

These four steps may seem like a bit more work than simply placing all the source codes for all the functions in the same file. There are several advantages, however. If we later write another program that could take advantage of the `Sort3()` function, we need only perform steps 3 and 4 (adding the `#include "sort.h"` line and placing the `sort.cpp` filename into the project in order to reuse the `Sort3()` function). If it has been previously debugged and verified, we can be sure it will perform well in our new program and we have that much less to debug. By using this mechanism, we are not in danger of introducing mistakes by incorrectly copying the source text from one file to another.

In addition, the program development environment is intelligent enough to know it only needs to compile or translate the `sort.cpp` file once. An intermediate file (usually named `sort.obj` or `sort.o` depending on the type of system you are using) is automatically created to contain the translated instructions in machine form. Each time a make is performed on a project that references `sort.cpp`, the compiler simply uses the already translated form (`sort.obj` or `sort.o`) and the process runs much faster. If a programmer ever edits `sort.cpp` to make changes, the PDE will be intelligent enough to recompile it the next time it is needed. This is particularly helpful when working on large program systems of many functions.

If a function is referenced or used and the appropriate `#include` is found at the top, but the function source file is not part of the project, the compiler will search a default file—the standard library. This is the reason we did not need to place the source file for the `sqrt()` function into a project to use it in a program. The `math.h` header file simply contains the function headers of the math functions in the standard library.

A function then consists of a prototype declaration and the function definition (the actual function implementation). The rule is that a function prototype must be encountered by the compiler prior to any calls to that function. The function implementation can be anywhere in any of the program files. What about the functions we wrote back in Chapter 3? These functions did not utilize a prototype. When a function implementation is above the main program or other functions which invoke that function, no separate prototype is needed—the heading of the function implementation serves as a prototype.

5.4.b   File scope

You might be thinking that one could simply include the `.cpp` file and forget the whole idea of a `.h` file:

```
#include "sort3.cpp"
```

This would cause the contents of the file `sort3.cpp` to be copied into your main program file as if you had typed it there. Wouldn't that work? Well, yes it would—in this case. There are a variety of situations, however, when trouble can be caused, and this is a poor practice.

Here is just one: Consider for a moment that you wish to make the `Sort3()` function available to another programmer. This friend doesn't use good practice and simply includes the `sort3.cpp` file in his program. Unfortunately, he doesn't know you have a private function in the file and he has written a function named `Swap()` for a different purpose. When his program is compiled, he sees error messages about two functions having the same name and becomes confused. If this other programmer had followed good practice and included the `.h` file, this private `Swap()` function of yours would have been hidden and not caused an error.

5.5 Introduction to files

At this point, you are ready to consider that input does not always come via the keyboard. Suppose you were asked to write a program to produce a table of cosines for a list of 50 different randomly ordered angles. No problem. Your program might look like the following:

```
// Calculate a table of cosines
#include <iostream.h>
#include <math.h>
void main( )
{   const float LOOPCOUNT = 50.0;
    float angle, count=0;
    while (count < LOOPCOUNT)
    {   cout << "enter an angle in radians: ";
        cin >> angle;
        cout << "angle: " << angle << " cos: " << cos(angle) << endl;
        count = count + 1.0;
    }
}
```

Certainly, nothing is new here. You might, however, tend to become somewhat frustrated while testing your program during development. Each time you test, you need to type in another list of 50 different angles! With just a couple of small modifications, we can type in a list one time and have this program *reuse the same list* each time it runs.

We'll start by typing in the list of angles once. Using your program development system, enter the angles list into a new file with one angle per line. Save this file under the name "input.dat" in the same directory as your program. Now we'll modify the program so that it reads the 50 angles from the file rather than from the keyboard. There are four changes (in bold):

```
// Calculate a table of cosines
#include <iostream.h>
#include <fstream.h>                    // 1. add this header file
#include <math.h>
void main( )
{   const float LOOPCOUNT = 50.0;
    float angle, count=0;
    ifstream infile;                    // 2. declare a file variable
    infile.open ("input.dat");          // 3. open "input.dat" for input
    while (count < LOOPCOUNT)
    {   infile >> angle;                // 4. read from infile, not cin
        cout << "angle:  << angle << " cos:  << cos(angle) << endl;
        count = count + 1.0;
    }
}
```

CONCEPT

reading input from a file

There are four simple steps to change a program to read from a file rather than from the keyboard. First, another header file was added. Second, the line `ifstream infile;` was added to the declarations. Third, the line `infile.open ("input.dat");` was added at the top of the instructions. Fourth, we changed the input lines that previously used `cin` to use `infile`. (Notice also that the prompt line in the original program is no longer needed.) Now when this program is executed, it will expect to input the angles from the file rather than from the keyboard. The file can be read over and over again.

This is a very elementary introduction, but these four steps can be used to convert any program that normally receives input from the keyboard to receive input from the file `"input.dat"`. The file should contain the input in the same order and format that you would have used when entering from the keyboard. In other words, the file should contain the same keystrokes. Naturally, it would be a mistake to provide an input file with less than the needed 50 angles or to include characters or data the program does not expect. The input file is not a C++ program file, so don't attempt to add comments! We'll return to this topic in much more detail in Chapter 8.

5.6 Example project

As one becomes involved with borrowing money, it is always a revelation how much of a payment on a loan goes to interest. Suppose a couple borrows $30,000 for a home on a 30-year loan at 8% annual interest. At the end of the first month, a check for the first monthly installment of $220 is mailed, but only about $20 actually go toward reducing the amount owed —the rest is for interest.

For this reason, it is usually helpful to generate an amortization table showing the payment amount, the amount of loan remaining, and the accumulated interest paid after each monthly period. The three formulas for these values are the following:

$$Bal_k = \frac{1}{(1 + rate)^{-k}} \left[\frac{P(1 + rate)^{-k} - 1}{rate} + PV \right]$$

$$Acum_k = Bal_k + (k)P - PV$$

$$P = PV \left[\frac{rate}{1 - (1 + rate)^N} \right]$$

where: Bal_k is the loan balance after payment k,

  $rate$ is the periodic interest rate,

  PV is the principal or initial loan value,

  P is the periodic payment amount,

  $Acum_k$ is the accumulated interest paid after payment k, and

  N is the total number of payment periods.

In designing a program to generate an amortization table, the first step is to determine what inputs the program will need. The values for the periodic interest rate, the principal value, and the number of payments are the basis for the three formulas. The main program should prompt the user for these values and output a table with one line for each payment. Note that the periodic rate is not necessarily the yearly interest rate. For example, if the yearly rate is 8% but payments are made monthly, the periodic rate is 0.08/12.

It seems the logical way to partition the problem is to assign a function to calculate these three formulas. Now all functions could be placed within the same file, but these functions will probably be useful in other applications, and we choose to place them inside a separate project file appropriately named `finance.cpp`. The associated header file will be `finance.h`. The main program will reside in the file `amortize.cpp`. Using a top-down approach, we will start with the main program.

After prompting for the necessary inputs and reading values from the user, the main program first calculates the monthly interest rate from the yearly rate and then calculates the monthly payment. An output title line is then displayed. Next, using a counting loop with the variable `month` going from 1 to the number of payments, the program (a) calculates a remaining balance to date, (b) calculates an accumulated interest to date, and (c) outputs a display line of this information. Remember, this main program is in the file `amortize.cpp` (Listing 5.5).

Listing 5.5

```cpp
// FILE: amortize.cpp  Display an amortization table for a loan
// ASSUMPTION: loan rate is yearly, payments are made monthly
#include <iostream.h>
#include "finance.h"

const float MONTHS = 12.0;

void main ()
{   float rate, principal, num_payments, accum;
    float yearly_rate, balance, payment, month=1;
    cout << "enter loan principal, rate, and number of payments: ";
    cin >> principal >> yearly_rate >> num_payments;

    rate = yearly_rate / MONTHS;
    payment = Payment (principal, rate, num_payments);
    cout << "Payment: " << payment << endl;
    cout << "Amortization of " << principal << " over " <<
        num_payments << " at a rate of " << rate << endl;
    cout << " Month      Balance      Accumulated Interest" << endl;
    cout << " ---------------------------------" << endl;

    while (month <= num_payments)
    {   Amortize (accum, balance, rate, payment, principal, month);
        cout << month << "    " << balance << "    " << accum << endl;
        month = month + 1.0;
    }
}
```

Now a separate file `finance.cpp` is created wherein these two functions can be defined or implemented. At first, we will just stub them in so that they do little but return constants. Note that the `Amortize()` function must affect two values: an accumulated interest and a new balance.

```
float Payment (float principal, float rate, float num_payments)
{   return (1.0);
}

void Amortize (float& accum, float& bal, float rate, float pmnt,
                         float prin, float num)
{   bal = 2.0;
    accum = 3.0;
}
```

A third file finanace.h is now created containing the prototype lines of these two functions (ending with semicolons), as in Listing 5.6.

Listing 5.6

```
// FILE:  finance.h  Header for loan calculation functions
float Payment (float principal, float rate, float num_payments);
void Amortize (float& accum, float& bal, float rate, float pmnt,
                         float prin, float num);
```

At this point, the project (consisting of the two files amortize.cpp and finance.cpp) can be made. The resulting executable program will not produce a very meaningful table, but it will allow us to verify that the project has been set up correctly, the number of arguments in the calling statements match the number of parameters in the function declarations, the table is formatted appropriately, the correct number of table lines are being generated, and so on. Before going on to more detail within the functions, these basic features and constructs of the program are first tested.

Now it is time to flesh out the functions. We notice that the subexpression $(1 + rate)^{-x}$ is used in several places. Rather than implement this subexpression in each location, we will again just refer to a function, named RateExpr() for want of a more descriptive title (Lising 5.7).

Listing 5.7

```
// FILE:  finance.cpp

#include <math.h>
// RateExpr()  Return an interest subexpression
// IN:rate is the periodic interest rate
//     k is a payment number
float RateExpr (float rate, float k)
{   float temp;
    temp = 1.0 + rate;
    return (pow (temp, -k));
}
```

```
// Payment()  Return the payment on a loan given the prin-
// cipal, rate, and number of payments
// IN:  rate is the periodic interest rate
//      principal is the original loan value
//      num_payments is the number of equally spaced payments
float Payment (float principal, float rate, float num_pay)
{  float paymnt;
   paymnt = principal * (rate / (1.0 - RateExpr (rate, num_pay)));
   return (paymnt);
}


// Amortize()  Update the accumulated interest and balance
// of a loan given principal, rate, payment, and payment number
// IN:  rate is the periodic interest rate
//      prin is the original loan value
//      num is the current payment number
// OUT:  bal is the current loan balance after the current payment
//        accum is the accumulated interest after payment
void Amortize (float& accum, float& bal, float rate, float pmnt,
                       float prin, float num)
{  float temp;
   temp = RateExpr (rate, num);
   bal = (1.0 / temp) * ((pmnt * (temp-1.0) / rate) + prin);
   accum = bal + num * pmnt - prin;
}
```

Notice that the `RateExpr()` function is not part of the `finance.h` header file since the main program does not need to invoke this function or even be aware that it exists. If two separate programmers were to work on this project, the one responsible for the `finance.cpp` file could decide to remove the `RateExpr()` function and perform this calculation directly each time it was needed. The other programmer would not need to be aware of this change and would not see any difference in the project. The two files are encapsulated. The only interaction between them is through the parameters of the functions named within the `finance.h` header file.

Notice also that the header file `math.h` is included at the top of the `finance.cpp` file since the `pow()` library function is needed within this file by the `RateExpr()` function.

5.7 Summary

KEY TERMS   Several new terms were introduced in this chapter:

1. *encapsulated*—a function that does not modify anything in the bigger program except through parameters and a return value is said to be encapsulated.

2. *reference parameters*—function parameters that refer back to an associated argument. Changes to a reference parameter actually cause changes to the associated argument.

3. *assumption* — a comment statement placed at the top of a function indicating assumptions that must be true if the function is to perform correctly.

4. *stubs* — functions that have appropriate headings but do no useful work. They are simply used to facilitate stepwise debugging and top-down design.

5. *algorithm* — a sequence of instruction steps that leads to an expected solution. An algorithm is usually expressed in symbolic or natural English form and is simply a way of organizing solutions prior to coding.

6. *prototype* — a function declaration line specifying the function type, function name, and list of parameters for a function.

CONCEPTS   Only one new syntax form was introduced: The addition of the & symbol after a parameter type changes it to a reference parameter. Conceptually, one can think of reference parameters as having a value copied from an argument variable when the function is called and having the parameter value copied back to the argument variable when the function returns. Constants, literals, expressions, or **const** identifiers are not appropriate arguments for a reference parameter since they are not changeable.

In addition, you learned that placing quotes around a header file name in an #include statement causes the system to search the current directory for the named header file.

Several concepts were suggested to help the beginning student save time during program development and debugging:

1. Modularize your program into a simple main program and short functions.

2. Provide adequate documentation at the beginning of each function to remind readers of assumptions and the purpose of parameters.

3. Check the status of function calls with the debugger at the top and bottom of each function. Debug first with functions written as stubs.

4. Debug your program with test data for which you have a hand-calculated answer.

A successful program is correct, efficient, easy to use, and most important, developed quickly and maintained easily. To reduce program complexity, simplify debugging and testing, and make code reuse easier, programs are most efficiently designed with small modular functions. Stepwise debugging and top-down design are facilitated through the use of function stubs. Header files and projects can be used to simplify the reuse of functions in other independent programs. Only the functions in the header file are seen by the including file. Functions not given prototypes in the header are private and not available to the including file.

A simple approach was introduced whereby a program can be changed to receive input from a separate file rather than the keyboard.

To input information from a disk file, the #include <fstream.h> statement must be added at the top of the program. Next, a file identifier must be declared and the file opened to prepare for input. For example, if the disk file is named "input.dat":

```
ifstream infile;
infile.open ("input.dat");
```

To input values just as if they had been typed from the keyboard, utilize the extraction >> operator with the file identifier. For example, to input a number into the variable `angle`:

```
infile >> angle;
```

Table 5.1 **Example segments**

`void CalcCost (float &age)`
`{`
`}`
	Changes to age in this function will cause corresponding changes to the calling argument.

`float SumAges ();`	A function prototype specifying this function returns a value but has no parameters.
`float NewCost (float &);`	A prototype indicating the function returns a value and has a single reference parameter.

`float OldCost (float x)`
`{ return (0);`
`}`
	A function stub for debug purposes.

`// ASSUMPTION:`	A header comment to document function assumptions.

5.8 Exercises

5.8.a   Short-answer questions

1. When a function is called, the variables or values within the parentheses are called _____.
2. The variables within the function parentheses in the function heading are called _____.
3. The heading of a function without the body or instructions is called a function _____.
4. Explain what should be stated in an ASSUMPTION comment.
5. Briefly explain the purpose of ASSUMPTION comments.
6. Briefly explain the purpose of a function stub.
7. Briefly explain why good programmers attempt to reuse code.
8. Consider the function Letterhead() in Listing 3.1. Give a prototype.
9. Give a prototype for the function GetValueBetween() in Listing 3.3.

10. Give a possible prototype for the `sqrt()` library function which might be found in the `math.h` file.

11. Four types of arguments in a function call are not appropriate matches for reference parameters. The first is a constant. What are the other three?

12. Explain why an arithmetic *expression* would not be appropriate as an argument match for a reference parameter. For example:

```
Swap (x, y*2)
```

13. Briefly explain when it is and when it is not appropriate to use a reference parameter when concerned with keeping functions encapsulated and modular.

14. The first step in program testing is usually to verify the ASSUMPTIONs and IN values at the top of each function as it is called. Explain briefly why this might help to localize a bug quickly.

15. Explain why testing a program with a set of hand-calculated data may not reveal some bugs in a program.

16. Briefly explain two advantages of using separate files for the main program and functions of a project.

17. Explain why using stubs for functions allows a programmer to simplify the process of debugging a program.

18. Which function prototypes should be listed in a header file? Which need not be listed?

19. Which system header file should be included to perform input from a disk file?

20. Briefly explain why a globally accessible variable is not a good alternative to a reference parameter. Also briefly explain why a globally accessible `const` variable may be a good alternative to passing a constant to each function that needs it.

5.8.b Projects

1. Reuse the `finance.cpp` functions in another program to simply calculate the payments of a loan and the total interest accumulated at payoff without generating an amortization table.

2. Using the `Sort3()` and `Swap()` functions in this chapter, write a program to sort a list of four different values input by the user.

3. Write a function named `AveCount()` which inputs a list of positive numbers representing test grades from the user. The user should enter a negative value as a sentinel that the list is complete. The function should return the average and the number of grades (`count`) to the calling program. Use the following simple `main()` program, which calls this function and displays the results to demonstrate your function:

```
void main()
{   float ave, count;
    ave = AveCount (count);
    cout << " ave is " << ave << " count is " << count << endl;
}
```

4. Write a function to input a list of 25 grades from the user and return a count of the number of As, Bs, Cs, Ds, and Fs to the calling program. An A grade is a score 90 or above, a B is 80 up to below 90, a C is 70 up to below 80, and so on. Use the following simple `main()` program, which calls this function and displays the results to demonstrate your function:

```
void main()
{   float A=0, B=0, C=0, D=0, F=0;
    CountGrades (A, B, C, D, F);
    cout << "grades (A, B, C, D, F): "
    cout   <<A<< ",", <<B<< "," <<C<< "," <<D<< "," <<F<< endl;
}
```

5. Two observers separated by distance C both note a building in the distance. Each observer measures the angle between a line from his position to the building and a line to the other observer. Write a function to accept the distance C and the two angles and return the two distances from each observer to the building. In other words, from the diagram, the function should accept as parameters the distance C and the angles a1 and a2. It should then calculate and return the distances A and B. Write a `main()` program to call this function and display the results for several different situations.

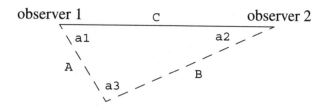

The appropriate formulas are the following:

$$A = \frac{C \sin(a1)}{\sin(a3)}$$

$$B = \frac{C \sin(a2)}{\sin(a3)}$$

$$a3 = 180° - (a1 + a2) \quad \text{(if angles are measured in degrees)}$$

Remember that `sin()` functions require the argument to be in radians (there are 2π radians for 360 degrees).

6. The two roots of a quadratic equation are defined as those two values of x for which the following equation is true:

$$ax^2 + bx + c = 0$$

Write a function that will accept values for the constants a, b, and c and return a status value indicating whether the roots are real and the values of the two roots. The appropriate formulas are:

$$x1 = \frac{-b + \sqrt{b^2 - 4ac}}{2a}$$

$$x2 = \frac{-b - \sqrt{b^2 - 4ac}}{2a}$$

If the value $(b^2 - 4ac)$ is positive, the roots are real. Your function should return a positive status value. If not, the roots are imaginary and your function should return a negative status value. Use the following `main()` program to test your function with several different constants for a, b, and c. Notice that this program contains an infinite loop—it continues to prompt for values. Occasionally, this is a desired effect. To terminate this program, simply press and hold the Ctrl key and then press capital C. This is known as a manual abort.

```
void main()
{    float a, b, c, status, root1, root2;
     while (1)
     {    cout << "enter values for a, b, and c: ";
          cin >> a >> b >> c;
          status = Roots (a, b, c, root1, root2);
          if (status > 0)
               cout << " roots are: " << root1 << " " << root2 << endl;
          else cout << " imaginary roots" << endl;
     }
}
```

7. A complex number contains two parts: a real part and an imaginary part. It can be written as a pair of numbers with a comma between. For example, 5,6 is a complex number with 5 as the real component and 6 as the imaginary component. Write a function to calculate and return the product of two imaginary numbers. Naturally, the product is also a complex number. Write a simple `main()` program to test your function. The formula is:

$$(a, b) \times (c, d) = (ac - bd), (cb + ad)$$

8. A problem with two equations and two unknowns can be solved using Cramer's rule. If the first equation is $ax + by = e$ and the second is $cx + dy = f$ (where x and y are the variables and a, b, c, d, e, and f are coefficient values) provided by the user, then the solution is the following:

$$x = (ed - bf)/(ad - bc)$$

$$y = (af - ec)/(ad - bc)$$

Write a function to accept values for the coefficients and return the values for x and y as well as a status value. If $ad - bc = 0$, then there is no solution and your function should return a negative status value. Otherwise, the function should return a positive status value and the values for x and y. Write a simple `main()` program to input coefficient values from the user, call your function, and display the results if a solution exists or display an appropriate error message otherwise.

9. **Creative Challenge:** The example project of this chapter (Listings 5.5, 5.6, and 5.7) assume the user will input a whole number for the number of monthly payments for a loan. There is no guarantee of this, however. Modify the project files so that the user sees an error message if something other than a whole number is entered for this value.

10. **Creative Challenge:** Write a program to manipulate nonnumeric data. Suppose the user has a paper list of student letter grades. The user should be able to use your program to enter this information in some way and then generate a summary table of the number of As, Bs, Cs, Ds, and Fs.

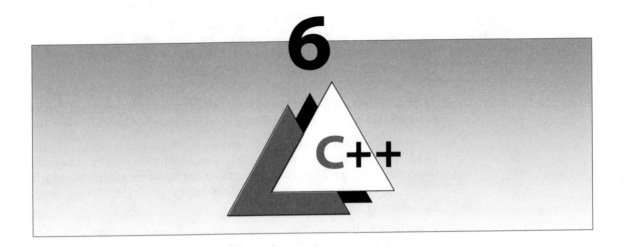

More Data Types

All of the programs examined and written to this point have used **float** variables. You need to understand that such variables are not infinitely accurate, but have bounds on accuracy and range. In addition, they make it difficult to enforce the use of whole numbers or allow simple representation of textual data. How would you write a program to calculate the number of quarters in a given amount of money? The program output must reasonably be a whole number. Wouldn't it be more friendly to prompt a user to `enter y to continue, n to stop` rather than `enter 1.0 to continue, 0 to stop`? This chapter introduces several additional variable types and points out where they are appropriate in programming problems and solutions. In addition, two more relational comparison operators are introduced.

6.1 Floating-point variables

Up to this point, variables have all been declared using the reserved word **float**. If functions returned a value, they were declared with this same **float**. The reserved word **float** is actually the definition of a variable or function *type*. In this case, the type is a decimal number. Before pointing out that there are actually several other available types in the C++ language, we should better understand the meaning of the type **float**.

6.1.a Representation

Floating-point values are stored internally using a form of scientific notation. If you will remember back to earlier math classes, scientific notation is a method of expressing very large or very small numbers using a small decimal number and a power of 10. For example, the value 1,234,560,000,000,000,000.0 would be expressed as:

```
0.123456 x 10¹⁹
```

The number 0.000,000,000,000,123,456 would be expressed as:

```
0.123456 x 10⁻¹²
```

The advantage of this approach is that fewer digits need to be written down *if the number ends or begins in a lot of zeros*. If a very long number does not end or begin with zeros, there is no savings in the number of digits that must be written down, *unless we decide to round the number to a smaller number of digits*. Suppose you decide you only need six digits of accuracy in your numbers. The value 1,234,567,890,123,456,789.0 would be written as:

```
.123457 x 10¹⁹
```

If you decide on the convention that every number in this form of scientific notation is to be written with the decimal point before the first nonzero digit, then you really only need to write down two simple integer numbers: the digits of the decimal number and the digits of the power of 10. The preceding value could be expressed with a pair of integers as:

```
123457, 19
```

The net result of this notation is that you can express very large or very small numbers with only a few digits—in this case, eight. You need to keep in mind that this representation is only an approximation, however, accurate to the first six digits of the actual number. This means that two very different numbers may have the same notation, as long as they are within six digits of accuracy of each other:

```
123,456,000,000,000,000.0      represented as 123456, 18
123,456,400,000,000,000.0      represented as 123456, 18
```

Even though these two numbers are 400 billion apart, this notation represents them in the same way.

KEY TERMS
characteristic,
mantissa

C++ represents floating-point numbers using a form of scientific notation. Each floating-point number is rounded to about six or seven significant digits and represented as two integers: The first represents the fractional part with an assumed point to the left of the digits; the second is the power to which this fraction would need to be multiplied to arrive at the correct value. (Actually, it turns out to be simpler to use powers of 2 instead of powers of 10 in a binary computer, but the principle is the same.) The details of this representation may differ slightly between computers and versions of C++, but the concept is similar. The fractional part (with the implied point) is called the *characteristic* and the power is called the *mantissa*.

6.1.b E-notation

To save typing some keystrokes, floating-point constants can be written using *E-notation* in C++. In this form, we simply use the letter e to represent the phrase $\times 10$ or *times ten*. So, 0.9×10^{25} would be written as 0.9e25 and 0.5×10^{-8} written as $0.5e - 8$ using this notation. Consider the following program segment used to input a **float** value from the keyboard:

```
float y;
cin >> y;
```

Suppose the value of 0.00000000054 is to be input. Typing any of the following would result in the correct number being placed into variable y:

```
0.00000000054
5.4e-10
0.54e-9
54.0e-11
```

6.1.c Precision and range

The key point to remember is that to save space and force all **float** numbers to require the same amount of memory space, *values are rounded to a predetermined accuracy*. For example, in Microsoft Visual C++, that is about seven digits. You may be thinking that is close enough for most applications, and you are right. It certainly has been for programming problems up to this point. This method of representing decimal numbers has some definite limitations, however. On most C++ systems, **float** variables are assigned 32 bits of memory space. Of that space, the characteristic utilizes enough bits to represent about seven digits, leaving only enough room for the mantissa to be in the range of about 10^{-38} to 10^{38}.

The reason I'm not being very definitive here and saying "about seven" digits and "about" −38 to +38 is that **float** values are stored as binary numbers. Binary numbers in this range do not always convert to an exact number of decimal digits. If you want to know the exact range, it is 1.175494×10^{-38} to 3.362103×10^{38} on 32-bit C++ systems. This may vary with other systems, but the point remains: There is a limit to accuracy in **float** variables. If you write a constant or input a value in a C++ program with more than about seven digits of accuracy, the system may round it to the correct number. If you perform a calculation with two **float** variables, the system may need to round the result.

KEY TERMS

overflow, underflow

CONCEPT

rules for `float` constants

What if you need to express a number with a characteristic larger than will fit, say, 0.9×10^{40}? The answer is that you can't with the **float** data type. We call this variable *overflow*. The very small number 0.9×10^{-40} will not fit either and would result in *underflow*. We will see later that there is another variable type more appropriate for such extremely large or small numbers or numbers where seven digits of accuracy are insufficient.

Three important rules to remember when inputting or writing **float** constants are:

1. Always use a decimal point, but never use a comma.

2. When using E-notation, the mantissa (exponent) must be a whole number.

3. If you write more than about seven digits in the decimal part, the system may round the number.

6.1.d Rounding errors

To illustrate the importance of understanding that **float** variables are rounded to just a few significant digits, consider the following program intended to add the salaries of a few software company CEOs to the national debt. The national debt is a very large number, and the generous CEO salaries are (individually, of course) quite small in relation. This program was run using Borland C++ 4.0, but the concept is applicable to any system (Listing 6.1).

Listing 6.1

```
// addsal.cpp  Add 6 salaries to the national debt.
#include <iostream.h>
void main ()
{   float sal1, sal2, sal3, sal4, sal5, sal6, debt;
    debt = -5.0e12;                    // about 5 trillion dollars
    cout << "The debt is now: " << debt << endl;
    cout << "Enter 6 salaries: ";
    cin >> sal1 >> sal2 >> sal3 >> sal4 >> sal5 >> sal6;
    debt = debt + sal1;
    debt = debt + sal2;
    debt = debt + sal3;
    debt = debt + sal4;
    debt = debt + sal5;
    debt = debt + sal6;
    cout  << " Thank you, the debt is now only  " << debt;
}
```

Now suppose the following salaries are input when this program is executed:

```
The debt is now: -5e12
Enter 6 salaries: 403405.0 1204000.0 1210000.0 376000.0
    1240000.0 607000.0
Thank you, the debt is now only -5e12
```

Two important points to notice from this program execution are the following:

1. When a floating-point number is very large or very small, it will be output using E-notation. Notice how `debt` is displayed.

2. After the addition of all six salaries, there was no change in the `debt` value. In other words, when a significantly smaller number is added to a very large number, the result may not be different from the original large number. The sum of `debt` and any one salary was not different from the original value of `debt` within the precision of a **float** variable (the first seven or so digits).

For example, consider the first assignment statement which adds the first salary to `debt`. The following shows the stages this addition will go through:

```
  - 5,000,000,000,000.0
  +               403,405.0
     ──────────────────────

  - 4,999,999,596,595.0

    after rounding to seven significant digits:
  - 5,000,000,000,000.0
```

KEY TERM

rounding error

When the result of the addition is rounded to seven digits of accuracy, the effect of the small salary is lost. We call this a *rounding error*. In other words, it would not matter in this program how many salaries we added into the national debt. As long as each salary is less than the debt by more than the precision of a **float** variable, the national debt would never change! I suppose some may think this adds credence to the thought that we will never be able to pay off the national debt, but the purpose here is to illustrate a situation when the limited accuracy of **float** variables can cause a significant problem. (This math demonstration uses decimal numbers. The computer uses binary values, so the exact rounding is somewhat different.) The concept you should understand is that the computer will round to the precision limit of a variable. The exact results of this little demonstration may vary from system to system since the precision and range of **float** variables may vary. Nevertheless, there is a set of numbers that will demonstrate this same concept on any system.

Suppose we *first* added all six salaries together to form a much larger composite salary. If this composite salary were then added into the national debt, it might be large enough to make a difference. Consider the changes made in Listing 6.2.

Listing 6.2

```cpp
// addsal.cpp  Add 6 salaries to the national debt.
#include <iostream.h>
void main ()
{   float sal1, sal2, sal3, sal4, sal5, sal6, debt, totalsal;
    debt = -5.0e12;
    cout << "The debt is now: " << debt;
    cout << "Enter 6 salaries: ";
```

```
    cin >> sal1 >> sal2 >> sal3 >> sal4 >> sal5 >> sal6;
    totalsal = sal1 + sal2 + sal3 + sal4 + sal5 + sal6;
    debt = debt + totalsal;
    cout   << " Thank you, the debt is now only  " << debt;
}
```

The execution of this program would now appear as follows:

```
The debt is now: -5e12
Enter 6 salaries: 403405.0   1204000.0   1210000.0   376000.0
    1240000.0   607000.0
Thank you, the debt is now only  -4.99999e+12
```

The answer is not exact; it is correct only to six significant digits. But at least we made a difference in the debt. The reason is, of course, that the total of the six salaries is over \$5 million. The paper calculation does not give the same answer since the computer is using binary values, but we can see from the following that the total salary amount reduces the debt so that rounding to about seven digits now changes the sum:

$$
\begin{aligned}
-\ & 5{,}000{,}000{,}000{,}000.0 \\
+\ & \phantom{5{,}000{,}000{,}0}5{,}040{,}405.0 \\
\hline
-\ & 4{,}999{,}994{,}959{,}595.0
\end{aligned}
$$

rounded to seven significant digits:
$$-\ 4{,}999{,}995{,}000{,}000.0$$

6.1.e Double-precision variables

As we have seen, the limitations of **float** variables can be significant. When either more digits of precision or a larger range than that available with **float** variables is needed, the type **double** can be used. The type **double** is short for "double precision." While Microsoft Visual C++ uses 32 bits to represent a **float** value, 64 bits are assigned for a **double** value. This increased space allows more digits of precision for the mantissa and more room for a larger characteristic. The largest value for a **double** variable is about 1.797693000000000e308 and the smallest is 2.2250738585072014e-308. Instead of just 7 digits of precision, **double** values are stored with about 15 or 16 digits of precision. Both **double** and **float** constants are written the same way, using decimal or E-notation. Consider now what would happen if we change the variable declaration line in Listing 6.2 to the following:

```
double sal1, sal2, sal3, sal4, sal5, sal6, debt, totalsal;
```

The user doesn't need to know the difference between **float** and **double** variables, just that a decimal number is used to represent salaries:

```
The debt is now: -5e12
Enter 6 salaries: 403405.0  1204000.0  1210000.0  376000.0
1240000.0  607000.0
Thank you, the debt is now only:   -4.99999e+12
```

This is surprising because we expected the answer to be nearly exact with about 15 digits of precision! What we see is still rounded to six digits. The reason for there being only six digits displayed has to do with the << output operation. In fact, the **double** variables in the program do contain 15 digits of precision and the debt variable does end up containing the exact answer. Since we rarely need more than six digits of precision in program output values, the *default* for the << output operation is to display all **float** or **double** values rounded to a maximum of six digits of precision. We will see in Chapter 8 how this default can be changed or overridden to produce as many digits of precision as we desire in output displays.

Usually, we wish a program to perform calculations with great precision but need only six digits of precision displayed in results. In these cases, most programmers will use **double** variables but expect the answers to be rounded to six digits of precision by the << output statement. This is particularly true for engineering and scientific work. (Consider for a moment that even the most precise scale or micrometer is usually accurate to only four digits.) In mathematical calculations, however, we may wish more precision displayed (such as when calculating the value of π), and the default for the << output operation would need to be changed.

You may ask: Why don't we always use **double** instead of **float**? Well, many programmers do just that. You need to understand, however, that a **double** variable requires twice as much space in most systems as a **float** variable. In future programs which manipulate large numbers of decimal values, that may be a concern. In some systems, however, the size of **float** and **double** variables is exactly the same! All you can count on are the following:

CONCEPT

double-precision data type

- The precision of **double** variables will be greater than or equal to that of **float** variables.
- The range of **double** variables will be greater than or equal to that of **float** variables.

6.2 Integer variables

CONCEPT

int data type

From the previous section, we learned that decimal or floating-point variables have limited precision but an extremely large range. Not all the world's data contain a decimal point, however, and another variable type is provided for values that are always whole numbers or integers: the type **int** (short for "integer").

6.2.a   Range

On many C++ systems, an **int** variable is allocated 16 bits of memory space and is capable of storing a whole number in the range of –32,768 to +32,767. (The reason for these particular limits will be made clear in Chapter 14.) Typically, **int** variables are used to represent values from the real world which must be whole numbers such as the count or size of a list, the number of people in a room, the number of loan payments, and so forth. Declaring a variable to be type **int** is a programmer's way of documenting that this variable will only represent whole numbers and ensuring that nonwhole numbers are not used in important calculations.

Integer constants are written without decimal points, of course, and users should enter values for **int** variables without decimal points.

```
int a;
a = 256;        // proper
```

It is incorrect to write an integer constant with a leading zero:

```
a = 0256;
```

CONCEPT

avoid leading zeros

This assignment does not produce an error message, but a value very different than 256 will be assigned to variable a. The reason is that C++ interprets constants that begin with a leading zero as representing a base-8 number and not a base-10 number as you are accustomed to dealing with. (The use of such numbers will be clearer in Chapter 14.)

6.2.b Mixed-Mode Expressions

KEY TERM

mixed-mode expression

Often, we need to utilize **int** and **float** or **double** variables in the same assignment statement or expression. Any expression (mathematical calculation) that uses both **int** and **float** or **double** variables or values is called a *mixed-mode expression*. There are three important rules to remember for mixed-mode expressions:

CONCEPT

rules for mixed-mode expressions

1. If a program statement attempts to assign a floating-point value to an **int** variable, the system will truncate the fractional part of the floating-point value and store only the integer part into the **int** variable:

```
float x;
int y;
x = 3.14159;
y = x;
cout << y;        // will display 3
cin >> y;         // if the user enters 6.9876, the next line
cout << y;        // will display 6
```

EXPERIMENT

What would happen if you assigned an **int** variable to a **float** variable?

2. *Any mathematical operation involving two integers always results in an integer.* That may seem obvious; the product of two integers is an integer, the sum of two integers is an integer, and so on. Where it becomes extremely important is when we *divide* two integers—the result is an integer. Remember, an expression or calculation in an assignment statement must be calculated before the result is assigned to the variable on the left-hand side of the = operator. For example:

```
int a, b, c;
float x;
a = 2;
b = 7;
c = b / a;     // 'c' now contains 3, not 3.5
cout << c;     // output will display 3, not 3.5
x = b / a;     // 'x' will contain 3, not 3.5
x = 1 / a;     // 'x' will contain 0, not 0.5
```

3. The corollary to rule 2 is that *any mathematical operation involving a floating-point value always results in a floating-point value.* In other words, if at least one of the two operands of a mathematical operation is a floating-point value, the result will be a floating-point value. So, a floating-point value times an integer results in a floating-point value. An integer divided by a floating-point value results in a floating-point value and so on.

```
int a;
float x;
a = 2;
x = 1.0 / a; // 'x' will contain 0.5, the result of the division
```

CONCEPT

rule of thumb for integer division

These three rules can be condensed into a single rule of thumb that many students find easier to remember:

An integer divided by an integer is always an integer.

The reason this simple statement is a nice condensed version of the three rules is that the only time you will get into trouble is when you divide an integer by an integer! Any other operation will result in the correct answer you expect, and whether it is an integer or floating-point value won't matter. Assigning an integer to a **float** variable produces a floating-point number, but appending .0 to an integer does not change the value (as long as the range and precision of the **float** variable are appropriate).

This rule of thumb can serve a useful purpose in some programs. Suppose we need a function to return the number of quarters in a given amount of money. The function in Listing 6.3 accepts as a parameter a decimal amount of money and returns the integer number of quarters in this amount. For example, if called with the amount 13.45, it should return 53.

Listing 6.3

```
// NumQuarters () Calculate the number of
// quarters in the money represented by the parameter
// IN:   amount -- a decimal amount of money
// RETURNS: the number of quarters
int NumQuarters (float money)
{   int quarters, cents;
    cents = money * 100;          // convert to pennies
    quarters = cents / 25;        // number of whole quarters
    return (quarters);
}
```

This function first converts the decimal money amount into cents. Any fractional cents would be dropped by truncation. By dividing the number of cents (an integer) by 25 (another integer), the integer number of quarters is determined. Any fractional amount left over is dropped by truncation.

6.2.c Parameters

CONCEPT

function call rules

Now that you are aware of several different variable types, let's clarify the rules for calling a function at this point in your career:

- The number of arguments must match the number of parameters (you know this already).

- The type of each argument *should* match the type of the corresponding parameter.

In other words, an **int** argument should be used for an **int** parameter, a **float** argument should be used for a **float** parameter, and so on. If this is not the case, you may or may not see a warning message when compiling your program. In any case, the system will consider the argument a type of mixed-mode expression and perform a conversion as described earlier. If the function parameter is a reference, however, you may find that changes to the parameter within the function are not reflected back to the corresponding argument. Consider this little example:

```
void SomeFunc (int& b)
{   b = 99;               // should change argument
}                         // to 99, but doesn't!
void main ()
{   float a = 5.6;
    SomeFunc (a);
    cout << a << endl;    // 'a' is still 5.6
}
```

WRONG WAY!

The reason you do not see the expected change in the argument variable a is that the system creates a temporary **int** variable to be the matching or corresponding argument to parameter b. This temporary variable is initialized to 5 (truncated from

5.6). The function changes the temporary variable, but this change is not reflected in variable a. The best advice is to make sure your argument types match your parameters so this effect does not occur.

6.2.d More comparison operators

Back in Chapter 2, we learned to use four basic comparison operators in an **if** or **while** statement test: >, <, <=, and >=. These comparison operators are most appropriate for **float** variables and values because they make *relative* comparisons. With **int** variables or values, it is also appropriate to test *exact* relationships. Two additional operators that allow such comparisons are:

```
== equal to
!= not equal to
```

For example:

```
int a, b, c;
cin >> a >> b >> c;
if (a == b)
    cout << "the first two numbers are exactly equal" << endl;
else ;
if (b != c) cout << "the last two are not exactly equal" << endl;
else ;
```

Tests for exact equality may not be appropriate for **float** or **double** variables since they might be *rounded* to a limited number of digits:

```
float d, e;
cin >> d >> e;
if (d == e)
    cout << " these numbers are exactly equal";
else ;
```

Suppose for this segment of code the user were to enter the two decimal values of 1.000000005 and 1.0. This segment would state that these numbers are exactly equal, which would surprise the user.

The exact comparison operators == and != are very useful. Be particularly careful, however, in noting that the test for exact equality (==) is not the same operator used for assignment (=). It is a common mistake to do something similar to the following:

```
if (a = b)
    cout << " these are equal";
else ;
```

CONCEPT
embedded
assignments

While this segment is obviously wrong since the = operator was mistakenly used in place of the intended == operator, it may produce only a warning message when compiled. The reason is that C++ *allows an assignment statement to be used anywhere an expression is expected.* The value of the expression is simply the value assigned. In other words, the preceding segment first assigns the value of b to a and then tests the value assigned to see if it is true (nonzero) or false (zero) to determine whether to execute the << output operation statement. We'll return later to this concept.

6.2.e Long and short integers

**CONCEPT
integer variations**

Just as there are several types of decimal representations for variety in precision and range (**float** and **double**), there are also several varieties of integer representations. Variables declared to be of type **short** are integers probably represented with fewer digits than **int** variables. Variables of type **long** are integers probably represented with more digits than **int** variables.

```
int time, period;
short age, count;
long months, miles_to_moon;
```

You have undoubtedly noticed the number of times the word *probably* occurs in the preceding paragraph. The actual number of bits or the size of memory used to represent variables of type **int**, **short**, and **long** depends on the system you are using. Just like **float** and **double**, all you can count on are the following:

■ The range of **short** will be less than or equal to the range of **int**.
■ The range of **int** will be less than or equal to the range of **long**.

In some systems and for some programs, it is to the advantage of the programmer to use the smallest-sized variable type available to conserve memory. To make these programs portable to other systems, all C++ compilers or program development environments support these types. They just may not all do so as efficiently.

6.3 Character variables

In Creative Challenge problem 10 at the end of the previous chapter, you were asked to write a program to manipulate *nonnumeric* data. In that problem, the user had a list of student letter grades. The program was to be used to output a summary table showing the number of As, Bs, and so on. Having only **float** variables in your bag of skills, about the only approach to this problem is to *code* the letter grades in some way—convert them to some numeric form so they could be stored in **float** variables. Consider the following attempt at a solution (Listing 6.4).

Listing 6.4

```
// grades.cpp  Compile a table of student grades
#include <iostream.h>
void main ()
{   int a=0, b=0, c=0, d=0, f=0, grade;
    cout << "Enter grades (ending with -1)" << endl;
    cout << "enter 0 for F, 1 for D, 2 for C, 3 for B, and 4 for A";
    cin >> grade;
    while (grade >= 0)                        // sum each grade
    {   if (grade >= 4)  a = a+1;             // category...
        else if (grade >= 3)  b = b+1;
            else if (grade >= 2)  c = c+1;
                else if (grade >= 1)  d = d+1;
                    else f = f+1;
        cin >> grade;
    }
    cout << " A: " << a << " B: " << b << " C: " << c << " D: "
        << d << " F: " << f << endl;
}
```

CONCEPT

char data type

This is a very clumsy solution because it forces the user to perform a mental conversion for each grade on the list. Entry mistakes would be quite likely if the list was very long. A more appropriate solution is to represent the grades just as they are—as letters. C++ provides the variable type **char** (short for "character") which can be used to store a single letter. Character constants in a program are written using single quotes. A more appropriate solution to the problem is given in Listing 6.5.

Listing 6.5

```
// grades2.cpp  Compile a table of student grades
#include <iostream.h>
void main ()
{   int a=0, b=0, c=0, d=0, f=0;
    char grade;
    cout << "Enter grades (ending with the letter X)" << endl;
    cin >> grade;
    while (grade != 'X')                        // sum each grade
    {   if (grade == 'A')  a = a+1;             // category...
        else if (grade == 'B')  b = b+1;
            else if (grade == 'C')  c = c+1;
                else if (grade == 'D')  d = d+1;
                    else if (grade == 'F')  f = f+1;
                        else ;                  // (ignore others)
        cin >> grade;
    }
    cout << " A: " << a << " B: " << b << " C: " << c << " D: "
        << d << " F: " << f << endl;
}
```

Since **char** variables are exact, the == and != operators are appropriate for comparisons. Typically, a program will use **char** variables for input, output, testing, and assignment. They are not usually appropriate for arithmetic operations such as * or /. (We will see later, however, when such arithmetic manipulation of **char** values is occasionally useful.)

6.C.a Representation

You might ask how letters are stored in the memory reserved for a **char** variable. Well, they're not actually stored. Memory cells are simply collections of bits that allow representation of numbers. To store a letter, the character is simply represented by a number code. For example, assigning the letter A to variable grade in the statement:

```
grade = 'A';
```

CONCEPT

character
representation is
by ASCII codes

is interpreted by the compiler as assigning the *code* for the letter A to the variable grade. Character constants (or actual letters) are always expressed within single quotes.

When a **char** variable is output or input, you might think of the << or >> operator statements as essentially using a table to look up the appropriate code or letter for storage or display. There are several different tables of character codes in use today. The most common, and the one utilized by C++ systems on PCs, is the ASCII table in Appendix E.

Take a moment and look at this appendix table. Note that there are codes assigned for 127 different characters: uppercase letters, lowercase letters, numeric digits, punctuation, and so on. Most of these are printable, but some are not. Note also that the codes for letters follow the alphabet. In other words, the code for the letter A is less than the code for the letter B and so on. This means that it is quite appropriate to compare **char** variables for alphabetical order:

```
char grade1, grade2;
   cin << grade1 << grade2;
   if (grade1 < grade2)
      cout << " the first grade is better than the second";
   else ;
```

In this program segment, the code in grade1 is compared to the code in grade2. If grade1 contains the code for a B and grade2 contains the code for a D, then the **if** statement will be true—the first grade is less than (alphabetically before) the second grade. Note from the ASCII table, however, that the code for a lowercase a is greater than that for an uppercase B.

EXPERIMENT

What would happen if you add an integer to a **char** variable? Try the following:

```
char c;
c = 'A';
c = c+2;
cout << c;
```

6.3.b I/O with `char` **variables**

KEY TERM

white space

When you wrote programs for **float** variables, input with the `>>` operator statement was straightforward. During input, the `>>` operator statement would skip over blank spaces or Returns (Enter keys) to find the decimal numbers to be input. Any nonprinting character such as a blank, tab, or Return is called a *white space*. The same holds true for **int** variables; the `>>` operator statement will skip white spaces to locate the integer values to be input. This is easy to do since nonprinting characters are not a part of numbers.

CONCEPT

white spaces are skipped

When we perform input to **char** variables, the situation is the same. To find the next character for input, the system will skip over blanks, tabs, and Returns. In other words, the system *is assuming you do not wish nonprinting characters to be input*. For example, consider the following program fragment which inputs and echos back out the characters that are typed at the keyboard until a pound sign is pressed:

```
char letter;
cin >> letter;
while (letter != '#')
{   cout << letter;
    cin >> letter;
}
```

Now, if the input is

```
this is    a    line    of    many            blanks #
```

the output is the following:

```
thisisalineofmanyblanks
```

That is well and good, of course, if you do not need to consider the white-space characters. What if you do? Suppose you need a program to count the number of all characters up to the next pound sign. The following won't work because any and all white-space characters would be ignored:

```
int count=0;
char c;
cin >> c;
while (c != '#')
{   count = count + 1;
    cin >> c;
    }
```

EXPERIMENT

What would happen if you typed a number when **cin** was expecting a character? Try an entry of 8 7 for:

```
char c;
cin >> c;
cout << c;
```

Some systems allow an option in the programming development environment to override this normal operation of character input so that white-space characters are read as normal data. Fortunately, there is a simpler approach to this problem which will be covered in Chapter 9.

6.3.c Character library functions

It would be quite difficult to memorize the ASCII table and remember the codes used to represent characters. Often, however, we may need a good understanding of such information. For example, consider the problem of determining if a character is a lowercase letter. From the ASCII table, we know that the codes for all lowercase letters are between the code for lowercase a and lowercase z (inclusive). Let's write a function that could be used to make such a test. The function islower() returns the integer 1 if the character argument is a lowercase letter; otherwise, it returns the integer 0 (Listing 6.6).

Listing 6.6

```
// islower()  Return 1 if the char. argument is a lower-
// case letter, otherwise return 0.
int islower (char c)
{   if (c >= 'a')
        if (c <= 'z') return (1);
        else return (0);
    else return (0);
}
```

This function might be utilized in a main program in the following manner:

```
char x;
cin >> x;
if (islower(x) == 1)
    cout << "this is a lowercase letter" << endl;
else ;
```

CONCEPT

true means nonzero

Actually, we do not need to compare the value returned by the islower() function with the constant 1. Anytime an expression is found within a test (such as an **if** or **while** statement) without a comparison being made, the expression itself is assumed to be true if nonzero and false if zero. In other words, the following segment is equivalent to the preceding one:

```
char x;
cin >> x;
if (islower(x))
    cout << "this is a lowercase letter" << endl;
else ;
```

There is an existing library of useful character functions as a part of every C++ system. Some are listed in Table 6.1. Note that this list also includes a similar is-lower() function. They are used just like other library functions and are associated with the ctype.h header file which must be included.

Suppose we needed a function to input and convert a word of text so that all lowercase letters become capitals. The function in Listing 6.7 uses a sentinel loop to input the word one character at a time. If a lowercase letter is detected, the equivalent uppercase letter is output; otherwise, the input character is output without modification. When complete, the function will return the count of the number of characters in the word to the calling program. We'll use the # character as the sentinel to indicate the end of the paragraph.

Table 6.1   Some standard character functions

Function	Returns
islower(c)	true if c is a lowercase letter, otherwise zero
isupper(c)	true if c is an uppercase letter, otherwise zero
isalpha(c)	true if c is an alphabet letter, otherwise zero
isdigit(c)	true if c is a digit character, otherwise zero
isspace(c)	true if c is a white-space character, otherwise zero
ispunct(c)	true if c is a punctuation character, otherwise zero
isprint(c)	true if c is a printable character, otherwise zero
isalnum(c)	true if c is a letter or digit character, otherwise zero

The function Toupper () utilizes the fact that the numeric difference between any pair of upper- and lowercase letters is the constant 32. Refer to the ASCII table in Appendix E. The letter f and letter F have codes different by 32. When we assign integers to **char** variables, the values are interpreted as ASCII codes. When we use char variables or constants in an expression, the values used are the corresponding ASCII codes. So, simply subtracting 32 from a lowercase letter changes the code (and hence the character) to uppercase.

Listing 6.7

```
// Capitalize()  Capitalize the lowercase letters of a word
// Returns the count of word characters
#include  <ctype.h>

 const char UPPER_LOWER_DIFF 32;

char Toupper (char c)
{   c = c - UPPER_LOWER_DIFF;
    return (c);
}

int Capitalize ()
{   int count=0;
    char c;
    cout << "Enter word, ending with #:" << endl;
    cin >> c;
    while (c != '#')
    {   count=count+1;
        if (islower(c))
             cout << Toupper(c);    // output all uppercase
        else   cout << c;
        cin >> c;
    }
    return (count);
}
```

The operation of this function is simple: The function islower() is used to test if a character is a lowercase letter. If it is, the uppercase equivalent is output using Toupper(), otherwise, the character (whatever it is) is output.

Be aware that the ctype.h header also contains a declaration for a toupper() library function, along with a tolower() function. These are available and perform a similar operation, but return int values instead of **char** values. If we were to utilize the toupper() library function instead of our own Toupper() function, the *integer codes* for uppercase letters would be output and not the letters themselves:

```
cout << toupper(c);      // output codes of uppercase
```

Now, if we were to assign the integer code for an uppercase letter to a `char` variable, wouldn't it represent the letter itself? The following would allow the standard `toupper()` library function to be used in place of our own:

```
c = toupper(c);
cout << c;                // output uppercase letters
```

6.4 Variables in other systems

As we have seen, the amount of memory allocated to each type of C++ variable is not a standard. The range and precision mentioned in this chapter for **float**, **char**, and **int** variables are not specific to all C++ systems, and you may find some differences if you attempt to compile and run your program on another system. There are some general relationships, however, that are standard, as was pointed out. The range of a **short** is less than or equal to that of an **int,** which is less than or equal to that of a **long**. The range and precision of a **float** is less than or equal to that of a **double**.

For example, there are several C++ systems that utilize 32 bits for all variable types: **char**, **int**, **short**, **long**, **float**, and **double**. In such a system, the range for integers is much larger than it is for those which use 16 bits for integers. However, there is no additional precision or range to be gained by using **double** over **float** and no advantage to using **long** over **int**.

There are some helpful standards, however. Many systems maintain two header files which contain defined constants representing important range and precision numbers: `limits.h` for integers and `float.h` for floating-point values. (Some systems only provide `limits.h`.) A defined constant is similar to a **const** identifier, and you may treat them as such at this point. By including these header files, a programmer can determine the nature of the system being used. Table 6.2 summarizes the names of these constants.

For example, the program in Listing 6.8 displays the number of precision digits for **float** variables and the smallest allowed integer on any C++ system.

Table 6.2 Defined precision and range constants for C++

Name	Definition
INT_MIN	smallest value for int variables
INT_MAX	largest value for int variables
FLT_MIN	smallest value for float variables
FLT_MAX	largest value for float variables
FLT_DIG	number of precision digits for float variables
DBL_MIN	smallest value for double variables
DBL_MAX	largest value for double variables
DBL_DIG	number of precision digits for double variables

Listing 6.8

```cpp
// prec.cpp  Display float precision digits
#include <iostream.h>
#include <float.h>
#include <limits.h>
void main()
{   cout << "float precision is: " << FLT_DIG << " digits" << endl;
    cout << "the smallest integer is: " << INT_MIN << endl;
}
```

6.5 Example project

Suppose a user has a log of information regarding 100 medical patients involved in a medication research study. Patients have been asked to record their age, weight, and sex on a separate line in the log. Gender was recorded as F or M, age was prefixed with A, and weight was prefixed with W. Unfortunately, the patients were not instructed in the order in which these data were to be recorded. As a result, the lines in the log do not consistently record information in the same sequence. The following might be an example of the first few lines:

```
F   A26   W110.5
A31   M   W235.4
W156.3   A29   F
F   W209.8   A41
...
```

A program is needed to accept these data and generate a report in a more readable and consistent format. In addition, the report is to specify both a recommended drug dose and an actual drug dose for each patient. The recommended drug dose is to be calculated according to the following criteria:

```
Males:          0.5 mg per each 10 lb of body weight
Females:        0.3 mg per each 8 lb of body weight
```

In other words, a 235-lb male should be given (23)(0.5) mg, or 11.5 mg., while a 143-lb female should be administered (17)(0.3) mg, or 5.1 mg. (Note that 143 / 8 is 17 plus a little.) Now, the pills in this study only come in even mg weights. The actual drug dose to be given is determined using the closest pill weight *not exceeding* the dose. So, if a patient is recommended for a dose of 5.1 mg, the report should suggest the 4-mg pill for the actual dose. The desired report would look like the following for the four input lines given:

```
Patient Drug Dose Report
Sex   Age   Weight   Dose       Pill
F     26    110.5    3.9 mg     2 mg
M     31    235.4    11.5 mg    10 mg
F     29    156.3    5.7 mg     4 mg
F     41    209.8    7.8 mg     6 mg
```

Using a top-down approach, we begin with the main program (Listing 6.9). Here, 100 patients must be read and processed. Each patient will result in one line of output. In other words, the main program is just a counted loop. We will use one function to read the data and others to calculate recommended and actual doses. We will put the main program into file "drugdose.cpp" and the functions in file "drugcalc.cpp". The interface header file for functions will be "drugcalc.h".

Listing 6.9

```cpp
// Drugdose.cpp  Generate a recommended and actual drug
//   dose for study patients.

#include <iostream.h>
#include "drugcalc.h"
const int NUMPATS = 100;

void main()
{   int count=0;                    // counter for patients.
    float recommend;                // recommended and actual
    int actual;                     // drug doses.
    char sex;                       // patient gender,
    float weight;                   // patient weight, and
    int age;                        // patient age.

    cout << "Patient Drug Dose Report" << endl;
    cout << " Sex    Age    Weight    Dose    Pill" << endl;

    while (count < NUMPATS)
    {   ReadPatient (sex, age, weight);
        recommend = RecomDose (sex, weight);
        actual = ActualDose (recommend);
        cout << sex << "  " << age << "  " << weight << "  " <<
            recommend << "   " << actual << endl;
        count = count + 1;
    }
}
```

As can be seen, the main program is primarily responsible for generating the report heading or title, calling functions to do the real work, and then outputting a line for each patient. The main program is often the easiest to write!

Once again, we will use stubs for the three functions. This will allow us to check that we have the project set up correctly and our arguments match our parameters. It will also help us set up the interface header file "drugcalc.h"(Listing 6.10)

Listing 6.10

```
// drugcalc.h  Header file for drug dose calculations
void ReadPatient (char& sex, int& age, float& weight);
float RecomDose (char sex, float wt);
int ActualDose (float recommend);
```

The stubs might look like the following, using a hypothetical fixed patient. Using these stubs (in the file "drugcalc.cpp"), we would make our project and run the program. Our expectations are to see a valid report with 100 lines representing the same patient.

```
void ReadPatient (char& sex, int& age, float& weight)
{   sex = 'M';
    age = 21;
    weight = 185.5;
}

float RecomDose (char sex, float wt)
{   cout << "params to RecomDose(): " << sex << "," << wt <<
    endl;
    return (9.0);
}

int ActualDose (float recommend)
{   cout << "params to ActualDose(): " << recommend << endl;
    return (8);
}
```

Once the stubs and main program are tested, the first problem is reading in the data on the study log. Rather than have a human transcribe the data into a consistent order for each patient, why not let the ReadPatient() function do that? This sort of free-form input problem is quite common. There are actually three items per line—a gender, an age, and a weight. Taking the top-down approach a step further, we will simply assume a function that can read a complete item, which we will call ReadItem(). For each item read, this function will save information in the appropriate variable (sex, age, or weight) depending on which item is read (Listing 6.11).

Listing 6.11

```
// ReadPatient()  Input a free-form line of patient data
// ASSUMPTION: input lines conform to the documented format
// OUT: sex will be returned as the letter 'F' or 'M'
//      age will be returned as an integer following the input 'A'
//      weight will be returned as a float following the input 'W'
void ReadPatient (char& sex, int& age, float& weight)
{   ReadItem (sex, age, weight);
    ReadItem (sex, age, weight);
    ReadItem (sex, age, weight);
}
```

What have we really accomplished? We have taken a complex problem of three parts and broken it down into three separate smaller problems, each of which is much easier to solve.

The function `ReadItem()` expects an item to begin with a letter. An A indicates that this item must be completed by next reading an integer age. A W indicates that this item must be completed by next reading a decimal weight. A F or M is simply a complete item on its own (Listing 6.12).

Listing 6.12

```
// ReadItem()  Input a single data item from a patient log line
// ASSUMPTION: input lines conform to the documented format
// OUT: sex is returned as the letter 'F' or 'M' (if input)
//      age is returned as an integer following the input 'A' (if input)
//      weight is returned as a float following the input 'W' (if input)
#include <iostream.h>
const char WEIGHT = 'W';
const char AGE = 'A';
const char MALE = 'M';
const char FEMALE = 'F';
void ReadItem (char& sex, int& age, float& weight)
{   char prefix;
    cin >> prefix;                              // first get the item prefix
    if (prefix == WEIGHT)
        cin >> weight;
    else if (prefix == AGE)
            cin >> age;
        else if (prefix == MALE)
                sex = prefix;
            else if (prefix == FEMALE)
                    sex = prefix;
                else cout << " ** illegal data item in patient input **" << endl;
}
```

That takes care of the free-form input problem. Now we must address the problems of calculating a recommended and actual drug dose. The `RecomDose()` function will take advantage of the fact that when assigning a **float** value to an **int** variable, the fraction is truncated. For men, the question is: How many 10s are there in weight? This can be determined simply by dividing weight by 10 and truncating the result. The recommended dose is this answer times the 0.5 mg dose increment. The calculations for females are similar (Listing 6.13).

Listing 6.13

```
// RecomDose()  Return a drug dose based on wt. and sex
// ASSUMPTION: sex is 'F' or 'M', weight is a positive value
const float F_INC = 0.3;
const float M_INC = 0.5;
const int F_DOSE = 8;
const int M_DOSE = 10;

float RecomDose (char sex, float wt)
{   int size;                        // number of dose units
    float dose;                      // recommended dose

    if (sex == 'M')
    {   size = wt / M_DOSE;          // truncates on assignment!
        dose = size * M_INC;
    }
    else
    {   size = wt / F_DOSE;
        dose = size * F_INC;
    }
    return (dose);
}
```

The conversion of a recommended dose to an actual pill size requires that the ActualDose() function determine the first even number at or below the recommended dose. This can be accomplished in two steps. First, we will convert the decimal recommended dose value (Listing 6.14). Second, we will test if this integer is even and, if not, decrement the value by 1. The first step is easy—just use truncation. The second step (test for an even number) seems a bit more difficult, so we take the standard programmer's way out: call a function, which we will name IsEven().

Listing 6.14

```
// ActualDose()  Convert a recommended dose to a pill size
//  IN: recommend is the decimal recommended dose

int ActualDose (float recommend)
{   int intdose;                     // integer recommended dose
    intdose = recommend;
    if (IsEven(intdose))
        return (intdose);
```

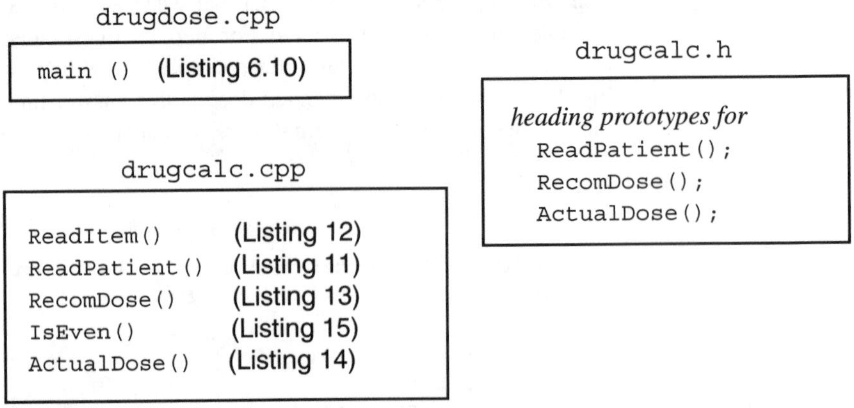

drugdose.cpp

main () (Listing 6.10)

drugcalc.h

heading prototypes for
  ReadPatient();
  RecomDose();
  ActualDose();

drugcalc.cpp

ReadItem()	(Listing 12)
ReadPatient()	(Listing 11)
RecomDose()	(Listing 13)
IsEven()	(Listing 15)
ActualDose()	(Listing 14)

Figure 6.1 Files and contents of the drug dose project

```
    else return (intdose-1);      // if not even, decrement by 1
}
```

Well, the project isn't finished yet, but we are continually getting closer to the final program by dividing big problems down into smaller and more manageable functions. The test for evenness can be made by noting that an even number has no fraction when divided by 2 (Listing 6.15). So, we will divide the number by 2 and truncate off the fraction. This result will then be multiplied by 2. If the original number was even, the result will be exactly the same number. Remember, an integer divided by an integer is an integer. (There is actually a library function to accomplish this called *iseven().*)

Listing 6.15

```
// IsEven()  Return true if parameter is an even value
// IN:  x is any integer.

int IsEven (int x)
{   if ((x/2)*2 == x) return (1);
    else return (0);
}
```

The project is now completed and consists of three files with these functions in the order indicated in Figure 6.1.

6.6 Summary

KEY TERMS Several new terms were introduced in this chapter:

1. *characteristic, mantissa*—the fraction and power or exponent of a number stored in scientific or E-notation.

2. *E-notation* — the representation of a very large or very small number using a characteristic and mantissa.

3. *overflow, underflow* — the error that occurs when an attempt is made to store a value too large or too small for a particular variable type.

4. *rounding error* — the error that results when a floating-point number is rounded to a limited number of precision digits.

5. *mixed-mode expression* — an arithmetic expression involving both floating-point and integer variables or values.

6. *white space* — the nonprinting characters for tab, carriage return, and blank.

CONCEPTS In addition to the **float** variable type previously used, several additional variable types were introduced: **double**, **int**, **short**, **long**, and **char**. Two additional comparison operators were also introduced for exact comparisons: == (equal to) and ! = (not equal to).

When an **if** or **while** statement contains only an arithmetic expression within the parentheses instead of a comparison, the expression is considered true if nonzero and false if zero. C++ allows an assignment statement to be used anywhere a simple expression is expected.

float values are rounded to a predetermined number of digits, usually about 7. **double** values have at least as great a range and precision as **float**, and usually much more. In many C++ systems, float values have a range from about 10^{-38} to 10^{38}. double variables are accurate to about 15 digits and have a range from about 10^{-308} to 10^{308}.

int variables are exact, but have a more limited range than **float** — only –32,768 to 32,767 in systems that use 16 bits for integers. Neither floating-point or integer constants are written with a comma. **long** integers have at least the same range as **int**, and usually much more (requiring more storage). **short** variables may require less space than **int** and may also have a much smaller range. Integer values should not normally be written with a leading zero, as this implies a base-8 number.

char variables are used to store codes for any of 255 different characters. The ASCII table in Appendix E lists the first 127. Character constants are written inside of single quotes. Both **int** and **char** variables and constants are appropriately compared using the == and ! = exact comparison operators. Exact comparisons with floating-point values may not be appropriate since they represent rounded accuracy.

It is important that the types of function arguments match the corresponding function parameter types. Also, a function call must pass the correct number of arguments.

The three rules for mixed-mode expressions are:

1. If a program statement attempts to assign a floating-point value to an **int** variable, the system will truncate the fractional part of the floating-point value and store only the integer part into the **int** variable.

2. Any mathematical operation involving two integers always results in an integer.

3. Any mathematical operation involving at least one floating-point value always results in a floating-point value.

The most important concept to remember about these rules is that *an integer divided by an integer always results in an integer.*

When inputting **char** variables, it is important to remember that input operations skip over white-space or nonprinting characters.

The assignment statement may be used anywhere the compiler expects to find an expression. This may lead to inadvertent errors since the following two if statements may appear similar, but have very different meanings:

```
if (x == y) ...      // test for exact equality
if (x = y)  ...      // test of the value assigned to x (zero or nonzero)
```

Table 6.3   Example segments

`double x, y;`	x and y are to be double-precision real variables.
`x = 5.3E-5;`	x is to be assigned 0.000053.
`char c;`	c is to be assigned the ques-
`c = '?';`	tion mark character (code).
`if (c < 'z')`	
`   cout << "yes";`	Output yes if the character assigned to c is less than the letter z.
`int a;`	Since 3/2 is an integer calculation, the 5.8 is added to 1
`a = 5.8 + 3 / 2;`	(1.5 truncated). a is then assigned 6 (6.8 truncated).
`if (done) ...`	True if done is not zero.
`int a;`	
`a = 6.3 / 2.9;`	The division results in 2.17. This is truncated to 2 for assignment.

6.7 Exercises

6.7.a   Short-answer questions

1. Which type of variable in C++ has a more limited range—**int** or **float**?
2. Which type of variable in C++ may only approximately represent the following decimal input number 1.2345678
3. The following number is in scientific notation. Identify the characteristic.
   3×10^5
4. Identify the mantissa in the scientific notation number in question 3.
5. What is wrong with the following assignment statement?

   ```
   cost = 1,234;
   ```

6. Briefly explain rounding error.
7. The arguments in a function call must match function parameters in both
   order and _____.
8. When float or double variables are output, the << operation by default will round the values to __6__ decimal places.
9. When inputting characters into **char** variables, the << operation will skip over
   _____.

10. Briefly explain what a white-space character is.
11. What values would be assigned to the **int** variable x in each case?
    a. x = 5 + 7.6;
    b. x = 5 / 7.6;
    c. x = 7 / 5;
    d. x = 7.6 / 5.5;
12. What values would be assigned to the **float** variable y in each case?
    a. y = 5 + 7.6;
    b. y = 5 / 7.6;
    c. y = 5 / 7;
    d. y = 5.5 / 7.6;
13. Express each value in E-notation:
    a. 0.00000576
    b. 576000000000.0
14. Write a segment of program to appropriately add the following five variables to the value in sum. Assume each of these variables contains a relatively small number, while sum contains a relatively large number:

    ```
    float small1, small2, small3, small4, small5, sum;
    ```

15. Briefly explain a situation where variable overflow could occur.
16. Briefly explain why it may not be appropriate to compare two **float** variables with the exact comparison operator ==.
17. Propose a small segment of program that could be used to test whether the **float** variable x contains a whole number.
18. Explain briefly why the variable type **double** does not guarantee a decimal representation with more precision and more range than a comparable **float** variable in any given C++ system. Explain why **double** does guarantee more precision and range in Borland C++.
19. Using the ASCII table, determine the possible character values for c for which the following **if** statements would output yes.

    ```
    if (c > 'Y')
        if (c <= 'b') cout << "yes";
        else ;
    else ;
    ```

20. For your particular C++ system, determine the minimum and maximum allowed for **long** integers.

6.7.b Projects

1. Write a program to calculate and output the number of dollars, quarters, dimes, nickels, and pennies in a given amount of money using the smallest number of coins and bills possible. The input should be a floating-point value representing a decimal value. For example, for the input 63.87 (for 63 dollars 87 cents), the output should be: 63 dollars, 3 quarters, 1 dime, 0 nickels, and 2 pennies.

2. Write a function named `IsOdd()` to return 1 or true if an integer parameter is odd. The function should return 0 or false otherwise.

3. Write a function named `IsDivisibleBy5()` to return 1 or true if an integer parameter is evenly divisible by 5. It should return false or 0 otherwise.

4. A researcher has a list of weights for two different rats in a nutrition study. These rats are named X and Y. Each line in the list contains a rat name and a weight for a different study day. Each rat has five weights, but the list is in no particular order. Write a program to input such a list and output the average weight for each of the two rats.

5. Write a program to input a sentence of characters ending with a period and output the number of printable characters in the sentence (including the period).

6. Modify project 5 so that in addition to the number of characters, the program outputs the number of lowercase letters and uppercase letters.

7. Take another look at the example project at the end of this chapter. Modify the drug dose rule so that men receive 0.5 mg for each 10 lb of body weight *or fraction thereof.* In other words, a 186.5-lb man should receive (19)(0.5) mg since 10 divides into 186.5 18 times *plus a fraction.* A 180.0-lb man should still receive (18)(0.5) mg, of course.

8. Write a program to input text characters from the keyboard and output the equivalent Morse code. The translation table is as follows:

```
A   . -        B  - . . .     C   - . - .
D   - . .      E  .           F   . . - .
G   - - .      H  . . . .     I   . .
J   . - - -    K  - . -        L   . - . .
M   - -        N  - .          O   - - -
P   . - - .    Q  - - . -      R   . - .
S   . . .      T  -            U   . . -
V   . . . -    W  . - -        X   - . . -
Y   - . - -    Z  - - . .
```

9. **Creative Challenge:** Write a program to input a paragraph ending with a Return keystroke and then output the same paragraph with the first letter of the first word of each sentence capitalized.

10. **Creative Challenge:** Write a function to input a paragraph and then count and return the number of times a spelling mistake is made because this rule was not followed: *i before e except after c.* (Yes, there is more to the rule, but this is enough of a challenge as it is!)

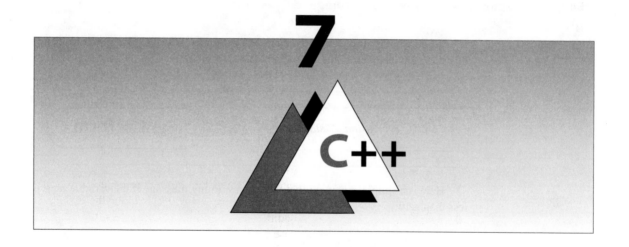

More Control Structures and Operators

Your programs are becoming sufficiently complex that you need to learn more of the control structures and operators available in C++. These extra capabilities will not necessarily enable you to write programs that you could not have written before, but they will allow you to write them more concisely, express your ideas more clearly, and develop programs faster. They will also lower the probability of mistakes in complex programs and allow such programs to be more easily maintained.

7.1 The single-choice `if`

CONCEPT
a variation of the
`if` statement

Up to now, we have used an `if` statement form that provided both a true and a false alternative for each program choice. There is a second form of the `if` statement that is best used when there is only a single choice to be made (without an alternative). In this form, the `else` clause is simply omitted. In other words, if the expression within the parentheses is true, the statement associated with the `if` is executed and control is then passed to the following statement. If the expression is false, control is just passed to the following statement. Naturally, the statement associated with the `if` can be a compound statement enclosed within { } braces. The general form of this statement is given in the following syntax form box.

> if (*expression*) *statement*   **Syntax form**

Here is a simple statement that outputs a warning message if the variable `age` is less than zero:

```
if (age < 0)
    cout << " Warning, age is negative" << endl;
```

This may seem like a very simple statement to learn, after having learned the **if** statement with two choices, but there is a subtlety here when we nest the single-choice form inside the two-choice form. Consider Figure 7.1.

According to this diagram, the message `a is smallest` should be output when a is less than both b and c. The message `a is not smallest` should be output when a is not less than b. If a is less than b, but not less than c, no message should be output at all. The first condition appears to be the familiar two-choice **if** since something needs to be done for both a true and a false choice. The second condition appears to be a single-choice **if** since there is nothing to be done when false. Your first attempt at coding this diagram in a top-down fashion might be the following:

```
if (a < b)
```
> *statements if true*

```
else
```
> *statements if false*

Here the two ovals represent the true and false sides of the outer two-choice **if**: The false side is the output for the message `a is not smallest`. The true side is the single-choice **if**. Now, when you fill these ovals in, you come up with something like the following:

```
if (a < b)
    if (a < c)
        cout << "a is smallest";
else
    cout << "a is not smallest";
```

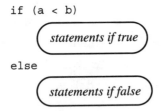

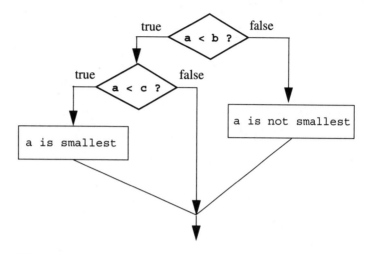

Figure 7.1   Symbolic diagram of a desired nested-`if`

CONCEPT

associating an
else with an if

When this code is run, you find that when a is not less than b, nothing is output even though you expected the second message to appear! The reason has to do with which **if** the **else** belongs to. Take another look at the preceding code segment. Even though you have written the code with the proper indentation to show that the **else** belongs to the top **if**, the compiler doesn't consider indentation or spacing. *An **else** will always be associated with the closest **if** possible.* Notice that when you tab the bottom two lines over a bit, you can see what the compiler is assuming.

```
if (a < b)
    if (a < c)
        cout << "a is smallest";
    else
        cout << "a is not smallest";
```

CONCEPT

placing braces
around both
choices

Figure 7.2 shows what logic is really being expressed by this nested-**if** segment. You can see why the results were not as expected. How can such errors in logic be avoided so that an **else** is always associated with the **if** you intend? There are several methods. A good rule of thumb here is *always to place { } braces around both choices* of a two-choice **if** as follows:

```
if (a < b)
{   if (a < c)
        cout << "a is smallest";
}
else
{   cout << "a is not smallest";
}
```

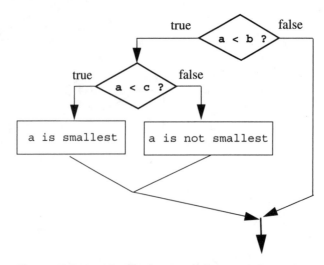

Figure 7.2 Symbolic diagram of nested-if as written

Notice that now the **else** can only be associated with the top **if,** which is what you originally had in mind.

7.2 Compound comparisons

Suppose you would like to display an error message if the user inputs a value for a variable age that you consider to be outside expected limits. The purpose, of course, is to warn the user that an entry error may have occurred. Let's say that an age value should lie between the values of 0 and 100. With what you have learned so far, this is probably going to require two **if** statements and two **cout** statements:

```
cin >> age;
if (age > 100)
    cout << " ERROR; age is outside expected limits";
if (age < 0)
    cout << " ERROR; age is outside expected limits";
```

CONCEPT

using compound comparisons

Actually, C++ allows you to combine these two tests in a single **if** through use of the operators || and **&&**. The || operator represents the logical OR of two expressions: If *either* expression is true, the entire test is true. The **&&** operator represents the logical AND of two expressions: If *both* expressions are true, the entire test is true. Both of these operators have a precedence lower than any of the comparison or arithmetic operators. The **&&** operator has a precedence greater than the || operator. (Of course, anytime you are not sure in what order the operators of a particular expression will be evaluated, simply use parentheses to indicate your desires.) The above segment of code could be expressed much simpler with a single **if**:

```
cin >> age;
if ((age > 100) || (age < 0))
    cout << " ERROR; age is outside expected limits";
```

KEY TERM
Boolean

These two operators are called *Boolean* operators because they compare two expressions, which are true or false themselves to determine whether an entire test is true or false. A Boolean expression or value can only take on the values true or false. It should be obvious now that an **if** or **while** statement treats the expression inside the parentheses as a Boolean value even if the expression is arithmetic. (Remember that any arithmetic expression or variable is considered true if nonzero and false if zero.) Table 7.1 summarizes the use of these operators.

Now, suppose you wish to test if the variable a is smaller than both b and c;

```
if (a < b && a < c)
    cout ("a is smallest");
else
    cout ("a is not smallest");
```

CONCEPT
be careful with
English statements

Be sure to use these operators correctly. A single & or | means something quite different, just as a single = is quite different than the == operator. (The | and & operators are used for bitwise manipulation and testing and are covered in Chapter 14.) Another common error is to try and translate an English statement of a test into C++ directly. For example, in English you might express a test by saying "a is less than b or c." Coding this directly into C++ produces:

```
if (a < b || c) ...
```

The Boolean operators **&&** and **||** are used to combine two expressions or tests that are already true or false. In other words, the operands on either side of a Boolean operator are assumed to represent true or false themselves. The English statement in the preceding paragraph actually implies that we are testing that "*a* is less than *b* and *a* is also less than *c*." The correct coding is:

```
if (a < b && a < c) ...
```

Table 7.1   Boolean && and || operators

a	b	a && b	a || b
true	true	true	true
true	false	false	true
false	true	false	true
false	false	false	false

Always make sure that you intend both sides of a **&&** or **||** operator to be true/false comparisons or tests themselves. Remember, both sides of a Boolean operator are considered as Boolean expressions. The **if** statement marked WRONG WAY! actually does not produce an error message. If you think about it, this statement tests whether (a is less than b) OR whether (c is true or nonzero).

CONCEPT

Boolean operator precedence

In the above example, the less-than operator has precedence over the **||** operator. In general, all comparison or relational operators have precedence over **&&**, which in turn has precedence over **||**. Rather than memorize these rules, a simple strategy of always using sufficient parentheses ensures that operators will be performed in the order you intend.

CONCEPT

NOT operator

There is one more Boolean operator—the **!** or NOT operator. This is a unary operator in that it is placed just before a single operand. The effect is to *complement* the operand or take its opposite. The **!** operator has precedence over the relational or comparison operators and the other Boolean operators. For example:

```
!a        true if a is not true
!(a<b)    true if a is not less than b (a is greater or equal to b)
!(a==b)   true if a is not equal to b
!(a>=b)   true if a is not greater or equal to b (a is less than b)
```

Remember, the opposite or complement of "less than" is not "greater than," but "greater than or equal to." Expressions involving the **!** operator become a bit more complex when used in compound expressions with **&&** and **||**. For example, consider the following expression:

```
!((a<b) && (b>= c))        same as        (a>=b) || (b<c)
```

You can convince yourself this is the case with Table 7.2, which examines all the possibilities.

CONCEPT

comparison conversions

In general, any Boolean expression with a **!** operator in front of it can be converted to an equivalent Boolean expression without the preceding **!** by first complementing every operator within the expression. In the expression, < is changed to >=, && is changed to ||, >= is changed to <, and so on. Next, if any subexpressions are themselves Boolean (with && or || operators), complement each operand.

KEY TERM

DeMorgan's theorem

This is known as *DeMorgan's theorem*. Here are some simple examples of equivalent Boolean expressions generated with this theorem.

Table 7.2 Comparison of ! ((a<b) && (b>=c) and (a>=b) || (b<c)

a<b	b>=c	a>=b	b<c	!((a<b)&&(b>=c))	(a>=b)||(b<c)
true	true	false	false	false	false
true	false	false	true	true	true
false	true	true	false	true	true
false	false	true	true	true	true

```
! (!a)           same as      a
!(a == b)        same as      (a != b)
!(a || b)        same as      (!a && !b)
!(a && b)        same as      (!a || !b)
!(a < b)         same as      (a >= b)
```

When there are ! operators inside the expression, it is best to convert these sub-expressions first and then convert the entire expression. For example:

```
!((a>b) && !(c<d))        same as      !((a>b) && (c>=d))
                          same as      (a<=b) || (c < d)
```

7.3 The for loop

The definite or *counted loop* is very common in programming. If you remember, this is a loop where the number of iterations is known beforehand. An example is when you need a function to input exactly *N* decimal values and then return the average to the calling program. With your current knowledge and skills, you would use a **while** statement. Your counted loop would probably consist of segments that perform three operations—initialize, test, and update:

1. Initialize a counting variable to 0 prior to the loop.

2. At the beginning or top of the loop, test the counting variable against the limit *N* for each loop iteration.

   (*loop body*)

3. At the bottom of the loop, update (increment) the counting variable.

Your function might look like Listing 7.1.

Listing 7.1

```
// AverageInput1 ()  Input N values and return average.
// IN:  N -- the number of values to input and average.
// ASSUMPTION: at least one value is entered.

float AverageInput1 (int N)
{   float sum = 0.0, value;

    int count = 0;              // 1. initialize counter to 0
    while (count < N)           // 2. test count against limit
    {   cin >> value;
        sum = sum + value;
        count = count + 1;      // 3. update counter
    }
    return (sum / count);
}
```

There is a C++ statement that combines all three operations of the counted loop—the **for** statement.

> for (*expr₁*; *expr₂*; *expr₃*) *statement*   **Syntax form**

CONCEPT

the **for** statement

As you can see, the **for** statement contains three expressions within parentheses. The statement following the parentheses is the body of the loop. Naturally, this statement body can be a single statement or a compound statement within { } braces. There are three rules governing the execution of a **for** statement:

1. The first expression is evaluated *prior* to the loop.
2. The second expression is tested at the *beginning* of each loop iteration to determine if the statement body should again be executed.
3. The last expression is evaluated *after* each loop iteration.

Remember that an assignment statement can be used where an arithmetic expression is expected. Consider now the following segment:

```
for (count=0; count < N; count=count+1)
     statement;
```

The statement (or compound statement inside of { } braces) will be repeatedly executed in a counted-loop fashion: First, count is initialized to 0. Next, count<N is tested. If true, the loop is entered and the *statement* body of the loop is executed. At the bottom of the loop, count=count+1 is executed, and control returns to the top of the loop to retest count<N. The loop continues to execute until the test is false. At this point, control is passed to the next statement. Suppose N is 3. This **for** loop is shorthand for the following intended operations (in English):

```
set count to zero                (first expression)
is count < N? yes, so do:        (second expression)
     statement;
set count to count+1             (third expression) [1]
is count < N? yes, so do:        (second expression)
     statement;
set count to count+1             (third expression) [2]
is count < N? yes, so do:        (second expression)
     statement;
set count to count+1             (third expression) [3]
is count < N? no,                (second expression)
     continue with rest of program . . .
```

So, if N is 3, the statement body of the loop is executed three times. If N were 5, the statement body would be executed five times. At this point, you could rewrite the function of Listing 7.1 as in Listing 7.2.

Listing 7.2

```
// AverageInput2 ()   Input N values and return average.
//    IN:   N -- the number of values to input and average.
//  ASSUMPTION: at least one value is entered.

float AverageInput2 (int N)
{   float sum = 0.0, value;
    int count;
    for (count=0; count < N; count=count+1)
    {   cin >> value;
        sum = sum + value;
    }
    return (sum / count);
}
```

The **for** statement is not limited to just counted loops, however. Any type loop can be implemented as long as the three rules are considered. For example, Listing 7.3 is a variation of Listing 7.2 with a *sentinel loop* using the **for** statement. The purpose of the function is to input and average an indeterminate number of positive values ending with a negative number as the sentinel value.

Listing 7.3

```
// AverageInput3 ()   Input positive values until a negative sentinel value is
// encountered. Return the average.
// ASSUMPTION: at least one value is entered.
// OUT:   count -- the number of values averaged

float AverageInput3 (int& count)
{   float sum = 0.0, value;
    cin >> value;
    for (count=0; value > 0.0; count=count+1)
    {   sum = sum + value;
        cin >> value;
    }
    return (sum / count);
}
```

It could be argued that this version of a sentinel loop is no less complex than what would have been written using a **while** statement. Generally, a good programmer will use a **for** statement for a definite loop (such as a counted loop) and a **while** statement for an indefinite loop (such as a sentinel loop).

To help ensure that you understand the three rules for evaluating **for** statements, consider the following code segment in which two **for** statements are nested:

```
for (n=0; n<3; n=n+1)
    for (k=n; k<3; k=k+1)
        cout << n << " " << k << end;
```

First, let's represent the segment in a top-down fashion and look at the top loop:

```
for (n=0; n<3; n=n+1)
```

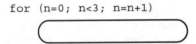

The oval now represents the statement body of this top or outer loop. By examining this **for** statement, you can see that the statement body will be executed three times, once for each value of n (0, 1, and 2). The following diagram represents these three iterations as three ovals labeled A, B, and C:

A	iteration, n=0
B	iteration, n=1
C	iteration, n=2

Let's now look at the first iteration of the oval (A) when n = 0. The statement inside this oval is the second **for** loop. During this oval, n is 0;

```
for (k=(0);   k<3;   k=k+1)
    cout << (0) << " " << k << end;
```

This is just a simple **for** loop which will execute the output statement three times with k having values of 0, then 1, and then 2. For each output statement, the values of n (0) and k are output:

```
0   0
0   1
0   2
```

Now look at the second iteration or oval (B) when n = 1;

```
for (k=(1); k<3;   k=k+1)
    cout << (1) << " " << k << end;
```

This loop will execute the output statement two times with k having values 1 and then 2:

```
1   1
1   2
```

Next, look at the last iteration or oval (C) when n = 2:

```
for (k=(2);   k<3;   k=k+1)
    cout << (2) << " " << k << end;
```

This loop will execute the output statement one time with k as 2:

```
2   2
```

Finally, just put all the oval results or outputs together in order:

```
0   0
0   1
0   2
1   1
1   2
2   2
```

To illustrate this concept of loops within loops, let's write a function that could be used to graph the cosine from 0 radians to π radians. We will begin using a top-down design approach. We decide that our graph should have 20 plot points, which means angle steps of $\pi/20$. Recognizing that screen output goes from top to bottom and left to right, we choose to orient the output graph vertically. The main() program is now ready (Listing 7.4).

EXPERIMENT

What would happen if you initialized the counter to a value that is greater than the limits of the test? Try:

```
for (n=5; n<4; n=n+1)
    cout << n << endl;
```

Listing 7.4

```cpp
// drawcos.cpp  Plot the cosine function horizontally on the
// screen for angles from 0 to 3π.
#include <iostream.h>
#include <math.h>
void main ()
{   float angle;
    const float anglestep = 0.1885;          // 3π / 50
    const float limit = 9.42478;             // 3π
    PlotYAxis();                             // draw the Y axis
// plot a point for each angle from 0 to 3p in steps of 3p/50
    for (angle=0.0; angle < limit; angle = angle+anglestep)
        PlotPoint (angle);
}
```

The function PlotYAxis() simply draws the Y axis (now horizontal) and fiducial marks across the top of the screen (Listing 7.5)

Listing 7.5

```
// PlotYAxis()  draw a Y axis and fiducial marks on screen
void PlotYAxis()
{    cout << " -1.0              0.0                 1.0" << endl;
     cout << "---------------------------|-----------------------" << endl;
}
```

At this point, you might stub in the function PlotPoint() simply to output the parameters and ensure that the program was working to that stage. In any case, let's now approach the PlotPoint() function. It must accept an angle as a parameter and draw a horizontal line with a plotting point in the appropriate position for that angle. In other words, each plot point becomes a line on the screen. Suppose you choose to use the asterisk * as a plotting point.

First, walk through the problem with an example angle value, say, 0.786 radians. Your calculator will indicate the cosine is 0.707. You know the cosine goes from a maximum of 1.0 to a minimum of –1.0, and these must fit within your line. The 1.0 should be on the far right of the screen, with –1.0 on the far left. The horizontal screen is about 70 characters wide. So a cosine of 0.707 should correspond to about position 60. The only trick now is to output 59 blanks and then an asterisk!

To scale any cosine value to fit in the appropriate proportional position along these 70 characters, you might use the following calculation. Your function now becomes Listing 7.6.

```
position = cos(angle) * 35 + 35;
```

Listing 7.6

```
// PlotPoint ()  Plot the cosine of the angle parameter
// on a line across the screen
// IN:  angle -- the angle in radians to be plotted

void PlotPoint (float angle)
{   int blanks, position;
    position = cos (angle) * 35 + 35;
    for (blanks=0; blanks<position; blanks=blanks+1)
        cout << " ";
    cout << "*" << endl;
}
```

When you run the program project developed using Listings 7.4, 7.5, and 7.6, you will see a plot similar to Figure 7.3 on your screen.

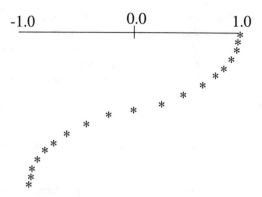

Figure 7.3 Plot of cosine from 0 to π using drawcos.cpp

7.4 Shorthand operators

Now is a good time to introduce an interesting concept that you haven't seen before: C++ generally allows the use of an assignment, input, or output statement anywhere an arithmetic expression is expected. This feature has a number of useful applications. For example, consider Listing 6.5. It required five assignment statements to initialize the five variables all to zero. Look at the following statement:

```
a = (b = 0);
```

This may appear quite strange at first glance. Actually, it is just an example of the feature mentioned earlier. The variable a is being assigned the value of the expression within the parentheses. This expression is just the result of the enclosed assignment statement. In other words, zero is assigned to b and then the value of that expression (the value assigned or zero) is copied into a. The net effect is to assign zero to both a and b in one simple statement.

An assignment operator on the right has precedence over any to the left. Thus, the parentheses in this example are actually not needed. We could now combine all five assignment statements from Listing 6.5 with the following:

```
a = b = c = d = f = 0;                   // initialize all to zero
```

This shorthand notation can easily be abused, however. The following statement is quite legal, but in poor style:

```
a = (b = c+2) * (d = 5);                 // POOR STYLE!
```

CONCEPT

we avoid nesting nontrivial assignments

Here, the value of c+2 is assigned to b, next the value of 5 is assigned to d, and then the two values assigned (c+2 and 5) are multiplied together and assigned to a. This is poor style for several reasons. First, this statement is difficult to read at first glance. It must be examined carefully to determine the intended effect. Second, it is more difficult to debug since it is more difficult to examine the intermediate operation results. Be careful with nesting assignment statements as a shorthand method. You are undoubtedly learning by now that it may take a bit more typing to be clear and simple when writing a program, but it tends to *save a lot of time in the debugging stage* of program development.

CONCEPT

shorthand operators

Several other shorthand notations or operators are allowed in C++:

---

variable **op** = *expression* (**same as**)

 variable = *variable* **op** *expression*

where op is any arithmetic operator

Syntax form

This syntax form indicates that the following pairs of assignment statements mean exactly the same thing; one is just a shorthand notation for the other.

a *= b;	same as	a = a * b;
x += y+z;	same as	x = x + (y+z);
z += 1;	same as	z = z + 1;

CONCEPT

++ and --operators

The last statement simply increments or adds 1 to a variable. This operation is very common, and there is another shorthand notation to do just that:

---

variable **++**   (**increment the variable after use**)

++ *variable*   (**increment the variable prior to use**)

variable **--**   (**decrement the variable after use**)

-- *variable*   (**decrement the variable prior to use**)

Syntax form

This syntax form indicates that the following line represents three different ways of saying exactly the same thing—add 1 to the current value of a:

a++;   a += 1;   a = a + 1;

This is actually where the language gets its name: C++ is intended to be an incremental advancement over the C language. In any case, when the increment operator follows a variable, it is called a *postincrement*. When the operator precedes the variable, it is a *preincrement*. When the increment (or decrement) operator is used by itself, it doesn't really matter which of the two forms is used. The difference between pre- and postincrementing (or decrementing) is important, however, when the operator is used *within* another statement such as is illustrated by the following segments:

```
b = a++;      // 'a' is assigned to 'b', then 'a' is incremented
```

If we assume a initially contains 5, b would be assigned 5 and a would be incremented to 6. In other words, a is incremented after it is used in the assignment. But if you were to use the other form

```
b = ++a;      // 'a' is incremented, then assigned to 'b'
```

then a would first be incremented to 6 and then used in the assignment; b would be assigned 6. In both cases, a changes to 6. The only difference is whether to use the original value of a or the incremented value of a in the assignment. By the same token, the following statement

```
cout << a++;   // output 'a', then increment
```

would output the current value of a, and then increment a. If a were to originally contain 5, that is the value which would be output. After the output, however, a would contain 6.

Many good programmers find that time is saved in the long run if the increment and decrement operators are generally used alone rather than within another statement. Breaking a statement such as the above output into two separate statements may require a few extra keystrokes, but it tends to save debugging time downstream. When this rule of thumb is followed, it really doesn't matter which form of increment (or decrement) is used:

```
cout << a;
a++;
```

EXPERIMENT

What would happen if you attempted this?

```
int a;   ++a = 5
```

How is this different from the following?

```
a++ = 5
```

CONCEPT

avoid using =, ++,
or -- in a compound
test

Be very careful not to embed assignment or increment/decrement operators within an **if** or **while** test. (Later, we will see there are other operators that can change the value of a variable, and these are to be avoided here too.) The reason is that a compiler will usually attempt to optimize the machine instructions generated from a C++ program so that no unnecessary instructions are performed. For example, consider the following **if** statement:

```
if (a<5 && (b>a++)) ...
```

WAY!
WRONG

The intent with this statement is to test whether (a is less than 5) AND (b is greater than a). After a is referenced on the right side of this compound comparison, it is to be incremented. The compiler, however, may generate instructions such that if the left part of the expression (a<5) is not true, the *rest of the test is skipped* since the entire test is guaranteed to be false. The result is that the right part of the test (b>a++) is never considered and the value of a is never incremented. This rule of thumb holds for any operation that you expect to be evaluated. If it should always be done, do not place it inside a test.

KEY TERM

optimization

While a complete discussion of *optimization* is beyond the scope of this text, you should be aware that this may include the aforementioned short-circuiting of compound expressions as well as actual reconstruction of some code segments to make a program faster or require less space. For example, which of the following segments do you think will execute faster (given the same machine and compiler)— segment 1 or segment 2?

```
a = (b * c) + d / e + 5;          // segment 1
x = (b * c) + d / e + 6;

temp = (b * c) + d / e;           // segment 2
a = temp + 5;
x = temp + 6;
```

Actually, there will probably be little difference in execution time. Even though the first segment seems to contain more operations, a good compiler will optimize or reconstruct the first segment to be as efficient as the second without further programmer effort.

CONCEPT

the modulo
operator

There is another arithmetic operator that has not yet been covered. It isn't really a shorthand operator, but we'll present it here anyway. You know, of course, that the / operator results in the dividend of the first or left operand divided by the right operand. The % or *modulo* operator results in the *remainder* of the left operand divided by the right operand. For example:

```
int a=3, b=4, c=5;
cout << a%b;              // (3/4) has remainder 3; outputs 3
```

Table 7.3 **Precedence and associativity of operators**

Operators	Associativity
(highest) ++ -- !	right to left
* / %	left to right
+ -	left to right
>> <<	left to right
< <= > >=	left to right
== !=	left to right
&	left to right
|	left to right
&&	left to right
||	left to right
(lowest) = *= += -= &= |=	right to left

```
cout << c%a;              // (5/3) has remainder 2; outputs 2
cout << 27 / c;           // outputs 5
cout << 27 % c;           // outputs remainder 2
```

In a previous problem, we needed a method of determining whether a given integer was even. The modulo operator provides a simple solution. An **if** statement can be used to check the remainder after division by 2 for a true (nonzero) or false (zero) value:

```
if (a % 2)
    cout << "a is not even";
else
    cout << "a is even";
```

Table 7.3 summarizes the precedence and associativity (order of evaluation for equal precedence operations) of many common operators.(We'll cover the & and | later in the text.)

7.5 Multiple choice and the `switch`

Occasionally, many more than two choices are needed in a program decision. We can accomplish this with many **if** statements, but it is usually much easier to employ the **switch** statement. For example, take another look at Listing 6.5, used to compile a list of grades. It required four nested if statements to determine whether an input grade was an A, B, C, D, or F. This program becomes much simpler to code using the **switch**. The syntax for this statement is:

```
switch (expression)
{ case value₁ : statements₁
    case value₂ : statements₂
    case value₃ : statements₃
    ...
    default     statementsₙ ;
}
```

Syntax form

CONCEPT

the switch
statement

Although it may appear complex, the interpretation of the **switch** is quite simple: When a **switch** statement is executed, the *expression* is compared to each of the listed **case** values from the top down. At the first match, the program begins execution of the statements at that entry point (at the *statements* associated with that **case** value). For example, if the value of the expression matched *value₂*, then *statements₂* would be executed, followed by *statements₃* and so on down through the list of statement groups. The values associated with each **case** must be integer or character constants. The *expression* must result in an integer or character value. Decimal or **float** values are not allowed. In this syntax form, *statements* can be a single statement, a sequence of statements, or a compound set of statements in **{ }** braces. For example:

```
int x;
cin >> x;
switch (x)
{   case 1:          cout << "first line";
                     cout << " continued first line" << endl;
    case 2:          cout << "second line";
                     cout << " continued second line" << endl;
    case 3:          cout << "third line" << endl;
    default:         cout << "last line" << endl;
}
```

Suppose when this segment is executed, the user enters 2. The output would be as follows:

```
second line continued second line
third line
last line
```

The *statements* associated with a **case** *value* are actually optional. This allows several **case** values to be associated with the same statement. In addition, the **default** clause is optional. For example:

```
switch (x)
{   case 0:
    case 1:              cout << "first line" << endl;
    case 2:              cout << "second line" << endl;
    case 3:
    case 4:              cout << "third line" << endl;
}
```

In this example, a value of 0 or 1 for x would cause all three messages to be displayed. A value of 3 or 4 would cause the third line message to be displayed. A user entry of 5 (not in the list) would have no associated **case** value, and the **switch** statement would be ignored.

CONCEPT
the break
statement

Frequently, a programmer will desire that the rest of the *statements* in a **switch** not be executed. To accomplish this, we need another C++ statement—the **break**.

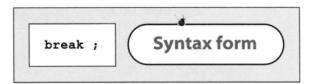

```
break ;          Syntax form
```

When the program encounters a **break** statement, it exits the current control statement (in this case, a **switch**) and moves to the following statement. Consider this modification to the previous code segment:

```
int x;
cin >> x;
switch (x)
{   case 1:              cout << "first line" << endl;
                         break;
    case 2:              cout << "second line" << endl;
                         break;
    case 3:              cout << "third line" << endl;
                         break;
    default:             cout << "last line" << endl;
}
```

CONCEPT
use break only
for the switch
statement

Now when the user enters 2, only the second line message is displayed. As mentioned, the **break** can be used to exit several control structures, including the **for** and **while**. In practice, however, a good programmer only needs it for the **switch** statement. In these other control structures, the test associated with the statement determines when the statement is finished, just as we have done all along.

Let's rewrite the program of Listing 6.5. If you turn back to Chapter 6, you will remember that this program allowed the user to enter a list of letter grades and then output a summary table with the number of As, Bs, and so forth (Listing 7.7).

example in class

Listing 7.7

```
// grades3.cpp  Compile a table of student grades
#include <iostream.h>

void main()
{   int a, b, c, d, f;
    char grade;
    a = b = c = d = f = 0;
    cout << "Enter grades (ending with letter x)" << endl;
    cin >> grade;
    while (grade != 'x')
    {   switch (grade)
        {   case 'A':                a++;  break;
            case 'B':                b++;  break;
            case 'C':                c++;  break;
            case 'D':                d++;  break;
            case 'F':                f++;  break;
            default:                 cout << "illegal grade";
        }
        cin >> grade;
    }
    cout << "A: " << a << " B: " << b << " C: " << c << " D: " <<
        d << " F: " << f << endl;
}
```

7.6 The do-while loop

CONCEPT

the do-while
statement

When using the **while** statement for a loop, the test for continuing is always made at the top of the loop. It is possible that the loop body might not be executed at all if the test is initially negative when the loop is reached. Occasionally, it might be desired that a loop execute at least once regardless of the initial value of the test. In these cases, a programmer would use the **do-while** statement.

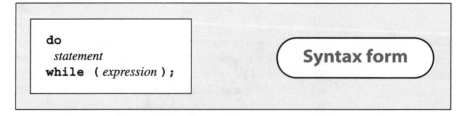

```
do
   statement
while ( expression );
```

Syntax form

Naturally, the *statement* body of the loop can be a single statement or a block of statements enclosed within **{ }** braces. The **do-while** is just a variant of the **while** statement, the only difference being that the test is made at the bottom of the loop instead of at the top. There are some situations where this type of loop corresponds better to the structure of an algorithm or design. Consider the problem of inputting an uppercase letter. If a character that is not an uppercase letter is input, the program should reject that input and wait for the user to reenter a correct character. The function in Listing 7.8 might be utilized.

Listing 7.8

```
// GetLetter()  Prompt the user for an uppercase letter. Ignore
// all entries that are not valid letters until one is entered.
// Return the first valid uppercase letter entered.
char GetLetter()
{   char letter;
    cout << "Enter an uppercase letter: ";
    do
        cin >> letter;
    while (!isupper(letter));
    return (letter);
}
```

In this function, a value must first be input prior to testing for a valid letter (the loop must execute at least once), and the **do-while** statement is used. The function remains within the loop until the test is false, indicating a valid uppercase letter has been entered.

7.7 Example project

A common problem in scientific research is attempting to classify items based on a set of measurements. For example, a laboratory rat might be measured for weight, age, the number of hours of activity per day, and the number of times the rat feeds each day. It is likely that no two rats in a study will have the same four measurements, but nevertheless, rats can be clustered into similar groups.

Suppose a particular researcher has devised the following set of rules to classify study rats into one of four groups:

```
Group A:   weight <= 5 grams and
           age < 2 months and
           activity <= 4 hours and
           feedings <= 5 times.
Group B:   weight <= 7 grams and
           age >= 2 but < 4 months—if activity < 4 hours or
           age >= 4, but < 6 months—if activity >= 4 hours.
Group C:   any weight and
           feedings>=6 times, but < 10 times—if age > 6 months or
           < 3 months or feedings > 10 times—if age >= 6 months.
Group D:   all others
```

Suppose you now decide to write a program to input these four measurements for each of 25 rats and then output the appropriate classification decisions for the researcher. The main program could simply be a **for** loop for 25 iterations (Listing 7.9).

Listing 7.9

```
// classify.cpp  Output classifications for rat features
// ASSUMPTION: 25 lines of input, 4 measurements per line;
// consisting of age, weight, feedings, and activity

#include <iostream.h>
const int NUMRATS = 25;

void main ()
{   float age, weight, activity;
    int feedings, count;
    char group;
    for (count=0; count<NUMRATS; count++)
    {   cin >> age >> weight >> feedings >> activity;
        group = Classify (age, weight, feedings, activity);
        cout << "rat " << count << " is group " << group << endl;
    }
}
```

As usual, the main program was easy to write. The real work is done in the Classify() function. To begin this function, you realize that these groups should be mutually exclusive—a rat cannot belong to two groups. If a rat qualifies for more than one group, you assign it to the first group in which it fits. Next, recognize that the notation used for these rules may make sense in English, but not in C++. Take a look at the first group. By expressing four criteria with one on each line, the researcher is indicating that all four must be true. Each individual criterion must then be combined with the && operator. Take a look at the following expression:

```
(wt <= 5.0) && (age < 2.0) && (activity <= 4.0) && (feedings <= 5)
```

That appears to be near the limit of complexity that a reader can easily follow! Unfortunately, the next group is even more complex. You might decide to evaluate these criteria in two steps. There is no reason why you cannot save the result of a Boolean operator in an **int** variable and then refer to it later. The English statement "a <= b < c" simply implies that "a<=b" and "b < c":

```
class1 = ((2 <= age) && (age < 4)) && (activity < 4);
class2 = ((4 <= age) && (age < 6)) && (activity >= 4);
```

In these criteria, lines 2 and 3 are obviously combined with an OR or || operator. These subexpressions can then be combined into a complete test for Group B as follows:

```
((wt < 7.0) && (class1 || class2))
```

The next group (C) doesn't care about weight. Either of two criteria must be met as represented on lines 2 and 3 of this group of rules. We will combine these with the || operator. Take a look at the line =2 criteria. Feedings must be between 6 and 10 but only if the age is greater than 6 or less than 3. Let's form a test for the right age group first.

```
ageclass1 = (age > 6.0) || (age < 3.0);
feedclass = (6 <= feedings) && (feedings < 10);
class 2 = (feedings > 10) && (age >= 6.0);
```

The complete test for Group C is then as follows:

```
((ageclass1 && feedclass) || class2)
```

We can visualize the entire function as a single **if** statement. A rat is in Group A or not (which makes it a member of B, C, or D):

```
if  ( test for group A )
    class = 'A';
else
{
    check for membership in other 3 groups          1.
}
```

The oval labeled 1 is itself a single `if` statement. A rat is in group B or not (which makes it a member of C or D):

```
if ( test for group B )
    class = 'B';
else
{
    check for membership in other 2 groups          2.
}
```

The oval labeled 2 is another **if** statement to separate the remaining rats into two groups. The complete function in Listing 7.10 now combines these three tests into a cascading **if** statement.

Listing 7.10

```
// Classify()  Return a group letter using classification rules

char Classify (float age, float wt, int feedings, float activity)
{   int ageclass1, feedclass, class1, class2;
    char group;
    if ((wt<=5.0)&&(age<2.0)&&(activity<=4.0)&&(feedings<=5))
        group = 'A';
    else
    {   class1 = ((2 <= age) && (age < 4)) && (activity < 4);
        class2 = ((4 <= age) && (age < 6)) && (activity >= 4);
        if ((wt < 7.0) && (class1 || class2))
            group = 'B';
        else
        {   ageclass1 = (age > 6.0) || (age < 3.0);
            feedclass = (6 <= feedings) && (feedings < 10);
            class2 = (feedings > 10) && (age >= 6.0);
            if ((ageclass1 && feedclass) || class2)
                group = 'C';
            else group = 'D';
        }
    }
    return (group);
}
```

7.8 Summary

KEY TERMS The new terms introduced in this chapter are the following:

1. *Boolean*—an expression that is considered to have only two possible values: true or false.

2. *DeMorgan's theorem*—a rule stating that the complement of any expression can be formulated by changing every relational and Boolean operator to its opposite.

3. *pre-, postincrement*—incrementing a variable before or after it is used in an expression (same for decrement).

4. *optimize*—a compiler's induced changes to a program to make it more efficient or to require less space.

CONCEPTS Several new statements were introduced. First, the single-choice **if** statement:

if (*expression*) *statement*

The **for** loop is convenient for counted loops;

for (*expression*$_1$ **;** *expression*$_2$ **;** *expression*$_3$)
    statement

In the **for** statement, *expression*$_1$ is evaluated prior to the loop, *expression*$_2$ is the test at the beginning of each iteration, and *expression*$_3$ is evaluated after each loop iteration.

The **switch** statement provides a simple means to express multiple choices. In this statement, the expression is compared against each case value to determine entry into the list of statements.

```
switch ( expression )
{   case value₁ :    statements₁
    case value₂ :    statements₂
    ...
    default :   statementsₙ
}
```

The **break** statement provides a means to exit out of a switch statement without continuing through the entire list of statements.

break ;

Finally, the **do-while** statement provides a loop with the test at the bottom of each iteration.

```
do
    statement
while ( expression ) ;
```

Several new operators were introduced. The || and && Boolean operators allow the combination of several simple tests. The expressions on both sides of a Boolean operator are also considered Boolean expressions. The ! operator is used to complement an expression value. DeMorgan's theorem can be used to form the complement of a Boolean expression.

A shorthand notation was introduced for common arithmetic operations. For example a+=b is shorthand for a = a+b. In addition, the increment and decrement operators were introduced for integer variables. When placed prior to a variable (such as ++a), preincrement (or decrement) is indicated. When placed after a variable (such as a++), postincrement is indicated.

The % or modulo operator results in the remainder of an integer division operation.

A few important programming hints were given:

■ Avoid nesting ++ or -- operators within other statements and avoid complex nesting of assignment (=) operators.

■ Be careful not to confuse the && and || operators with the & and | operators, which have very different meanings.

■ To avoid having an **else** matched with the wrong if when nested, always enclose the true choice of a two-choice **if** inside { } braces.

■ Be sure you intend both sides of a Boolean && or || operator to be Boolean (true or false) expressions in themselves.

Table 7.4 **Example segments**

`if (a<2 || (c==5 && d>3))...`
`{ ...`
`}`
	True if a is less than 2 or *both* of the following: c is 5 and d is greater than 3.

`for (n=0; n<10; n++) ...`
`{ ...`
`}`
	Repeat this block 10 times as n goes from 0 to 9.

`a++;`	Increment a.
`c = ++b;`	First increment b, then assign to variable c.
`c = b--;`	First assign b to c, then decrement b.
`c *= (b+a);`	The current value of c is multiplied by (b+a) and then stored back into c.

7.9 Exercises

7.9.a   Short-answer questions

1. A good rule of thumb is always to place ⟨⟩ around both choices of a two-choice **if**.
2. When deciding which **if** is associated with an **else**, the compiler will always choose the ⟨closest⟩ **if** possible.
3. A condition in an **if** or **while** statement is considered to be true if it is ⟨any non-0 value⟩.
4. When a condition contains both **&&** and **||** operators (with no additional parentheses), the ⟨&&⟩ will be evaluated first.
5. Which Boolean operator should be used in a condition to test if either variable a or variable b is true? ⟨|| -or⟩
6. Which Boolean operator should be used in a condition to test if both variable a and variable b are true? ⟨if⟩
7. Consider the following **for** loop:

   ```
   for ( n=0; n<10; n++ )
       cout << "hello" << endl;
   ```

   How many different lines will the above loop produce?
8. Which section of the **for** loop will be executed once at the top of the loop?
9. Which two sections of the **for** loop will be executed each iteration?
10. Rewrite the following definite loop using a **for** statement.

    ```
    int count;
    count = 0;
    while (count < 25)
    {   cout << "count is " << count << endl;
        count++;
    }
    ```

11. What would be output as a result of this segment?

```
int n, j;
for (n=0; n<5; n++)
    for (j=n; j<5; j++)
        cout << n << "," << j << endl;
```

12. What would be output as a result of the execution of this segment?

```
int x, y;
for (x=1; x<=5; x++)
    {    cout << x << endl;
         for (y=2; y<x; y++)
             cout << y << endl;
    }
```

13. Indicate which of the following expressions are true and which are false:

```
int a=5, b=7; c=0;
```

a. (a <b || c)
b. (a && c)
c. (c && b || a)

14. Determine an equivalent expression using DeMorgan's theorem.
a. ! (a<b)
b. ! (a && b)
c. ! a || ! b

15. Give an example of two different variable types that might be used in a **switch** statement.

16. Propose a **switch** statement using the variable N to output messages according to the following table:

```
N      message
1      "too small"
2      "small"
3      "just right"
4      "large"
5      "too large"
```

17. Describe what occurs if the expression in a **switch** statement does not match any of the **case** options.

18. Briefly describe the primary use of the **break** statement.

19. Convert the following statements to shorthand notation.
a. a = a + 1;
b. b = b * 2;
c. c = c + (a = a+1);

7.9.b   Projects

1. The Acme Shipping Company uses the following rate schedule:

Weight	Charge	Surcharge for Hazardous Material
0 – 5 lb	$5/lb	$17
>5 – 10 lb	$20 + $6/lb for wt over 5 lb	$22
>10 lb	$41 + $7/lb for wt over 10 lb	$27

For example, a package of hazardous material weighing 7 lb would be charged $54 ($20 plus 2 * $6 plus the $22 surcharge). A package of nonhazardous material weighing 17 lb would be charged $97 ($41 plus 8 * $7). Write a function to implement this rate schedule and demonstrate your function with a driver program to input package weights and contents and output charges.

2. The GoodHands Insurance Agency determines auto insurance rates based on the driver's age, ticket history, and the value of the car. The base rate is 6% of the car value. Male drivers under age 25 pay an extra 17%, and female drivers under age 21 pay an extra 4% of the base charge. A driver with more than three tickets pays an extra $100. Write a function to calculate insurance rates based on this information. Test your function with a main program to input driver information and output rates.

3. Listing 6.5 represented a method of compiling a summary table of student grades. Rewrite this program to utilize a **switch** statement to test a letter grade and determine which count should be incremented.

4. Using a **for** loop, write a small program to generate a table of squares and square roots for whole numbers from 1 to 25. For example, your output might begin something like the following:

```
N       square root    square
1       1               1
2       1.41421         4
3       1.73205         9
. . .
```

5. Write a program to generate a table of integer powers for the numbers 1 through 10 in steps of 0.5. On each table line, output the powers from 2 through 5. You may need to use **long** variables to avoid overflow. The output table should look similar to the following:

```
N       2       3        4         5
1       1       1        1         1
1.5     2.25    3.375    5.0625    7.59375
2       4       8        16        32
2.5     6.25    15.625   39.0625   97.6563
. . .
```

6. Write a function to calculate N! using a **for** loop:

```
N! = 1 if N <= 1, else N! = N * (N-1) * (N-2) * (N-3) * ... 1
```

Write a main program to allow a user to input a list of positive integers. The list should begin with a count of the size of the list. For each positive integer in the list, output the factorial. For example, the following might be used for input indicating a list size of 5 elements. The output should consist of 5 factorials for 7, 3, and so on.

```
5
7
3
4
2
6
```

7. Write a program to graph the following function from 0 to 2 in increments of 0.1.

$$y = \frac{1}{1+x}$$

8. The value of the mathematical constant e can be calculated using the following converging series:

$$e = 2 + \frac{1}{2!} + \frac{1}{3!} + \frac{1}{4!} + ...$$

Each term in this series is smaller in magnitude than the previous one. Thus, the accuracy of the result depends only on the number of terms you calculate. Write a function to calculate the value for e by summing the first 25 terms of this series. Note: The last few terms will have very large numbers in the denominator. You may wish to use **double** variables. You may also wish to consider that 1/4! is (1/4) * (1/3!).

9. The value of the cosine function can be calculated using the following converging series:

$$\cos(x) = 1 - \frac{x^2}{2!} + \frac{x^4}{4!} - \frac{x^6}{6!} + ...$$

Each term in this series is smaller in magnitude than the previous one. Thus, the accuracy of the result depends only on the number of terms you calculate. Write a function to calculate the cosine of a positive real value (in radians) by summing the first 25 terms of this series. Note: You may want to review project 8.

10. **Creative Challenge:** Refer to project 3. As you develop this program in a stepwise, top-down fashion, you will probably need to enter a list of grades repeatedly as you debug and verify your program. Assume your list (for which you have hand-calculated a result) consists of 20 grades. This would be a time-consuming and error-prone process (not to mention boring). Devise a method so that the list of scores does not need to be entered each time during development. In other words, each time you run the program, it should have access to the list without needing the user to enter the values.

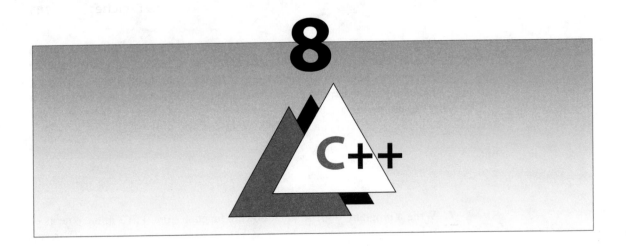

Simple File I/O

Back in Chapter 5, you learned a basic set of steps that could be used to have a program read input from a file rather than the user keyboard. You still expect all output information to be displayed on the screen or perhaps with a printer. In this chapter, you will learn much more about versatile ways to create and use disk files to store program input, how to read such data in future programs, and how to save program output to disk files.

8.1 External stream files

By now, you have become somewhat comfortable with what a disk file represents. In your program development environment (PDE), you have used disk files to save your program source and perhaps the executable version. You have seen a simple way to direct a program to read input from a file named `input.dat`. While some use of files for program input and output (I/O) can be controlled from several operating systems using redirection (see appendixes), we will take a more complete look at using disk files for both input and output data. This approach has the advantage of not requiring special operating system commands or special skills on the part of the user.

KEY TERM
oracle testing

An important use of external input files is in *oracle testing*. During development, a program is frequently tested with a predetermined set of input data for which the output has been hand-calculated or predicted. The idea is that if the program output matches the predicted output, you are on the right track. This input data for which the output is known are referred to as an oracle file. Often, this oracle file is quite large if many different aspects or situations within a program are to be exercised. Naturally, it would be very inefficient to reenter this oracle data each time a program is tested. The potential for an entry error by the operator may be large. It is much simpler to have the program read the oracle data from the disk.

We will begin our discussion by learning how to specify and declare file variables and then learn how to use disk files for program output. After that, we will learn how to return to such files and use them in later programs for input.

8.1.a Filenames and file variables

The first step in using a disk file for program output is to choose an appropriate filename. Appropriate file naming conventions depend on the operating system you are using. (You may want to review the appropriate appendix.) For example, under DOS, a filename may be a maximum of eight letters or digits in length and must begin with a letter. Each filename may also have an extension, which is a period followed by up to three letters or digits. There are several standard filename extensions: C++ program source files usually end with .CPP, and program executable files end with .EXE. The PDE recognizes appropriate extensions and knows what to expect for the *type* of information they hold.

Disk files used to store program output information may represent a wide range of information types, and no standard file extensions are defined in the commonly used operating systems. Often, files that end with the extensions .DAT (short for "data") and .TXT (short for "textual information") are used by programmers to hold general program output or data files, but these extensions are only a convention. In practice, a programmer may decide to use any extension. It should not, however, conflict with predefined extensions expected by the PDE or the operating system. Table 8.1 lists a number of common file extensions which are assumed by DOS and Windows to contain certain specific types of information. General program output files should avoid the use of these extensions.

Table 8.1 Some common DOS and Windows file extensions

Extension	Expected File Content
.CPP	C++ source file
.EXE	Relocatable execution file
.COM	Execution file
.OBJ	Object binary file
.INI	Windows information file
.BAT	DOS batch command file
.SYS	System file
.PRJ	Borland C++ project file
.IDE	Borland C++ environment file
.DSP	Microsoft Visual C++ project file
.DSW	Microsoft Visual C++ workspace file

As you previously learned, a good programmer always attempts to name things descriptively. Choose a filename that reflects the type and purpose of the information contained within the file. By convention, most programmers use the filename to reflect the *purpose* and the file extension to reflect the file *type*. For example, a file containing grades in text form might be named `"grades.txt"`, whereas a file containing a list of numeric student ages might be named `"students.num"`. Following this convention, a file containing textual descriptions of students and a file containing numeric grades might be `"students.txt"` and `"grades.num"`, respectively.

Now, there are several different methods of accessing disk files. In this text, we will learn *stream* access and leave the other methods for another course of study.

The first step in accessing external files using the stream access method is to include the appropriate header file which contains the definitions and interface information necessary to access the file manipulation functions.

```
#include <fstream.h>
```
Syntax form

It turns out that including this file will also provide all the interface information found in the `iostream.h` header file we have been using. The reason is that the `fstream.h` file contains a `#include <iostream.h>` line, which will be conditionally used if you haven't already included this file yourself. In other words, if you include `fstream.h`, you do not also need to include `iostream.h` in a program file—it has already been done. *It doesn't hurt, however.* Some programmers prefer to explicitly include both header files if both keyboard/screen and external file I/O are to be performed.

In any case, the next step to using external files in a program is to declare a *file stream variable* (often called a file variable). This variable is used by C++ to keep track of the state of the file during program execution. Among other things, this means where the program is with respect to reading or writing position within the file. A file variable for output files is declared using the type **ofstream** (short for "output file stream"):

```
ofstream variable ;
```
Syntax form

A *stream* is C++ jargon for a flow of information where lines are expected to end with Return keystrokes and numbers are expected to be separated with white spaces. Doesn't that sound familiar? These are also the expectations we have used when dealing with **cin** and **cout**.

After a file variable has been declared, a specific disk file must be *opened* and associated with this file variable through use of the following syntax:

---

variable.**open** (*filename*) ;   **Syntax form**

CONCEPT
**effect of opening
a file**

Keep in mind that C++ does not perform file operations but simply sends requests or commands to the underlying operating system which has responsibility for the actual file manipulation and storage. In other words, the open() command causes C++ to formulate a request to the operating system to open the indicated file. The filename is expressed as a literal or a text string enclosed within double quotes. The open() request causes the operating system first to determine if the file already exists. If it does, the existing file is emptied and prepared to accept new data. If it does not exist, an empty file is created on the disk and prepared to accept data. Consider the following simple example:

```
ofstream newfile;
newfile.open ("students.txt");
```

As a result of this segment, a disk file named "students.txt" will be created (or emptied if one already exists) and readied to accept data from the program. The system will use the file variable newfile to keep track of the state of the file during execution.

Remember that a filename may also include a disk drive specifier and/or a directory path. The file in the previous segment contains neither of these and will be created on the *default disk drive and directory*. If the file is to be created explicitly on disk drive A, for example, the following could be used within DOS or Windows:

```
newfile.open ("a:students.txt");
```

CONCEPT
**be careful of the
backslash**

You need to be very careful when including a directory path in the filename under DOS or Windows since these operating systems interpret the backslash (\) character differently than C++. Since a filename is expressed as a literal, a **\n** would be interpreted by C++ as a Return character just as it is in any literal. Consider the following filename, which includes a directory path:

```
newfile.open ("a:\newstudents");
```
WRONG
WAY!

The literal within the double quotes is a valid DOS or Windows filename, but C++ would change it before passing it along to the operating system! In this example, C++ would first replace the **\n** with a Return white-space character. Subsequently, the request passed to DOS or Windows would contain a path that would be incorrectly interpreted. The solution is to use two backslashes for each directory separator in the path. When C++ sees two slashes, they are treated as a single slash and no control or white-space characters are assumed. In other words:

```
newfile.open ("a:\\newstudents");
```

Once the .open command has been executed, the disk file is waiting for information. Output is accomplished through use of the << operator symbol just as it was with **cout**. The difference is that you simply use the file variable in place of **cout** when you want information to be written to the disk file:

```
newfile << "this is written to the disk file" << endl;
cout << "this is written to the screen" << endl;
```

These commands cause C++ to send the two literal strings to the operating system for output to the disk file associated with newfile and the screen, respectively. If you think about this example for a minute, the similarities between outputting to a disk file and outputting to the screen can tell you something about the true nature of **cout**—it is really also a stream file variable! When you preface a C++ program with the #include statement for iostream.h

```
#include <iostream.h>
```

you are indicating your intention to send output to the screen (as well as input from the keyboard) within the program. The header file iostream.h actually contains the declaration for **cout** as a file variable. In addition, the C++ system effectively adds the appropriate cout.open() statement to your program to prepare the screen for output. The screen display is really a sort of *write-only* file.

KEY TERM
insertion operator

As you might have guessed, the << symbol is really an operator just like + or *. More formally, we refer to << as the *insertion operator*. The right side operand of << indicates where the output information is coming from, and the left side operand indicates where the output information is to be sent or inserted.

In any case, you are now ready for a complete example. Suppose you wish to create a disk file on the B drive containing a list of account numbers and balances for maintaining company finances (Listing 8.1).

Listing 8.1

```
// accounts.cpp  Create disk file B:ACCNTS.DAT for
// accounts and balances
#include <iostream.h>
#include <fstream.h>
void main ()
{   char done = 'y';
    int acntnum;                            // an account num.
```

```
    float balance;                  // an account balance
    ofstream outfile;               // a file var.

    outfile.open ("b:accnts.dat");  // prepare file for writing

// Now input values from keyboard and write to the disk file...

    while (done != 'n')
    {   cout << "enter an account number and balance: ";
        cin >> acntnum >> balance;
        outfile << acntnum << " " << balance << endl;
        cout << "another account?"
        cin >> done;
    }
}
```

KEY TERM
database

The example in Listing 8.1 prompts the user to enter an account number and balance. These are then written to the disk file named "b:accnts.dat". The program continues with the next account until the user indicates that no more accounts are to be entered. When the program terminates, the disk file will contain a *database* of account information. While this example is somewhat simplistic, a database is just a disk file (or often a collection of files) of information that can be repeatedly accessed by other programs—alleviating the need to reenter the information into each program that might need it.

The data in the "b:accnts.dat" file will be formatted just as directed by the output line; each line would contain an account number, followed by a blank, followed by a balance, followed by an end-of-line character (a Return):

```
outfile << acntnum << " " << balance << endl:
```

For example, consider the following demonstration and resulting file:

```
enter an account number and balance: 345   678.90
another account? y
enter an account number and balance: 123   456.78
another account? y
enter an account number and balance: 901   234.56
another account? n
```

The file "b:accnts.dat" would contain the following text. (Refer to the appropriate appendix on how to display the contents of a text file to the screen.)

```
b:accnts.dat:
              345   678.90
              123   456.78
              901   234.56
```

What would happen if the output for Listing 8.1 did not include (a) the `endl` or (b) the `" "`?

KEY TERM
record

The data in the `"b:accnts.dat"` file represent three accounts. Each account is represented by two pieces of information: an account number and a balance. We often refer to each group of related information as a *record*. In other words, each account is represented by a record. It just so happens in this example that each record ends with a Return—there is one record per line. In some cases, a record might consist of more than one line. Suppose we needed 27 different values to represent an account (an address, some dates, etc.). Suppose also that we used five different lines to store these 27 values. Each group of 27 values (a group of five lines) related to one account would be considered a record.

8.1.b   Input files

Input files are used in a similar manner with one minor difference: An input file variable is declared using **ifstream** (which stands for "input file stream").

ifstream *variable* ;	**Syntax form**

After declaring a file variable, you need to open the file to allow the system to prepare for reading using the `open()` syntax, just as was done with output files. Naturally, it does not make any sense to attempt to open a disk file that does not exist. Later in the chapter, we will look at what occurs when one mistakenly attempts to do such an illogical thing.

KEY TERM
extraction
operator

Input is accomplished using the `>>` operator, just as we have done with the **cin** file variable. (Remember **cin** and **cout** are simply stream file variables opened to the keyboard and screen, respectively.) While the `<<` is called the insertion operator, the `>>` is referred to as the *extraction operator*. The left side operand indicates where the information is to be extracted from while the right side operand indicates the variable where the extracted information is to be stored.

Suppose now we wish to use our simple database file to supply input to a program intended to report the total value of all accounts. A program can be written to open and read the information from the `"b:accnts.dat"` file just as if it had been typed from the keyboard. *Let's first assume we are aware that this file contains exactly three accounts.* Consider Listing 8.2.

Listing 8.2

```
// total.cpp  Report the total of all accounts
#include <iostream.h>
#include <fstream.h>
void main ()
{   int acntnum;                      // an account num.
    float balance;                    // an account balance
    int n;
    float sum = 0.0;
    ifstream infile;                  // a file var. for the input

    infile.open ("b:accnts.dat");   // prepare file for reading

    for (n=0; n<3; n++)               // sum 3 accounts...
    {   infile >> acntnum >> balance;
        sum += balance;
    }
    cout << "The total of all accounts is: " << sum << endl;
}
```

You might ask what the programmer could do if the number of accounts in the database file was not known. We will return to this problem later. In any case, several other applications might also use the same "b:accnts.dat" file. For example, a program could be developed to report the balance of a specific account. Consider Listing 8.3.

Listing 8.3

```
// report.cpp  Report the balance of a specific account
#include <iostream.h>
#include <fstream.h>

void main ()
{   int acntnum, search;                     // account numbers
    float balance;                           // an account balance
    ifstream infile;                         // input file variable
    int n, done = 0;

    infile.open ("b:accnts.dat");            // prepare file for reading...
    cout << "Enter account number: ";
    cin >> search;                           // get accnt num. from user
    for (n=0; n<3 && !done; n++)
    {   infile >> acntnum >> balance;        // read an account...
        if (acntnum == search)               // found!
        {   cout << "balance is: " << balance;
            done = 1;
        }
    }
}
```

The program in Listing 8.3 prompts the user for an account number and then reads the account lines in the `"b:accnts.dat"` file until that particular account is found or all accounts have been examined. The program then displays the balance associated with that account. Other programs could be developed to generate a report of all accounts and so on. The advantage of using an external disk file is that the account information does not need to be entered each time one of these programs is executed.

EXPERIMENT

What would happen in Listing 8.3 if the desired account entered by the user did not exist?

8.1.c Shorthand notations

The actions of declaring a file variable and opening a file can actually be combined into a single statement. In the following syntax form box, these single statements take the place of a file variable declaration and an `open()` command:

---

ifstream *variable* (*filename*, `ios::in`);
ofstream *variable* (*filename*, `ios::out`);

Syntax form

The `ios::in` and `ios::out` can be thought of as simple key phrases indicating whether a file variable is to be used for input or output. For example, the following block of statements

```
ifstream infile;
infile.open ("b:accnts.dat");
```

accomplishes the same thing as this single statement:

```
ifstream infile ("b:accnts.dat", ios::in);
```

8.2 End-of-file loops

An interesting and important concern is raised in the preceding section: What if the number of records is not known when a file is to be read? Also, what if the number of records changes? Is there some way to write programs that read this file so that they will work without a prior knowledge of the number of file records? There is: *The results of an input or extraction expression can be tested for success or failure.* An extraction operator expression will be false if the associated file is empty, closed, or does not contain the correct type or number of data values you have indicated should be read. For example, consider the following segment, which could be used in Listing 8.2:

```
infile.open ("b:accnts.dat");        // prepare file for reading

while (infile >> acntnum >> balance)// sum all accounts...
    sum += balance;
cout << "The total of all acounts is: " << sum << endl;
```

The **while** statement contains the extraction expression within its parentheses. The net result is that the extraction (or input) is attempted, and then the success or failure of that attempt is tested to determine whether the body of the **while** statement should be entered. In other words, if the system was able to input an acntnum and a balance, the expression would be true and the balance would be summed. If the system was not able to input another record (perhaps because all records have been read and the system is at the end of the file), the expression would be false and the **while** statement would exit.

Remember, an extraction expression may also fail if the type or number of data items does not match the variables that are to be filled. Suppose the "b:accnts.dat" file contained the following three lines:

```
b:accnts.dat:
                345    678.90
                X      456.78
                901    234.56
```

This code segment would report that The total of all accounts is: 678.90, which is just the first account balance. The reason is that the extraction failed on the second record or line. The system expected to find an integer and a real number. Instead a character was encountered. At that point, the sum of account balances was just the balance of the first record.

8.3 Closing files

Basically, a disk (coated with a magnetic medium) is rotated under a read/write head within the disk drive system. Information is magnetically written or encoded on concentric rings or *tracks* of the disk surface. To access information previously written, the program must wait for the disk to mechanically position the head over the correct track and then wait for the correct segment of that track to rotate under the head. These waiting times are quite large with respect to the actual data access. Consequently, a good operating system will often attempt to minimize the number of times a disk access is made by pooling operations until a larger number of requests can be blocked together. DOS, Windows, and UNIX all use this approach.

KEY TERM
buffer

For example, if a program performs many insertion (or output) operations, an operating system will pool or temporarily store this output in a reserved location in memory called a *buffer*. When the buffer is full, the system will then perform one disk access to write the entire buffer. The program may make many insertion operation requests. The operating system often combines them into only a few disk accesses. (There are additional reasons for buffering, but they are not important now.)

A problem may occur, however, when a programmer desires to read back what has just been written to a disk file. Consider the following segment which attempts to create a new file, write values to it, and then read those values back:

```
ofstream outfile;                       WAY!
ifstream infile;                        WRONG

outfile.open ("somefile.dat");          // open the output file
outfile << 55 << 66 << 77;              // write 3 integers

infile.open ("somefile.dat");           // now open for reading
infile << x << y << z;                   // and read them back
```

The problem is that while the three integers have been written or inserted into the file as far as the program is concerned, the operating system may have simply put this output into a buffer. It may not actually be written to the disk until the buffer is full. Either the `infile.open()` statement would not make sense because the file does not yet actually exist on the disk, or the extraction operation would be invalid because the disk file does not yet contain the integers.

For this reason, most systems will only allow a file to be opened with one file variable at a time. Fortunately, there is a way to indicate that no more output is to be expected and cause the system to flush the buffer out to the disk. This is done through use of the `close()` syntax:

```
variable.close();
```

Syntax form

CONCEPT
the close statement

Naturally, no more output or insertion actions may be performed once a file is closed (without reopening the file). The method of correcting the problem with the preceding segment is then simply to add a `close()` action between the writing of the integers and the subsequent reading:

```
ofstream outfile;
ifstream infile;

outfile.open ("somefile.dat");    // open the output file
outfile << 55 << 66 << 77;        // write 3 integers
outfile.close();                  // flush the system buffer!

infile.open ("somefile.dat");     // now open for reading
infile << x << y << z;            // and read them back
```

CONCEPT
automatic
closing of files

What about the programs in Listings 8.1, 8.2, and 8.3? They do not contain a `close()` statement. It is obvious to the operating system that when a program terminates, no more output should be expected. As a result, all file buffers are automatically flushed to respective disk files on program termination. The net result is that one only really needs to use a `close()` statement when output is to be subsequently read before the program terminates. Of course, it does not hurt to place `close()` statements for output files at the end of a program even when they are not immediately to be reopened. In fact, it is considered by some to be proper style because it expressly states what is to occur without the need of the reader to be aware of any default actions. If a program needs to access many files, it might also be necessary to close a file to allow buffer space to be reused by the next file to be opened.

8.4 Output formatting

Up to this point, we have accepted the default way in which the insertion operation formats the output. Often, however, an application will need to output information in some other well-defined format. Perhaps the output is to form a table with evenly aligned columns, or the values of real numbers are to be rounded to a consistent number of decimal points. An output stream responds to several control functions for such formatting. We will introduce a few of the most commonly used ones here.

```
variable.width (n) ;
variable.precision (n) ;            Syntax form
variable.fill (c) ;
```

CONCEPT
formatting rules

In this syntax form box, n refers to a positive integer and c refers to a character. The width control function allows the number of positions or columns used for the next numeric value to be changed; the next numeric value is output in a field of at least n columns. Fortunately, if the number to be output requires more columns than you specify, C++ will override such a request and a sufficient number of columns will be used. Thus, *n* is just a requested *minimum* number of columns. If the number to be output will fit in fewer columns, the value is right justified within the *n*-column field and the remaining positions are filled with the default fill character (which is normally a space). Remember, this control function only changes the number of positions for the next value. Subsequent values will be output again using the system defaults.

The precision control function allows the programmer to change the maximum number of significant digits used for a real or **float** value. This change remains in effect until the next `precision()` statement (or of course, the end of the program). For example, if precision is set to four digits, a float value less than 99.0 would be rounded to two decimal places to produce four significant digits. Numbers that have more than four digits to the left of the decimal point would be expressed in E-notation with four significant digits. Numbers that are less than 1 (< 1.0) may be output in decimal notation or E-notation, but rounded to four significant digits.

```
cout.precision(4);        // set precision to 4 significant digits
cout << 45.6789;          // produces 45.68
cout << 1234567.89;       // produces 1.234e06
cout << 0.00987654;       // produces 0.009877
cout << 45.0;             // produces 45
```

The `fill()` control function allows the programmer to change the default character used to fill unused positions or columns. Remember, the default value for the fill character is just the space or blank character. Once set with a `fill()` function, a new default remains in place until the program terminates or a new fill character is set by a subsequent `fill()` call.

Suppose a **float** variable is to be output in the next 12 columns, rounded to two decimal places and preceded with dots (as might be the case in a financial report) to fill the remaining columns not needed. If the variable `value` has the value of 789.357, the desired output should look like this:

```
Item Cost . . . . . . 789.36
```

The correct output segment could be:

```
cout << "Item Cost";
cout.fill('.');
cout.precision(5);
cout.width(12);
cout << value;
```

Suppose one needed to have a program input a sequence of numbers from a disk file and display the associated square roots of each of these numbers with four digits of precision in a table on the monitor display. The above formatting control statements might be used to ensure that this table lines up nicely under appropriate column headings. Consider Listing 8.4.

Listing 8.4

```cpp
// roottbl.cpp   Display a table of square roots for a list of
// input values from the disk file "a:values.dat"
#include <iostream.h>
#include <fstream.h>
#include <math.h>
const int PRECISION = 4;        // output precision
const int WIDTH1 = 10;          // width of values column
const int WIDTH2 = 15;          // width of root column

void main ()
{   float value, root;
    ifstream infile ("a:values.dat", ios::in);

    cout << "  value          square root" << endl;

    cout.precision(PRECISION);   // set precision
    while (infile >> value)      // loop through file values...
    {   root = sqrt (value);
        cout.width(WIDTH1);      // input values use these cols
        cout << value;
        cout.width(WIDTH2);      // roots use next WIDTH2 cols
        cout << root << endl;
    }
}
```

Now if the file contains the following values:

a:values.dat:
```
25.0
16.5
18.4
199.233
234.567
123452.3
```

The execution of the program of Listing 8.4 would produce the following output:

```
value          square root
25               5
16.5             4.062
18.4             4.29
199.2            14.11
234.6            15.32
1.235e+05        351.4
```

EXPERIMENT:

What would happen if the `.precision` control statement were used with `int` or `char` variables?

These three format control functions are perhaps the most useful. Others are available, but are not covered in this text.

8.5 The standard error stream

Most popular operating systems such as DOS, Windows, and UNIX allow the user to redirect the output (or input) of a program. (You might want to look at the appropriate operating system appendix if you have not already done so.) For example, under DOS, if a program named `myprog.exe` is executed with the following command

```
c:> myprog
```

KEY TERMS
standard output
and input streams

then all `<<` output using **cout** would send lines to the *standard output stream* or the display screen. All `>>` input using **cin** would come from the *standard input stream* or the keyboard. The special `<` and `>` redirection symbols in DOS, UNIX, and Windows allow the user to override these defaults. For example,

```
c:> myprog >output.dat
```

would cause all program output using **cout** to be redirected to the file `output.dat`. The command

```
c:> myprog >output.dat <input.dat
```

would cause all program output from **cout** statements and all input using **cin** statements to be redirected. Output would still go to the `output.dat` file, and now input would come from the `input.dat` file. Remember, these changes in program I/O are done without any changes to the program itself.

What if portions of the program output should not be redirected away from the display? Suppose you have a program that might produce error messages to warn the user if a data entry error occurs. Consider this fragment:

```
cin >> age;
if (age < 0)
        cout << "**ERROR; an illegal age has been entered";
```

KEY TERM
standard error
stream

If the user had redirected all program output to a file, this error message would be sent to that file and consequently not be seen by the user until the file was later examined. C++ provides a simple means of preventing this particular problem. Another output stream known as the *standard error stream* is not affected by the normal > redirection. This means that there are a total of three streams that are declared and opened by default in a simple C++ program. This standard error stream is for output and uses the **cerr** stream variable. Now, it does not have to be used for error messages, but that is the most common application. The bottom line is that any output using the **cerr** stream variable will normally go to the screen even if the **cout** output has been redirected. If the preceding fragment is changed to the following

```
cin >> age;
if (age < 0)
    cerr << "**ERROR; an illegal age has been entered";
```

then the error message would appear on the screen regardless of whether standard output redirection is used or not.

Be careful: This does not mean that **cerr** output cannot be redirected away from the screen—it can in most operating systems. It just isn't done with a simple > symbol.

8.6 An introduction to member functions

You may have noticed that we have slipped in a new concept in this chapter (other than just those dealing with file input and output). The open(), close(), precision(), and so forth commands or statements appear to be function calls, but they are not invoked using the simple method introduced in Chapter 3. In particular, they are all preceded with a variable name and a dot.

In Chapter 3, functions were invoked with a set of arguments within the parentheses and could be used with any appropriate variables as long as the types of each parameter and associated argument were the same. We refer to these as general functions.

KEY TERM
class

In C++, there is a concept much broader and more powerful than representing things in nature with simple variables. It is called a *class*. While a variable might represent some state or value of an item in nature, a class might be used to represent a state *and all the operations, activities, and uses* associated with that item in nature. A simple variable might hold or *own* a value, while a class might also own a set of functions which act on that value. The study of classes and their uses will occupy a great deal of your advanced study of programming and software engineering methods.

KEY TERM
member function

For now, you should understand just a couple of important facts. First, **cin** and **cout** are not instances of some simple variable type (like **int** or **float**), but rather instances of a class; **cin** is an instance of the **ifstream** class, whereas **cout** is an instance of the **ofstream** class. Second, each class instance is allowed to have its own set of functions—appropriately called *member functions*. In other words

```
ofstream outfile;
outfile.precision(4);
```

invokes not just any `precision()` function, but the one that specifically belongs to `outfile`. Likewise

```
Tool lathe;
lathe.precision(10);
```

would invoke the `precision()` function belonging to `lathe`, which is an instance of a completely different class named `Tool`. One is designed to work specifically with the **cout** instance of an output stream, while the other `precision()` might be designed to work specifically with instances of some representation of industrial tools. The dot is how one specifies which particular function is to be invoked. These two `precision()` functions probably both deal with changing precision, but changing precision on a `lathe` is a very different operation than that for an output stream.

Now this might seem a bit esoteric, but it is really quite useful. We will come back to this concept with a lot more explanation, examples, and uses in Chapter 12. For now, simply remember that the functions dealing with files (`open()`, `close()`, `precision()`, `width()`, and `fill()`—must all be invoked by preceding them with the associated file variable name (the class instance) and a dot.

8.7 Example project

Suppose a pharmacist needs to manage medications being given to a set of patients. In particular, he would like to enter a drug code and a patient ID into a program and have the program output a warning if the patient was currently taking any other medications that might adversely interact with the new drug. This would be particularly helpful in a hospital where patients might be treated by several different physicians and simultaneously be taking numerous drugs.

To approach this problem, we will first define our database of files. We will establish a file containing patient records named `"patients.txt"`. Each record in this file will consist of a four-digit patient ID followed by a sequence of two-digit drug codes ending with the sentinel value of `-1`. A patient may have any number of different drug codes. Here is a possible `"patients.txt"` file. For example, the first line of this file indicates that patient `3647` is currently taking three drugs with codes `25`, `91`, and `46`:

```
patients.txt:
              3647  25  91  46 -1
              4732  46  13  92  11 84 -1
              6673 46 -1
              ...
```

Now, a second file will be created for drug interactions named `"drugs.txt"`. Each line in this file will consist of a drug number followed by a list of the drugs (numbers) that should not be taken concurrently with this medication. This list will end with the same sentinel of -1. For example, here is a possible "drugs.txt" file. The first line indicates that drug 46 should never be taken with drugs 18 or 75:

drugs.txt:

```
46    18    75    -1
13    91    -1
18    46    23    -1
...
```

Now, the program will need to go through the following steps:

1. Get a patient ID number and a new prescription drug number from the user.
2. Find the patient record in "patients.txt" for this ID. Make a list of the drugs the patient is currently taking.
3. Find the drug record in "drugs.txt" for this new drug.
4. Compare each conflicting drug in the drug record (for the new prescription) with the list of drugs currently being taken. If a match is found, output a warning to the pharmacist.

Notice that the list of drugs currently being taken (from the "patients.txt" file) will need to be repeatedly searched—once for each conflicting drug in the new drug record (from the "drugs.txt" file) to verify the patient is not currently taking any of these contraindicated medications. To simplify this process, we will make a new temporary file (named "temp.txt") that contains just this list of drugs the patient is currently taking. Each time we need to search the file, we will need to re-open this temporary file to start the system off at the file beginning. The main program (Listing 8.5) will simply be an implementation of the four steps listed. (We will see in Chapter 9 that there is an easier and more efficient way of keeping track of a patient's drug list.)

Listing 8.5

```cpp
// drugtest.cpp   Compare new prescription with currently
// prescribed meds for dangerous combinations.
// ASSUMPTION: the files "patients.txt" and "drugs.txt" exist.
#include <iostream.h>
#include <fstream.h>
const int END = -1;

void main ()
{   int patID, newdrug, contradrug;
    ifstream patfile ("patients.txt", ios::in);      // patient records
    ifstream drugfile ("drugs.txt", ios::in);        // drug records
    ofstream outfile ("temp.txt", ios::out);         // list of current meds
```

```
    cout << "enter patient ID and drug number: ";
    cin >> patID >> newdrug;
// Make a list of the current medications for this patient in file "temp.txt"
    MakeList (patID, patfile, outfile);
    outfile.close();
// Find the new drug in the "drugs.txt" database file
    FindDrug (drugfile, newdrug);
// Search the contraindicated drugs for each drug the patient is taking ("temp.txt")
    if (drugfile)
        if (drugfile >> contradrug)
            while (contradrug > 0)
            {   if (CurrentlyTaking (contradrug))
                    cout <<
                        "*WARNING; drug interaction possible!"<< endl;
                drugfile >> contradrug;
            }
}
```

Notice that after calling FindDrug(), the program checks to verify that the file variable is true, indicating that the function did not reach the end of the file or encounter an error while searching for the drug. Attempting to read values from a stream file after reaching the end or encountering an error can cause a program to fail or produce incorrect results. Throughout this project, we will first verify that an input file variable is true before attempting to read another record of information from the file.

Let's take these functions one at a time. First, consider MakeList(). When this function returns, the file "temp.txt" should contain a list of drug numbers this patient is currently taking. The first step is to find the correct patient record in the "patients.txt" file using the patfile file variable. Now, remember that files are read just as you read a book—from left to right and from top to bottom. We will think of the file variable as an index or bookmark into the current position of the file. The first task is to move the index for "patients.txt" to just after the correct patient ID. Next, the drug numbers are read and output to the "temp.txt" file until the sentinel is reached. Notice that when file variables are passed to a function, they should be declared as reference parameters since they are subsequently changed when used (Listing 8.6).

Listing 8.6

```
// MakeList () Make a list of current meds in file "temp.txt"
// ASSUMPTIONS: patfile is opened to the file "patients.txt". outfile is
// opened to the file "temp.txt". Lowest patID is 1111, highest drug
// number is 99. Assumes patient is in file. Sentinel is END.
// IN: patID is the patient ID number.
// IN/OUT:  patfile is opened to "patients.txt", outfile to "temp.txt"
```

```
void MakeList (int patID, ifstream& patfile, ofstream& outfile)
{   int drug, id;
    patfile >> id;
    while (patfile && id != patID)         // find the correct patient
        patfile >> id;
    if (patfile)                           // (be sure patient was found)
    {   patfile >> drug;                   // make list of current meds
        while (drug > 0)                   // in file using 'outfile'
        {   outfile << "   " << drug;
            patfile >> drug;
        }
    }
}
```

Finding the correct drug in `FindDrug()` is a bit more difficult. One cannot simply search for a match since only the first drug on a line should be examined. We'll use an indefinite loop. First, read the first drug on a line. If it does not match the new drug, skip the rest of the drugs on that line until the sentinel is found. Again read the first drug (now on the next line) and so on until the correct match is found (Listing 8.7).

Listing 8.7

```
// FindDrug()  Locate the correct drug record in "drugs.txt"
// ASSUMPTIONS: file "drugs.txt" is opened to 'drugfile'.
// List sentinel is END. newdrug must be found in file.
// IN: newdrug is the drug to be found.
// IN/OUT:  drugfile is opened to "drugs.txt"

void FindDrug (ifstream& drugfile, int newdrug)
{   int thisdrug;
    drugfile >> thisdrug;                      // first drug for each record
    while (drugfile && thisdrug != newdrug)
        {   drugfile >> thisdrug;              // if wrong drug, skip over list
            while (thisdrug > 0)
                drugfile >> thisdrug;
            drugfile >> thisdrug;              // and get next drug record
        }
}
```

Finally, to test if the patient is currently taking any of the contraindicated drugs now in "`temp.txt`", the function `CurrentlyTaking()` must read the drugs in "`temp.txt`" and compare them one by one against the new drug. Each time this function is called, the "`temp.txt`" file must be opened, read, and closed to prepare for the next call (Listing 8.8).

Listing 8.8

```
// CurrentlyTaking()  Test if newdrug is in the file "temp.txt"
// IN: contradrug is a drug the patient should not take.
int CurrentlyTaking (int contradrug)
{  int currently_taking, found = 0;
   ifstream fin ("temp.txt", ios::in);
   while (fin >> currently_taking && !found)
       if (currently_taking == contradrug)
           found = 1;
   fin.close();          // close so file might be reopened in a subsequent call
   return (found);
}
```

8.8 Summary

KEY TERMS   Quite a few new terms were introduced in this chapter;

1. *oracle testing*—the use of a re-usable file with test input during program development and debugging. The file contains a set of input that demonstrates and tests, all important aspects of the program.

2. *file variable*—a disk file used in a program must first be associated with a specific file variable in the **open()** command. Subsequent references to the disk file are via this file variable.

3. *stream*—a flow of textual information where lines are expected to end with Return keystrokes and numbers are expected to be separated with white spaces. The keyboard (read-only) and the screen (write-only) are special open-ended stream files.

4. *insertion, extraction operators*—the << is the insertion operator and is used with a stream file variable to request an output operation. The >> is the extraction operator and is used with a stream file variable to request an input operation.

5. *database*—a file or set of files that contains a collection of related records of information of long-term value and is read and written by a collection of related programs.

6. *record*—a single set of related data within a database file. This is often a single line in a stream file.

7. *buffer*—an intermediate storage location for file data usually within the operating system memory space used to reduce physical disk accesses.

8. *standard input, standard output, standard error streams*—file names associated with the default file variables cin, cout, and cerr. Unless overridden by redirection, they correspond to the keyboard, display, and display files respectively.

9. *class*—a term barely introduced in this chapter with much more to be learned. At this point, we understand that a class is a much more expressive way to describe some item in nature. A class instance may contain not only a set of variables, but a collection of related functions used to perform operations on those variables. The classes introduced in this chapter are `ifstream` and `ofstream`. The file variables `cin`, `cout`, and `cerr` are instances of these classes.

10. *member function*—a function that belongs to a class and is used to operate on the variables of a class instance. Member functions are invoked using the class instance name and a dot preceding the function name.

CONCEPTS   To reference disk files within a program, the **`<fstream.h>`** header must first be included at the top of the program to bring in the definitions and interface information necessary for the stream classes and member functions. Then, a file variable must be declared for each disk file. Next, the file must be opened with the `open()` member function. For input files, this function or command requests the operating system to locate the file on disk and prepare it for reading. For output files, any existing file is purged to prepare for new data. If an output file does not yet exist, one is created. The operations of file variable declaration and file opening can be combined into a single shorthand declaration statement.

Input and output from files are accomplished using the extraction `>>` and insertion `<<` operators with the appropriate file variable, just as we are accustomed to using with `cin` and `cout`. An input or extraction operation will fail and assign a false or 0 to the file variable if (a) the end of the file (EOF) is reached or (b) a character other than white space is encountered which cannot logically be a part of the intended destination variable.

During program execution, the operating system may use system buffers as intermediate holding areas for disk input or output to reduce the number of physical disk accesses necessary. When a program terminates, any open files are automatically closed, causing any associated output buffers to be flushed out to the disk file. Files can be manually closed with the `close()` member function. If a program needs to read data just written to a disk file, a `close()` function must be called to ensure the output buffer is first flushed.

The formatting of output can be controlled to a certain extent with three member functions. The `width()` member function allows the minimum number of columns to be specified for the next numeric value. If the numeric value actually requires more columns than the program has specified using the `width()` function, the request will be overridden. Any unused columns are filled with the default fill character, which is usually the space. The default fill character can be specified, however, with the `fill()` member function. The `precision()` function allows the number of significant digits of all subsequent numeric values to be specified.

A couple of important hints were presented. First, remember to use filenames with appropriately descriptive names and extensions. Avoid the use of extensions that are normally associated with other types of files. Second, be careful when including the full path of a filename in an `open()` or shorthand declaration-and-open call under DOS or Windows. Since C++ interprets the backslash character differently than DOS and Windows, the actual filename passed by C++ may be different than expected. The solution is to use a double backslash for each backslash. This protects the slash and warns C++ that it is not part of a control character.

Table 8.2 Example segments

`#include <fstream.h>`	Program will be utilizing file I/O.
`ofstream thisfile;`	`thisfile` is a file stream variable.
`thisfile.open ("a:data.txt");`	The disk file `"a:data.txt"` is opened to (used with) `thisfile`.
`ifstream input ("text.txt", ios:in);`	`input` is a file stream variable opened to the disk file `"text.txt"`.
`input.close();`	The disk file opened to `input` is closed.
`thisfile.precision(5);`	The next value output using `thisfile` will be expressed with 5 significant digits of precision.
`input.open ("a:\\progs\\text");`	The disk file `"a:\progs\text"` is opened to `input`. Note the use of the double backslash in a literal.

8.9 Exercises

8.9.a Short-answer questions

1. Suggest an appropriate filename and extension for the following files:
   a. a file to hold student grades for an entire term of a class
   b. a permanent file to hold student addresses
   c. a temporary file to hold a letter until it is printed
   d. a file to be continually updated to hold account balances
2. Disk files with extension `.DAT` typically hold what type of data?
3. Disk files which hold executable programs are typically labeled with what three-letter extension?
4. Disk files with extension `.DSW` typically hold what type of data?
5. What variable is used by C++ to keep track of the state of the file during program execution?
6. What term or jargon is used in C++ for a flow of information where lines are expected to end with Return keystrokes and numbers are expected to be separated with white spaces?
7. What symbol is used for the insertion operator? The extraction operator?
8. Briefly explain how the results of an input or extraction operation can be tested for success or failure.
9. The _____ control function can be used to change the default number of significant digits displayed during output with the insertion operator.

10. During a program execution, the operating system may use _____ as intermediate holding areas for disk input or output to reduce the number of physical disk accesses necessary.

11. While a variable might represent some state or value of an item in nature, a _____ might be used to represent a state *and all the operations, activities, and uses* associated with that item in nature.

12. Assume a program has been written to input records from a payroll file and calculate paychecks. Each record consists of an employee ID, the number of hours worked, and the current hourly rate. The program is designed to detect illogical values in the last two values of each record. Suggest a good oracle file for testing this program with enough valid and invalid records to completely exercise the program.

13. Give a shorthand file variable declaration and opening statement for the disk file `"b:\accounts\payroll.dat"`.

14. Declare appropriate variables and give the input or extraction statement(s) that could be used to read one record from the file described in questions 12 and 13.

15. Declare an appropriate file variable and give the `open()` function call that might be used to create the disk file of question 13.

16. Consider the following input or extraction statement:

```
int a, b;
if (!(cin >> a >> b)) cout << " error! ";
```

Describe two specific situations where this statement would output the `error` message.

17. Give the formatting function calls that could be used to output the next numeric value in ten columns with five significant digits using `cout`.

18. Describe the output that would occur as a result of the following statements:
    a. `int x = 55;   cout.precision(6);   cout << x << endl;`
    b. `int x = 666;   cout.precision(2);   cout << x << endl;`
    c. `float y = 876.54321;   cout.precision(4);   cout << y << endl;`
    d. `float y = 0.00000876;   cout.precision(4);   cout << y << endl;`
    e. `float y = 1234500000.0;   cout.precision(3);   cout << y << endl;`

19. Describe the output that would occur as a result of the following statements:
    a. `int x = 7777;   cout.width(3);   cout << x << endl;`
    b. `int x = 7777;   cout.width(8);   cout << x << endl;`
    c. `float y = 876.54321;   cout.width(8);   cout << y << endl;`
    d. `float y = 123.4567;   cout.precision(4);   cout.width(4);   cout <<y << endl;`
    e. `int x = 55;   cout.fill('.');   cout.width(10);   cout << x << endl;`

20. Briefly describe the purpose of including the `<fstream.h>` header in a program referencing external files.

8.9.b Projects

1. Write the program described in short answer question 12.
2. Use the DOS edit program, the Windows notepad program, or the C++ editor to create a text file containing a personal letter. Write a C++ program to use this file as input. The program should output a summary table containing the count of each of the following punctuation marks: exclamation point, comma, colon, semicolon, question mark, and period.
3. Refer to the letter file described in project 2. Write a program which could be used as a primitive spelling checker. The program should output a warning message if the letter contains a violation of the following rule:

   ```
   'i' before 'e' except after 'c'
   ```

4. Write a program to input the characters of a text file (such as the personal letter file of project 2) and output the characters to a newly created file with all lower-case letters converted to uppercase.
5. Refer to the data file described in short answer question 12. Write a program to read this data file and create a new output file with just the records of employees who worked overtime—more than 40 hours.
6. Write a program to input the characters of a text file (such as the personal letter file of project 2) and output a count of the number of times the word the is found.
7. Refer again to the problem described in short answer question 12. Modify the problem so that the input file records may exist in one of two different formats. Regular employees have records in the form described in question 12, whereas management employees have records where the ID is a four-character code word. Write a program that could still process this file and produce adequate paycheck information. Remember, these records are *randomly intermixed* throughout the input file. For example:

   ```
   122     5.62    35
   DONW    12.95   43
   7326    6.25    44
   876     4.95    21
   PHIL    15.25   46
   ...
   ```

8. The example project in this chapter implicitly assumed that the patient entered by the pharmacist would be found in the "patients.txt" file. It also assumed that the drug entered would be found in the "drugs.txt" database file. Modify this project to make it more robust and user-friendly. Detect when a patient is not found in the patient database or when a drug is not found in the drug database. Issue an appropriate warning to the user if either situation occurs.
9. **Creative Challenge:** All program examples and demonstrations to this point have processed input records in the order in which they were read. For example, consider the programming problem described in short answer question 12. It is a

straightforward program that simply contains a loop to read a record, perform a calculation, and output a result. When all records have been processed (EOF is reached), the program terminates. Consider now a more complex problem. Write a program to read this data file and create a new output file with the same records or information, *but sorted in numeric order by employee ID*. In other words, the first record in the new file should be the employee in the original file with the lowest ID number. For this problem, you may assume the input file contains fewer than ten employee records. Hint: One approach involves repeatedly reading the same file.

10. **Creative Challenge:** Refer to the example given in Listing 8.4. In this problem, the output is to be formatted to line up appropriately in columns. Suppose the output is to line up by decimal point, as is frequently done in math tables. Rewrite the program of Listing 8.4 so that the output is formatted with each value rounded to have exactly one digit to the right of the decimal point. For the given example data file, the output should appear as the following:

```
value              square root
    25.0               5.0
    16.5               4.1
    18.4               4.3
   199.2              14.1
   234.6              15.3
123400.0             351.4
```

11. **Creative Challenge:** So far, the variable type you have in your repertoire for handling textual information is **char**. Often, however, programs are needed to manipulate textual information at a much higher level. Write a program that allows the user to enter a list of names (first name, followed by a space, followed by last name). The program should output the list with the names in formal order (last name, followed by a comma and a space, followed by first name).

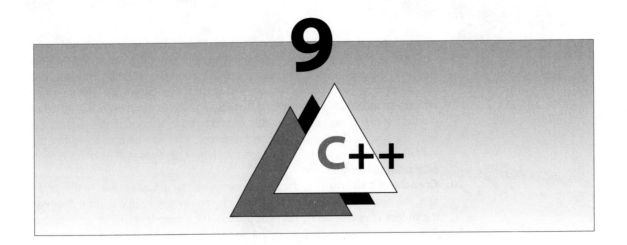

Strings and the string Class

Up to this point, we have dealt primarily with numeric data. Programming examples have used literal strings within output statements, but no methods have been introduced to efficiently input and manipulate textual data (other than single characters). As you can imagine, applications that need this capability are very common. How would you write a basic word-processing program? How would you allow a user to input an individual's name? In this chapter, we learn some basic string handling capabilities.

To the Instructor: The `string` class is a fairly recent standard and not all schools will have program development environments to support it. If you choose to teach string handling using character arrays, you may skip this chapter. Character arrays are introduced in the next chapter.

9.1 Strings and string declarations

As you remember, we have defined *literals* to be fixed textual data placed within a set of quotes. More appropriately, we might have used the term *string* literal. Literals have been quite handy in placing annotation messages within output such as:

```
cout << " the answer is: " << ans << endl;
```

You have also used literals when declaring or opening file variables as in:

```
ofstream outfile ("a:somefile.dat", ios::out);
```

As yet, however, there has been no method of manipulating textual information within a program, except as single characters. Take another look at Creative Challenge project 11 at the end of the previous chapter. In this program, the user is to enter a list of names, one name per line, with the first name first. The program is to output this same list, but with the names in formal order: last name first. As you may have discovered, this is a bulky and somewhat complex problem when this program is attempted using simple **char** variables. Fortunately, there is a much simpler method of handling textual data.

KEY TERM
string

First, you need to learn a broader term for textual data (which encompasses literals): A *string* is simply a representation of textual data. A sentence can be a string, a single word can be a string, even a single character. When a string is represented as a specific sequence of characters (enclosed in quotes) within a program, it is called a literal. You might think of a literal as a kind of string constant. Just as there are numeric variables, however, there can also be string variables. Thus, strings can be input into variables, manipulated with a variety of operations, and output from variables. There are many ways of manipulating strings in C++. We will examine one very useful method which uses the **string** data type.

9.1.a Standards for strings

The **string** is a new data type to be added to the types you already use such as **float**, **int**, **char**, and so on. The **string** is a fairly new data type standard in the C++ language, however. Most older program development environments (PDEs) provided slightly different syntax for strings, but with the adoption of a standard, programming is becoming much more portable. Recent or current versions of the most common C++ systems support this standard. That does not mean that, if you are using an older C++ PDE, some type of string variables will not be supported. You may just need to learn a slightly different syntax and semantics, and your programs may not be as portable as you would wish. We'll proceed on the assumption that your PDE is sufficiently up-to-date to support the current standard.

In spite of the C++ standard, there are still some minor differences between PDEs as to how one gains access to the **string** type. With some systems, you need to include an additional header file at the top of your file:

```
#include <iostream.h>
#include <string>
```

standard form

CONCEPT
two header file
forms

This additional header provides the prototypes and access to this new data type. Notice that this header is different from what you are used to: *There is no* .h *extension*. Do not mistakenly add the .h to the string header file—such a file exists in most C++ systems but has a very different purpose and would cause many confusing error messages! Newer editions of header files and newer standards follow this practice of having no extension on a system header file.

With Microsoft Visual C++, you will need to change the `iostream` header file to a newer edition as well as include the `string` header. Also, you will need to add one more line:

```
#include <iostream>
#include <string>
using namespace std;
```

Notice that neither header file has an `.h` *extension.* The last line is required to have the PDE recognize `string` as a standard data type name. (Further explanations of `namespaces` are left for future courses.) If any other stream or I/O header files are needed (such as `fstream`), they must also use the newer editions.

Your instructor will indicate which of the two approaches you should use or if another variation is required for your particular PDE.

9.1.b   String declarations and assignment

Variables are declared with the data type **string**:

string *variable, variable, ... ;*   **Syntax form**

You need to be careful here to differentiate between two uses of the word *string*. As you learned previously, we refer to a sequence of characters as a string. You have just learned that the other use is as a variable type. We'll use computer-font **string** to indicate the variable type and standard-font string to indicate a sequence of characters. This multiple use of the word is traditional, and we are stuck with it if we want to converse with other programmers. This is similar to referring to an integer as a whole number and an **int** as a variable that can hold a whole number. A **string** variable can hold a string.

Stop to think for a moment: This is the first variable type you have seen that is associated with a sequence of things as opposed to a single thing. We will look at more of these kinds of variables in the future.

A **string** variable can be used anywhere a literal is appropriate. Also, **string** variables can be initialized with literals as part of a declaration just as **int** or **float** variables can be initialized when declared. For example:

```
string word1, word2 = "hello", word3 = "goodbye" ;
```

Similarly, **string** variables can be assigned from other **string** variables or from literals just as you would expect. For example:

```
word1 = "Fred Smith";
word2 = word3;
```

CONCEPT

char vs. string
variables

Remember, **string** variables are not the same as **char** variables. The latter can hold or represent only a single character, while a **string** represents a sequence of zero or more characters. Character constants are represented with single quotes; string constants or literals are represented *within double quotes*. Remember that if a **float** value or variable is assigned to an **int** variable (or vice versa), there is an automatic conversion that occurs. If a **char** variable or character constant is assigned to a **string**, the character is converted to a string. However, there is no definition for automatic conversion from a **string** to a **char** variable. Carefully consider the following example:

```
string s;       // s is a variable for strings
char c;         // c is a variable for a single character
s = "%";        // s is assigned the string containing a percent
c = '%';        // c is assigned the percent character
```

A literal may contain only a single character, *but it is still a string*.

```
s = '%';        // OK, character is converted to a string
c = "%"         // ILLEGAL
s = c;          // OK, character is converted to a string
c = s;          // ILLEGAL
```

It should be obvious why a long literal may not be assigned to a **char** variable, but you may need to memorize that a literal or string of only one character may not be assigned to a **char** variable.

Another point of confusion for some students is the difference between a number and a literal containing the digit characters of that number. Consider the following:

```
string text = "123.45";
float number = 123.45;
```

These are actually very different because the internal representation of **float** and **string** variables is different. The variable number contains the numeric representation of this value. The variable text actually contains the sequence of digit characters. Again, there are ways of calling functions to convert a **float** to a **string** and vice versa. *There is, however, no automatic or default conversion:*

```
number = text;
text = number;
```

WRONG WAY!

The upshot of all this is that **string** variables and literals are a separate representation of data and are not automatically compatible with the other data types you have learned. This is not really a restriction; the more data types we have, the more different kinds of data we can represent. If you need to represent real numbers and need the kinds of operations one performs on real numbers, just choose **float** in the first place.

A **string** variable may be assigned the null or empty string. The *null string* is just a string containing no characters. When a **string** variable is declared, this is the default initialization:

```
string word = "hello";     // word contains hello
string none;               // none contains the null string
word = "";                 // word now contains the null string
```

The null string is not the same as a string containing only blanks. Remember, a blank is not "nothing"; it is a specific character. It just doesn't use any ink when printed! For example, consider the following:

```
string word = "hello", spaces = "          ", name = "fred";
cout << word << spaces << name;
```

The output produced by this segment contains the blanks in the string `spaces` between the strings of `word` and `name`:

```
hello          fred
```

9.2 I/O with `string` variables

As you noticed in the preceding paragraph, the insertion << operator can be used with **string** variables just as it is with the **float**, **int**, and **char** variable types you have learned. The extraction >> operator is also available. When a **string** variable is output, the system will use exactly as many columns as are required for the text within the string. For example:

```
string phrase = "a man and", object = "his dog.";
cout << phrase << object << endl;
```

This code outputs these two strings immediately adjacent to each other to produce the following:

```
a man andhis dog.
```

Naturally, if the first **string** variable contained a blank at the end of the text, it would read more clearly:

```
string phrase = "a man and ", object = "his dog.";
cout << phrase << object << endl;
```

Table 9.1 **Examples of** `string` **variable input** (`<R>` **represents return**)

User Inputs	word1	word2	Comments
`hello my friend<R>`	`hello`	`my`	`friend` has not yet been read.
`hello <R>` `Jack<R>`	`hello`	`Jack`	Return is just a white space.
`constant: 123.456`	`constant:`	`123.456`	word2 contains the digits, not the numeric value of `123.456`.
`( Jack Smith )`	`(`	`Jack`	`Smith )` is still in the input buffer.
`(Jack Smith)`	`(Jack`	`Smith)`	Note: There is no space before or after the parentheses.
`hello <R><R><R>` `fred`	`hello`	`fred`	several white spaces are the same as one.

CONCEPT

I/O with `string` **variables**

When **string** variables are input using the extraction >> operator, the next sequence of keyboard characters *up to the next white space* is placed within the variable. Remember, a white space is any nonprinting character such as the space or Return. Another way to look at this is *the next word* is placed into the variable. For example, consider the following code fragment and Table 9.1 showing the values that would be assigned to these two variables for a variety of user inputs.

```
string word1, word2;
cin >> word1 >> word2;
```

Because the extraction >> operator only inputs text for a **string** variable up to the next white space, there can be a significant difference between assigning a **string** variable with a literal or inputting the text via the keyboard. The following assigns an entire name to the **string** variable:

```
string name;
name = "Fred J. Smith";
```

But an input statement with the user keying the name from the keyboard would only read the first name into the variable:

```
cin >> name; // if user types Fred J. Smith, 'name' receives Fred
```

To allow a user to input a full name (first and last) and have it stored into a single **string** variable, three variables could be used in the input statement:

```
string name, mi, lastname;
cin >> name   >> mi >> lastname;    // name contains "Fred"
              //mi contains "J." and lastname contains "Smith"
```

CONCEPT

strings and white-space characters

string variables and literals may contain sequences with any character from the keyboard, including the alphabetical characters, the digits, symbols, the space, and even the Return and Function keys (Fn). (The Control, Alt, and Shift keys are actually character modifiers and not special characters in themselves.) The keys used for editing — such as Backspace, Home, and Delete — are usually captured and interpreted by the operating system and are not normally passed on to a C++ user program.

We now have enough tools to go back to Creative Challenge problem 11 of the previous chapter and develop a fairly simple solution. We'll use the Microsoft Visual C++ access method. Consider Listing 9.1.

Listing 9.1

```
// names.cpp   Changes a list of names from <last-name-last> to
// <last-name-first> format.
// ASSUMPTION: The disk file "names.txt" contains a list of names in last-
// name-last order. All names are separated with white spaces. The last and
// first name are separated by white spaces.

#include <iostream>
#include <fstream>
#include <string>
using namespace std;

void main()
{   ifstream infile ("names.txt", ios::in);
    string firstname, lastname;

    while (infile >> firstname >> lastname)
        cout << lastname << ", " << firstname << endl;
}
```

Not much of a challenge at all when using **string** variables! Notice that the insertion << operator statement of Listing 9.1 contains a literal with a comma and a blank. Without that blank, the first name would immediately follow the comma.

If you wish to have an entire line of text input to a **string** variable regardless of white spaces or blanks, there is a built-in function called getline(). The first argument is either cin or a file stream variable and the second argument is the **string** to be filled.

```
string name;
getline (cin, name);          // an entire line is input to name
```

This function returns a false if the end of a file is reached (just as the >> extraction operator) and can be used in a `while` loop to process all lines in a file:

```
while (getline(infile, line))
    cout << "line read: " << line << endl;
```

9.3 `string` operations

CONCEPT
concatenation of strings

A **string** variable may be concatenated with another string using the + operator. Concatenation means that the two strings are joined or pasted together. As a result, a new string is formed from the first string operand followed by the second string operand. For example:

```
string first = "Fred",  last = " Smith", name;
name = first + last;
cout << name << endl;           // outputs "Fred Smith"
```

Naturally, a literal may be concatenated onto the end of a **string** variable, or vice versa:

```
string first = "Fred", name;
name = first + " Smith";
cout << name << endl;           // outputs "Fred Smith"
name = "Smith, " + first;
cout << name << endl;           // outputs "Smith, Fred"
```

You cannot concatenate two literals into a **string**:

```
string name;
name = "Fred" + "Smith";
```

WRONG WAY!

Be careful of this important rule. These concatenation operations can be nested or grouped as long as you ensure at least one side of the + concatenation is always a **string** variable. The reason for this restriction will become clear in Chapter 12. For example:

```
string word1 = "hello", word2 = " good ", word3 = " friend", line;
line = (word1 + " my") + ("good" + word3);

cout << line << endl;       // output is "hello my good friend"
```

The shorthand notation operator += may also be used:

```
name += ", DDS";// same as: name = name + ", DDS";
```

This code results in the string , DDS being appended onto the end of the string in name.

Now, you might be wondering why C++ is not confused by the use of the + operator, which we previously thought was associated only with arithmetic plus operations. The reason this operator can also be used for **string** concatenation is fundamental to the C++ language. We will spend nearly a whole chapter on this concept (Chapter 12), but think about the following until we get there: Basically, the **+** is just a symbol. In C++, a function can be called using a name *or an operator symbol*! By looking at the operator symbol and the types on the left and right sides of the symbol, the system knows which function to call. When you use the **+** operator between two **string** variables (or a **string** variable and a literal), the system calls the concatenation function. A programmer can add to or change the meaning of the existing operator symbol functions! Now, that must surely generate a number of questions, but at least you have a glimpse of the fact that a lot of interesting concepts are yet to come.

9.4 Functions for string

CONCEPT

class member
notation

There are a number of useful functions available for dealing with **string** variables. These particular functions are invoked *using the class notation* you were introduced to at the end of the previous chapter. You have probably guessed that **string** is not a simple variable type like **int** or **float**, but a *class* more like **ofstream** or **ifstream**. Just like the precision() function, the name of the class instance (or **string** variable name) and a dot are added to the front of a function call.

The current length of a **string** variable can be determined using the length() function. There are no arguments. For example:

```
string name = "Fred Smith";
int size;
size = name.length();
cout << " length of name is: " << size;// outputs 10
```

Another available function is max_size(). Again, there are no arguments. This function returns the maximum length of a string that can be input or assigned to a string variable on your particular system. This is always a very large number. (Using Microsoft Visual C++, one could save this entire book in a single **string** variable.)

The last function we will look at in this chapter is quite useful. The find() is used to determine if a string variable contains a particular word or other subsequence of characters. There are a number of ways to use it; we will look at one simple use in this chapter. In this simple use, the find() function returns an integer less than max_size() if the subsequence is found and an integer greater than max_size() if not.

There are two arguments. The first is the string or literal representing the subsequence and the second is just 0. This is best illustrated by example. Suppose we wish to know if the name Pam is anywhere to be found in an input line:

```
string line;
getline(cin, line);                      // input an entire line
if (line.find("Pam", 0) < line.max_size())
    cout << "The name was found!" << endl;
```

Suppose the following line is entered:

```
The angry nanny sent Pam to bed without dinner.
```

Then the preceding program fragment would output

```
The name was found!
```

since the string Pam is in the line. Now, suppose, the line reads:

```
The angry nanny sent Pamela to bed without dinner.
```

The string `Pam` is still found since the `find()` function doesn't look for an independent word—just the sequence of characters P, a, and m.

Let's look at a more complete example of these **string** functions. Suppose you are a CIA operative and wish to quickly examine a large document in a disk file to see if the word `"nuclear"` or phrase `"atomic energy"` is ever mentioned. One approach is to write a program to read each line of the file and use the `find()` function to check for each string in turn (Listing 9.2).

Listing 9.2

```cpp
// CheckFor.cpp Checks a disk file for occurrences of "nuclear" or "atomic energy"
// ASSUMPTION: The disk file contains a text.
#include <iostream>
#include <fstream>
#include <string>
using namespace std;

const string word = "nuclear";
const string phrase = "atomic energy";

void main( )
{   string line, filename;
    ifstream infile;
    cout << "enter a filename: ";
    cin >> filename;
    infile.open(filename);
    while (getline(infile, line))
    {    if (line.find(word, 0) < line.max_size())
            cout << "WORD FOUND!" << endl;
        else if (line.find(phrase, 0) < line.max_size())
            cout << "PHRASE FOUND!" << endl;
    }
    cout << "file completely examined" << endl;
}
```

9.5 `String` comparisons

In addition to the five operation functions just described, **string** variables and literals can be compared using the relational operators (==, !=, <, >, <=, >=). The first two operators make an exact comparison and are easy to understand: Two strings are equal if they contain exact copies. To be exact copies, both strings must contain the same characters in the same case. The last four operators make a relative comparison of two strings: One string is less than the other if it comes *alphabetically before* the other. In other words, to determine if one string is less than another, ask yourself if it would come before the second string in a dictionary or phone book. If two strings start out the same but one is longer, the shorter string is alphabetically before the longer. Caution: All uppercase letters are alphabetically prior to any lowercase letters. In other words, Zeek is alphabetically prior to adam.

```
if (thisword < "computer") ...
if (thisword >= thatword) ...
```

CONCEPT

literals may not be compared

While the relational operators may be used to compare two **string** variables or a **string** variable with a literal, they should not be used to compare two literals for alphabetical ordering. (Actually, I'm not quite sure why it would even be useful to do this.) Nevertheless, if you did attempt this, you would find the relational comparison of two literals has a very different meaning, as you will learn in the next chapter. You will not necessarily get an error message, but you won't get the results you expect:

```
if ( "hello" < "goodbye" ) ...
```

WRONG WAY!

Let's take a look at an interesting example of **string** variable comparisons. Listing 9.3 represents a complete program to compare any two words entered by the user:

Listing 9.3

```cpp
// compare.cpp   Compare two words entered by the user
#include <iostream>
#include <string>
using namespace std;

void main()
{   string firstword, secondword;

    cout << "enter two words: ";
    cin >> firstword >> secondword;
    if (firstword==secondword)
        cout << "words are exactly equal" << endl;
    else if (firstword < secondword)
        cout << "first word is alphabetically less" << endl;
```

```
        else cout << "second word is alphabetically less" << endl;
}
```

The comparison of two **string** variables is relatively straightforward if the associated string values contain only letters. What if a string contains digits or symbols or, even worse, the nonprinting characters such as the space, Return, or control characters? The comparisons are still well defined. C++ looks for the *first position in the two strings to contain different characters*. The first string is less than the second if its character in that position has an ASCII code less than the corresponding character in the same position in the other string. This is sometimes confusing if the strings contain digits. Consider the comparison of the two following strings (not integers):

```
string num1 = "  9999", num2 = "123";
if (num1 < num2)
    cout << num1 << " is less than " << num2 << endl;
```

Here, the first string *is less than* the second string since it begins with a blank (which is less than the character 1). In other words, a string is a sequence of characters (letters, punctuation, digits, etc.), and C++ makes no attempt to determine what these characters represent in nature. As the programmer, that is your job.

9.6 Parameter passing with strings

string variables may be used as parameters to functions just as you have used **int**, **float**, or any previously learned variable type. Again, if the parameter may be changed by a function, the & operator is appended to the string declaration. Take a look at the following simple function which has two string parameters (Listing 9.4). It swaps these two strings if they are not in alphabetical order and returns the *shorter* of the two.

Listing 9.4

```
// Order()   Accepts two strings and swaps them if not in order
// ASSUMPTION: Both string parameters have been assigned by the
// caller.  Returns the shorter of the two.
string Order (string& first, string& second)
{   string temp;
    if (first >= second)
    {   temp = first;                   // swap if not in order
        first = second;
        second = first;
    }
    if (first.length() < second.length()
        return first;
    else return second;                 // return shorter
}
```

9.7 Example project

Consider now a more significant programming example using **string** variables. A common example of string processing is in the area of spelling checkers—programs which determine if a word is correctly spelled. This, of course, would be fairly difficult (at least in English) through the use of spelling rules. A more straightforward solution simply uses the same method you or I might use: Look up the word in question in a dictionary and assume if it is found that it must be correctly spelled. In Listing 9.2, a program was presented which simply compared two words entered by the user. In Listing 9.5, this concept is expanded to compare a word entered by the user with the words of an entire file (representing a dictionary). If the word is not found in the dictionary file, the user is informed the word is spelled incorrectly.

As usual, the main program is easy to write: The approach of this program is to prompt the user to enter a word to be checked. A function is then called to check whether this word has a match in the disk file `"a:dict.txt"`.

Listing 9.5

```
// spelchk.cpp   Check the spelling of a word entered by
// the user against the file "a:dict.txt" to verify spelling.
#include <iostream>
#include <fstream>
#include <string>
using namespace std;

void main ()
{   ifstream infile ("a:dict.txt", ios::in);// dict. file variable
    string user_word;                       // word in question

    cout << "Enter word to be checked (lower case): ";
    cin >> user_word;
    if (InDictionary(infile, user_word))    // true if in dictionary
        cout << "Spelling is correct!" << endl;
    else cout << "Incorrect spelling!" << endl;
}
```

All we now need is the `InDictionary()` function. This function simply reads the words from the disk file one at a time and makes a comparison with the user's word. There are three possible reasons to stop reading words from the disk file (and making comparisons): (a) a match is found, (b) the disk file is exhausted (end of file is reached), and (c) the search proceeds past where the user word would have been found in the alphabetized dictionary. We will use a simple **int** variable as a flag indicating if any of these three conditions has been reached (Listing 9.6).

Listing 9.6

```
// InDictionary()  Accept an istream file var. for a disk file
// and a string var. for a word. Return true if the word is
// found in the dictionary disk file (else false).
// ASSUMPTION: file has already been opened
// IN: infile is file variable to an alphabetized lowercase dictionary
// IN:user_word is a lowercase word.

int InDictionary (ifstream& infile, string user_word)
{   int done = 0;                                // loop completion flag
    int found = 0;                               // word-found flag
    string dict_word;                            // var for dictionary words
    while (!done)
    {   if (infile >> dict_word)                 // get next dict. word...
        {   if (user_word == dict_word)          // do words match?
            {   done = 1;
                found = 1;
            }
            else if (user_word < dict_word)
                done = 1;                         // searched too far.
        }
        else
            done = 1;                             // end of file.
    }
    return (found);
}
```

CONCEPT

using a single loop control variable

The multiple conditions for ending the **while** loop are expressed in one simple integer variable done. Each of the three possible situations that can end the loop was considered in separate **if** statements to set done. Some programmers give in to the temptation to combine several conditions with Boolean operators. The problems this can cause have been previously examined.

Notice that the disk file "a:dict.txt" was opened in the main program, even though it was only accessed within the InDictionary() function. The file variable infile was passed to the function for this purpose. Why not simply declare and open the file within the function itself? In other words, why not do something similar to the following?

```
int InDictionary (string user_word)
{   ifstream infile ("a:dict.txt", ios::in);
    ...
}
void main()
{   ...
    if (InDictionary(user_word))
    ...
}
```

This change would certainly work. In addition, the interface to the function has one less parameter and is less prone to error. The question is more one of *style*. The name of the disk file is globally important. A reader should not need to hunt down through embedded functions to determine the disk filename. By placing the file variable declaration at the top of the main program, this global piece of information is readily accessible. Second, the function would not be as self-contained if it relied on implied information not expressly stated in the parameter list. Any changes to the disk filename would require changes to the function.

CONCEPT

using string
constants

There is an even better solution that combines the best of both approaches. By placing a declaration of a global constant **string** above the main program, the name of the disk file is readily accessible, but the file variable does not need to be declared prior to the function call. Because the filename is passed as a string, the function remains self-contained and general.

```
const string filename = "a:dict.txt";

int InDictionary (string filename, string user_word)
{   ifstream infile (filename, ios::in);
    ...
}
void main()
{   ...
    if (InDictionary (filename, user_word))
    ...
}
```

9.8 Summary

KEY TERMS   Only a couple of new terms were introduced in this chapter:

1. *string*—a representation of textual data (a literal is a constant string).

2. *null string*—a string containing no characters.

CONCEPTS   In this chapter, a new data class was introduced: the **string**. Access to this new data type varied somewhat between program development environments, but the use of **string** variables and the operations available are standard. The header file for string access does not have an .h extension.

Several important rules were presented concerning the use of **string** variables. A **string** variable may be initialized at declaration, just like **int** or **float** variables. Also, **string** variables may be passed as arguments to functions whenever literals are expected. When **string** variables are used as function parameters, they may match other **string** arguments or literals.

String variables may be input and output using the extraction >> and insertion << operators, just as other data types. On input, the extraction operator assigns keyboard characters up to the next white space. The library function getline() may be used to input an entire line into a **string** variable. Literals may be assigned to **string** variables.

String variables or a **string** variable and a literal may be concatenated using the + operator. *Do not attempt to concatenate two literals.* Strings containing numeric digits are not numbers.

The length of a **string** may be determined using the length() function. This function is called using the class member notation: the variable followed by a dot and the function name. The maximum length of a string variable can be determined with max_size(). Whether or not a string variable contains a particular substring or sequence can be tested with the find() function.

Any of the six relational comparison operators may be used to compare two strings or a string with a literal. Strings are ordered alphabetically, just as in a dictionary or phone book. C++ looks for the first position in the two strings to contain different characters. The first string is less than the second if its character in that position has an ASCII code less than the corresponding character in the same position in the other string.

Several important hints or points to remember were presented. Two literals should not be compared for alphabetical ordering using relational operators. This may not produce an error message, but it represents something far different than the comparison of **string** variables.

String variables are not the same as **char** variables. The latter can hold or represent only a single character, while a **string** represents a sequence of characters (even if that sequence is only a single character long). Even if a string contains the digit characters of a number, it is still a string. There is no automatic conversion between **string** variables and **int** or **float** or **char** or any other data representation.

A sequence of any characters may be stored in a **string** variable, including the alphabetical letter characters, the digits, symbols, the space, and even the Return and Function keys (Fn).

It is often less prone to error to control a conditional expression (in a loop or if statement) using a single variable than it is to combine many subexpressions with Boolean operators. Each of the subexpressions are then examined in separate **if** statements.

Table 9.2 Example segments

`#include <string>`	Provides access to **string** variables.
`string word2 = "help";`	The declaration and initialization of a **string** variable.
`word2 = "thanks";`	Assignment of a string.
`if (word2 != "help")...`	The comparison of a **string** variable with a literal.
`cout << word2.length();`	The output of the length of the current string in word2.

9.9 Exercises

9.9.a Short-answer questions

1. The _____ variable type may be used to hold a sequence of values as opposed to a single value like **int** or **float**.
2. Show an = statement to assign the null string to **string** variable x.
3. The >> extraction operator reads a character sequence into a string variable until a _____ _____ is detected.
4. The `getline()` function reads a character sequence into a `string` variable until the end of a _____ is reached.
5. The operator that joins two strings to form a new longer string is called the _____ operator and is represented by the _____ symbol.
6. To test if a **string** variable contains a particular word, the _____ function can be used.
7. The `length()` function is called using class member notation, which is the name of the **string** followed by a _____ followed by the name of the function.
8. One **string** variable is less than a second if its character sequence would be found _____ the second in a dictionary or phone book.
9. Explain what must be true in order for two **string** variables to be considered equal.
10. Give the function that can be called to input an entire line into a `string` variable.
11. Indicate which of the following represent illegal initializations and indicate the nature of the problem:
    a. `string word = "        ";`
    b. `string word = "12345";`
    c. `string word = 12345;`
    d. `string word = 'x';`
    e. `string word = "x";`
12. What is the initial value of a **string** variable that is not initialized?
13. What header file must be included to use or access the **string** variable class?
14. What function will return the current length of a **string** variable?
15. What is the result of a concatenation operation that joins a string of 50 characters and a string of 45 characters?
16. What will be the result of the following code segment?

```
string a = "1234";
string b = "    2345";
if (a < b)
   cout << "yes";
else cout << "no";
```

17. Can a single character be assigned to a **string** variable?
18. Can a **string** variable be assigned to a **char** variable?
19. Indicate which of the following represent illegal operations and indicate the nature of the problem:
    a. a literal assigned to a **string** variable
    b. a number typed at the keyboard for input to a **string** variable
    c. use of a **string** variable as an argument to an `open()` call

20. Indicate whether the following expressions are true or false:

```
string word1="goodbye", word2="hello", word3;
```

a. `word1 <= word2`
b. `word2 != "Hello"`
c. `word3.length()`
d. `word2 > word1`

9.9.b Projects

1. Write a simple program to enter two words and have the program print these words in alphabetical order.
2. Word processing is a common computer application. Write a program to allow a user to perform a find/replace operation on a disk file. The user should be prompted to enter a *search* word and a *replacement* word. Create a new disk file for output. For each occurrence of the search word in the original file, substitute the replacement word in the new file.
3. Write a program to perform a password verification. The user should be prompted to enter a password using any keyboard characters except white spaces (blanks, tabs, Return, etc.). The case of letters should not be significant. The program should then output `verified` if the entry matches any of several passwords found in a separate disk file `"passwd.txt"`.
4. Suppose a text document `"letter.txt"` contains a number of requests to a subordinate. Write a program to make these requests more polite by inserting the word `please` in front of each occurrence of the action verbs `request`, `submit`, `ask`, and `instruct`.
5. Write a function `Insert()` that could be used to insert a string into a file. The function should have three parameters: the **string** variable containing the text to be inserted, a **string** variable containing the filename, and the integer word number after which the new text should be inserted. This function should insert the new text after the appropriate word into a new copy of the file. Test your function with a small driver main program.
6. The example program in Listing 9.6 allowed a user to enter a word and have the spelling checked. A more appropriate program would allow a user to specify a filename and have the program check all words in that file for correct spelling. Write and demonstrate such a program. Be sure to allow words to possibly be capitalized and perhaps end with punctuation marks.
7. Build a database text file for the World Wide Widgets Company containing four lines for each employee. These lines should contain the following information:

```
first line:    firstname lastname (two words)
second line:   job title (one word)
third line:    phone number (one word)
fourth line:   pay rate (a real number)
```

For example, here are a couple of possible employees:

```
Fred Smith
   clerk
   789-1234
   7.75
Janet Anderson
   supervisor
   789-2345
15.50
```

Write a program to prompt the user for an employee name and a number of hours worked. Search this database file and output (a) the appropriate title and phone number and (b) the calculated paycheck (number of hours worked times the pay rate).

8. The Example Project at the end of the previous chapter allowed a pharmacist to check a newly prescribed drug against currently prescribed medications for a patient and a drug database file to verify that no drug interactions are predicted. The database used two-digit codes to represent drugs. Modify this program so that the database and program use actual drug names.

9. **Creative Challenge:** The relational operators allow a simple comparison between two strings. Suppose, however, that a file of ten different words needed to be examined and a new file created *with these words in alphabetical order.* Write and demonstrate such a program. Hint: One approach would make use of repeated passes through the file, each time finding and outputting just one word.

10. **Creative Challenge:** Write a program to read a text file and output a table of occurrences for each word in the file. This is not a trivial problem with what you know so far, so make whatever assumptions you need to regarding the number of possible different words in the file.

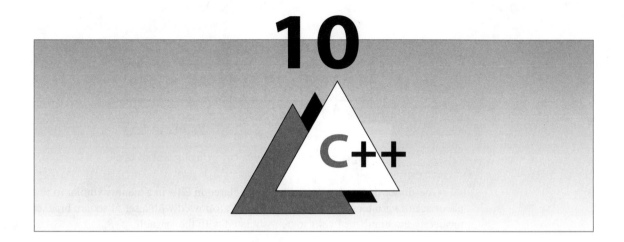

Simple Arrays

A simple variable is one that is associated with a single value or object. Each variable is associated with a name in a declaration statement. Unfortunately, some problems are clumsy or even quite difficult to solve using simple variables. For example, how would you write a program to sort a long list of values or names? In this chapter, you will learn that general-purpose programming languages such as C++ allow more than one value to be associated with a variable. Such a variable is called an array. The individual values of an array are stored in adjacent memory locations and are indexed just as one might index a table. Arrays are very common and are found in nearly all useful or meaningful programs.

10.1 Array declaration and referencing

An array variable might best be thought of as a kind of table. For example, consider the paper table of shirt costs for seven different styles, which might be found next to a cash register at a local clothing shop (Figure 10.1).

KEY TERM
dimension

A cashier who knows the style number of a particular shirt can quickly look up or find the cost by referring to the appropriate cell. Since there is only one index (the shirt style number), this is called "one-dimensional" table or array. (Tables can, of course, have more than one *dimension*. We'll return to that later.) Notice that the table begins with an index of 0 rather than with 1 as might be expected. One-dimensional arrays are very common. In fact, it is rare to find a meaningful program without at least one such array.

Shirt Cost Table

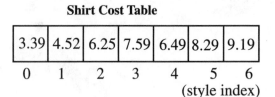

3.39	4.52	6.25	7.59	6.49	8.29	9.19
0	1	2	3	4	5	6

(style index)

Figure 10.1 A simple one-dimensional table

One-dimensional array variables are declared in C++ in a manner similar to simple or scalar variables. For arrays, the name is followed with a set of square brackets to specify the number of cells to be associated with the variable:

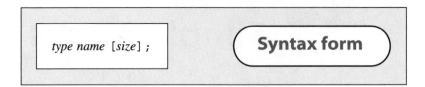

type name [*size*] ;

Syntax form

The array variable type can be any available data type such as **int**, **float**, **string**, or **char**. We will see later that C++ also allows the creation of new data types if the available types are not adequate for the needs of a program. In any case, the table of shirt costs might be declared as:

```
float shirt_cost [7];
```

CONCEPT

indexes start at 0

This declaration establishes an array variable `shirt_cost` with a total of seven different cells. Just as the table in Figure 10.1 has an index that begins with 0, all *C++ arrays have indexes that begin with 0*. All index values must be ordinal. At this point, the ordinal data types you are familiar with are **int** and **char** or any expression that results in an **int** or **char** value. If an array has *N* cells, the last cell for an array will always be numbered *N*–1. This is an important rule to remember and is the cause of many an error in a beginning student's program. Now, you might ask, "Why not start at 1?" It turns out that executable programs can be made slightly more efficient if indexes begin at 0. Some historical figure decided that the trade-off was worth the inconvenience to beginning programmers.

Within a program, a specific `shirt_cost` cell is referred to by following the array variable name with brackets containing the specific cell index. The following examples show some possible uses of this array in a program:

```
cin >> shirt_cost[0];          // input a cost into cell 0
sum += shirt_cost[4];          // add cell 4 into 'sum'
cout << shirt_cost[0]
     << shirt_cost[1];         // output the first two cells
shirt_cost[3] = 15.75;         // set cell 3 to 15.75
```

So, the first cell has index [0], the next cell has index [1], and so on. A good way to remember this is to refer to the index as the number of cells beyond the initial cell of the array. For example,

```
shirt_cost[4]
```

CONCEPT

array size

refers to the cell 4 beyond the initial cell of the array. Don't be confused: *The integer in brackets in the declaration of the array variable specifies the total number of cells in the array. The integer in brackets in an executable statement refers to a specific cell in that array.*

When using an array in an assignment, condition, input, or output statement, always add the brackets and index at the end of the variable name to indicate which cell of the array you are referencing. Normally, you will not use an array name in an assignment, condition, input, or output statement by itself without the brackets and index. For example, the following statements are not appropriate:

```
shirt_cost = 5.6;      // which cell??
cout << shirt_cost;    // which cell??
```

WAY!
WRONG

The index need not be an integer constant. It is often useful to use an integer variable or even a small integer expression. The only requirement is that whatever you place within the brackets evaluates to a valid ordinal index. The following are also legal references to the array. In this fragment, the costs associated with cell 0, cell 3, and cell 5 are added together:

```
int a=0, b=3, c=6;
sum = shirt_cost[a] + shirt_cost[b] + shirt_cost[c-1];
```

As mentioned earlier, any valid data type can be used for an array variable. In addition, more than one array may be specified in a single declaration line. Consider a program which needs to keep a table of correct test-question answers for a five-question true–false quiz and a table of the number of students who got a particular question correct:

```
char answer[5];
int number_right[5];
```

KEY TERM

parallel arrays

In this example, the character (T or F) in cell N of the answer array is the correct answer for a particular quiz question, provided the questions are numbered 0 to 4. The integer in cell N of the number_right array is the number of students who got this question correct. Since N relates to the same question in both arrays, we sometimes refer to these as *parallel arrays*. The correct answer to question 2 is T and 9 students answered correctly.

The actual quiz questions themselves might even be stored in a **string** array:

```
string question[5];
```

KEY TERM
subscripted
variable

In this array, `question` can hold 5 different strings. Another name for an array is a *subscripted variable*. We often refer to the index of an array variable cell as the *subscript*. For example, when verbally discussing program code, `answer[3]` may be referred to as "answer subscript 3" or an even more shortened form "answer sub 3."

10.2 Array initialization

If you recall, a simple variable can be initialized when declared. In addition, variables can be declared to be **const** or read-only. For example, let's return to the quiz information and initialize the arrays to hold the values indicated in Figure 10.2. We'll also initialize the `question` array. The `answer` and `question` arrays will be declared as **const** or read-only so that they cannot be inadvertently changed in the program:

```
const char answer[5] = { 'T', 'F', 'T', 'F', 'F' };
int summary[5] = { 10, 14, 9, 11, 13 };
string question[5] = { "Kennedy was a democrat", "Nixon was a
    democrat", "Carter was a democrat", "Bush was a democrat",
    "Ford was a democrat"};
```

In a like manner, any array variable can also be initialized in the declaration statement. The expanded syntax form is the following:

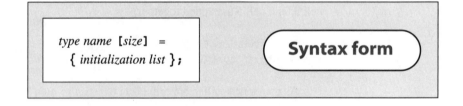

type name [*size*] =
  { *initialization list* };

Syntax form

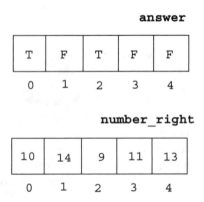

answer

T	F	T	F	F
0	1	2	3	4

number_right

10	14	9	11	13
0	1	2	3	4

Figure 10.2 Example of parallel arrays

The initialization list is a list of appropriate values separated by commas. Naturally, it would be an error to specify too many initialization values. If you do not initialize an array, the cells may contain arbitrary values (garbage) on some systems (until you make specific assignments). It is not required that an entire array be initialized. For example, if the number of right answers for the last two questions is not yet known (and will be determined later when the program is run), a shortened initialization list can be used. In the following example, only the first three cells are initialized. *The remaining cells default to an initial value of 0*:

```
int summary[5] = { 10, 14, 9 };
```

A common use of this concept is demonstrated in the following statement. Here, the first cell is specifically initialized to 0 and the remaining cells *default* to an initial value of 0. In other words, the entire array is initialized to 0.

```
int summary[5] = { 0 };                // initialize all cells to 0.
```

CONCEPT
omitting array size

If the array is fully initialized, the number of cells in the brackets can actually be omitted; C++ will infer the number of cells from the number of initialization values in the braces. This is not necessarily a good programming practice, however. First of all, it may force another reader to count the values in the initialization list. Second, it may lead to inadvertent mistakes that are hard to discover if the list is incorrectly typed. The use of this option is not encouraged. A basic form of good programming style is to "state explicitly what you intend."

10.3 Array processing with loops

Ask yourself how you would initialize a very large array, or how you would initialize an array at run time. Often, of course, the values of an array are not known when the program is written. Suppose there are two disk files. The file "key.txt" contains a list of the correct answers to a quiz. The file "students.txt" contains a list of student records or lines, each line containing a student ID number and the answers to the quiz from that student. We will assume one student per file line. Our goal is to write a program to initialize the answer array from the correct answers in the "key.txt" disk file. Next, the program is to input student records, grade each student's answers against the correct key answers, and output a score for each student. The program is also to tabulate the number of students who get each question correct into the summary array. Let's call the program "gradtest.cpp".

Now suppose the disk file "key.txt" contains the following characters:

key.txt:

```
T F T F F
```

Assume the disk file `"students.txt"` contains the following lines:

students.txt:

1234   TFFTF
6543   TFTTT
5344   TFTFF
8765   FTFFF
2983   TFTTF

The output of the proposed program should look like this:

```
student: 1234   score 3
student: 6543   score 3
student: 5344   score 5
student: 8765   score 2
student: 2983   score 4
correct answers summary for each question: 4 4 3 2 4
```

This is a reusable program, of course. By simply changing the contents of the two disk files, one could grade subsequent quizzes. Using top-down design methods, this program really consists of three parts (Figure 10.3).

Consider oval (a) first. In this problem, we need to process or fill the `answer` array cells in sequence from the `"key.txt"` disk file. The first character read goes into cell 0, the next character into cell 1, and so on. The simplest approach is to use a **for** loop variable as the index of an array. This is a very common construction or mechanism in high-level programs and you will use it repeatedly. We'll again assume a **char** array of five cells named `answer` into which we read the correct quiz answers. For example, suppose the disk file is opened to file variable `keyfile_in`. Oval (a) might become:

```
for (int n=0; n<5; n++)
   keyfile_in >> answer[n];
```

Table 10.1 illustrates the steps that would be executed as the loop variable n goes from 0 to 4.

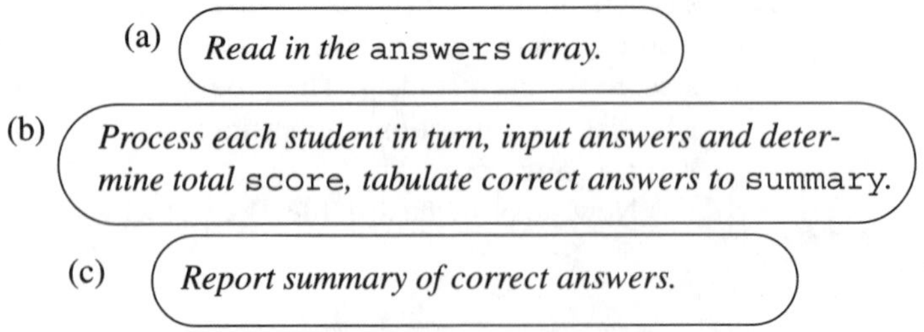

(a) *Read in the* answers *array.*

(b) *Process each student in turn, input answers and determine total* score, *tabulate correct answers to* summary.

(c) *Report summary of correct answers.*

Figure 10.3 Master design chart of "gradtest.cpp"

Table 10.1 Example execution of array loop

value of `n`	effective loop statement	effect on `answer`	remaining `chars` in file
0	`cin >> answers[0]`	T, ?, ?, ?, ?	FTFF
1	`cin >> answers[1]`	T, F, ?,.?, ?	TFF
2	`cin >> answers[2]`	T, F, T, ?, ?	FF
3	`cin >> answers[3]`	T, F, T, F,?	F
4	`cin >> answers[4]`	T, F, T, F, F	

Now let's take a look at oval (b). This is obviously a loop structure since we need to consider each student in turn. Since we are inputting student records from a disk file and we don't know how many records exist, we will choose a **while** loop that terminates on reaching the end of file. Assume the disk file `"students.txt"` is opened to file variable `studentfile_in` (Figure 10.4).

Here we are assuming the variable `score` now contains the sum of correct responses for the current student. Oval (b.1) represents the grading of one student to place the correct count into `score`. We don't need all student answers in the program to grade one student, just one student's answers. In fact, we only need one student answer at a time. In that way, the processing of one student represents the processing of five answers—a **for** loop. Now, assume we have an **int** array of five cells named `summary`, all initialized to 0. We could decompose oval (b.1) in the following manner:

```
score = 0;                          // assume a 0 score
for (ans=0; ans<5; ans++)           // loop over 5 answers...
{   studentfile_in >> thisanswer;   // get next answer
    if (thisanswer == answer[ans])  // is it right?
    {   score++;                     // if so, increase grade
        summary[ans]++;              // and tabulate in summary
    }
}
```

After grading all students, the array `summary` now contains the number of correct answers for each of the five quiz questions.

```
        while (studentfile_in >> id)
        {
(b.1)       ⟨ Process one student; for each answer, sum correct
              answers and store in score. Tabulate in summary ⟩
        }
        cout << "student: "<<id<<"  score: "<<score<<endl;
```

Figure 10.4 Further decomposition of oval (b)

Oval (c) is to report the number of correct scores in the `summary` table. Since there are five scores, we will output them sequentially, again using a **for** loop to output each `summary` cell in turn.

```
cout << "correct answers summary for each question:";
for (n=0; n<5; n++)
    cout <<summary[n];
```

Consider the program of Listing 10.1, which puts the whole problem together into a complete program with appropriate declarations. Notice that the number 5 has been removed from the program and defined at the top as a global constant.

Listing 10.1

```
// gradtest.cpp  Grade student quiz answers in file 'students.txt' against
// the key in disk file 'key.txt'. Report each student's score and a class
// summary of the number correct for each question.
#include <iostream.h>
#include <fstream.h>
const int SIZE = 5;

void main ()
{   ifstream keyfile_in ("key.txt", ios::in);
    ifstream studentfile_in ("students.txt", ios::in);
    char answer[SIZE], thisanswer;
    int ans, summary[SIZE] = {0};
    int  id, n, score;

for (n=0; n<SIZE; n++)
    keyfile_in >> answer[n];               // input answer key array

while (studentfile_in >> id)               // loop over students
{    score = 0;                            // assume a 0 score
    for (ans=0; ans<SIZE; ans++)           // loop over answers
    {    studentfile_in >> thisanswer;     // get next answer
        if (thisanswer == answer[ans])     // is it right?
        {    score++;                      // if so, increase grade
            summary[ans]++;                // and tabulate
        }
    }                                      // end of loop over answers (ans)
    cout << "student: "<< id <<"  score: " << score << endl;
}                                          // end of loop over students (while)

cout << "correct answers summary for each question: ";
for (n=0; n<SIZE; n++)
    cout << summary[n] << " ";             // output summary table
}
```

> **EXPERIMENT**
>
> What would happen if you output an array without initialization or without assigning values to each cell?

10.4 Common errors

Keep in mind that a C++ expression should still refer to array variable cells individually. If you need to store a constant in all five cells of an array, you will need five assignment statements or a loop that causes one assignment statement to be executed five times. If you need to output the contents of an array, you will need multiple output statements or a loop. The following, for example, will not output all five cells of the cost array:

```
int cost[5] = { 11, 22, 33, 44, 55 };
cout << cost;
```

WRONG WAY!

Unfortunately, it will not produce an error message when compiled or a run-time error when executed. You will just see garbage for output. Using an array name without a subscript is not invalid; it just has a much different (but useful) meaning that will be examined later.

Take another look at the last **for** loop of the program in Listing 10.1. Since the indexes range from 0 to 4 (a total of five cells), the following would be inappropriate:

```
for (ans=0; ans<=5; ans++)
    cout << summary[ans];
```

WRONG WAY!

CONCEPT
out-of-bounds
indexes

This **for** statement attempts to output a value from a cell of the array which does not exist—summary[5] or the sixth cell! You probably will not see a compiler error or warning with the prceding statement during a program build or make, however. In addition, you may not even see an execution error when the statement is executed. C++ makes no attempt to ensure that the indexes you use are valid. That is your responsibility. The statement asks the system to output a value from a cell that is beyond (or outside of) the array declared. The system is simply going to trust you and will output whatever value happens to be found just past the end of the array—garbage to you.

powers

1	2	4	8	16	32	64	128	256	512
0	1	2	3	4	5	6	7	8	9

Figure 10.5 Diagram of `powers` array

That type of error might be fairly easy to detect and correct. After all, it just results in some extra output. A much more serious problem occurs when we attempt to *store* a value in a cell that doesn't exist. Suppose we were to construct a table of 10 successive powers of 2 (Figure 10.5):

```
int powers[10] = { 1 };
for (n=1; n<10; n++)
    powers[n] = powers[n-1] * 2;
```

Now go back and change this simple loop so that it stores one more value beyond the end of the `powers` array:

```
int powers[10] = { 1 };
for (n=1; n<=10; n++)
    powers[n] = powers[n-1] * 2;
```

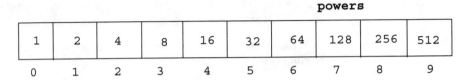

This action will write over some other location containing whatever happens to be stored just after the array. There are several possibilities: The overwritten cell was another variable, a program instruction, or part of the system. If you are lucky, this program will terminate with a run-time error at the assignment statement. Unfortunately, it is much more likely that this section will execute fine but cause a serious run-time bug to occur *in another part of the program* when the overwritten memory cell is needed. This bug might manifest itself in completely unpredictable ways. For example, a section of program that was running fine yesterday now produces the wrong answers. The program crashes whenever an output statement is attempted. The `int` variable x is assigned 5, but when output, 6 is displayed.

CONCEPT
consider index errors

Almost any type of problem may be manifest if an index goes beyond an array. The bottom line is this: Whenever a strange bug is detected that is not quickly resolved, check to see if you have an array index that has gone out-of-bounds.

10.5 Arrays as arguments and parameters

10.5.a Passing entire arrays

Just as simple variables (`int`, `float`, and `char`) or class variables (such as `string` and `ofstream`) can be passed to functions, arrays can be used as function parameters as well. To specify an array as a function parameter, the array is declared inside the function parameter list, but no array size is placed within the brackets.

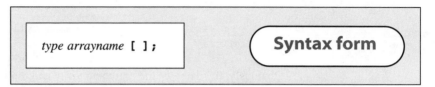

CONCEPT

arrays as parameters

Within the function, the parameter array is referenced in the normal manner. The & operator does not need to be used to make the array a reference parameter because *array parameters are automatically reference parameters*. This means, of course, that any changes in the parameter array are reflected in the corresponding argument array. For example, consider the simple function in Listing 10.2 intended to return the sum of the cells in the parameter array.

Listing 10.2

```
// SumArray ()  Returns the sum of the integer parameter array
// IN:  this array is a one-dimensional array of integers
//      size is the number of cells to be summed

int SumArray (int thisarray[ ], int size)
{   int sum=0, n;
    for (n=0; n<size; n++)          // loop over each array cell
        sum += thisarray[n];        // keep a running sum
    return (sum);
}
```

Notice that the `size` of the array is expected as a second parameter in the function. This is to allow a parameter in the function to indicate how many cells are to be added. Without this parameter, the **for** loop could not be set to sum the correct number of cells. This is because *a parameter array can be used for any sized argument array as long as the array type is the same*. It is common practice when passing arrays to include another integer parameter that can be used to indicate the size of the array being passed.

To call a function and pass an array argument, *only the name of the array is placed into the function argument list*. For now, this is the one time you will use an array name without an accompanying subscript. Consider the following three arrays and accompanying function calls:

```
int weights[10], ages[20];
int sum5, sum10, sum20;
...
//  sum10 is assigned to be the sum of all 'weights' cells
```

```
                  sum10 = SumArray (weights, 10);
                  ...
                  // sum5 is assigned to be the sum of the first 5 cells of 'ages'
                  sum5 = SumArray (ages, 5);
                  ...
                  //  sum20 is assigned to be the sum of all 'ages' cells
                  sum20 = SumArray (ages, 20);
```

Obviously, the name of the argument array and the name of the parameter array do not need to be the same (just as with other parameters). Notice that if a `size` argument is less than the number of cells in the array, the function simply sums that many cells from the beginning of the array. In other words, the function trusts the caller to supply a meaningful number for the `size` parameter. This has two features: (a) The function can be used to sum a variety of different **int** arrays. (b) If the caller supplies a `size` value that is beyond the parameter array, garbage will be summed.

Let's return to the test-grading program designed in Figure 10.3 and implemented in Listing 10.1. This program has become somewhat complex and is reaching the level where it may be difficult for another to read and understand. If we use modular functions, however, the implementation of the design chart of Figure 10.3 becomes quite simple (Listing 10.3).

Listing 10.3

```cpp
// gradtst2.cpp  Grade student quiz answers in file 'students.txt' against
//     the key in disk file 'key.txt'. Report each student's score and a class
///     summary of the number correct for each question.
#include <iostream>
#include <fstream>
#include <string>
using namespace std;

const string KEYFILE = "key.txt";
const string STUDENTFILE= "students.txt";
const int SIZE = 5;
void InputAnswerKey (string, char[ ], int);              // prototypes
void  GradeStudents (string, char[ ], int[ ], int);
void ReportSummary (int[ ], int);

void main ()
{   char answers[SIZE];
    int summary[SIZE] = {0};
    InputAnswerKey (KEYFILE, answers, SIZE);
    GradeStudents (STUDENTFILE, answers, summary, SIZE);
    ReportSummary (summary, SIZE);
}
```

The only task now is to write the three functions that the main program references. As you can see, this is actually a way of performing top-down design without the need for temporary ovals. The three functions represent ovals (a), (b), and (c). The first function is being passed a string and a character array of five cells, as in Listing 10.4.

Listing 10.4

```
// InputAnswerKey()  Reads a disk file for a quiz answer key and
// sets the correct answers in the array 'answers'.
// ASSUMPTION: input file exists and contains 5 answers
// IN: keyfile is a string for the input file name
//      size is the array size
// OUT: ans is an array for the correct quiz answers

void InputAnswerKey (string keyfile, char ans[ ], int size)
{   istream infile (keyfile, ios::in);
    for (int n=0; n<size; n++)
        infile >> ans[n];
}
```

The second function is responsible for grading each student record from the "student.txt" file using the test answer key array (Listing 10.5).

Listing 10.5

```
// GradeStudents ()  Using the 'answers' test key, grade
// each student quiz in file STUDENTFILE. Print score.
// ASSUMPTION: file STUDENTFILE exists and contains
// one record per student.
// IN: studfile is a string filename
// answers contains (size) test key answers
// size is the size of the answers and summary arrays
// OUT:  summary will be a count table of correct answers.

void  GradeStudents (string studfile, char answers[ ], int summary[ ], int size)
{   ifstream studentfile_in (studfile, ios::in);
    int id, score, ans, thisanswer;
    while (studentfile_in >> id)              // loop over students
    {   score = 0;                            // assume a 0 score
        for (ans=0; ans<size; ans++)          // loop over answers
        {     studentfile_in >> thisanswer;   // get next answer
            if (thisanswer==answers[ans])     // is it right?
            {   score++;                      // if so, update grade
                summary[ans]++;               // and tabulate
            }
        }                                     // end of loop over answers (ans)
        cout << "student: "<< id <<"  score: " << score << endl;
    }                                         // end of loop over students
}
```

The last function has the simple responsibility of generating the output report from the summary array (Listing 10.6).

Listing 10.6

```
// ReportSummary() Generate output report from 'summary'
// IN:  summary, a table of correct answer counts; SIZE is cells in 'summary'

void ReportSummary (int summary[ ], int size)
{   cout << "correct answers summary for each question; ";
    for (int n=0; n<size; n++)
        cout << summary[n] << " ";
}
```

As we are continually seeing, using functions to implement design ovals allows the programmer to neatly compartmentalize each task. Debugging is made simpler by allowing the programmer to check ASSUMPTIONS, IN, and OUT conditions at the top and bottom of each function.

10.5.b   Passing individual cells

In the previous section, entire arrays were used as arguments and declared as parameters. What if only a single cell of an array is to be passed? In this case, a single array cell is just like any other simple variable, and the same approach used in Chapter 3 applies. Namely, the matching parameter is declared as a simple variable. If parameter changes are to be reflected back in the single cell argument, the parameter is declared as a reference parameter using the & modifier.

Consider the function in Listing 10.7, which simply swaps the contents of any two **string** variables. Swapping the values in two cells requires a third temporary cell.

Listing 10.7

```
// Swap()  Exchange the two parameter strings
// IN/OUT:  word1 and word2 are two strings

void Swap (string& word1, string& word2)
{   string temp;
    temp = word1;
    word1 = word2;
    word2 = temp;
}
```

The function of Listing 10.7 can be called with individual **string** variable arguments or with individual cells of a **string** array. The only requirement is that the arguments must represent individual strings:

```
string thisword, thatword, manywords[50];
...
Swap (thisword, thatword);                // valid call
Swap (thatword, manywords[5]);            // valid call
Swap (manywords[3], thisword);            // valid call
Swap (manywords[7], manywords[11]);       // valid call
```

If an argument does not represent a single **string** variable, an error will occur. The reason for this error will be more apparent in Chapter 14.

```
Swap (thisword, manywords);
```
WRONG WAY!

10.6 Sorting an array

Take another look at the Creative Challenge problems at the end of the previous chapter. One task was to input ten words and then output them in alphabetical order. Using arrays, this project is significantly simpler to solve than it probably was for you at that time. Ordering the elements of an array is called sorting. The design chart for this program solution is quite simple. The top and bottom ovals of Figure 10.6 are simple enough to implement directly. We will set the problem of oval (b) into a function (Listing 10.8) and come back to it later.

KEY TERM
selection sort

After debugging this program using a stub function for Sort (), it is time to figure out how to order the array words. There are numerous methods to solve this problem, some more efficient than others. The approach or algorithm we will apply is known as a *selection sort*. The approach is not particularly fast or efficient, but it is easy to program.

Repeat the following steps as index k goes from 0 to SIZE-2:

1. Find the smallest array value in the index range k to SIZE-1. Assume it is found at index small_pos.

2. Swap the old value at position k with the value at position small_pos.

(a)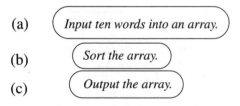
(b)
(c)

Figure 10.6 Design chart for the word-sorting project

Listing 10.8

```
// wordsort.cpp  Sort and output a list of 10 words from a list
provided by the user.
#include <iostream>
#include <fstream>
#include <string>
using namespace std;

const int SIZE 10;
void Sort (string words[ ], int size);
void main ()
{   string words[SIZE];
    int n;
    cout << "enter " << SIZE << " words: ";
    for (n=0; n<SIZE; n++)           // input the list of words
        cin >> words[n];

    Sort (words, SIZE);              // sort the list

    cout << "sorted words are:" << endl;
    for (n=0; n<SIZE; n++)           // output the list
        cout << words[n] << endl;
}
```

In essence, we are considering each cell in sequence. For each cell, we search the remaining array to find the smallest value (from this cell on to the end) and then exchange or swap values with the smallest found. (Actually, we do not need to consider the last cell—that is why the index k only reaches SIZE-2. By the time the last cell is reached, the array is already in order). Figure 10.7 diagrams how this might proceed for a given array of five integers.

Having the index k go from 0 to SIZE-2 is just a **for** loop. Searching for the smallest value from k to SIZE-1 is another **for** loop which is nested within the first loop. The example in Figure 10.7 deals with integers; the same algorithm would, of course, work for **string** or **float** values. The Swap () function called in Listing 10.9 is just the one implemented in Listing 10.7.

Listing 10.9

```
// Sort()  Order the values in the array
// IN:  words is a String array of size values

void Swap (string& x, string& y);
void Sort (string words[ ], int size)
{   int n, k, small_pos;
    string smallest;
```

```
for (k=0; k<size-1; k++)              // repeat; each cell but last.
{   smallest = words[k];              // assume this is smallest
    for (n=k; n<size; n++)            // compare with other words...
        if (words[n] <= words[k])     // if smaller, save position
        {   small_pos = n;            // and word...
            smallest = words[n];
        }
    Swap (words[k], words[small_pos]);// swap these cells
}
}
```

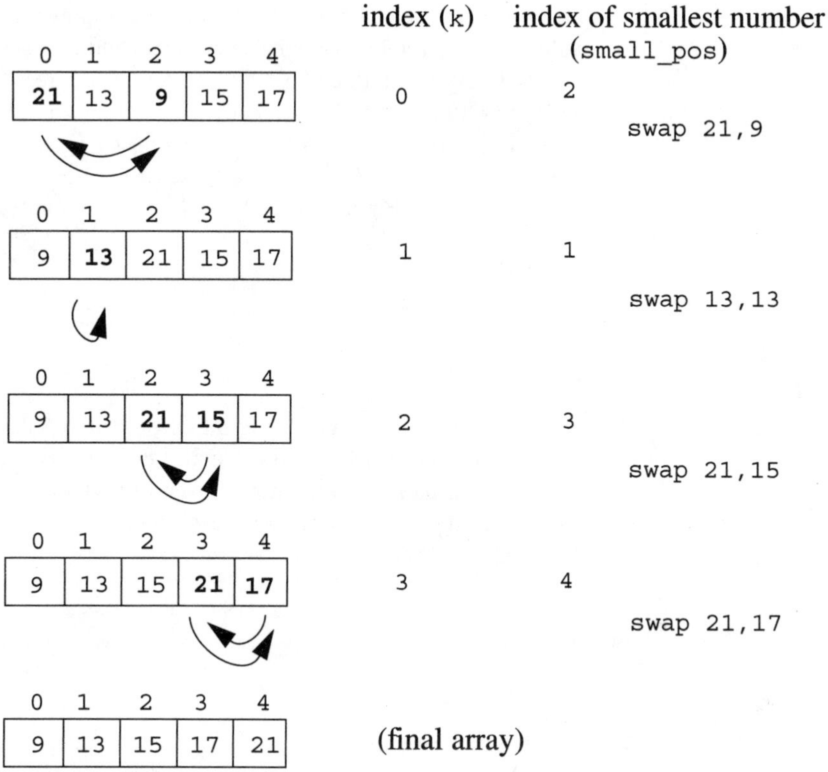

index (k)   index of smallest number
(small_pos)

	0	1	2	3	4
	21	13	**9**	15	17

0   2

swap 21,9

	0	1	2	3	4
	9	**13**	21	15	17

1   1

swap 13,13

	0	1	2	3	4
	9	13	**21**	**15**	17

2   3

swap 21,15

	0	1	2	3	4
	9	13	15	**21**	**17**

3   4

swap 21,17

	0	1	2	3	4
	9	13	15	17	21

(final array)

Figure 10.7 Selection sort of an array of five int cells

10.7 Introduction to pointers

Although it is not important to understand how arrays are physically represented in the computer in order to use them (as we have in the examples of this chapter), it will help you understand later topics. Keep in mind that what is presented in this section does not in any way change how you have learned to use arrays in programs and functions in the first part of this chapter.

10.7.a Bracket notation

KEY TERM

pointer

A useful model that will help you understand bracket notation and pointers is the following: When an array is declared to contain, say, 10 cells, visualize C++ as establishing *11 cells*—the 10 cells of the array and another cell containing a *pointer* to the beginning of that array sequence of 10 cells. This single cell is associated with the name of the array. Consider Figure 10.8.

"Okay," you are thinking, "what is a pointer?" A pointer is just an address; these are interchangeable terms. While each different computer architecture may utilize a different address form, these addresses are just integer numbers (or occasionally pairs of numbers). Each cell in computer memory has two attributes: a value (stored or held inside the cell) and an address (specifying where the cell is located). Every memory cell has its own unique address. A physical memory address really has little meaning outside the execution of a program. In fact, it may change each time a program is run as the operating system allocates different areas of memory for variables. We normally represent pointers in diagrams of this text using arrows, as in Figure 10.8. The following assignment statement

```
void main ()
{   float y, x[10];
    ...
    y = x[5];
```

translates to the system as "assign to y the value 5 cells beyond where x is pointing." Now, you may be thinking about how we pass arrays as arguments simply by using the name of the array. If you are wondering if the value we are really passing to the function is just the pointer, you're right. Consider the following function:

```
void SomeFunc (float z[ ])
{   z[5] = 99.9;
}
```

The function argument declares z to be a pointer to a sequence of floating-point cells. You are probably beginning to understand why this function could deal with many different sized arrays as arguments: The function doesn't know how many cells are in the array; it only knows where the array starts.

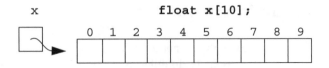

Figure 10.8 Physical representation of the declaration `float x[10];`

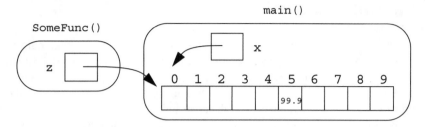

Figure 10.9 Passing array pointers

You might also begin to see why array parameters are automatically reference parameters (without the & modifier). Suppose this function were invoked from a main program:

```
void main ()
{   float x[10];
    . . .
    SomeFunc (x);
    . . .
}
```

The argument x represents a pointer to an array of 10 cells (Figure 10.9). The parameter z of SomeFunc will receive a copy of this pointer when the function is invoked. Inside the function, the statement z[5] = 99.9 translates to "assign 99.9 at 5 cells beyond where z is pointing." Since z and x are actually both pointing to the same array, assigning a value to a cell in z actually changes a cell in x. The net effect is that the cell x[5] is assigned the 99.9 value.

The pointer cell named x that we are visualizing for the array should actually be considered a **const** pointer. In other words, it does not make sense ever to think of changing this pointer value to point to some other array of cells. It can only point to the 10 cells of the array that were established when the array was declared. The parameter pointer cell named z within the function is a variable pointer, since the array it will point to may change if the function is called with a different array pointer argument.

When an array is declared in C++, the system can be visualized as creating a pointer variable with the array name that points to the sequence of cells representing the array values. When an array name is used in a function call argument list, a pointer to the array is actually all that is being passed. Declaring a corresponding parameter array with an empty set of brackets (no size) actually declares only a pointer. The parameter array pointer is then set to point to the argument array. This is why we say that arrays are automatically passed by reference even though the & modifier is not used in the parameter declaration.

This is just a brief introduction to an important and interesting topic. You don't need to understand pointers just yet. We will spend the better part of Chapter 14 on this subject.

10.8 Multi-dimensional arrays

Let's return to the shirt cost table from the beginning of the chapter. Suppose the company now comes out with a new improved line of shirts with each style in four different colors (Figure 10.10).

Now you need to know two indexes to determine the appropriate shirt cost: the style index and the color index. Obviously, this is a two-dimensional table. A word of caution: Some students tend to think of array dimensions as a *physical reality*. As a result, they artificially label these two-dimensional table indexes as the *row* index and the *column* index. In this way of thinking, a three-dimensional table is viewed as a *cube*. Keep in mind that use of the term *dimension* really has little to do with physical diagrams or figures: it is simply a way of specifying how many different indexes there are.

You can easily see that if the table in Figure 10.10 were reorganized so that the color index went from left to right and the style index went from top to bottom, it would still contain the same information. In other words, given a color and style index, the look-up cost would be the same. Another reason this particular labeling should be avoided is that it falls apart when tables have higher dimensions. For example, consider a collection of books of shirt costs. Each volume corresponds to a particular manufacturer, each chapter in a volume corresponds to a particular fabric, each section within a chapter is a particular size, and each page in a section contains a two-dimensional table of style and color indexes. This is obviously a five-dimensional table. To look up a shirt cost, you need to know the manufacturer, fabric, size, style, and color. While this analogy is simple to envision, trying to imagine a hypercube of five dimensions as a physical construction could give one a real headache.

You can easily imagine that the shirt cost volumes could be rearranged in a number of different ways. For example, each volume could be organized to contain a particular fabric and each chapter could be a specific manufacturer. Regardless of how publication is organized, *if you know the ordering of indexes*, the look-up cost for a particular shirt will be the same. Suppose now the company decides on the first ordering: manufacturer, fabric, size, style, and color. If you were asked to look up the cost of a shirt using the index group (3, 6, 4, 2, 1), you can easily recognize that this refers to a manufacturer index of 3, a fabric index of 6, a size index of 4, a style index of 2, and a color index of 1.

Improved Shirt Cost Table

	0	1	2	3	4	5	6
0	3.45	4.59	7.39	9.45	6.78	2.84	4.56
1	3.47	4.63	7.41	9.49	6.83	2.99	4.75
2	3.53	4.66	7.45	9.53	6.89	2.54	4.99
3	3.69	4.69	7.56	9.65	6.98	3.05	5.76

(color index) — rows 0–3
(style index) — columns 0–6

Figure 10.10 A simple two-dimensional table

Let's return now to C++. Multidimensional array variables are declared by using sets of brackets after the variable name to specify the number of cells for each array index:

$$type\ name\ [size_1]\ [size_2]\ ...;$$

Syntax form

In the syntax box, $size_1$ refers to the number of possible values for the first index, $size_2$ refers to the number of possible values for the second index, and so on for as many indexes as are needed. The *type* refers to the type of individual cells. The declaration

```
float improved_shirt_cost [4][7];
```

declares a two-dimensional array named `improved_shirt_cost` that is associated with two indexes. The first has four possible values (numbered 0 to 3) and the second index has seven values (numbered 0 to 6), as in the table of Figure 10.10. This is often called a uniform array, since all rows are the same size and all columns are the same size. (You will learn later that there are ways of establishing ragged arrays where each row may have a different number of values. There are also ways of establishing arrays where the cells may represent a variety of different types!)

CONCEPT
index associations

Which index is for color and which index is for style? That is the programmer's responsibility to remember and document! C++ does not care how you choose to order indexes to represent tables. As far as the computer is concerned, it is just a two-dimensional array of **float** values. The CPU has no idea what a shirt is.

When a two-dimensional array cell is referenced within a program, the reference needs to index values in the correct order. Each index is enclosed with brackets. For example, if we associate the first index with color and the second with style

```
thiscost = improved_shirt_cost [2][4];
```

refers to the cost of the shirt with color number 2 and style number 4. (Remember again that all indexes begin with 0.)

CONCEPT
multidimensional parameters

When passing multidimensional arrays as arguments to functions, again only the name of the array is used (which, of course, represents a pointer to the array). While many differently sized one-dimensional arrays may be passed as arguments to a function expecting a one-dimensional parameter, much less latitude is allowed when passing uniform multi-dimensional arrays. When declaring a multidimensional array as a parameter, only the first set of brackets is empty. The second (and any subsequent brackets) set must contain the correct size. Generally speaking, multidimensional argument arrays and corresponding parameter arrays are nearly always exactly the same size in all dimensions.

For example, the following function expects a two-dimensional array as a parameter. Only arrays with a second index size of 7 may be passed as arguments:

```
void SomeFunc (int table[ ] [7]);
```

Suppose this information has been stored in the disk file `"shirts.txt"` and we need a program to perform lookups for a user. Assume each line in the file represents one of four different styles. There are seven costs for each of seven different colors for each style:

shirts.txt:

3.45	4.59	7.39	9.45	6.78	2.84	4.56
3.47	4.63	7.41	9.49	6.83	2.99	4.75
3.53	4.66	7.45	9.53	6.89	2.54	4.99
3.69	4.69	7.56	9.65	6.98	3.05	5.76

Consider the following simple implementation in Listing 10.10. The first function `ReadTable()` reads the table information from the disk file. Since C++ reads input streams from left to right and top to bottom, this function first reads an entire line of style values for each style: the costs for each of seven different colors. The second function `DoLookUps()` prompts the user for color and style indexes and then outputs the appropriate cost.

Listing 10.10

```cpp
// widcost.cpp  Output the cost of a shirt given the color and style indexes.
// ASSUMPTION: file "shirts.txt" contains the 4x7 cost table
#include <iostream>
#include <fstream.>
#include <string>
using namespace std;

const string filename = "shirts.txt";
const int COLORS = 7;
const int STYLES = 4;

// ReadTable() Fill a 2-D cost table from the 'filename' file
// ASSUMPTION: file exists.
// IN:    filename is the correct filename string
// OUT:   table is a 2-D array of costs
void ReadTable (float table[ ][COLORS], string filename)
{   ifstream infile (filename, ios::in);
    int color, style;
    for (style=0; style<STYLES; style++)
        for (color=0; color<COLORS; color++)
            infile >> table[style][color];
}
```

```
// DoLookUps()  Output a cost for a given style and color
// IN: table is the 2-D array of costs.
void DoLookUps (float table[ ][COLORS])
{  int color, style;
   cout << "enter color and style (Ctrl-C to end)";
   while (cin >> color >> style)
   {    if (color >= COLORS || style >= STYLES)
            cout << "invalid color or style...";
        else cout << " cost for color: "<<color<<" and style "<<style
            <<" is "<< table[style][color] << endl;
   }
}


void main ()
{  float cost_table[4][7];              // color is second index, style is first

   ReadTable (cost_table, filename);    // input the table from disk
   DoLookUps (cost_table);              // perform lookups for user
}
```

Notice in Listing 10.10 that the DoLookUps () function has a **while** loop doing input from the keyboard. This loop will terminate when the input is unsuccessful. In this case, the user may press Ctrl-C (hold the Ctrl key while pressing C) to terminate input. Notice also that the values for style and color number are first checked to ensure they are within correct table range before they are utilized.

Now we are ready for the big five-dimensional table example. Suppose you choose the ordering: manufacturer, fabric, size, color, and style. Suppose also there were 8 different manufacturers, 4 fabrics for each manufacturer, 2 sizes for each fabric, 4 colors for each size, and 7 styles for each color. The following declaration would be appropriate. Notice the importance of documenting the ordering of the indexes:

```
// Table of shirt costs.
// Ordering of indexes; manufacturer, fabric, size, color, style
    float shirt_cost_volumes [8][4][2][4][7];
```

In practical programming, one-dimensional and occasionally two-dimensional arrays are often sufficient for most problems. It is rare that higher-dimensioned arrays are used. There are much more powerful ways of declaring and using complex tables, as you will learn in the next chapter.

10.9 Example project

Even **long** variables are quite limited in the range of integers that can be expressed. Occasionally, a program is needed to manipulate very large integers with exact precision. For example, if you needed to calculate this year's interest on the national debt, the principal is too large for **long** and the debt needs to be more accurate than can be calculated with **double**. You may decide to use an integer *array* for a large number—representing each digit with a single cell. Let's write a program that could input two 20-digit integers and output the correct sum. As usual, the main program is a snap to write (Listing 10.11).

Listing 10.11

```
// BigInt.cpp  Adds two Big Integers (20-digit integers)
#include <iostream.h>
const int NUMDIG = 20, NUMDIG2 = 21;   // digit size of large
                                          integers
void ReadBigInt (int b[ ]);                  // prototypes...
void SumBigInt (int x[ ], int y[ ], int sum[ ]);

void main ()
{   int x[NUMDIG], y[NUMDIG], sum[NUMDIG2], n;
    ReadBigInt (x);
    ReadBigInt (y);
    SumBigInt (x, y, sum);               // sum two large integers
    cout << "the sum is: ";
    for (n=0; n<NUMDIG2; n++)
        cout << sum[n] << endl;
}
```

Reading in a big integer requires that 20 smaller, single-digit integers be input. We will read these in as characters and convert each character to an integer by utilizing the fact that the ASCII code for the character 5 is five more than the ASCII code for 0, the code for 7 is seven more than 0, and so on. We will simply subtract ASCII codes (Lisiting 10.12).

Listing 10.12

```
// ReadBigInt()  Read in a Big Integer of NUMDIG digits
// OUT: array b contains the NUMDIG digits

void ReadBigInt (int b[ ])
{   int n;
    char c;
    cout << "enter a 20-digit integer: ";
    for (n=0; n<NUMDIG; n++)          // input a large integer one
    {   cin >> c;                     // char at a time.
        b[n] = c - '0';               // convert to digit value.
    }
}
```

The function `SumBigInt()` simply sums digits the same way you do when adding: The rightmost digit is the sum of the two rightmost digits. If the sum is greater than 10, subtract 10 and carry 1 over to the next column. The sum has one more digit than the other two arrays to allow for a carry on the leftmost digits sum (Listing 10.13).

Listing 10.13

```
// SumBigInt()  Sums two Big Integer arrays into a third
// IN:   x and y are NUMDIG arrays containing Big Integers
// OUT:  sum is a NUMDIG2 array containing the arithmetic sum

void SumBigInt (int x[ ], int y[ ], int sum[ ])
{   int n, carry=0;
    for (n=NUMDIG-1; n>=0; n--)
    {   sum[n+1] = x[n] + y[n] + carry;
        if (sum[n+1] >= 10)
        {   sum[n+1] -= 10;        // perform long addition
            carry = 1;             // digit-by-digit in the arrays
        }
        else carry = 0;
    }
    sum[0] = carry;
}
```

10.10 Summary

KEY TERMS   Several new terms were introduced in this chapter:

1. *dimension*—the number of indexes needed to reference an array.

2. *parallel arrays*—two (or more) arrays in which cells with corresponding indexes are related.

3. *subscript*—another name for the index of an array.

4. *selection sort*—an algorithm for ordering the cells of an array.

5. *pointer*—the numeric address of a memory cell.

CONCEPTS   A number of new concepts and forms were also presented. Arrays must be declared with the size of the array in brackets. Array cells are numbered beginning with 0. When referencing an array in an executable statement, the index is placed within brackets. Arrays may be initialized when declared by assigning an initial-value list within braces. C++ does not check to ensure that an array reference is valid (that the cell referenced really is within the declared array). That is the programmer's responsibility. Writing to cells beyond the end of an array can result in serious and difficult-to-find bugs.

Table 10.2 Example segments

`int x[10];`	Declaration of a 10-cell array.
`int y[5] = {15, -3, 77, 0, 9};`	Declaration and initialization.
`for (n=0; n<10; n++)` `   cout << x[n] << endl;`	Output of a 10-cell array.
`int x[10];` `   cost = SumArray(x);`	Passing array x to a function.
`int SumArray (int y[ ])`	Declaring an array parameter.
`char name[10] = "Jim Black";`	Initializing a character array.
`cout << name;`	Output of a character array provided that the array ends with \0.
`float z[2][3] = {{1,2,3},{9,8,7}};`	Declaration and initialization of a two-dimensional array.

When one-dimensional arrays are passed as arguments to function calls, only the name is placed within the call list. When declaring one-dimensional arrays as function parameters, an empty set of brackets is used. This allows a one-dimensional array parameter to be used for one-dimensional argument arrays of differing sizes. Naturally, the *type* of the argument and parameter array must still be the same.

Array arguments to function calls are automatically passed by reference. Any changes to the parameter array are reflected in the argument array in the calling program. When passing multidimensional arrays to functions, the corresponding parameter arrays are declared with the same size constants (in brackets) for all but the first dimension. The name of an array by itself represents a **const** pointer to the cells of the array.

The most common problem associated with programming with arrays is having an index go out-of-bounds. When a cell outside of the range of an array is examined, often no run-time error will result. The program will simply retrieve a garbage value. When a value is written to a cell outside of the array range, a serious bug can result which can be difficult to find. Such a bug may manifest itself in a completely different part of the program. A good rule of thumb is that whenever a difficult bug presents itself in a program, immediately suspect an array index. It may be *any* array index *anywhere* in the program. A good programming practice in some situations is to check the values of indexes with an **if** statement before they are used in subsequent program segments.

When an array is fully initialized at declaration, the size of the array may be omitted, but this is not necessarily a good programming practice.

10.11 Exercises

10.11.a Short-answer questions

1. Give a declaration statement for each of the following:
    a. An array of 10 integer cells,
    b. An array of 5 `float` cells initialized to 5.6, 7.8, 9.1, 2.3, and 4.5.
    c. An array of 12 `char` cells initialized to the string `"hello world"`.

2. Can one array be copied into another array with a simple assignment statement as shown here? Explain your answer.

```
int x[5], y[5];
...
x = y;// copy array y into array x
```

3. The ordinal constant or variable within brackets used to reference a particular one-dimensional array cell is called the array _____.

4. The number of different indexes required to reference a single array cell is called the array _____.

5. The index or subscript of an array must be what type of variable or constant?

6. If an array is not initialized at all, the cells will initially contain _____.

7. If an integer array is partially initialized, the unspecified cells will be set to _____.

8. Do array parameter declarations in a function need to use the & operator if the array is to be changed or modified?

9. List two common programming errors associated with using one-dimensional arrays.

10. Does the C++ system check to verify that an array index is within bounds before executing a statement containing an array reference?

11. Write a simple **for** loop segment to output the following array:

```
int values[20];
```

12. Write a simple **for** loop segment to allow the user to input new values in the array of question 11.

13. Write a **for** loop segment to sum the integers in the array of question 11 into the following variable:

```
int sum = 0;
```

14. Show how the array of question 11 should be passed to the function `SomeFunc()`.

15. If the function `SomeFunc()` expects a single integer array parameter, show how the declaration of the parameter should be stated.

16. What happens when an array is not fully initialized? For example:

```
int numbers[5] = { 33, 44, 55 };
```

17. What is the primary difference between the following two declarations?

```
char word[6] = "hello";
char word[6] = { 'h', 'e', 'l', 'l', 'o' };
```

18. What is the most common programming error when using arrays?

19. Write a segment of code to declare and fill a two-dimensional array using the following table showing the percentages of ages for males and females of three different heights:

```
                        Height
                    <5'      5-5.5'   >5.5'
        Sex     M   0.13     0.52     0.35
                F   0.26     0.54     0.20
```

20. Declare a two-dimensional array to hold the powers of integer positive numbers. One index should represent the number itself and have the range 0 to 5. The other index should represent the power and have a range of 0 to 4. For example, the two indexes power = 3 and number = 4 should represent a cell for 4^3. *This question has two equivalent answers.*

10.11.b Projects

1. Create a text disk file containing 20 integers. Write a program to input this array of 20 integers from the disk file and output the sum and average.

2. Write a program to encrypt a text file by substituting characters using the following parallel arrays. Each input character is to be located in the plaintext array, and the corresponding character in the encrypted array is to be output to a separate file. Input characters not found in the plaintext array are to be output as is. Notice that plaintext begins with a blank.

```
char plaintext[40] =
    {" abcdefghijklmnopqrstuvwxyz1234567890,.:;"};
char encrypted[40] =
    {"1qaz2wsx3edc4rfv5tgb6yhn7ujm8i k9ol0p!@#$"};
```

3. Write a function to fill a one-dimensional table with the first 100 Fibonacci numbers. A Fibonacci number is simply the sum of the previous two Fibonacci numbers. The first two numbers in the sequence are 1 and 1. The next few numbers are 2, 3, 5, 8, and so on. Now write a main() program to call this function and pass it to an array to be filled. When the function returns, the main() program should output these Fibonacci numbers *backward*.

4. Create a text disk file containing a list of 50 student records. Each record (or line) should contain two values: an integer ID number and a name. Write a program to read this file and allow the user to look up the ID number for a given name.

5. Create a text disk file containing a list of 50 integer values. Write a program to read this list and issue a warning message to the user for each duplicate found in the list.

6. Using the disk file created for project 5, write a program to input this file, sort the numbers, and output the resulting array.

7. Using the disk file created for project 4, write a program to input this file, sort the records by ID number, and output the result to another disk file. This new file should contain the same records as the original (one ID and name per line), but the ID numbers should be in numeric order. Be sure to keep names and ID numbers together.

8. Since C++ does not have a built-in power operator, it might be convenient to have a two-dimensional table of integer powers. Declare two-dimensional array for ten integers (0 through 9), each integer having four different powers (1 through 4). Write a function to fill this table with appropriate values. In the `main()` program, allow the user to enter an integer and a requested power and have the program then look up and display the appropriate answer. If the user enters a request outside of the table, display an error message. Notice that the power index is to run from 1 through 4.

9. The Game of Life is a traditional computer science program, and you are now ready to give it a try. It is a simple simulation approach to the interaction of primitive life forms such as bacteria colonies. Colonies live out their existence on a two-dimensional matrix. The immediate neighbors of a cell are those eight horizontally, vertically, and diagonally adjacent cells. The life of a colony in the next generation is determined according to a set of simple rules:

a. If a colony cell (containing life) has fewer than two neighbor colony cells, the colony will die of isolation in the next generation.

b. If a colony cell has more than three neighbor colonies, it will die of over-crowding in the next generation.

c. If an empty cell has exactly three colony cells adjacent to it, a new colony will be born there in the next generation. For all other cases, a cell continues unchanged into the next generation.

The game is played by initializing the matrix with initial colonies and then calculating and outputting the matrices of generations as time passes. For example, the following diagram shows five generations of a given initial matrix:

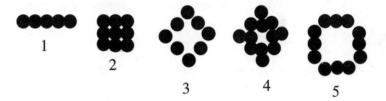

10. Creative Challenge: At this point, you know how to use arrays that have integer indexes beginning with 0. What about tables with indexes that are not even integers? Write a program to read a text file and then output a table of occurrences for each word in the file—the number of times *the* was found, the number of times *in* was found, and so on for each different word in the file.

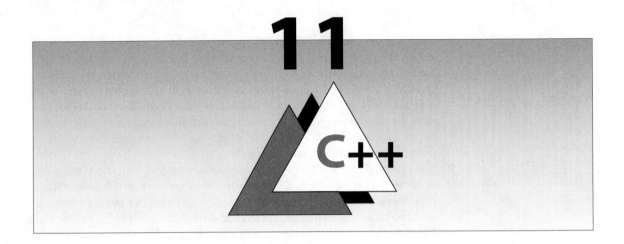

String Processing

Many computer programs deal with processing textual data as opposed to strictly numeric data. You encounter such programs in word processors, interactive role-playing games, e-mail programs, and a variety of other applications. With a basic understanding of arrays, you are now ready to learn some very useful ways to process strings.

11.1 Strings as arrays

In Chapter 9 you learned that an entire string could be stored in a `string` variable. The string stored was considered as a single entity. A **string** variable could be input, output, assigned, and compared with other `string` variables or literals.

You may also think of a **string** variable as being an array. The [ ] operator may be used to reference the individual characters from a **string** variable just as if the **string** variable were actually an array:

```
string q = "lemon";
q[0] = 'd';                      // q now contains "demon"
```

Now, a string variable is actually not a simple array, *but you may conceptually think of it as such*. One of the important features of the C++ language is that more complex objects may be made to appear as simple objects that use familiar operators in familiar ways. This is known as object-oriented programming, and you will learn the basics of this strategy in Chapter 12.

CONCEPT
class objects may
be assigned

As mentioned previously, a **string** variable is actually a class object. *A class object may be assigned*. As a result, you remember that one **string** variable may be assigned to another:

```
string name1, name2 = "programming";
name1 = name2;                         // perfectly legal
```

You would, of course, never attempt this with a simple data type array of **int**, **char**, or **float**:

```
int ages1[5], ages2[5] = {11,22,33,44,55};
ages1 = ages2;
```

WAY!
WRONG

So, in other words, when you are referring to the entire string contents of a **string** variable, you simply use the name of the variable. When you are referring to a single character within the string, you use the [ ] array operator after the variable name.

You may of course, not reference a character beyond the current contents of the variable. For example, in the previous code, the length of string variable q is 5 and the last character that may be referenced is q[4]:

```
cout << q[4];                 // outputs the last character; 'n'
```

Just as an example, here is a snippet of code to output the word associated with the variable name *backward*—producing DERF:

```
string name = "FRED";
int n;
for (n=3; n>=0; n--)
   cout << name[n];
```

The integer variable n goes from 3 down to and including 0. The character D is output, followed by E, followed by R until the character in position name[0] (F) is output last.

Writing a new character to a position in a string variable that does not exist is a serious error:

```
name[56] = 'x';
```

WAY!
WRONG

What about arrays of strings? Consider an array of five different names which we'll call people:

```
string people[5];         // an array of five different strings
```

A simple set of rules applies:

1. When you use the string array name by itself, you are referring to the entire array.

2. When you use a single set of brackets [n], you are referring to a single string in cell n.

3. When you use a double set of brackets [n] [m], you are referring to the string in cell n and a single character m of that string.

For example, to pass the entire `people` array to a function, you might do the following:

```
SomeFunc (people, 5);
```

The function would need to declare a parameter similar to the `people` array. Just as you remember from the chapter on arrays, you do not specify the size of the parameter array and leave the brackets empty:

```
void SomeFunc (string these_people[ ], int size)
{  ...
```

Generally, another parameter (in this case, `size`) is used to indicate the number of cells in the parameter array. Back to the main program, the following outputs the name in cell 2 of the `people` array:

```
cout << people[2];          // output name in cell 2
```

To pass this single name to a function, you might do the following:

```
OtherFunc (people[2]);
```

This function would need to declare a parameter similar to a single string in the name array. For example:

```
void OtherFunc (string one_person)
{  ...
```

Now the fun part: To output just the first letter of the name in cell 2 of the `people` array, use a double set of brackets:

```
cout << people[2][0];       // outputs first letter of one name
```

To pass this single letter to a function, you might do the following:

```
LastFunc (people[2][0]);
```

This last function would need to declare a parameter to be the appropriate type—a single character:

```
void LastFunc (char c)
{   ...
```

It is as if an array of **string** is a two-dimensional array of **char**. This is not actually the case, but the analogy helps one understand the previous statements.

Note: It may initially appear that string arrays are referenced in some special way. While you cannot assign simple data type arrays of **int**, **char**, or **float**, you can refer to components of these arrays in the same manner when passing parameters. This is not a common thing to do at your current stage of programming knowledge, but it is an interesting fact to store away for future reference. For example:

```
int x[3][4] = {{11,22,33}, {44,55,66}, {77,88,99}};// 3 sets of 4 integers
FirstFunc (x);          // passes entire 2-d array
SecondFunc (x[2]);      // passes set 2 (a 1-d array of 4)
ThirdFunc (x[2][3]);    // passes set 2; integer in cell 3 (a single int)
```

This is as far as the analogy goes. You certainly cannot assign or output components other than individual cells for these types of arrays:

```
int x[3][4] = {{11,22,33}, {44,55,66}, {77,88,99}};// 3 sets of 4 integers
int y[3][4];

y = x;
y[2] = x[1];
cout << x;
cout << x[2];
```

Returning back to **string** variables, let's do an example program that inputs a word and then outputs this word with the first letter capitalized (Listing 11.1). You will remember from a previous chapter that there is a library function islower() which returns true if a character argument is a lowercase letter. You also learned the character function toupper() which returns the integer code for the uppercase equivalent of a character argument. This integer code can be assigned to a single character cell to become a **char**. The prototype for these functions is in the <ctype.h> header.

Listing 11.1

```
// Capitalize.cpp   A program to input a word and output the capitalization
#include <iostream>
#include <string>
#include <ctype.h>
using namespace std;
```

```
void (main)
{   string word;
    cout << "enter word to be capitalized: " ;
    cin >> word;
    if (islower(word[0]))
        word[0] = toupper(word[0]);
    cout << "capitalized word is: " << word << endl;
}
```

11.2 Member functions

Remember, a **string** variable is a class object. Quite a number of member functions are available for **string** objects. Several useful functions are described in Table 11.1. Assume a **string** variable s, string expression sexp, a **char** c, and integers pos and n.

As you remember from Chapter 9, the find() member function is used to locate a string expression. Instead of always being zero as in the previous examples, the second parameter pos is actually used to indicate the character position in the string where the search should begin. If a given string expression is found, find() returns the location index. If not found, find() returns an **unsigned long** value greater than max_size(), or greater than the number of characters in the string. For example:

```
string r="this is a test string", s="test", t="NOT FOUND";
cout << r.find(s, 0);    // outputs 10, the location of "test"
cout << r.find(t, 0);    // outputs a very large number
cout << r.find(s, 11);   // outputs a very large number
```

The insert() member function can be used to insert a string expression into an existing **string** variable. For example, using the above r, s, and t variables:

Table 11.1 Useful member functions of the class string

Member Function	Purpose
s.find(sexp, pos);	Returns the first occurrence of sexp in s starting at pos or an unsigned long greater than max_size().
s.find(c, pos);	Returns the first occurrence of c in s starting at pos or an unsigned long greater than max_size().
s.insert(pos, sexp);	Inserts a copy of sexp into s beginning at pos.
s.replace(pos, n, sexp);	Replaces n chars of s beginning at pos with sexp.
s.substr(pos, n);	Returns a copy of the substring of s beginning at pos for n chars.
s.length();	Returns the current length of s.
s.max_size();	Returns the maximum size for s as an unsigned long.

```
r.insert(s, 5);
cout << r;                  // outputs "this test is a test string"
```

The `substr()` function is used to make a copy of a portion of a string. Consider the following:

```
string u;
u = t.substr(4, 5);         // copy beginning at cell 4 for 5 cells
cout << u;                  // outputs "FOUND"
```

The variable u now contains a copy of the substring of t beginning at cell 4 and going for 5 characters.

Variables of type **string** can be quite large, but this limit is actually system dependent. All C++ development systems of which I am aware allow at least 2^{16} characters for each `string` variable. In some, the limit is much larger. For example, Microsoft Visual C++ 6.x allows just slightly less than 2^{32} characters, which is sufficient to store this entire text in a single **string** variable. The member function `max_size()` may be used to find the limit for a given system. This function returns an **unsigned long**:

```
cout << u.max_size();  // maximum size for any string variable
```

11.3 Character arrays for strings

CONCEPT

char arrays for
strings

This section may be omitted without loss of continuity. It is placed here for historical perspective and convention.

Since the last chapter, you've learned the use of **string** variables for textual representations. There is another older method of representing strings using **char** arrays. (This is the only practical way of doing text processing in the C language and older versions of C++ where the more modern **string** class standard is not supported.) To represent strings, one simply declares a **char** array of enough length to hold the intended text — plus one. This last cell is used to hold an end-of-string marker character, which is just the null character or \0. These string arrays may be initialized during declaration. For example:

```
char name[14] = "Fred A. Smith";
```

Initializing with a literal ensures the correct termination. The system automatically places \0 at the end of the text in the array. This is different from the following statement, which simply initializes the word array with the individual characters specified. Both the plea array and the word array contain sequences of characters, but only the plea and name arrays are terminated with \0 (Figure 11.1).

```
char word[4] = { 'h', 'e', 'l', 'p' };
char plea[5] = "help";
```

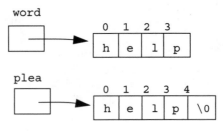

Figure 11.1 The effect of using a literal for `char` array initialization

CONCEPT

string array I/O

If you use a pointer to a **char** array with the insertion << output operator, C++ assumes the array holds a null-terminated string and will subsequently output characters *until the null character is encountered*. If you use a **char** pointer with the extraction >> input operator, the system assumes you wish to input a string and will fill the array with the next word from the input stream and then *add a null character at the end*. (A word means all characters up to the next white space.) Pretty convenient! For example:

```
char text[10];
cin >> text;  // input a word into the 'text' array (end with null)
cout << text; // output characters up to the null
```

EXPERIMENT

What would happen if you used a **char** array in an output statement that did not end with the null character? Try outputting the following:

```
char word[4] = {'h', 'e', 'l', 'p' };
```

CONCEPT

string arguments

Character arrays (appropriately terminated) may be used as arguments to function calls anywhere a literal or **string** variable is expected. (The opposite is also true.) The reason this works is interesting: The compiler actually creates a character array for each literal found in an executable statement. The literal in the executable statement is then replaced with a pointer to this character array just prior to translating the statement. So, for example:

```
char filename[13];
ofstream outfile;
cin >> filename;
outfile.open (filename);
```

If the file name `"thisfile.txt"` were input, the `open()` statement would be exactly the same as the following, since both are passing pointers to character arrays that contain the string `"thisfile.txt"`:

```
outfile.open ("thisfile.txt");
```

These are the only built-in capabilities to support this type of string representation. None of the other operators such as + concatenation or = assignment or the relational comparison operators correctly manipulate these **char** array strings. All other **char** array operations must be accomplished with a function. Consider the following two common mistakes. Suppose a programmer needs a segment of code to determine if two words entered by a user at the keyboard are the same. The following might be attempted:

```
char word1[10] , word2[10];
cin >> word2 >> word1;
if (word1 == word2)
    cout << "yes";
```

Look at the **if** statement. While the programmer intended to check if the arrays contained the same string, this comparison tests *if the two pointers are equal*. Even if these two arrays contain the same word, they will be in different locations and the two pointers will never be equal.

Fortunately, this older method of representing strings has led to the construction of an extensive library. Table 11.2 summarizes the more useful functions of this library. The interface header file needed to access the library is `"string.h"`. Notice that the header file has an `.h` extension. Do not confuse this header with the one used for **string** variables.

Table 11.2 Library of string manipulation functions

Prototype	Operation
void strcpy (char **dest[]**, char **source[]**)	Copies chars from source array to dest array up to and including null char.
void strcat (char **dest[]**, char **source[]**)	Concatenates chars from source array onto end of dest array up to and including null char.
int strlen (char **source[]**)	Returns the integer length of the string in source.
int strcmp (char a[], char b[])	Alphabetically compares two strings; returns 0 if strings are equal, <0 if a is before b, and >0 if a is after b.
int atoi (char **source[]**)	Returns the first digit chars in source as an integer.
float atof (char **source[]**)	Returns the first digit decimal chars in source as a float value.

None of these functions do any significant checking for error conditions. For example, if you attempt to use `strcat()` to concatenate a long string onto the end of another string without sufficient room, the destination array will simply be overwritten. All functions assume the character array parameters are correctly terminated with the null character.

11.4 Example project

Suppose one needs to process a text file so that all occurrences of a given word are replaced with another. For example, suppose a form letter is generated to be sent to CUSTOMER. The letter might look like Figure 11.2. Now suppose this document is saved in a text file named `"letter.txt"`.

A list of customers to which this letter is to be sent is in a file named `"customers.txt"`. Suppose the names in the `"customers.txt"` file contain two words—a title and a last name—such as Figure 11.3.

World Wide Widgets
123 Center Place
New York, NY 01234

Dear CUSTOMER:

Your account is past due. Please remit the entire balance at once, CUSTOMER, or we will be forced to turn the matter over to the law firm of Dewey, Cheatem, and Howe. CUSTOMER, this is your last chance.

Have a nice day!

E. Scrooge,
President.

Figure 11.2 Possible `"letter.txt"` file

Mr. Samuelson
Mrs. Edwards
Mr. Libowitz
Ms. Crawford
Mr. Jones
Miss Persimmon

Figure 11.3 Possible `"customers.txt"` file

The company needs a program to input this letter and send a copy to each customer with the customer's actual title and name replacing CUSTOMER in each case. The first design of the program has the following components:

> *input the letter from* `"letter.txt"`.

> *loop through all customers in* `"customers.txt"`; *for each customer, make a copy of the letter with the customer's title and name replacing* CUSTOMER *and then output that letter copy.*

Let's attack the first pseudocode oval to input the letter from the disk file. We recognize that the letter is more than one line. One approach would be to input each line of the letter into an array of strings. In that manner, each line preserves the white-space formatting of the original letter. (If we were to input each word into an array, the white spaces would be lost.) We'll assume the letter never contains more than 100 lines:

```
string letter[100];
```

The input operation for the letter needs to be done until the file is empty. This requires an indefinite input loop—something we have done before. Assume a file variable `letter_in` has been opened for the disk file:

```
number_lines = 0;
while (getline (letter_in, letter[number_lines]))
    number_lines++;
```

The next pseudocode oval represents the actual processing of the letter for each customer. This is obviously a loop with one iteration for each customer in the `"customer.txt"` file. Again, this is an indefinite input loop. We'll need some `string` variables for a title, a last name, and one for the combined name. In this case, we'll let the white spaces be ignored since we don't need to preserve any formatting for a customer name. We'll input each word — the title and the last name — as a separate string and then concatenate them to form a customer name. Assume a file variable `customer_in` has been opened for the `"customer.txt"` disk file:

```
number_customers = 0;
while (customer_in >> title)
{   customer_in >> lastname;
    customer = title + " " + lastname;
```

> *make a copy of the letter, replacing* CUSTOMER *with this customer and then output this letter copy.*

```
    number_customers++;
}
```

This last pseudocode oval is a bit detailed, so we'll postpone the effort and simply call a function to do this job. The completed `main()` program is in Listing 11.2.

Listing 11.2

```cpp
// FormLetter.cpp    A program to generate customized form letters.
// ASSUMPTION: file "letter.txt" contains the form letter template with the word
// CUSTOMER in the place of an actual customer name. The file "customers.txt"
// contains titles and last names of customers.
#include <iostream>
#include <fstream>
#include <string>
using namespace std;

void main()
{   string letter[100], title, lastname, customer;
    int number_lines, number_customers;
    ifstream letter_in ("letter.txt", ios::in);
    ifstream customer_in ("customer.txt", ios::in);

    number_lines = 0;
    while (getline (letter_in, letter[number_lines]))
        number_lines++;
    number_customers = 0;
    while (customer_in >> title)
    {   customer_in >> lastname;
        customer = title + " " + lastname;
        Generate_Letter(letter, number_lines, customer);
        number_customers++;
    }
}
```

This main program would first be debugged and tested with a stub for the `Generate_Letter()` function to verify that the letter is being correctly input and the customer names are being correctly input and formed. Now we can turn attention to the function itself. The heading is implied from the way the function is called:

```cpp
void Generate_Letter (string letter[ ], int num_lines, string thisname)
{   ...
```

The function needs to process `num_lines` of letter lines—a definite loop. For each line in the letter, the function needs to determine if the word CUSTOMER is found. If so, that word needs to be replaced with the new last name provided as a parameter. Finally, the function needs to output the line. We can use the `find()` member function to determine if CUSTOMER is in the line, the `replace()` member function to replace CUSTOMER with a null string, and `insert()` to put in the correct customer name (Listing 11.3).

Listing 11.3

```
// Generate_Letter()  Replaces "CUSTOMER" with new name in letter
// ASSUMPTIONS: letter contains num_lines, lastname is a new customer
void Generate_Letter (string letter[ ], int num_lines, string thisname)
{   unsigned long max, pos;
    max = letter[0].max_size();
    for (int n=0; n<num_lines; n++)
    {   if ((pos = letter[n].find("CUSTOMER", 0))  < max)
        {   letter[n].replace(pos, 8, "");
            letter[n].insert(pos, thisname);
        }
        cout << letter[n] << endl;
    }
}
```

Let's examine these function lines with an example. Suppose, the form letter is in parameter `letter` and the name `Mr. Samuelson` is in `thisname`. The `num_lines` variable will be 15. The first function line sets `max` to the very large number representing the maximum **string** variable length for this system. The **for** loop then considers each line in `letter` in turn. For each line, the **if** statement will be true if CUSTOMER is found in the line being examined. Consider when the following line is tested:

```
firm of Dewey, Cheatem, and Howe. CUSTOMER, this is your last
```

In this case, `pos` is set to 34—the cell containing the C of CUSTOMER. The 34 is certainly less than `max` and the **if** is true. Now, the eight characters of CUSTOMER beginning at cell 34 are replaced with a null string:

```
firm of Dewey, Cheatem, and Howe. , this is your last
```

Finally, the new last name is inserted into this string beginning at cell 34 to form the new letter line:

```
firm of Dewey, Cheatem, and Howe. Mr. Samuelson, this is your last
```

You might ask why the program did not simply use the `replace()` **string** member function. It could have. This function replaces a number of characters in the current string with a new string *that does not need to be of the same length*. In other words, the following two lines in the `Generate_Letter()` function

```
letter[n].replace(pos, 8, "");
letter[n].insert(pos, thisname);
```

which replace CUSTOMER with a null string and then subsequently insert the actual customer name in the same position, could be replaced with a single line for the same effect:

```
letter[n].replace (pos, 8, thisname);
```

Occasionally, a good programmer will use several statements to accomplish what could have been done with one in order to debug the program more easily if an error has been made. By breaking a complex operation into several simpler steps, the programmer is often better able to view which operation is associated with a bug.

11.5 Summary

CONCEPTS   In this chapter, you learned that a single **string** variable can be thought of as being an array. Since a **string** is a class object, you may assign an entire **string** variable to another with a simple = operator. In addition, the [ ] operator may be used to reference the individual characters of the **string** variable. It is important not to reference characters beyond the current length of the string stored in a **string** variable.

When you declare an array of strings, three simple rules help you to remember how to reference components of this array: (a) When you use the **string** array name by itself, you are referring to the entire array. (b) When you use a single set of brackets [n], you are referring to a single string in cell n. (c) When you use a double set of brackets [n] [m], you are referring to the string in cell n and a single character m of that string.

These rules only apply to **string** variables at this point. While you may pass subcomponents of other types of arrays, you may not assign, output, or input such components.

A variety of member functions are available from the string class which can be used to manipulate the contents of a string variable. Refer to Table 11.1.

There is another older method of representing strings using **char** arrays. To use this method, one simply declares a **char** array of enough length to hold the intended text—plus one. This last cell is used to hold an end-of-string marker character which is just the null character or \0. These string arrays may be initialized during declaration.

The I/O operators >> and << are able to support this approach. When inputting a string, the >> operator will read characters into the array pointed to until a white space is encountered. An additional null character is then stored at the end of these characters to mark the end of the string. It is the programmer's responsibility to ensure that the array is of sufficient size. The << output operator will output characters from the array pointed to until the null character is encountered.

Pointers to **char** arrays (appropriately terminated) may be used as arguments to function calls anywhere a literal or **string** variable is expected. The opposite is also true.

These are the only built-in capabilities to support string representation with a **char** array. None of the other operators such as + concatenation or = assignment or the relational comparison operators correctly manipulate these **char** array strings. All other **char** array operations must be accomplished with a function. In particular, it is important never to attempt to use comparison operators with **char** arrays, and **char** arrays may not be copied with the = assignment operator.

11.6 Exercises

11.6.a Short-answer questions

1. Is it legal to assign one class object variable to another?
2. Is it legal to assign an **int** array to another **int** array?
3. Indicate the output of the following statements:

```
string name = "Fred Jones";
cout << name;
cout << name[0];
cout << name[9];
```

4. When inputting a string into a **string** variable, the >> operator will stop reading characters when a _____ _____ is encountered.
5. Describe the effect of the following statements:

```
string name = "Sally Smith";
cout << name.find("Smith", 0);
```

6. Give an additional statement that could be used to insert the middle name Ray to the name variable in question 5.
7. Give a statement that could be used to output the current number of characters in the string variable sentence.
8. Give a statement that could be added to the following to output the length or number of characters of the *first word* in the variable sentence.

```
string sentence;
getline (cin, sentence);
```

9. Give a statement that could be added to the preceding code to output the length of the first name.
10. Give a statement that could be added to the preceding code to replace the last word in sentence with the word END.

   *These questions relate to string representation with **char** arrays. If this section of the chapter was skipped, ignore these questions.*

11. Declare a **char** array long enough to hold a word of ten characters.
12. What special character value does C++ use to mark the end of a **char** array string?
13. What is wrong with the following statement?

```
char word[8] = "longword";
```

14. What is wrong with the following statement?

```
char word1[10], word2[10];
cin >> word1;
word2 = word1;
```

15. Which library function might be used to copy the contents of one **char** array string into another?

16. Give a statement that could be added to output the length of the current string stored in the following array:

```
char line[80];
cin >> line;
```

17. What is wrong with the following statements?

```
char word1[10], word2[10];
cin >> word1 >> word2;
if (word1 == word2)
cout << "yes";
```

18. Show the correct way to determine if the two `char` array strings in the previous question contain the same word.

19. Give a statement that could be used to output the word `less` if the string contents of **char** array `word1` are less than the string contents of **char** array `word2`.

20. What is wrong with the following statements? Show an addition to these statements that would correct the problem.

```
char word[5] = {'h', 'e', 'l', 'l', 'o'};
cout << word;
```

11.6.b Projects

1. Write a simple program to input a line of text and then output this same line with a period added at the end.

2. A word is considered a palindrome if it reads the same forward as backward. For example, *madam* is a palindrome as is *did* and *boob*. Write a program to input a word and determine if the word is a palindrome.

3. Write a program to replace single digits in a text file with their appropriate words. You may assume that only single-digit numbers will be found. For example:

```
The box held 7 copies of 2 different books.
```

would be changed to

```
The box held seven copies of two different books.
```

4. Using a `string` variable, read the words of a disk text file and determine if there are any words that violate the following spelling rule: *i before e except after c.*

5. Generate a program to input a list of ten names and then output these names in alphabetical order.

6. In Chapter 9, you saw an example of a spelling-checker program to determine if the words of a file are correctly spelled. Redo this program to allow words in sentence structure. In other words, your spelling checker should ignore the case of words and ignore any punctuation that might follow or precede a word.

   *Projects 7, 8, and 9 relate to string representation with **char** arrays. If this section of the chapter was skipped, ignore these projects.*

7. The library function `strlen()` is used to return the length of the string stored in the **char** array argument. Write and demonstrate your own version of this function.

8. The library function `strcat()` is used to concatenate the second **char** array argument onto the end of the first. Write and demonstrate your own version of this function.

9. The library function `strcmp()` is used to compare the first **char** array argument with the second. Write and demonstrate your own version of this function.

10. **Creative Challenge:** Refer back to project 3, which required that single-digit numbers in a text file be replaced with their word equivalents. Expand this problem to allow multiple-digit numbers. For example:

```
The box held 27 copies of 648 different books.
```

would be changed to become

```
The box held twenty seven copies of six hundred forty eight
different books.
```

You may assume that no numbers larger than three digits will be found.

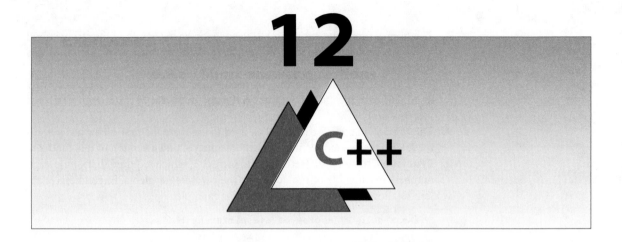

Designing with Simple Classes and Structures

The class is, of all the features and capabilities of C++, the construct that gives the language the most versatility and power. The concepts associated with designing and using classes are fundamental to the principles of object-oriented programming, a methodology of approaching programming projects that has been gaining significant acceptance in the software industry. Up to this point, we have dealt with simple variables and arrays of simple variables. Since the aspects of a real-world problem are not always easily described within those constraints, we need the more powerful features of classes.

`To the Instructor:` This chapter is divided into two sections: coverage of classes (beginning at Section 12.1) and coverage of `struct` (Section 12.10). They are presented basically as independent teaching units. Either can be covered first. For more traditional instructors who feel the `struct` is a natural steppingstone to classes, Section 12.10 can be covered first. For instructors who feel that classes encompass all of the functionality of the `struct` and are no more difficult to learn, the chapter sections should be covered in the given order. (C++ actually treats a `struct` as a class with minor syntax differences.) The section on `struct` can be omitted without loss of continuity, but inclusion is encouraged if for no other reason than historical perspective.

12.1 Object-oriented programming

If you will remember back to Chapter 4, the *software life cycle* was introduced. These are the stages a large software project passes through until it becomes obsolete: analysis, design, coding, testing, and maintenance. Whether or not a large project is profitable (on time, within budget, and functional) often depends on the choice of programming methodology. A methodology includes not only the choice of programming language but also the approach to designing and implementing the project code.

Interestingly, industry studies have shown that by far the greatest portion of a project budget is consumed in maintenance, which includes making modifications, correcting aspects of performance, upgrading to add new features, and so forth. A good methodology will certainly simplify the design and coding stages. Most important, a good methodology will lead to programs that are easily understood by others and efficiently modified.

KEY TERM
object-oriented
programming

Object-Oriented Programming, or OOP for short, is a methodology which is rapidly becoming the industry standard. OOP has been shown to simplify program design. More important, OOP leads to projects that are well organized, easy to design, flexible, easy to read, and easy to modify. The reuse of sections of code from other projects is facilitated. Algorithms or functions that are implemented for one representation of data are easily modified to be useful for a completely different type of information.

C++ is very popular with organizations who choose the OOP methodology. Several other languages support the OOP methodology as well: Java (popular in Internet applications), Ada (common in military and government projects), SmallTalk, and others. Even if you end up using another language, the principles of OOP that you will be exposed to in this course are basically the same. Keep in mind that C++ does not *require* the use of OOP methodology.

OOP has all the foregoing advantages *once you know how to use it correctly.* Just because C++ supports OOP doesn't mean that all C++ programs use the OOP methodology and are well organized, easy to understand and modify, and so on. The truth is far from it. You need to learn not only the features of the language that support OOP but also how they are intended to be used to achieve the OOP goals.

Unfortunately, providing support for OOP leads to a language that is a bit more complex to learn and efficiently use than other general-purpose high-level languages. It takes a lot more training and experience to become a good OOP C++ programmer than it takes just to become a good C programmer. In addition, the OOP features of C++ may tend to complicate the simple programs demonstrated and assigned in a text where the power of these features may not be visible or obviously needed. Keep in mind that the purpose of examples and assignment projects in this text is not necessarily the use of the finished program but rather the concepts and skill learned from solving the problem. We will not learn all the OOP supporting features of C++ in this text, just an introduction to the concepts of the methodology and the basic OOP features of C++.

KEY TERM
object

Fundamental to OOP is the concept of an *object*. An object is simply a self-contained representation of something useful in the real world. An object can be a student, a jet engine, a hotel reservation system, a bank account, or just about anything you can name. An object may contain variables and constants, but the concept is much larger and more encompassing. An object contains (a) all the necessary attributes or information to describe its nature and, just as important, (b) all the functions or operations that are necessary for the object to be useful. Application programs don't manipulate objects. They request that objects manipulate themselves. Application programs create objects, send them messages asking them to manipulate themselves for desired results, and destroy objects. These three operations are actually all that an object-oriented program performs. The methods used by an object to keep track of attribute information and to perform these operations are of no concern to the application program.

Think of an airline reservation clerk. Customers come to the clerk to ask that certain results be accomplished: book a reservation, buy a ticket, check a bag, return a ticket, and so forth. The customer is simply sending requests to the clerk. *How* the desired results are accomplished is not important to the customer. As a traveler (application program), you might know how to use the clerk object and accomplish all the desired results without understanding all the workings of the system. The clerk expects to interface with the public through a set of defined request messages. You only need to know the type and form of requests that can be honored. (You could ask the clerk to wash your socks, but you probably wouldn't get very far.) Any other traveler (another application program) can use the same clerk to accomplish the same set of results.

KEY TERMS

data abstraction,
encapsulation,
polymorphism,
inheritance

The basic concepts used in applying OOP methodology are:

- *Data abstraction*. The details of attribute or information representation are hidden from the program using an object. The application program becomes easier to write if the application programmer does not need to understand the internals of the object in order to use it.

- *Encapsulation*. An object's attributes or information and all the procedures that manipulate these attributes are encapsulated or wrapped together. The application programmer does not need to worry about writing functions to correctly manipulate an object. Those capabilities come packaged within the object itself.

- *Polymorphism*. A function or operator can be designed to work with a variety of different but similar objects. In addition, generic functions can be written which are independent from the type of object they will be passed as arguments.

- *Inheritance*. More complex objects can be created out of simpler objects without the need to understand the internals of these lower-level objects or the methods that are used for manipulation. The development of complex objects becomes a simple matter of combining or adding to lower-level objects that already exist.

Rather than present a more complete formal discussion of the entire OOP methodology, we will begin by learning some important features and capabilities provided by C++ and then, as we go, discuss how they lead to the goals of OOP: Programs that are well organized, easy to design, flexible, easy to read, easy to modify, and allow easy reuse of needed sections in other projects.

12.2 Simple function overloading

KEY TERM
overloading

An idea that is fundamental to the understanding of classes is the concept of *overloading*. C++ allows several different functions to have the same name. (You have been exposed to this concept in the last couple of chapters.) Using the same name or symbol for more than one operation is known as overloading. For example, a programmer might write two Sort() functions, one expecting a **float** array as a parameter and the other expecting a **string** array. Consider the following two prototypes:

```
void Sort (int values[ ], int size);
void Sort (string words[ ], int size);
```

KEY TERM
signatures

When a Sort() function is called, the system resolves the ambiguity (of which version to call) by comparing function *signatures*. A function signature consists of the function name, the function type, the number of parameters, and the type of each parameter. Each function within a program must have a unique signature. In other words, each function must be different from all other functions by at least one aspect of their signatures. The previous two Sort() functions differ in the type of the first parameter.

Consider how this might simplify program development in the larger sense. Suppose one were to develop a set of Sort() functions for **int**, **float**, **char**, and **string** parameters. This set of functions could be placed into the file "Sort.cpp". The prototypes for all the functions in this set could be placed in the file "Sort.h". In the future, any programmer in your business who needs to be able to sort an array simply includes "Sort.h" at the top of a program and adds "Sort.cpp" to the project file. For any of these different array types that need to be sorted, the call is simply:

```
Sort (array, size);
```

It appears to the new programmer that a generic function Sort() is available that is capable of sorting any type of array. In actuality, the system is choosing the appropriate member of the set of functions which match the calling signature.

12.3 The C++ class

KEY TERM
class

The mechanism used to implement OOP objects in C++ is the *class*. At this point in our study, a class is just a declaration for an object. The terms class and object are often used interchangeably. More properly, a class is a kind of template for an object or group of objects.

12.3.a Class declarations

CONCEPT
begin class names
with capital letters

Classes can be declared with quite a range of complexity and flexibility. The purpose of this chapter is not to document all the possibilities and syntax variations but to teach a few of the simple methods associated with basic classes. The basic class is declared with the form seen in the following syntax box. A common convention is to have class names begin with a capital letter. This helps application programmers differentiate between other variable types and class types. Notice the semicolon after the closing brace. This is often forgotten by beginning programmers and will cause the compiler great confusion.

CONCEPT

class declarations

In a basic class, members of a class are either attribute variables or functions. *Public members* are accessible to any part of the application program. *Private members* are accessible only within the class. No other access is allowed.

```
class Name
{ public: public members

  private: private members
};
```

Syntax form

Public members are usually attribute variables and functions representing the class to the public. Public functions are those used as the public interface to application programs using this class. In other words, public functions are used by the program as requests to the object. Private members are attribute variables and functions necessary for the object to represent and perform as it should. These members are not necessary or desirable for public knowledge. Private functions are those operations needed and invoked by the object itself, but they are not available to outside applications.

Let's start with the general concept and then approach a specific example. Using the earlier airline clerk example, public attributes might be the name of the airline being represented and the clerk's name. A private attribute might be the clerk's password used on the reservation computer. A public function might be a request for a reservation. A private function might be reconciling the till at the end of the day.

Consider now a specific example. Suppose a program needs to be able to manage student information: keeping track of names, addresses, GPAs, and so on. Take a look at the following partial class declaration for a **Student** object. Functions are listed as prototypes within the class definition. Variables are declared in the normal fashion:

```
class Student
{ public : void PrintName ();           // print the name
          void AddGrade (float grade); // add grade to GPA
          float GetGPA ();             // return student GPA
          void ChngAddr (char addr[ ]); // update address
          void ChngAddr (char addr[ ], char city[ ]);
                                       // change address and city

  private : ...
};
```

KEY TERM
application
interface

All an application programmer really needs to understand to effectively use this class is the purpose of the public functions and the use of the associated parameters. This is known as the *application interface* for the class. Proper documentation on these functions becomes a sort of application programmer user's manual for the class. Don't let this confuse you: The application interface for a class is really the interface between the class and the application program. The interface between the human user and the application program is called the *user interface*.

KEY TERM
instance

Instances of the class `Student` are created with a declaration in the application program using the class name. An instance is an actual **Student** object, whereas a class is a sort of template definition:

```
Student Fred, Jane, CS101[50];
```

You might say that when you declare variable `temp` as type **int**, you have created an instance of **int** named `temp`. The terminology is not all that important. Most students simply say "declare `temp` to be **int**." Here we have declared `Fred` and `Jane` each to be a **Student**. `CS101` is an array of 50 **Student**s. An individual **Student** is a collection of attribute variables and request functions. *Each individual instance has its own set of attribute variables and functions.* This is obviously true for attribute variables, but does this really mean that each **Student** declared causes a separate section of function code to be linked into the executable program? Does the above example have 52 different sets of identical request functions? This is actually a very good way to think of it, but it is not actually true. There are, of course, 52 different sets of attribute variables. The system links in only one copy of the actual function code for the class but manages this in such a way that *it appears* to the application that individual functions exist for each instance.

The application programmer knows from the public section that five different requests can be made. Notice that two of these requests are calls to the overloaded `ChngAddr()` function. You have already learned in previous chapters that member functions of a class are called using the class instance name followed by a dot. Let's say the member function `AddGrade()` is intended to add a grade to a student's records. Suppose also that `PrintName()` is used to display a student's name. To ask that `Jane` have a grade of 98.7 added and then print the full name of `Fred` would be done as follows:

```
Jane.AddGrade (98.7);
Fred.PrintName();
```

In the following requests, the 17th **Student** in the array `CS101` is to have his address changed, while Jane is to have her address and city changed:

```
CS101[17].ChngAddr ("appt. 27b, Moon Towers");
Jane.ChngAddr ("123 Oak Str", "Logan, UT.");
```

This dot notation serves to indicate the **Student** to whom the request is being made. In these two requests, the application programmer has no idea how the GPA is stored or how the new address is recorded *and doesn't care*.

Now let's go back and complete the class declaration to include some missing private members:

```
class Student
{ public :  void PrintName ();              // print the name
            void AddGrade (float grade); // add grade to GPA
            float GetGPA ();              // return student GPA
            void ChngAddr (char addr[ ]);// update address
            void ChngAddr (char addr[ ], char city[ ]);
                                          // change address and city
  private : float GPA;
            string address1, address2;
            int number_of_grades;
            string fullname;
};
```

These private variables enable each **Student** to keep track of important attribute information between requests from the application program. They are quite private, however. If the application program were to attempt to examine or change one, a compile-time error would result:

```
cout << Jane.GPA;
cout << Fred.fullname;
```

WAY! WRONG

Member attribute variables may not be initialized in the declaration. (We will later see a method of initializing attribute variables.)

```
private : float GPA = 4.0;
```

WAY! WRONG

Let's go back to the class definition and add a public attribute variable just to see how that might be accessed:

```
class Student
{ public :    same as above

              int ID;                    // student id number

  private :   same as above
};
```

The application program could now access the ID of Jane, Fred, or any of the 50 different CS101 students. Again, the dot notation allows one to specify which of the many different Student instances you are referring to:

```
cout << Fred.ID;                // output Fred's ID number
```

It should now be clear that if a programmer understands the application interface, he or she can declare and use the class instances without an understanding of how the public functions actually perform or how the attributes of the class are represented and stored. It should also become clear that a programmer can declare a new class and define an application interface without needing to know how the public functions will actually work. The class declaration only includes function prototypes, not the functions themselves. We will return to the implementation of these functions in a moment.

12.4 Managing projects that use classes

CONCEPT
recommended style

We will manage projects that use classes by separating files according to the following recommended style. (This is basically the same approach we have previously used in managing projects.) Other approaches are possible, but this approach is almost universally accepted as proper style:

■ Place the class declaration into an interface header file: *classname*.h.

■ Place the implementation of the functions of this class into a separate C++ implementation file: *classname*.cpp.

■ Place the application file(s) in separate .cpp files. Each application file that needs to utilize the class must include the header file.

■ All application files and the *classname*.cpp file should be listed as part of the application project file.

The goal of this approach is to make the class declaration and implementation readily available to application programs but preserve them as separate *and independent* files, which the application programmer does not need to examine or edit.

Let's now take a look at another class example. Suppose a program is needed to manipulate complex numbers, such as a complex-number calculator capable of addition, subtraction, and multiplication. The application program needs to input complex numbers and then add, subtract, and multiply them. Results are then displayed. Assume now that this program will be developed by a team of two programmers. Programmer A has the responsibility of providing the team with a new class—the **Complex** class. Programmer B has the responsibility of writing the application program and using the **Complex** class to achieve what the eventual application desires.

We'll start with A's job. The application interface to the class might first be declared as follows:

```
class Complex
{ public :
    void InputC (istream& in);      // input a complex number
    void OutputC (ostream& out);    // output a complex number
```

```
        Complex AddC (Complex x);      // add two complex numbers
        Complex SubC (Complex x);      // sub two complex numbers
        Complex MultC (Complex x);     // mult two complex numbers
      private:                         // to be completed later
    };
```

The interface just defined consists of five functions. The first two allow an application to input values into a **Complex** (or more properly, a **Complex** instance) or output values from a **Complex** using any **istream** or **ostream** file variables. The next three allow arithmetic operations to be performed on a **Complex** (adding another **Complex** to a **Complex** and so on). Now, the class declaration is not executable code; it just contains definitions. Programmer A places this class definition (to be completed later) into the file "complex.h".

With this interface, programmer B is ready to write the application program. Listing 12.1 is a possible example.

Listing 12.1

```
// cmath.cpp  A program to do complex math.
#include <iostream.h>
#include "complex.h"
void main ()
{   char choice;
    Complex a, b, c;                        // three Complex variables
    cout << "enter a complex number pair such as (5.1,2.3i):";
    a.InputC(cin);                          // input cmplx into 'a'
    cout << "enter a complex number pair such as (5.1,2.3i):";
    b.InputC(cin);                          // input cmplx into 'b'
    cout << "enter choice: (a)dd, (s)ub, (m)ult:";
    cin >> choice;                          // get user's choice
    switch (choice)
    {   case 'a' :  c = a.AddC (b);         // add 'b' to 'a', assign to 'c'
                    break;
        case 's' :  c = a.SubC (b);         // sub 'b' from 'a'
                    break;
        case 'm' :  c = a.MultC (b);        // mult 'b' to 'a'
                    break;
        default :   cout << "entry error";
    }
    c.OutputC(cout);                        // display results.
}
```

CONCEPT

request functions belong to a class variable

Notice in this Listing that the application programmer simply treats the **Complex** class as a sort of new variable type. Any manipulation of a **Complex** is handled through request function calls. In the program, every request function *belongs* to a class variable or instance using the dot notation. From the interface, programmer B knows that the AddC() function is called with the owner instance placed in front with the dot notation and that the **Complex** to be added to the owner is placed within parentheses as an argument. The function returns the sum and also a **Complex**.

CONCEPT

built-in capabilities

Notice now that a class variable may be assigned to another class variable with the = operator. This is such a common need that C++ has this capability built in without any need for special programming. In the program, the **Complex** value returned by AddC() is assigned to c. Also built in to C++ is the ability to pass class variables (or more appropriately, class objects) as arguments and parameters to functions or as returning values. The other operators of the language are not automatically available — >>, <<, the arithmetic operators, the relational comparison operators, and so on — without further programming. In the following fragment, the <<, +, and < operators are not built-in or defined for this new Complex class constructed by the programmer:

```
cout << a;        // '<<' is not defined
c = a + b;        // addition is not defined
if (a < b) ...    // '<' is not defined
```

Programmer B places this application program in file "cmath.cpp". At this point, there are two files: "complex.h" and "cmath.cpp".

12.4.a Function implementations

Programmer A now has the responsibility to complete the class declaration in "complex.h" and to actually write and implement the member functions in the file "complex.cpp". Let's do a little math review: A complex number is just a pair of values, one representing a real part and the other the imaginary part. They are often written as a pair with a comma between them. The imaginary value in the pair is usually suffixed with an i or j:

(5.6, 7.8i)

If we let the Greek symbols represent any numeric value, the math operations are defined as follows:

$(\alpha, \beta i) + (\chi, \delta i) \longrightarrow ((\alpha+\chi), (\beta+\delta)i)$
$(\alpha, \beta i) - (\chi, \delta i) \longrightarrow ((\alpha-\chi), (\beta-\delta)i)$
$(\alpha, \beta i) * (\chi, \delta i) \longrightarrow ((\alpha\chi - \beta\delta), (\beta\chi + \alpha\delta)i)$

Programmer A decides to use two **float** attributes to represent a **Complex** value, and "complex.h" is completed (Listing 12.2).

Listing 12.2

```
// complex.h  Declaration for the class Complex

class Complex
{ public :
    void InputC (istream& in);     // input a complex number
    void OutputC (ostream& out);   // output a complex number
    Complex AddC (Complex x);      // add two complex numbers
    Complex SubC (Complex x);      // sub two complex numbers
    Complex MultC (Complex x);     // mult two complex numbers
  private:  float real, imag;      // private attributes.
};
```

Programmer A now writes or implements the member functions for "complex.cpp". We will start with the addition function AddC(). This function must add a parameter (a **Complex**) to the owner of the function (a **Complex**) and return the **Complex** result. Since there may be other AddC() functions associated with other classes, a method is needed for specifying that this particular function belongs to the class **Complex**. (Remember that the class declaration is in a separate file "complex.h".) This is the purpose of the scope operator ::.

type classname::funcname
    (parameter-list)

Syntax form

CONCEPT

the default owner

Each member function name is preceded with the name of the class and the scope operator. Within a member function, anytime a member attribute variable is referred to without the owner dot specified, *it is assumed to belong to the function owner*. If a member variable of a parameter or local **Complex** variable is referenced, the owner dot must be specified. Within a member function, the entire owner instance can be referred to with the expression *this, a notation which will become clearer later on. For example, within a member function:

```
Complex temp;
temp = *this;                  // a copy of the owner
```

Since the "complex.cpp" function can be separately compiled, the file "complex.h" will need to be included for this file to use the **Complex** declaration. Listing 12.3 gives the functions in "complex.cpp" as written by programmer A.

Listing 12.3

```
// complex.cpp  Implementation file for class Complex
#include <iostream.h>
#include "complex.h"

// AddC()  Return the sum of the owner and the parameter
Complex Complex::AddC (Complex x)
{  Complex temp;
   temp.real = real + x.real;
   temp.imag = imag + x.imag;
   return (temp);
}

// SubC()  Return the diff. between the owner and parameter
Complex Complex::SubC (Complex x)
{  Complex temp;
   temp.real = real - x.real;
   temp.imag = imag - x.imag;
   return (temp);
}

// MultC()  Return the product of  the owner and the parameter
Complex Complex::MultC( Complex x)
{  Complex temp;
   temp.real = (real*x.real) - (imag*x.imag);
   temp.imag = (imag * x.real) + (real * x.imag);
   return (temp);
}

// InputC()  Input a complex pair into owner
void Complex::InputC (istream& in)
{  char i, paren, comma;
   in >> paren >> real >> comma >> imag >> i >> paren;
}

// OutputC()  Output the owner as a complex pair
void Complex::OutputC (ostream& out)
{  out << '(' << real << ',' << imag << "i)" << endl;
}
```

KEY TERM
function host

Remember, anytime a member variable is referenced without the owner-dot notation, it is assumed to belong to the owner. Another name for the owner of a function is the class *function host*.

The OutputC() and InputC() functions have a stream file variable as an argument. This would then allow I/O using files as well as the cin and cout variables. For example, the following could be done in an application program:

```
ifstream infile ("complex.dat", ios::in);
a.InputC(infile);
```

The complete project file for this application would include the `"cmath.cpp"` and `"complex.cpp"`. After building the project, the following is an example session with a user:

```
c:> cmath
enter a complex number pair/such as (5.1, 2.3i): (5.6, 7.2i)
enter a complex number pair/such as (5.1, 2.3i): (1.5, 9.3i)
enter choice: (a)dd, (s)ub, (m)ult: a
(7.1, 16.5i)
```

You may wish to explicitly state that the `AddC()` function does not modify the owner instance or the `Complex` argument by adding the **const** modifiers. Compare the following prototype with the corresponding `AddC()` function of Listing 12.2:

```
Complex AddC (const Complex x) const;
```

12.4.b Constructors

KEY TERM
constructor

For programmer B to write a more versatile application program, there needs to be some way of initializing **Complex** variables without requiring the user to enter data from the keyboard. You remember that when **int** variables are declared, they may be initialized with a constant value. The same is possible with class variables if a *constructor* function is provided in the class. A constructor is a special member function that allows initialization. The constructor is automatically invoked for each class variable that is declared with an initial value. Before we learn how to implement a constructor, let's see what this means to application programmer B. The initial values for each member variable are listed in parentheses following the new class variable name. The following would be allowed:

```
Complex a(5.6, 7.9), b(3.4, -8.2), c;
```

In the example, a would be initialized with a real value of 5.6 and an imaginary value of 7.9. The variable b would be initialized with a real value of 3.4 and an imaginary value of -8.2.

CONCEPT
using constructors

A constructor member function always has a special name, which is the same name as the class itself. Adding the following prototype to the **Complex** public functions (in `"complex.h"`) would add the constructor to the class declaration:

```
Complex (float initreal, float initimag);        // constructor
```

CONCEPT
constructors do not
return a value

Notice that the constructor prototype does not have a function return type declared (not **void**, not **Complex**, nothing!) Unlike other functions, a constructor is a special function that must not have a return type. It is never invoked or called directly by the application and so never returns to the application. It is simply used by the system when a class variable is declared. Here is a possible implementation of the constructor to be placed within the implementation file `"complex.cpp"`:

```
Complex::Complex (float initreal, float initimag)   // constructor
{   real = initreal;
    imag = initimag;
}
```

CONCEPT
**constructors must
be available for all
declarations**

Programmer A is not done yet. What about the declaration of c? This **Complex** variable does not have an initialization given. If you provide a constructor, *you must provide an overloaded signature for a constructor for all declarations to be used.* In other words, there is a problem: Programmer A has decided to allow initializations, but there is no constructor function for the declaration of a class variable without an initialization. To solve this problem, this other constructor doesn't need to do anything; but nevertheless, it must exist.

One may add a *default constructor* (which in this case does nothing) by adding the following to the header file:

```
Complex() { }
```

KEY TERM
default constructor

This is not just a prototype; it is a complete function implementation. A declaration may actually contain complete function definitions and not just prototype declarations, but that is not very good style. We previously decided that `.h` files would not contain executable code, but definitions and interfaces only. The segment does not violate that style rule since the function actually contains no executable code. Now, however, there is a constructor signature for both **Complex** declarations — with an initialization list and without a declaration list. If one also wished to allow initializations with only the real value specified and the imaginary value defaulting to zero, another overloaded constructor could be added for that signature.

CONCEPT
**invoking a
constructor**

Be careful. A constructor is invoked when you declare an instance of a class with a list of initial values in parentheses. The default constructor is not invoked with an empty set of parentheses:

```
Complex c();
```

WAY! WRONG

This line is actually a prototype declaration; c is declared to be a function that returns a **Complex**. The proper method of using the default constructor is just to do an uninitialized declaration:

```
Complex c;                      // an uninitialized class variable.
```

CONCEPT

a default
constructor may
be required

The bottom line is this: If you add a constructor to a class declaration, also add a default constructor. They nearly always come in pairs. If you do not add any constructors, the default constructor is not needed. (Actually, the system creates a default constructor for you. If you supply even one constructor, the system assumes you do not wish this standard default constructor and you must supply it explicitly.) Listing 12.4 is the new version of "complex.h" containing both constructors (one a complete function and one a prototype with the implementation in "complex.cpp")

Listing 12.4

```
// complex2.h  Improved Complex class with constructors

class Complex
{ public :
  Complex () { }                              // default constructor
  Complex (float initreal, float initimag);   // constructor
  void InputC (istream& in);                  // input a complex number
  void OutputC (ostream& out);                // output a complex number
  Complex AddC (Complex x);                   // add two complex numbers
  Complex SubC (Complex x);                   // sub two complex numbers
  Complex MultC (Complex x);                  // mult two complex numbers
  private:  float real, imag;                 // private attributes.
};
```

Now what about arrays of class variables? No initialization for individual members of arrays is supported other than that provided by the default constructor. In the following declaration, the default constructor is invoked for each cell of the array. Any other initialization must be done by assignment or input statements:

```
Complex group[50];        // must use the default constructor
```

12.5 Operator overloading

Let's go back and take a look at things from the application programmer's perspective (programmer B). To use the **Complex** class, the programmer needed to learn the interface and the appropriate method of calling the member request functions. How could things be made better so that the application program was (a) easier to design and code, (b) easier to read and understand, and (c) easier to modify and maintain by other programmers? The answer is simple: Make the interface to the **Complex** class as close as possible to what the application programmers already know and understand. Suppose we could tell application programmers that the **Complex** class was to be used just as one might use **int** or **float**? We will call this class version "complex3". Listing 12.5 shows what the application programmer would *like* to be able to write. We'll call this version "cmath3.cpp".

Listing 12.5

```
// cmath3.cpp  A program to do complex math.
// Assumption:
// Complex can be treated as any other simple numeric data type.
#include <iostream.h>
#include "complex3.h"

void main ()
{   char choice;
    Complex a, b, c;                            // three Complex variables
    cout << "enter a complex number pair: ";
    cin >> a;                                   // input cmplx into 'a'
    cout << "enter a complex number pair: ";
    cin >> b;                                   // input cmplx into 'b'
    cout << "enter choice: (a)dd, (s)ub, (m)ult: ";
    cin >> choice;                              // get user's choice
    switch (choice)
    {   case 'a' :   c = a + b;                 // add 'b' to 'a', assign to 'c'
                     break;
        case 's' :   c = a - b;                 // sub 'b' from 'a'
                     break;
        case 'm' :   c = a * b;                 // mult 'b' to 'a'
                     break;
        default  :   cout << "entry error";
                     exit (0);
    }
    cout << c;                                  // display results.
}
```

This certainly is easier for another programmer to read and understand. It appears as if **Complex** is just like other numeric data types. This is possible because C++ allows not only member functions to be overloaded *but operators as well*. Take a look first at the arithmetic operators *, +, and - to see how they are implemented in the following section.

12.5.a   Overloading member operators

CONCEPT

many operator symbols can be used for functions

Each of these operators can be thought of as a function that has two operands or arguments: one on the left and one on the right. The type of these arguments along with the operator symbol itself represent the signature of the operator function. Additional signatures can be added to overload a member operator using the phrase **operator** *symbol* as the name of the function.

```
type classname::operator  symbol
    ( right-side arg ) ;
```

Syntax form

Notice that only the right-side argument is declared as a parameter. *The left-side argument is always the owner or host of the operator.* For example:

```
c = a + b;
```

Here, the owner or host is a and the right-side argument is b. To locate this operator function, the system would search the operator functions declared within the class of a or **Complex** to locate the + operator with a **Complex** as the right-side parameter. To overload the + operator to handle **Complex** arguments, the following prototype might be used:

```
Complex Complex::operator + (Complex x);
```

The code specifies a + operator member of **Complex** that returns a **Complex** as the result of the operation. In other words, the sum of a **Complex** and a **Complex** is another **Complex**.

12.5.b Overloading nonmember operators

The extraction >> and insertion << operators present a bit of a problem in that the left-side owner of the operator is in the **ostream** or **istream** classes. To overload these operators so that a right-side argument of a **Complex** would be recognized and correctly handled, we would need to edit and modify these classes, which we did not write, do not really understand, or do not have easy access to. The solution is not to try and learn the internal workings of these classes but simply to *overload these operators outside any class*. The syntax for overloading an operator that is not a member of any particular class is as follows:

```
type operator  symbol
    ( left-side arg, right-side arg ) ;
```

Syntax form

Now, a function that is not a member of the Complex class cannot access any of the private attribute variables, but it certainly can *call the appropriate member function* to do so. The Output() and Input() member functions are already available. The overloaded insertion or extraction operator functions simply call these member functions and pass the appropriate stream variable.

KEY TERM
wrapper functions

These overloaded insertion and extraction operator functions are appropriately called *wrapper functions*, since all they do is call another function. The "complex3.cpp" file in Listing 12.6 replaces the previous request functions with overloaded operators for arithmetic calculations and adds wrapper I/O functions.

Listing 12.6

```cpp
// complex3.cpp  Implementation file for class Complex using
// overloaded arithmetic and insertion, extraction operators
#include <iostream.h>
#include "complex3.h"

// '+' operator  Returns the sum of the owner and the parameter
Complex Complex::operator + (Complex x)
{  Complex temp;
   temp.real = real + x.real;
   temp.imag = imag + x.imag;
   return (temp);
}

// '-' operator  Returns the diff. between the owner and parameter
Complex Complex::operator - (Complex x)
{  Complex temp;
   temp.real = real - x.real;
   temp.imag = imag - x.imag;
   return (temp);
}

// '*' operator  Returns the product of  the owner and the parameter
Complex Complex::operator * ( Complex x)
{  Complex temp;
   temp.real = (real * x.real) - (imag * x.imag);
   temp.imag = (imag * x.real) + (real * x.imag);
   return (temp);
}

// InputC()  Input a complex pair into owner
void Complex::InputC (istream& in)
{  char i, paren, comma;
   in >> paren >> real >> comma >> imag >> i >> paren;
}

// OutputC()  Output the owner as a complex pair
void Complex::OutputC (ostream& out)
{  out << '(' << real << ',' << imag << "i)" << endl;
}
```

```
// wrapper function for the extraction '>>' operator
istream& operator >> (istream& in, Complex& x)
{  x.InputC (in);
   return (in);
}

// wrapper function for the insertion '<<' operator
ostream& operator << (ostream& out, Complex x)
{  x.Output (out);
   return (out);
}
```

Notice that the I/O wrapper functions declare the stream variable as a reference parameter and return a reference to the same stream variable. There is an important reason for this. Normal use of the insertion operator allows one to cascade values to be output. For example:

```
float x=5.6;  int y=987;  char z='#';
cout << x << y << z;
```

Take another look at the output statement with appropriate parentheses inserted:

```
((cout << x ) << y) << z;
```

What occurs is this: First, the appropriate member insertion function << belonging to the **ostream** class that has a signature with a float as the argument is called with x. The **ostream** owner cout is updated and the function returns cout. The net result is:

```
(cout << y) << z;
```

The output of y occurs and the updated **ostream** owner cout is again returned to be used with z:

```
cout << z;
```

CONCEPT
updating the
stream variable

To make our overloaded insertion and extraction operators function in the same manner and allow cascaded use, they must update the stream variable and return it. Listing 12.7 is the associated header file "complex3.h".

Listing 12.7

```
// complex3.h  New and Improved Complex class with construc-
// tors and overloaded arithmetic operators
```

```
class Complex
{ public :
    Complex () { }                     // default constructor
    Complex (float initreal, float initimag);// constructor
    void InputC (istream& in);         // input a complex number
    void OutputC (ostream& out);       // output a complex number
    Complex operator+ (Complex x);     // add two complex numbers
    Complex operator- (Complex x);     // sub two complex numbers
    Complex operator* (Complex x);     // mult two complex numbers
  private:  float real, imag;          // private attributes.
};
ostream& operator << (ostream& out, Complex x);
istream& operator >> (istream& in, Complex& x);
```

CONCEPT
a standard idiom for class I/O

Notice that the overloaded I/O operator prototypes are declared outside of the **`Complex`** class. These prototypes and the associated overloaded function implementations *can be used as a standard idiom*. In other words, to overload the insertion and extraction operators for any new class you develop, simply use these two prototypes and their associated implementation functions with only the class name changed. Each new class must then have an appropriate `OutputC()` and `InputC()` function declared and implemented for these wrapper functions to call.

CONCEPT
only existing operators can be overloaded

Only existing operators can be overloaded or implemented with the **`operator`** *symbol* syntax. The language does not allow one to invent a new operator. For example, suppose one wished to add a power function to the language using the caret ^ symbol:

```
int operator ^ (int base, int exponent);
```

Nearly all C++ operators can be overloaded (you cannot overload scope `::` or `.` dot). In this chapter, we have covered only the overloading of binary operators—those with arguments on both sides. (This includes the = assignment operator and the compound-assignment operators such as +=, by the way.) The overloading of unary operators such as increment ++ and pointer resolution * as well as some special operators such as parentheses `( )` and brackets `[ ]` is an advanced topic and beyond the scope of this text.

12.6 `static` members

KEY TERM
`static` member

You have learned that each instance of a class has its own copies of attribute variables. C++ also allows all class instances or class variables to *share* certain designated attribute variables known as `static` *members*. A `static` member is not stored within any one class instance, but a single globally accessible copy is available to all instances of the associate class. To declare a `static` member, one simply uses the modifier **`static`**.

Consider the following class, which might be useful in managing a laboratory experiment with rats. The goal is to have the system automatically assign a new ID number to each new Rat declared:

```
class Rat
{ public :  Rat ( );              // constructor
                ...                // other member functions
   private : float weight;
             char sex;
             int ID;              // a different ID for each Rat
             static int nextID;   // a static global member
};
```

The static member must also be declared as a special global variable in the class implementation file. To ensure that there is not a conflict with any other variable of the same name, the scope operator is used to tie the static member to the correct class. The modifier **static** is used only in the class declaration and not in the global declaration. static members cannot be initialized with a constructor because there is only one global copy. They must be initialized with this global declaration:

```
// Rat.cpp implementation file for the Rat class
int Rat::nextID = 1;
```

Now when any **Rat** member function refers to the static attribute nextID, they are all referring to the single global copy. Consider how one might use the constructor for this class:

```
Rat::Rat ()
{  ID = nextID++;
}
```

As a result, each declaration of a new **Rat** variable will result in the constructor being automatically invoked. The constructor will assign the next available ID number to the member attribute ID and increment the static global member variable nextID by 1 to be ready for the next declaration.

```
Rat willard, peggy, sam;
```

In this example, willard will have an ID value of 1, peggy will be assigned an ID value of 2, and sam will have an ID of 3. The value of nextID will be 4, ready for any further declarations. (Since the constructor is going to be invoked for every declaration, this will include any temporary Rat variables as well as copies used for parameter passing. Each **Rat**, however, will have a unique ID value even though these might not be consecutive.)

This `static` member is still a private member of the class, even if there is only one copy. The application will not be aware of its existence or be allowed to make a reference using `nextID`. Only member functions have access.

12.7 Should you have `friends`?

C++ normally does not allow nonmember functions to access any private attribute variables. This is how the OOP principle of encapsulation is enforced. Without this encapsulation, application programs (over which the class author has no control) could corrupt important attributes and prevent member functions from operating correctly. The whole idea of encapsulation is that the application programmer does not need to understand the private workings of a class in order to use it. More specifically, the application programmer is not *allowed* to mess up the private workings of a class that he or she does not completely understand. An application program is assured that the class will work correctly because the only manipulation of the class is via member functions.

KEY TERM
friend functions

There is, however, a way to bypass this OOP principle through the use of `friend` *functions*. A `friend` function is one which is not a member, but which has been granted access to the private attribute members of a class. In a class declaration, the modifier **friend** is used to grant this access. Suppose one wished to compare a **Complex** with a **float**. For example, consider the following overloaded < operator which we'll assume has been defined to test the magnitude of a against b;

```
Complex a;  float b;
...
if (a < b) ...          // 'a' is the host, 'b' is the argument
```

This operator is easily implemented since the host is a **Complex**. For example, the following function could be added as a member function to the `"complex2.cpp"` file (as an implementation) and `"complex2.h"` file (as a prototype). Here, the magnitude of the **Complex** host is calculated and compared with the **float** value:

```
int Complex::operator < (float x)
{   float mag;
    mag = sqrt ((real * real) + (imag * imag));
    if (y < mag) return (1);
    else return (0);
}
```

The problem occurs when you decide to allow comparisons the other way around:

```
if (b < a) ...          // the left side 'b' is not a Complex
```

To do this, the operator must be overloaded outside the **Complex** class since the left-side argument is not a **Complex** host. If it is outside the class, it cannot have access to either the real or imag parts of a! This problem can be solved by making the function a friend to the class. In the class declaration:

```
class Complex
{ public :  friend operator < (Complex x, float y);
    . . .
```

The nonmember implementation is straightforward with no special syntax:

```
int operator < (float y, Complex x)
{   float mag;
    mag = sqrt ((x.real * x.real) + (x.imag * x.imag));
    if (y < mag) return (1);
    else return (0);
}
```

Note that the owner-dot notation must be used to specify the components of the **Complex** argument.

Now just a minute! Can't we solve this problem without bypassing the principles of OOP and without leaving the private members of the class open to noncontrolled access? There is a way. Let's return to the basic principle of encapsulation: Anytime a nonmember function needs access to private attributes, it must call a member request function. Suppose we add the following request functions to the class:

```
class Complex
{ public :  float GetReal ();   // return the real part of host
            float GetImag ();   // return the imag part of host
    . . .
```

These two functions have very simple implementations. Consider:

```
float Complex::GetReal ()
{   return (real);
}
```

Now the comparison operator < can be overloaded without needing to be a friend or having access to private attributes:

```
int operator < (float y, Complex x)
{   float mag;
    mag = sqrt ((x.GetReal() * x.GetReal() ) +
                (x.GetImag() * x.GetImag() ));
    if (mag < x) return (1);
    else return (0);
}
```

CONCEPT
use `friends`
judiciously

Some will argue that there are special cases when the `friend` exception is warranted. But these are few and far between. Use `friends` judiciously and sparingly. It is a great temptation to just make a `friend` when a more encapsulated request member access function would be more appropriate. Anytime a `friend` is used, it should be considered part of the class and controlled by the author alone. Application program functions should not be allowed to be `friends` to an encapsulated class.

The advantages of OOP and encapsulating a class may be difficult to see in these small examples, but when working with large projects and teams of many programmers, they will inevitably save you time and money. You will be judged as a programmer not by how quickly you can get a program running, but more by how much money that program makes or saves the company. A quickly written program that is prone to bugs and hard to read and modify will nearly always cost in the long run.

12.8 User-defined conversions

C++ knows about implicit conversions between dissimilar data types. For example

```
int x = 5;  float y = 3.4, z;
z = x + y;
```

is allowed because the value of x is implicitly converted into a **float** before the addition occurs. For class variables, one can define the functions that are to be implicitly invoked whenever the system needs to convert *to* or *from* a class instance to another variable type. Consider first the need to convert *to* a class instance:

```
Complex a;  float y = 4.5;
a = y;
```

This conversion can be accomplished with a *constructor* with a single **float** parameter. The system will automatically apply this constructor to create a temporary **Complex** that can then be assigned to a:

```
Complex::Complex (float somefloat)
{   real = somefloat; imag = 0.0;
}
```

CONCEPT
conversion
functions

To provide implicit conversion *from* a class variable, a special type-conversion function is needed using the following syntax:

operator *type* **( ) ;**	**Syntax form**

For example, to allow the conversion of a `Complex` variable into a **float**, one might use the following function (where the **float** is just the magnitude of the complex value):

```
Complex::operator float ( )
{  return (sqrt (real*real + imag*imag));
}
```

CONCEPT
avoid conversion
ambiguity

Special care needs to be taken to ensure that ambiguity does not result from these added conversion functions. For example:

```
Complex (3.4, 5.6);  float y = 4.5;
cout << (a + y);
```

Should the system convert a to a **float** or y into a **Complex** so that addition can occur?

12.9 `struct` **and user-defined structures**

KEY TERM
structures

There is another simple mechanism in C++ that can be utilized to define and declare new data types which are aggregates of existing types. We call such aggregates *structures* and the mechanism is called the **struct** (short for "structure"). While the C++ **struct** has many features in common with the class, we will focus on the more traditional uses that are compatible with the C language. There are several different syntax forms that can be utilized for defining structures. The following is one of the most common and versatile:

```
typedef struct
{ declarations using existing
    data types
} struct_type_name ;
```

Syntax form

CONCEPT
structure
declarations

The reserved word **typedef** indicates that this syntax form defines a *new data type*. It does not declare variables or instances of that type. The word **struct** indicates that the new data type is a composite or record of existing types. The variable members declared within this structure are a template of what actual instances of this structure will contain when they are later declared. Often, the declarations within a data structure are heterogeneous. For example, consider again the problem of defining a student data structure to consist of a GPA, an address string, a name, and a count of grades:

```
typedef struct
{   float gpa;
    string address;
    int grades;
    string fullname;
} StudentStruct;
```

It is a good idea to use a structure type name with the word struct as a suffix to remind you that this is a new data structure definition name. The segment specifies a new composite data *type* or structure consisting of the components listed. The word **StudentStruct** now represents this data type and can be utilized like the existing types of **int**, **char**, **float**, and so on. Structure definitions are normally placed in a header file in a manner similar to class declarations. This header file is then included in each source file that needs to declare variables using this structure type.

Each variable declared to be of this new type will be associated with this group of components. Actual instances or variables of this new data type are declared in the normal way:

```
StudentStruct Jerry, Greg, Jill;
```

A diagram of these variables would show each variable as a box with five subcomponents:

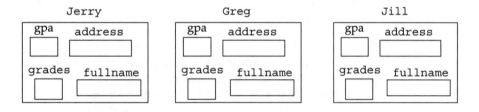

Arrays of structures are very common:

```
StudentStruct seniors[35];
```

Individual components of a **StudentStruct** variable are referenced using the same dot notation utilized for class objects. The variable name is followed by a dot and the subcomponent to be used. For example:

```
Jerry.fullname = "Jerry Smithers";
Jerry.gpa = 3.75;
Greg.grades = 5;
cout << "GPA for Jerry: " << Jerry.gpa << endl;
seniors[k].address = "Building A";
```

Variables declared with the same structure type can be copied with the assignment (=) operator. The effect is to copy all subcomponents of the right-side variable into the corresponding subcomponents of the left-side target variable:

```
Jill = Jerry;        // Jill's data are now the same as Jerry's.
seniors[21] = Greg;  // The 22nd senior is now the same as Greg.
```

Structure variables can be freely passed to parameters of functions if the structure type is the same:

```
void SomeFunc (StudentStruct& person)
{ ...
}
void main ( )
{   StudentStruct Sam;
    ...
    SomeFunc (Sam);
}
```

The other operations common to the primitive data types *are not built in* to C++. For example, without special overloading functions, there is no definition for stream input or output with structures or to compare structures. The components of a structure must be individually referenced:

```
cout << Jerry;
if (Jerry > Jill) ...
```

WRONG WAY!

It is important to remember that data structures with different structure type names are different even if they contain the same subcomponents. For example, the following structure type would not be compatible for assignment to a **StudentStruct** and could not be passed to a **StudentStruct** parameter:

```
typedef struct
{   float gpa;
    string address;
    int ngrades;
    string fullname;
} PersonStruct;

PersonStruct Fred;
Fred = Jerry;
```

WRONG WAY!

In this case, the individual subcomponents are compatible. For example:

```
Fred.gpa = Jerry.gpa;
if (Fred.ngrades < Jerry.ngrades) ...
```

12.10 Comparing `struct` with class

Now, after studying both the class and the **struct**, you may be thinking that a structure is just a limited class, and you are right. The same utility could be achieved with a class. A **struct** *is just a simplified class where all members default to public access*. Obviously, the previous **StudentStruct** could be implemented just as easily as a **Student** class:

```
class StudentClass
{   public:       float gpa;
                  string address;
                  int ngrades;
                  string fullname;
} ;
```

This **Student** class is certainly no more difficult to specify than the **StudentStruct**. In practice, *C++ systems treat a structure as if it had been declared as a class with default public access*. Does this mean that **struct** definitions could also include member functions and private members? Yes, but it is not commonly done. On the professional level, it is good programming practice to utilize classes if a user-defined type is to contain member functions or private components. The **struct** is generally reserved for user-defined data structure types consisting of only public variables. Contrary to what some may think, there are no size or efficiency advantages to using **struct** over classes.

If **struct** does not provide any new capability or isn't any easier to enter and use, why learn both models and notations? There are two very good reasons why this topic is useful to understand. First, the **struct** is the only mechanism available in C because that language does not support classes (although C does not allow **struct** declarations to contain member functions or private components). A good C++ programmer will often be called upon to understand C programs written by someone else. Second, many C++ programmers learned C first. Thus, they tend to utilize **struct** for simple aggregate types that do not require member functions or private attributes. You will frequently need to be able to read and understand C++ software written by others.

12.11 Example project

An integer set is a collection of integers in no particular order. An integer that is a member of a set exists only once within the set. The operations that might be needed to manipulate sets are union, intersection, and membership:

- union—form a new set from the combination of two argument sets.

- intersection—form a new set from the argument set members that belong to both of the two sets.

- membership—a test to determine if an integer is a member of a set.

Some high-level languages have sets as built-in data types. Unfortunately, C++ does not. Let's develop a **Set** class that could be used in a variety of application programs. We will start this project with a draft of the public interface manual:

1. Sets are declared with the type **Set**. Sets are initially empty: `Set a, b, c.`

2. Sets may be assigned to other `Set` variables using =: `b = a.`

3. The union of two sets may be achieved with +: `c = a + b.`

4. An integer may be added to a set with +: `a = a + 25.`

5. The intersection of two sets may be achieved with &: `c = a & b.`

6. The removal of an integer member may be achieved with -: `c = c - 25.`

7. A test for set membership may be achieved with the Boolean function *setvariable*.IsMember(*int*): `if (a.IsMember(25)) cout << yes.`

8. The maximum set size is 100 elements.

With these interface criteria, we are ready to build the "`Set.h`" definition file (Listing 12.8). First, we will use a default constructor to ensure that each declared `Set` instance is initially defined as empty. Since assignment of objects is built in to C++, we do not need to overload the = operator for list item 2. The + will need two implementations (as will -): one for another `Set` as an argument and one for an `int` argument. A Boolean function `IsMember()` will also be needed. We will use a simple **int** array to store set members.

Listing 12.8

```
// Set.h  A class for implementation of sets
class Set
{  public:   Set ();                   // default constructor
             Set operator + (Set s); // union of sets
             Set operator + (int n); // insertion of an integer
             Set operator & (Set s); // intersection of sets
             Set operator - (int n); // removal of an integer
             int IsMember (int n);   // test for membership
   private:  int members[100];
             int size;
};
```

The implementation will simply manipulate the private `members` array to manage `Set` elements (Listing 12.9).

Listing 12.9

```
// Set.cpp  Implementation file for Set class
#include "Set.h"

Set::Set ()                           // default constructor
{  size = 0;
}
```

```
// Union returns a new set containing members of either set
Set Set::operator + (Set s)                 // union of sets
{  int j;
   Set temp;
   temp = s;                                // copy of arg set
   for (j=0; j<size; j++)                   // now add owner set
       if (!IsMember(temp.members[j]))
           temp.members[temp.size++] = members[j++];
   return (temp);
}


//  Insertion returns a set with the arg. added (if not already a member)
Set Set::operator + (int n)                 // insertion of an integer
{  Set temp;
   temp = *this;
   if (!IsMember(n))
       temp.members[temp.size++] = n;
   return (temp);
}


// Intersection returns a set with members which were in both sets.
Set Set::operator & (Set s)                 // intersection of sets
{  Set temp;
   int n, value;
   for (n=0; n<s.size; n++)                 // check members of Set s
   {   value = s.members[n];                // and add if also members of host
       if (IsMember(value))
           temp.members[temp.size++] = value;
   }
   for (n=0; n<size; n++)                    // now check members of
   {   value = members[n];                   // the host set which are not already
       if (s.IsMember(value))                // in the temp set
           if (!temp.IsMember(value))
               temp.members[temp.size++] = value;
   }
   return (temp);
}


// Removes a number if it is a member
Set Set::operator - (int n)                 // removal of an integer
{  Set temp;
   int k;
   for (k=0; k<size; k++)
       if (members[k] != n)
           temp.members[temp.size++] = members[k];
   return (temp);
}
```

```
// Returns true if n is a member of the owner set
int Set::IsMember (int n)                        // test for membership
{   int k;
    for (k=0; k<size; k++)
        if (members[k] == n)
            return (1);
    return (0);
}
```

Naturally, the implementation of this function and the private attribute members of **Set** could be changed without requiring any application programs to be modified.

12.12 Summary

KEY TERMS Quite a few new terms were used in this chapter, and it will be worth your while to become familiar with them:

1. *object-oriented programming*—a methodology for software development that leads to projects that are well organized, easy to design, flexible, easy to read, easy to modify, and containing modules that are easy to reuse.

2. *object*—a self-contained representaiton of something useful in the real world.

3. *data abstraction*—the details of attribute or information representation that are hidden from the program using an object.

4. *encapsulation*—an object's attributes or information and all the procedures that manipulate these attributes are encapsulated or wrapped together.

5. *polymorphism*—a function or operator can be designed to work with a variety of different but similar objects.

6. *inheritance*—more complex objects can be created out of simpler objects without the need to understand the internals of these lower-level objects or the methods they use for manipulation.

7. *overloading*—several different functions may have the same name.

8. *signature*—a function signature is made of the function name, the number of parameters, and the type of each parameter.

9. *class*—the fundamental C++ implementation of an OOP object.

10. *application interface*—the purpose and parameters of the public functions of a class needed by an application programmer.

11. *instances*—specific variables of a class type.

12. *function host*—the class-instance owner of a member function.

13. *constructor*—a member function implicitly called to initialize instances.

14. *default constructor*—a member function implicitly called when an instance is declared without initialization.

15. *wrapper functions*—functions that simply call other functions.

16. *static member*—a member variable shared by all instances of a class.

17. *friend*—a non-member function that is granted access to private members of a class.

18. *structure*—a simple aggregate data type.

CONCEPTS　　In this chapter, the methods of declaring, implementing, and using classes were introduced.

In a basic class, members of a class are either attribute variables or functions. Public members are accessible to any part of the application program. Private members are accessible only within the class. No other access is allowed by application programs. Public members are most often request functions, and private members are most often attribute variables.

When member request functions are invoked, dot notation is used to associate the function call with a specific instance owner. In the implementation file, each member function name is associated with the correct class using the scope operator : :. Within a member function, a member variable referred to without the owner dot is assumed to belong to the function owner. If a member variable of a parameter or local object variable is referenced, the owner dot must be specified. Allowing a non-member function to be declared as a friend allows external access to private members of a class. This approach should be used carefully, since it is contrary to the concepts of object-oriented programming. Careful planning and wrapper functions are more appropriately used in place of friend functions.

A constructor member function always has the same name as the class itself. The constructor prototype does not have a function *type* declared. It is never invoked by the application and so never returns to the application. It is implicitly used by the system when a class variable is declared. No initialization for individual members of arrays is supported other than that provided by the default constructor.

A binary operator can be thought of as a function that has two operands or arguments: one on the left and one on the right. The type of these arguments along with the operator symbol itself represent the signature of the operator function. Additional signatures can be added to overload a member operator function using **operator** *symbol* as the name of the function. The left-side argument is always the owner or host of the operator. Nearly all existing operators can be overloaded. Some exceptions are the scope : : and . dot member operators. New operator symbols cannot be invented.

Implicit conversions *to* a class instance can be accomplished with a constructor. Conversions *from* a class instance to another type can be defined with a special **operator** *type* function.

The **struct** provides an alternate mechanism for declaring a new composite or structured data type. While it has no real advantages over classes, you will need to understand this mechanism to read programs written by others.

Table 12.1 Example segments

`class A ...`	The declaration of a new class.
`void A::Calc(int n);`	Prototypes for two overloaded
`void A::Calc(float x);`	functions with different signatures.
`A::A() { }`	A default constructor.
`A::A (char c, int m);`	Prototype for a specific constructor.
`A a,b,c('x',56);`	Creation of three instances of class A. The last `c` is initialized with a specific constructor.
`cout << a.visible;`	Output of the public member variable `visible`.
`a.SomeFunc();`	Calling the public member function `SomeFunc()`.
`b = a + c;`	Requires that the plus operator be defined (overloaded) for the class of variables `a`, `b`, and `c`.

A couple of important hints should be remembered when programming with classes. Class names should be declared in such a way as to differentiate them from other variable types. A common convention is to begin a class name with a capital letter.

Classes are best managed with separate files for class declaration (the `.h` file) and member function implementations (the `.cpp` file). Both the application program and the implementation should include the `.h` file. The application project must list the implementation `.cpp` file.

When declaring a class variable without initialization, do not use an empty set of parentheses. This would become a declaration of a function returning a class instance.

Whenever user-defined constructors are added to a class, be sure to explicitly add the default constructor.

The overloading of the insertion `<<` and extraction `>>` I/O operators is best done with the idiom wrapper functions presented in the chapter. Be sure to pass and return the stream variable by reference.

Special care needs to be taken to ensure that ambiguity does not result from too many explicit type-conversion functions.

12.13 Exercises

12.13.a Short-answer questions

1. The acronym OOP stands for _____ _____ _____.
2. The concept of hiding the details of an attribute or object representation is known as _____ _____.
3. The term used to note that a function or operator can be used for a variety of similar types and variables is _____.
4. List the four components of a function signature.

5. The purpose and signatures of the public member functions of a class are part of the _____ _____.

6. An appropriate constructor is automatically invoked by the system when a class object is _____.

7. Suppose the following line is observed in a program:

```
person.GetName();
```

Which is the object? Which is a public member function?

8. Which group of member attributes or functions is accessible to an application program? Which group of class attributes is only accessible to the member functions of the class?

9. Briefly explain where the : : operator is most commonly used.

10. List two operators or symbols that cannot be overloaded.

11. What symbol must immediately follow the closing } brace of a class declaration?

12. Under what circumstances *must* a default constructor be declared?

13. In what aspects is a constructor a special member function of a class?

14. Declare a class to represent a Fraction object. Each Fraction should be associated with a numerator and a denominator.

15. Declare a class to represent a Course object. Each Course should be associated with 50 student names, a teacher name, and an integer classroom location code. Declare what you think would be the appropriate request functions for this class.

16. Declare a class to represent a **Vector** object for possible applications programs dealing with graphics. Each **Vector** should be associated with an X, Y starting position on a graph, a direction angle, and a length or magnitude. Declare what you think would be the appropriate request functions for this class.

17. For the **Complex** class specified in this chapter, declare a Magnitude() function that would return the magnitude of the host.

18. Give an application program declaration that could be used to create an array of 50 **Complex** variables named Array. Show how the 21st cell could be assigned the value (2.5, 5.6i).

19. For the **Complex** class specified in this chapter, declare (overload) the member operator function = to allow an **int** to be assigned to a **Complex** object. For example, **Complex x; x = 9;**. This should result in the **Complex** value of (9, 0i) being assigned to **x**.

20. How can a nonmember function be allowed to access private attribute variables of a class? Under what circumstances should this approach be considered appropriate?

12.13.b Projects

1. Implement and overload a function named Power() to allow the calculation of powers of both **int** and **float** values.

2. Define and implement a class named **Cylinder** which has attribute members to represent the radius and length of a cylindrical object. Provide application programs with access functions to:
   a. Assign a radius and length to an object.
   b. Return the volume of an object of this class.
   c. Return the surface area of an object of this class.
   Write an application program to demonstrate the class.

3. Declare a class to represent a **Fraction** object. Each **Fraction** should be associated with an **int** numerator and denominator. Write an application program to demonstrate the class.
   a. Allow initialization of **Fraction** declarations as **Fraction x(3, 4);**.
   b. Allow output of **Fraction** variables with << such as **cout << x;**   (this should produce 3/4).
   c. Allow input of **Fraction** variables with >> such as **cin >> x;**   (this should expect the user to enter two integers separated by the / character).

4. Return to project 3. Add the following access-request functions to the class. Update the application program to demonstrate these additional features.

```
int Numerator ();          // return the host numerator
int Denominator ();        // return the host denominator
```

5. Return to project 3. Implement implicit conversions so that an integer can be assigned to a **Fraction** such as **Fraction x; x = 9;** (this should result in the fraction 9/1). Update the application program to demonstrate these additional features.

6. Return to project 3. Add the overloaded operators +, -, *, and / to allow arithmetic expressions involving fractions. Update the application program to demonstrate these additional features. Be sure to issue appropriate error messages and take appropriate action when a divide-by-zero attempt is made.

7. A business decides to computerize customer information. The same customer records are to be used for billing and generating mailing lists. Develop a class that has attribute members to represent an account balance, last name, first name, address, city, state, and zip code. The application program should be able to access an object instance of this class to (a) print a mailing label, (b) update a balance, (c) test if a customer is within a given zip code, and (d) access the current balance.

8. Return to short answer question 16. Fully implement the **Vector** class and provide access functions that would allow an application program to:
   a. Perform I/O using the insertion and extraction operators.
   b. Update any of the components of a vector.
   c. Test whether two vectors intersect.
   Write an application program to demonstrate the class.

9. Take another look at this chapter's Example Project. This implementation is not very robust in detecting the overflow of a set—trying to add too many members. You know that assigning a value beyond the end of an array can cause tricky bugs. Modify the project so that a **Set** can never be assigned more than 100 members.

10. **Creative Challenge:** This chapter's Example Project limits sets to 100 members. Regardless of how many members a set needs, each **Set** has an array of exactly 100 member cells. Change the implementation of the **Set** class so that the array declared for a set is only as big as it currently needs to be. This should also allow sets of more than 100 cells.

11. **Creative Challenge:** A Maze class can be defined with an attribute array representing a two-dimensional character table. Walls or filled spaces are marked with asterisks. Paths or open spaces are marked with the letter p. The goal in the maze is the letter g. All outside cells are walls. Diagonal moves are not allowed. Write an application program that will:

   a. Declare a Maze object.

   b. Read in the Maze object from a disk file.

   c. Allow the user to enter the indexes of a starting position in the maze (a cell containing a p) by calling the access function Start().

   d. Output the correct path to the goal by calling the access function Solve().

   Test your program with the following maze:

```
**********
*p**p**pg*
*pppp*pp**
***pp*ppp*
*ppp****p*
***pppppp*
*ppp******
***p****p*
***pppppp*
**********
```

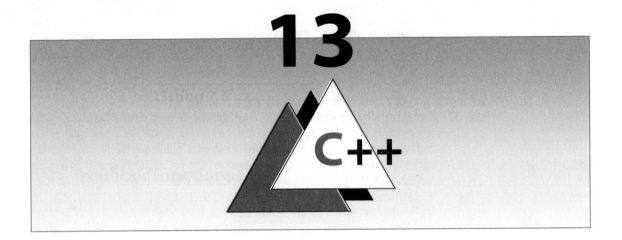

Recursion

Many of the programming problems examined so far in the text have used loops in the problem solution. At this point in your career, you tend to look for obvious ways to apply loops or iteration to help in the design of solutions. There are, however, other very different approaches to programming solutions to problems that generally do not use loops at all. This chapter introduces the concept of recursive solutions and points out the types of problems for which recursion is best suited. If you haven't looked at Creative Challenge problem 11 of the previous chapter requiring a solution to a maze, do so now. This chapter will show you a fairly easy solution using recursion.

13.1 Recursive definitions

A recursive definition is one in which the solution or answer to a problem is defined in terms of the same problem. Now, that may sound like a lot of double-talk, but consider the simple mathematical definition of a factorial operation for positive integers N:

```
If N ≤1 then N! = 1
otherwise,  N! = N(N-1)!
```

In other words, to apply this definition or rule to calculate the factorial of 5, one must know the factorial of 4 since 5! = 5(4!). The solution is stated in terms of the original problem (Figure 13.1). Fortunately, this definition is usable because (a) each successive application of the rule is applied to a smaller problem and (b) the final application is not recursive at all. So, in other words:

```
5! = 5(4!)
4! = 4(3!)
3! = 3(2!)
2! = 2(1!)
1! = 1
```

KEY TERM
useful recursive
definition

In general, a *useful recursive definition* is one with these two characteristics:

1. A recursive application of the rule should be applied toward a simpler problem.

2. At least one application of the rule toward a trivial problem must not be recursive.

For example, consider the following rule for calculating some strange value that we will call the Cannon of a positive number:

```
If N = 0  then   Cannon(x) = 1
otherwise,  Cannon(x) =  x * Cannon(x+1)
```

This isn't very useful because each application of the rule is toward a problem that is not closer to the simplest problem. No finite number of applications of this rule would ever lead to a solution to Cannon(5).

Now, many real-world problems can be expressed in similar recursive solutions or rules. For example, consider this almost trivial rule for climbing stairs:

```
climb (stairs):     if you are at the top, stop
                    otherwise,     step up one stair,
                                   climb (remaining stairs)
```

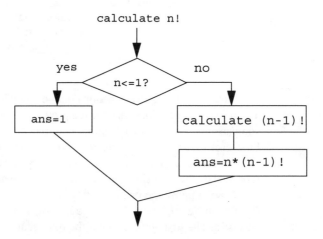

Figure 13.1 Chart of factorial calculation

To apply this rule for climbing stairs, you need only be able to perform two simple or primitive operations: *stop* and *step up one stair*.

Now you are probably thinking that a better rule would instruct the user to *repeat* a primitive operation such as step up one stair *until* the top was reached. That would be an iterative or looping rule. The purpose here is to illustrate that an alternative method of describing a solution or rule is possible—one which does not use iteration or looping. In general, a recursive solution will not contain terms such as *repeat* or *until*. We will entirely sidestep the question of which method of stating a rule is better for the moment. Interesting issues on that question will be considered later.

Let's try one more. Remember, the goal is to begin to see recursive rules or solutions. How about a rule for finding a certain name in an ordered (sorted) array of names? Think about how you might go about finding the correct entry in a phone book when looking up a friend: The book is first opened to some middle location and you put your finger on a name. If you just happened to pick your friend's name, you are done. If not, however, you must decide which half of the book to consider next. If the friend is listed alphabetically prior to the names you picked, you ignore the latter part of the book and consider only the part of the book prior to your present position. If on the other hand, your friend is listed after the name your finger is on, you consider only the names after your current position. Now what? You apply the rule again! You turn to some middle location in the remaining side of the book and continue.

Suppose you have an array of names in a computer program and wish to find a specific name. Here is a rule applied with two arguments—a name to be found and an array in which to search:

```
Find (name, array);
a) Find the middle of the array; call this position MIDDLE
b) If name matches the one at position MIDDLE; stop
   Else    i) call the names before MIDDLE the 'priorarray'
              and the names after MIDDLE the 'afterarray'.
          ii) If name is less than the name at MIDDLE
                  Find (name, priorarray)
              else if name is greater than name at MIDDLE
                  Find (name, afterarray)
```

Notice that the rule or function does not contain any commands to repeat anything. The primitive operations that are required are *stop*, *divide the array*, and a couple of comparisons. Are the two features required of a good recursive definition present? First, each time Find() is called within the rule, the array to search is smaller than the original array. Second, there is a nonrecursive solution to the trivial problem approached by the recursive applications. When the name is found, the rule stops.

Now, suppose the original array consists of ten names: array = Ann, Bill, Carl, Dan, Eve, Fred, Gary, Hal, Ian, and Julio. We wish to find the index of "Fred". The first application of the rule results in:

```
Find ("Fred", array);
a) MIDDLE = 4,
```

b) "Eve" is not the name, so
    i)   priorarray = Ann, Bill, Carl, Dan
         afterarray = Fred, Gary, Hal, Ian, Julio
   ii) "Fred" is greater than "Eve" so
        Find ("Fred", afterarray).

The second application of the rule has us searching this afterarray of the last five names for "Fred". The argument array is now Fred, Gary, Hal, Ian, and Julio.

```
Find ("Fred", array);
a) MIDDLE = 2,
b) "Hal" is not the name, so
        i)   priorarray = Fred, Gary
             afterarray = Ian, Julio
        ii) "Fred" is less than "Hal" so
                Find ("Fred", priorarray).
```

The third application of the rule has us searching this priorarray for "Fred". The argument array is now Fred and Gary.

```
Find ("Fred", array);
a) MIDDLE = 0,
b) "Fred" is found, so stop
```

KEY TERM
binary search

This particular rule for finding something in an ordered array is called a *binary search* and is a very common algorithm in computer science. It is very efficient; each time the rule is recursively applied, the new array is only about half the size of the original array. It is given here simply to help you see that many useful problems have recursive solutions which do not involve iteration. We will return to this algorithm for more details later in the chapter.

13.2 Recursive functions

KEY TERM
recursive function

A *recursive function* is one that calls itself. This may happen directly or indirectly. For example, suppose function FuncA() calls FuncB(), which in turn calls FuncA() before returning. FuncA() would be a recursive function. Suppose FuncA() calls FuncB(), which calls FuncA(), which again calls FuncB() before returning. In this case, both functions would be recursive. Anytime a function can be called a second time before the first call effects a return, the function is recursive.

Just like a good recursive definition, a good recursive function must have the same two features:

1. A recursive call of the function should be with arguments that represent a simpler problem.

2. At least one call of the function must be applied toward a trivial problem that will return without another recursive call.

In general, the body of a C++ function written for a recursive definition has the simple form of an **if-else** statement:

if (*trivial case*)
> *calculate answer;*

else
> *calculate answer with a recursive call on a simpler problem*

Listing 13.1 presents a C++ function to calculate the factorial of a number.

Listing 13.1

```
   // Fact()  Return the factorial of parameter n
1  //   IN:  n is a positive integer number
2  int Fact (int n)
3  {   int temp;
4      if (n <= 1)                        // trivial case
5          temp = 1;
6      else
7          temp = n * Fact(n-1);          // recursive case
8      return (temp);
9  }
```

Take a good look at this simple function. Notice that it is *nothing more than a restating of the rule* given earlier in the chapter. In a sense, it does not explain how a factorial is to be calculated; it simply states the recursive rule. Here are some examples of how this function might be invoked from an application program:

```
int value1 = 5, value2 = 4;
int ans1, ans2;
ans1 = Fact (value1);                      // should return 120
ans2 = Fact (value2);                      // should return 24
```

13.3 Tracing recursion

Let's now consider how the function of Listing 13.1 might be used or executed. We will first do this without the use of a computer as a paper-and-pencil exercise. If you have a reasonable understanding of how such a function might be evaluated or executed by a person, you will have a basic understanding of how it will be executed by a computer.

Suppose you are in a room full of desks. You are sitting at the desk closest to the door, which we will call desk A. The function of Listing 13.1 is written on the board. Upon each desk is a sheet of paper with three labeled boxes:

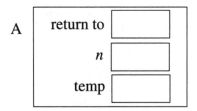

Your boss walks in the door and asks you to calculate the factorial of 5. She does this by writing 5 into the *n* box and Boss into the return to box to tell you to whom the answer is to be returned:

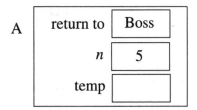

You simply follow the instructions on the board. Each time you need to invoke the rules recursively, you go to a new desk! When you go to a new desk, you must take with you two values: the number for which this rule is to calculate a factorial and the desk to which the answer is to be returned. You begin, and because 5 is greater than 1, you must first know the factorial of 4 before you can perform line #7: `temp = n * Fact (n-1);`. You leave this desk and go to desk B and write into the appropriate boxes:

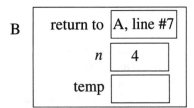

Sitting now at desk B, you begin the instructions (from the top): 4 is greater than 1 and you must perform the instruction of line #7. First, you must know the factorial of 3, so you leave this desk and go to desk C, taking with you the arguments indicating you need to return to C, line #7, and the value of 3. Arriving at desk C, you write into the appropriate boxes:

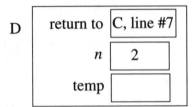

At desk C, you begin the instructions again from the start: 3 is greater than 1 and you must perform line #7. You go to desk D, taking the arguments indicating a return to C, line #7, and the value of 2:

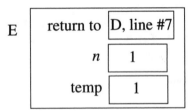

The same story is at desk D: 2 is greater than 1 and you pause at line #7. You go to desk E. At desk E, you find that n is equal to 1 and go to line #5 and write 1 into the temp box.

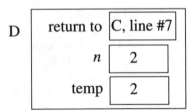

When you now come to the end of the instructions, you must take the value of temp and return to the indicated location—in this case, desk D, line #7. Arriving back at desk D, *you continue where you left off at line #7.* The calculation of n (2 at desk D) times 1 (just 1) is written into temp and you have completed the instructions at desk D:

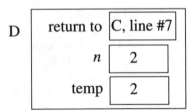

You memorize the value of temp and return to the indicated location (C, line #7) to report that the factorial of *n* (2) is 2. Arriving back at desk C, you continue where you left off at line #7. The product of *n* (3 at desk C) times 2 is written into temp and you are done at desk C:

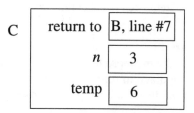

You report back (desk B, line #7) that the factorial of *n* (3) is 6. Back at desk B, you continue where you left off at line #7. The product of *n* (4 at desk B) times 6 is written to temp and you are done at desk B:

$$
\begin{array}{c|c}
\text{B} & \begin{array}{rl}
\text{return to} & \boxed{\text{A, line \#7}} \\
n & \boxed{4} \\
\text{temp} & \boxed{24}
\end{array}
\end{array}
$$

Almost done. You report back to desk A that the factorial of *n* (4 at desk B) is 24. At desk A, you continue at line #7 and calculate *n* (5) times 24 and write 120 into temp. Completing the instructions, you finally report back to the boss that *n* (5) factorial is 120.

One small difference between this procedure and how the computer actually executes this function to calculate Fact(5) is that the desks do not contain drawn and labeled boxes on paper. Each time the system goes to a new desk (so to speak), it must get out a clean sheet of "workspace" memory and draw the boxes before filling them in. With that minor symbolic change, this is analogous to how the computer would execute this function: Each time a function is called (recursively or not), the system sets up a new workspace of memory for local variables and parameters needed by that function—a clean sheet of paper, so to speak. Parameters are filled in, the return location is noted, and execution begins at the top. There is only one copy of the instructions, but there can be many different workspaces. Only one workspace is used at a time.

KEY TERM

call tree

Often, to debug or verify a recursive function, it is useful to diagram a solution in a manner similar to that just presented. To simplify the process and eliminate the need for textual descriptions (such as those used earlier), labeled arrows are usually employed. This diagram is known as a function *call tree*. The reason the term *tree* is used will become clearer in the following examples. The methods for building a call tree are:

1. When a function is called, draw an arrow from the calling to the called function. Label this arrow with the line number to be returned to (using the # symbol) and the values of arguments being passed.

2. When a function returns, draw an arrow back to the original function being returned to. Label this arrow with the value being returned.

The complete call tree for the previous example of Fact(5) is given in Figure 13.2. The line for return in the first call to Fact() from some other function or the main program is not important since this is not a recursive call. Each box in the diagram represents the variables of a workspace for a single function execution. Inside a box are the variables and parameters for a function.

CONCEPT

problems have both kinds of solutions

The factorial problem has a simple iterative solution that could have been used. In fact, the following is universally true: *For every recursive rule, there is an equally valid iterative rule. For every iterative rule, there is an equally valid recursive rule.*

In many cases, the iterative rule is easier to state and may be much more obvious to the programmer. There are some problems, however, where the recursive rule is easier to state! (We will soon see that there are some problems where one of these methods may be very difficult to see or state.) The programmer who is familiar with both approaches is in a stronger position to choose the more appropriate one. Some problems have very easy recursive solutions, but their iterative solutions are very complex and involved. Some problems, of course, are the other way around. You need both methods in your skills for problem solving.

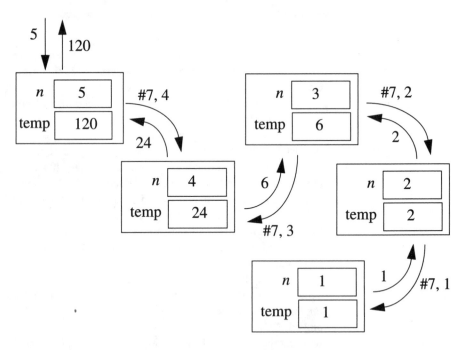

Figure 13.2 Call tree for the function call Fact(5)

It is possible that a function may contain more than one call to itself. Consider the rule for the Fibonacci series. A term in the series is defined as the sum of the previous two terms. The first two terms of the series are 1 and 1:

```
Fib(n) =  1  if n <= 2
          or Fib(n-1) + Fib(n-2)    if n > 2
```

The series starts out as follows:

```
1,  1,  2,  3,  5,  8,  13,  21,  34,  55, ...
```

Given any two successive terms in this series, it is a simple matter to calculate the next term. The other way around, however, is not as simple a task. That is, given a single term, calculate the previous two terms. More simply stated, given a value of n (the term position in the series), calculate the term. Since the rule is a useful recursive definition, we can write a function to calculate any Fibonacci number for a positive value of n (Listing 13.2).

Listing 13.2

```
    // Fib()  Returns the Fibonacci number corresponding to n
1   //  IN:  n is a positive integer
2   int Fib (int n)
3   {   int temp;
4       if (n <= 1)
5           temp = 1;                      // trivial case
6       else
7           temp = Fib(n-1) + Fib(n-2);    // recursive case with two calls
8       return (temp);
9   }
```

Once again, the function is just a restatement of the rule. Note that both required characteristics of a useful recursive rule are present: Each recursive call is for a simpler Fibonacci number (one closer to the trivial solution), and the trivial solution is not a recursive call. The call tree for the function call Fib(5) is given in Figure 13.3. Since each function call returns to line #7 (except the first call), the line numbers are left off this diagram for simplicity. Only the arguments passed and the values returned are given as arrow labels.

Note that there are two arrows out of each workspace box as a result of the two recursive function calls made. (In this case, the diagram really does look more like a tree.) As a result, each workspace has two arrows returning to it. The values being returned are then added together at line #7 (of Listing 13.2). Each function returns a single result, which is the Fibonacci number corresponding to the value of *n* within the function.

Let's go back to the Fib() function of Listing 13.2 and add an output statement at the beginning and end of the function.

```
int Fib (int n)
  {    int temp;
       cout << "preparing to calculate Fibonacci"<< n <<
       endl;
       if (n > 1)
           temp = Fib(n-1) + Fib(n-2);
       else temp = 1;
       cout << "Fibonacci"<< n << "is"<< temp << endl;
       return (temp);
  }
```

When this function executes, these output messages document the progress of the system through the numerous recursive calls. If this function were called as Fib(5) again, the following output diary would result:

```
preparing to calculate Fibonacci 5
preparing to calculate Fibonacci 4
preparing to calculate Fibonacci 3
preparing to calculate Fibonacci 2
preparing to calculate Fibonacci 1
 Fibonacci 1 is 1
preparing to calculate Fibonacci 0
 Fibonacci 0 is 1
 Fibonacci 2 is 2
preparing to calculate Fibonacci 1
 Fibonacci 1 is 1
 Fibonacci 3 is 3
preparing to calculate Fibonacci 2
preparing to calculate Fibonacci 1
 Fibonacci 1 is 1
preparing to calculate Fibonacci 0
 Fibonacci 0 is 1
 Fibonacci 2 is 2
 Fibonacci 4 is 5
preparing to calculate Fibonacci 3
preparing to calculate Fibonacci 2
preparing to calculate Fibonacci 1
 Fibonacci 1 is 1
preparing to calculate Fibonacci 0
 Fibonacci 0 is 1
 Fibonacci 2 is 2
preparing to calculate Fibonacci 1
 Fibonacci 1 is 1
 Fibonacci 3 is 3
 Fibonacci 5 is 8
```

You will quickly observe from this output that the process of determining the value to be returned from the first function call of Fib(5) is not at all efficient. Notice that many of the function calls are exact duplicates. The call to Fib(1) was made five

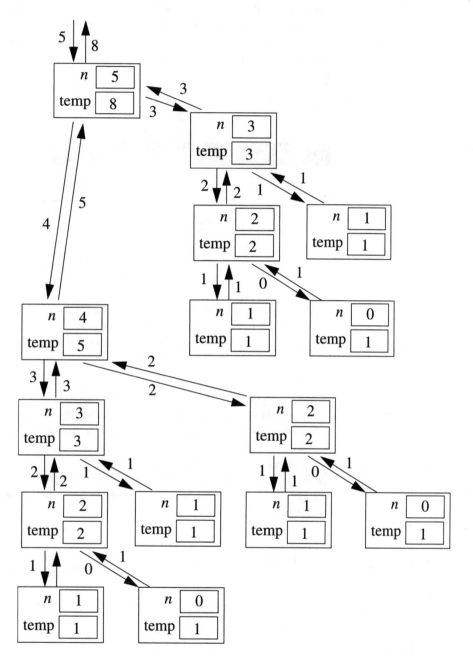

Figure 13.3   Call tree for the function call Fib(5)

times. The call to `Fib(0)` was made three times. An iterative solution to this problem would probably run much faster. Some will tell you that this is almost always the case; a recursive solution will usually be less efficient than an iterative solution. With a good optimizing compiler, however, that is not as true as it once might have been. You will find that many recursive solutions are approximately as efficient as a good iterative solution. Some recursive solutions may even be more efficient than iterative solutions.

EXPERIMENT

Would the `Fib()` function run faster if you were to test whether a call was necessary before making a recursive call? For example:

```
int a, b;
if ((n-1)>1) a = Fib(n-1); else a = 1;
if ((n-2)>1) b = Fib(n-2); else b = 1;
temp = a*b;
```

A simple way of timing a function is to call it in a large loop from the `main()` program (perhaps thousands of times). One execution is the time required for the loop divided by the number of iterations.

Regardless of which solution would run faster, this recursive function was very easy to write. Frequently, a judgment call must be made regarding which is more important in a particular project: program execution time or programmer development time. Quite often, programmer development time is the more important aspect of a project budget.

Not all recursive functions must return a value, of course. A recursive function could be type **void** and effect results through reference parameters. Consider a simple approach to counting the number of zeros in an array of integers. A recursive rule might be stated as follows:

```
if the array is nonempty;
    if the first cell value is zero, count it
    then count the number of zeros in the rest of the array
```

Listing 13.3 is a simple function to implement this recursive rule.

Listing 13.3

```
   // count()  Count the number of zeros in an array
1  // IN: array is an array of integers starting at index start, ending at index last
2  // OUT:  num is the integer count of zeros
3  void count (int array[ ], int start, int last, int& num)
```

```
4  {    if (start <= last)                          // array is nonempty
5       {    if (array[start] == 0)
                 num++;                              // count first value if zero
6            count (array, start+1, last, num);      // count zeros in rest of array
7       }
8  }
```

The function of Listing 13.3 might be called as follows:

```
int ages[6] = {3, 0, 4, 5, 0, 0};
int numofzeros = 0;
count (ages, 0, 5, numofzeros);
cout << "count of zeros is:"<< numofzeros << endl;
```

Line #4 tests for the trivial case. If the array is empty, the function does nothing and immediately returns. Line #6 is the recursive call with a set of arguments representing the rest of the array from the current starting point on. Now, there are several ways in which this function could be made much more efficient. Nevertheless, it is a straightforward implementation of the stated recursive rule and was easy to write. Naturally, you could have written this function without using recursion, but you wouldn't learn much.

The call tree for the preceding example function call in Figure 13.4 does not show any return values since this is a **void** function. (The array is not shown in each function

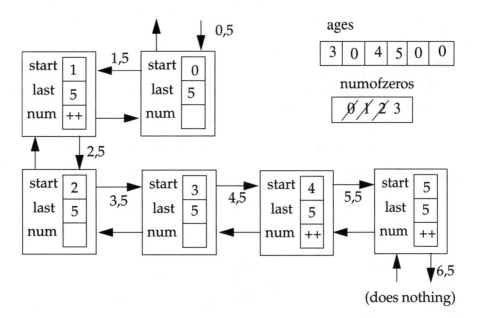

Figure 13.4 Call tree for count (ages, 0, 5, numofzeros)

box because it is the same as ages in all.) Since num is a reference variable, the diagram does not show a value in a box, but contains ++ to show when num would be incremented. The outside argument numofzeros of this calling example is shown beside the tree and is updated at each change to num. The returning line is always #6.

13.4 Binary search

Let's return to the binary search rule developed at the beginning of the chapter. To support this rule, we will first implement a simple method of calculating the middle of an array. Suppose we define the first index of the array as first and the last index of the array as last. We will define the middle index as:

```
middle = (last - first) / 2 + first;
```

Since these are integer values, the division will result in a truncation, and the final middle result will be an integer as well. Now we will express the function with four arguments: the name to be found, the array to be searched, and the first and last indexes of this array. In this manner, the function is more general than if we were simply to assume that every array is to be searched from index 0. The trivial case for this rule is when the name is found at the middle position. For this example, we will assume the name is always in the array. (Later, in the chapter projects, you may have the chance to investigate ways of adding another trivial case for when the name is not in the array at all.) The function will return the index of the cell where the name was found, as in Listing 13.4.

Listing 13.4

```
// Find ()  A binary search of an array. Returns the index of the
// cell matching the search name.
// IN: name is a string to be found and must be in the array
//     array is a string array to be searched (contains >1 name)
//     first, last are beginning and ending indexes of the search

int Find (string name, string array[ ], int first, int last)
{   int middle, found;
    cout << "searching from"<< first << "to"<< last << endl;
    middle = (last - first) / 2 + first;
    if (name == array[middle]) found = middle;
    else
    {   if (name < array[middle])
            found = Find (name, array, first, middle-1);
        else found = Find (name, array, middle+1, last);
    }
    return (found);
}
```

Again, the function is simply a restatement of the recursive rule and is easy to write. No iteration loops were needed. The bold output statement at the top of the function will serve to document the progress of the function during testing. Now suppose we have the following disk file containing a list of names:

namelist.txt:

```
Ann
Bill
Carl
Dan
Eve
Fred
Gary
Hal
Ian
Julio
```

The test program in Listing 13.5 could be used to verify the `Find()` function.

Listing 13.5

```cpp
// Perform a binary search of the names in file "namelist.txt"
#include <iostream>
#include <fstream>
#include <string>
using namespace std;
const int NUMNAMES = 10;

void main()
{   string name_array[NUMNAMES], name;
    ifstream infile ("namelist.txt", ios::in);
    int n;
    for (n=0; n<NUMNAMES; n++)
        infile >> name_array[n];          // read in names
    cout << "enter name to be found: ";
    cin >> name;                          // get name for search...
    cout << name << "found at index"
        << Find (name, name_array, 0, NUMNAMES-1);
}
```

Let's now demonstrate this test program to find `Fred`:

```
enter name to be found: Fred
searching from 0 to 9
searching from 5 to 9
searching from 5 to 6
Fred found at index 5
```

13.5 Example project

Up to this point, all the problems we have looked at had both iterative and recursive solutions that were relatively easy to see and understand. As mentioned earlier, however, there are problems where iterative solutions are not particularly easy to develop *but recursive solutions are natural!* One interesting example is Creative Challenge problem 11 at the end of Chapter 12.

This problem requires a programming solution to finding a new path through an arbitrary maze. For simplicity, we will assume the maze can be represented by a 10 by 10 array of characters. A wall or filled space is represented with the '*' character. Open spaces are marked with 'p'. The goal in the maze is marked with 'g'. We will assume that all outside cells are walls. The path must make vertical and horizontal movements; no diagonal jumps are allowed. Here is an example of one such maze:

```
**********
*p**p**pg*
*pppp*pp**
***pp*ppp*
*ppp***p*
***pppppp*
*ppp******
***p***p*
***pppppp*
**********
```

The user should be able to specify a starting cell (which must be a 'p') and have the program output a path to the goal. This problem has an iterative solution, but it is quite involved and difficult for most to envision. The recursive solution is quite simple!

The concept is this: The entire problem does not need to be addressed; only the decisions and actions for a single cell are considered. Suppose you were an explorer placed arbitrarily within the maze and tasked to report back whether your cell was part of a new path solution. There are several trivial situations that might occur:

1. If your cell contains a 'g', report YES.
2. If your cell contains an '*' it cannot be a part of a new path, so report NO.
3. If your cell has previously been visited as evidenced by footprints in the sand, it cannot be part of a new path, so report NO.

If none of these trivial solutions occur, it is possible that your cell could be part of a new path. In this case, *send our four assistant explorers*—one in each direction. If any assistant reports back that the visited cell is part of a new path, report in turn to your boss that you are part of this new path. How do these assistants know if they found a new path? You might say, "That is not my problem. I only know that if I am on a path, they are closer to the goal than I am." In other words, the assistants have a simpler problem to solve. You are beginning to think recursively!

To make our solution simple to use for a possible application program, we begin the solution to this problem by defining a `Maze` class in `"Maze.h"` (Listing 13.6).

Listing 13.6

```
// Maze.h  Header file for the Maze class

class Maze
{ public:   void Input (istream& in);      // read in the maze
            void Solve (int x, int y);     // solve the maze
  private:  char cells[10][10];
            int Recursive_Solve (int x, int y);
};

// wrapper function for the extraction operator
istream& operator >> (istream& in, Maze& m);
```

Notice that again the idiom wrapper function for input is prototyped in the header file to allow a `Maze` object to be input with `>>`. Suppose now that an application program wishes to solve the maze example starting at position (x=6, y=8). (Indexes begin with 0 and increase from left to right for x and from top to bottom for y.) For the application program, the programming is easy:

```
Maze thismaze;
cin >> thismaze;
cout << "The path is:" << endl;
thismaze.Solve (6, 8);
```

CONCEPT

avoid recursive public functions

The `Input()` is going to be straightforward, so let's take a look at `Solve()`. *It is good policy not to allow public functions to be recursive.* There is no C++ rule that says you can't, but it tends to make design and development more difficult than necessary. If a public function was recursive, it would be called by both the public and by itself. That is somewhat against the idea of public functions serving as the interface to applications programs. Rather than allow a public function to be invoked in more than one way, keep your public functions for nonrecursive calls only. *You will find that it often will simplify the number of necessary parameters.* We still need a recursive solution, however; let's just make `Solve()` a wrapper for the actual recursive function. Our actual `Recursive_Solve()` function does the real work. The user is not aware of this function and it is prototyped in the private area. The implementation now is just *a restatement of the recursive rule* developed earlier (Listing 13.7). We will define the letter `'f'` to represent a footprint.

Listing 13.7

// Maze.cpp   Implementation file for the Maze class

```cpp
#include <iostream.h>
#include "Maze.h"

void Maze::Solve (int x, int y)
{   Recursive_Solve (x, y);
    cout << " maze is solved" << endl;
}

int Maze::Recursive_Solve (int x, int y)
{    int success = 0;
    switch (cells[x][y])
    {    case 'g' :    success = 1; break;
         case '*' :    success = 0; break;
         case 'f' :    success = 0; break;
         default  :    cells[x][y] = 'f';  // leave a footprint...
                       success = Recursive_Solve(x+1, y) +
                       Recursive_Solve(x-1, y) +
                       Recursive_Solve(x, y+1) +
                       Recursive_Solve(x, y-1);  break;
    }
    if (success > 0) cout << x << "," << y << endl;
    return (success);
}

void Maze::Input (istream& in)
{   int col, row;
    for (row=0; row<10; row++)
        for (col=0; col<10; col++)
            in >> cells[col][row];
}

// wrapper function for the extraction operator
istream& operator >> (istream& in, Maze& m)
{   m.Input (in);
}
```

When we execute this program to solve the maze in file `"maze.txt"`, the following dialog occurs:

```
The path is:
8,1
7,1
7,2
6,2
```

```
6,3
7,3
8,3
8,4
8,5
7,5
6,5
5,5
4,5
3,5
3,6
3,7
3,8
4,8
5,8
6,8
maze is solved
```

Notice that the path is printed out backward. This makes sense if you think about it for a minute. Each explorer is also an assistant to the explorer who sent him out. The first assistant to actually determine that he is on the new path is the one that finds himself at the goal. As a result, that is the first cell location printed out. There are lots of other explorers waiting to hear if their assistants have found a path. This assistant that found the goal then reports back to the explorer that sent him. That explorer now understands that he also is on the path, and that cell location is printed out. He in turn reports back to the explorer that sent him and so on until the first explorer sent out by the public `Solve()` function reports back to the application.

EXPERIMENT

In the `Maze` implementation, the recursive function first marks a footprint before sending out assistant explorers. What would occur if the footprint were only marked just before the explorer returned to report?

If you plot the path in the maze, you will also see that the path is not necessarily the shortest path possible. It is, however, a valid path. Try the program with a number of different starting positions and convince yourself that it works. Now, take 30 minutes or so and try to come up with an idea for a programming solution that does not involve recursion. Don't waste more time than that because it's a tough problem without recursion. The exercise will, however, help you appreciate the fact that some problems are more appropriately solved with recursive rules.

13.6 Summary

KEY TERMS   Only a few new terms were introduced in this chapter. They are quite important to this new concept of recursion, however:

1. *useful recursive definition*—a rule for solving a problem with two characteristics: At least one application of the rule toward a trivial problem must not be recursive. A recursive application of the rule should be applied toward a simpler problem.

2. *binary search*—a method of searching a list by continually dividing the list into two halves and subsequently eliminating one half until the item is found.

3. *recursive function*—a function that calls itself or is called by another function before it returns.

4. *call tree*—a diagram of recursive calls showing arguments passed, individual workspaces with local variables, and values returned.

CONCEPTS   A recursive function will generally not contain a loop. A recursive function must always have two components or characteristics. First, the function will invoke itself, each time with a set of parameters that are closer to a trivial solution. Second, the function will contain a trivial case or base case, where a solution can be immediately returned without another recursive call.

There are several programming hints and important points of style to remember. For every recursive rule, there is an equally valid iterative rule. For every iterative rule, there is an equally valid recursive rule. The best rule to use may depend on which is easier and faster to implement and perhaps which is more efficient.

It is good policy not to allow public functions to be recursive. If you need a recursive member function, use a nonrecursive public function as a wrapper to call a private recursive function.

13.7 Exercises

13.7.a   Short-answer questions

1. What are the two characteristics of a useful recursive rule?
2. What two components or characteristics are found in a recursive function?
3. A _____ _____ is a paper-and-pencil diagram useful in designing and debugging a recursive function.
4. The _____ _____ algorithm is a method of searching an ordered list by continually dividing the remaining list in half and subsequently eliminating one of the halves from consideration until an item is found.
5. When implementing a class, it is good policy not to allow _____ functions to be recursive.

6. For every iterative rule, there is an equally valid _____ rule.

7. Each recursive function in C++ should take the form of what common statement?

8. What is the purpose of drawing a call tree?

9. Are there some problems for which an iterative solution is not possible? Are there some problems for which a recursive solution is not possible?

10. State a useful recursive rule (in English) for the multiplication of two integer values. Hint: Suppose you wish to multiply 7 * 23. Would you be able to calculate the result without using multiplication if you knew the answer to 6 * 23?

11. State a useful recursive rule (in English) for outputting a string in a **char** array. You may assume the string ends with the null \0 character. Hint: If you output the first character in the string, would outputting the rest of the string be a simpler problem?

12. Refer to the function `Fact()` of Listing 13.1. Draw the call tree for the following function call:

```
int n;   n = Fact(6);
```

13. Refer to the function `Fib()` of Listing 13.2. Draw the call tree for the following function call:

```
int n;   n = Fib(3);
```

14. The value of sin(x) can be calculated (in radians) for positive values of x using the following series formula:

$$\sin(x) = x\left(1 - \frac{x^2}{1^2\pi^2}\right)\left(1 - \frac{x^2}{2^2\pi^2}\right)\left(1 - \frac{x^2}{3^2\pi^2}\right)\cdots$$

Each succeeding series term will be closer and closer to 1.0, and the series converges to a correct answer. For example, when the absolute value of a new term is within 0.01 of 1.0, you can assume the series is correct to within 0.05. Write a useful recursive rule (in English) for calculating the value of sin(x) to within 0.05.

15. Suppose a sorted array of 64 names must be searched using the binary search algorithm. What is the worst-case number of names that must be compared to find a particular name?

16. The `Fact()` function of Listing 13.1 is not particularly efficient. Write a better recursive rule (in English) so that recursive calls are not made if n<=3. By drawing a call tree for `Fact(5)` for this new rule, determine how many recursive calls would be avoided.

17. The `Fib()` function of Listing 13.2 is not particularly efficient. Write a better recursive rule (in English) so that recursive calls are not made if n<=3. By drawing a call tree for `Fib(5)` for this new rule, determine how many recursive calls would be avoided.

18. Draw a call tree for a `count("fantastic", num)` call using Listing 13.3.

19. Draw a call tree for a `Find("Carl", list, 0, 9)` call using Listing 13.4 and the same name list used in the chapter example.
20. The maze implementation of Listings 13.5 and 13.6 is not particularly efficient. For example, an explorer sends out all four assistants at once. Would it be more efficient to send out one assistant (say, to the left) and then await the report? If successful, there would be no need to send out the other three assistants. Write a better recursive rule (in English) for a more efficient approach.

13.7.b Projects

1. Refer to short answer question 10. Implement this recursive rule for multiplication as a function. Provide a `main()` program to call this function for a variety of multiplication problems to test your implementation.
2. Implement a `Sin(x)` function using the useful recursive rule developed for short answer question 14. Provide a `main()` program to call this function for a variety of appropriate values of `x` to test your implementation.
3. Implement the improved recursive rule of short answer question 17. Write an appropriate driver program to test your implementation for several values of n. Compare the number of recursive calls made with your implementation to those made by the function of Listing 13.1.
4. The standard string library contains the `strlen()` function which returns the length of a string in a **char** array. Write a recursive implementation of this function. Hint: If you knew the length of the string following the first character, would you be able to determine the length of the entire string?
5. The maze implementation of Listings 13.5 and 13.6 is not particularly efficient. For example, an explorer sends out all four assistants at once. Would it be more efficient to send out one assistant (say, to the left) and then await the report? If successful, there would be no need to send out the other three assistants. Modify the `Maze.cpp` implementation to effect this change. Test your implementation against the implementation in this chapter for several different starting points to determine which makes the fewest recursive function calls.
6. The maze implementation of Listings 13.5 and 13.6 does not always find the shortest path to the goal. Suppose you knew that the goal was always up and to the right of the starting position. (It still, of course, may require a path that goes left or down for parts of the path to reach the goal.) Modify the `Maze.cpp` implementation to take advantage of this fact. Test your implementation against the implementation in this chapter for several different starting points to verify that the shortest path is always chosen if this fact is true.

7. A palindrome is a word or phrase (with punctuation and blanks removed) that is spelled exactly the same forward or backward. Some examples are *level* and *deed*, and, of course, the first sentence ever spoken, "Madam, I'm Adam" (*madamimadam*). You've seen this problem as a project in a previous chapter. This time, write a *recursive* function that accepts a string parameter in a **char** array and returns 1 if the string is a palindrome (0 otherwise). Hint: The first character must match the last, the second character must match the second to last, and so on.

8. The greatest common divisor (GCD) of two integers x and y is defined as the largest integer that divides both x and y evenly. Euclid's algorithm states that this GCD(x, y) is

   a. y if y divides x evenly

   b. otherwise, it is GCD(y, remainder of x divided by y)

   Write a function GCD() to calculate this value and test it with an appropriate driver application.

9. **Creative Challenge:** The Towers of Hanoi problem is a tradition in the computer sciences. Normally, these Creative Challenge projects involve some aspect of a problem you probably do not yet know how to solve completely. Not this time. You have all the tools you need to attack this one. It is not a trivial problem, however, and it involves learning to think recursively. (There is an iterative solution to this problem, but it is quite complex and requires that you first understand the recursive solution.) When you are done, you will be surprised at how concise the solution is.

   There are three pegs and N differently sized disks. Each disk has a hole so that it will fit over a peg. Initially, all disks are on the first peg in size order such that the largest is on the bottom and the smallest is on top. The goal is to move all disks from the first peg to the last peg following two simple rules:

   a. Only one disk may be moved at a time.

   b. A larger disk may never be place upon a smaller disk.

   Hint: A problem involving only one disk is trivial. So is the problem of moving only two disks. Suppose the pegs are labeled A, B, and C. To move two disks from A to C:

   ```
   Move the top disk from A to B.
   Move the other disk from A to C.
   Move the disk from B to C.
   ```

   Now suppose the problem involved moving three disks. If you could move two disks to an intermediate peg, move the bottom disk to the destination peg, and then move the two disks from the intermediate peg to the destination, you would have it. Now, moving two disks of course requires the preceding separate steps to move them one at a time, but that is a trivial problem. So, we have expressed a complex problem (three disks) into two trivial problems (two disks and one disk).

What about moving four disks? Move three disks to the intermediate peg, move the bottom disk to the destination, and finally move the three disks on the intermediate peg to the destination. We have expressed the problem in a simpler recursive problem (three disks) and a trivial problem (one disk).

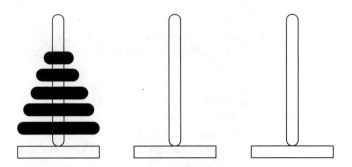

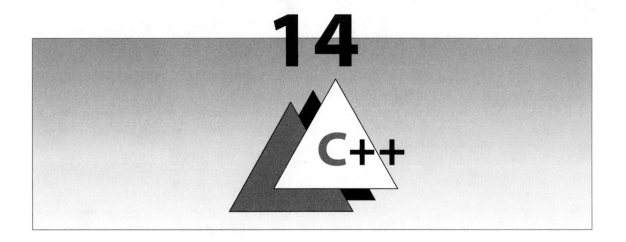

Internal Representations, Pointers, and Dynamic Memory

We have used `int` and `char` data types in many programming examples. Chapter 4 discussed the ranges and precision of each of these types, and we now need to extend understanding on the internal representation of such variables to allow the use of low-level or bitwise operators available in C++. You are familiar with the `const` declaration modifier, and there are two other modifiers that will be important additions to your skills. In addition, we will take a look at explicit conversions between data types with casting operators. Pointers have been introduced, but in this chapter, we discuss pointers in a more complete and useful manner. Finally, you will learn that arrays do not need to be fixed in size when a program is written because space can be dynamically allocated when a program determines just how much space is needed.

14.1 Binary representation

To the Instructor: This section can be skipped without loss of continuity.

In Chapter 6, you learned that the limits of `int` variables depend on the number of bits used for internal representation by the system. For 16-bit integers, values stored may range from –32,768 to 32,767. You may have wondered why such odd numbers. The reason is that integers (and real values as well) are stored in binary or base-2 form.

14.1.a Numbering systems

Let's review the base-10 number system you use every day. When writing an integer value such as 765, you imply that there are 7 hundreds, 6 tens, and 5 ones. This is very different from 567, which contains the same digits but in a different order. We call this a *positional* number system. (Roman numerals, on the other hand, are not positional.) A digit's position determines the power of 10 with which the digit is to be multiplied.

$$765 \ = \ 7 * 10^2 + 6 * 10^1 + 5 * 10^0$$

There are ten different digits (0 through 9) in a base-10 system. Suppose we decided, to use a base-8 system? There would be eight different digits (0 through 7 perhaps). Each digit in a number would represent the power of 8 with which the digit is to be multiplied. We often represent numbers written in different bases with a small parenthesized subscript. For example:

$$4236_{(8)} \ = \ 4 * 8^3 + 2 * 8^2 + 3 * 8^1 + 6 * 8^0$$

If you simply carry out the math of the right-side expression using a base-10 calculator, you will arrive at the equivalent value in a base-10 system (we usually do not use the small parenthesized subscript for base-10, which is our default system):

$$4236_{(8)} \ = \ 2206$$

We could, of course, place as many zeros in front of any number in any base without changing the value or meaning of the number.

Computers represent integers in base-2 since there are only two different digits in a *binary* digital circuit (1 and 0). The same positional system applies; it is just a different base than what we normally use. Instead of multiplying the digits against powers of 10, we multiply by powers of 2:

$$0000000011010110_{(2)} \ = \ 1 * 2^7 + 1 * 2^6 + 1 * 2^4 + 1 * 2^2 + 1 * 2^1$$

Carrying out this calculation using a base-10 calculator results in the equivalent value in a base-10 system:

$$0000000011010110_{(2)} \ = \ 214$$

KEY TERM
hexadecimal

Since it is often clumsy to write numerous base-2 or binary numbers because of the large number of digits they usually require, computer scientists often use base-16 notation or *hexadecimal*. In this system, we need 16 different digits. To augment the ten digits we are familiar with, the letters A, B, C, D, E, and F are used to represent values of 10, 11, 12, 13, 14, and 15, respectively. For example:

$$8A7C_{(16)} = 8 * 16^3 + A * 16^2 + 7 * 16^1 + C * 16^0$$
$$= 8 * 16^3 + 10 * 16^2 + 7 * 16^1 + 12 * 16^0$$
$$= 35,452$$

This is just a convenience for the computer scientist. Numbers are still stored in base-2 inside computer or disk memory. It just happens that 16 is a power of 2 (2^4) which allows one to group binary digits into four-digit segments and represent each segment with the equivalent hexadecimal digit.

binary	decimal	hexadecimal
0000	0	0
0001	1	1
0010	2	2
0011	3	3
0100	4	4
0101	5	5
0110	6	6
0111	7	7
1000	8	8
1001	9	9
1010	10	A
1011	11	B
1100	12	C
1101	13	D
1110	14	E
1111	15	F

For example, consider the following binary, hexadecimal, and decimal number equivalents. In writing the binary numbers, small spaces have been placed between groups of four binary digits to help you see the hexadecimal equivalents:

binary	hexadecimal	decimal
0100 1001 1011 1101	49BD	18,877
0111 1111 0001 1110	7F1E	32,542
0000 0000 1010 1000	00A8	168
0101 1011 1110 0011	5BE3	23,523

CONCEPT
converting between systems

Converting from binary to hexadecimal is quite simple because 16 is a power of 2. Thus, each group of four binary digits (counting from the least significant toward the most significant) corresponds to one hexadecimal digit. For example, the least significant group of four binary digits in the first number listed (decimal 18,877) is 1101. This is just $2^3 + 2^4 + 2^0$ or 13 decimal, which is D hexadecimal.

Converting from decimal to hexadecimal requires division by successively smaller powers of 16. The following are some simple steps for the process:

1. Pick a power of 16 that is just larger than the decimal value.
2. Repeat the following until the decimal value is zero: Divide the decimal value by the next lower power of 16; the dividend becomes the next hexadecimal digit and the remainder becomes a new decimal value to be converted.

For example, suppose the decimal value to be converted to hexadecimal is 23,523. Here are the steps and the result:

```
A power of 16 just larger than 23,523 is 16⁴ (or 65,536)

23523 / 16³ = 23523 / 4096 = 5 remainder 3043
3043 / 16² = 3043 / 256 = 11 remainder 227
227 / 16¹ = 227 / 16 = 14 remainder 3
3 / 16⁰ = 3 / 1 = 3 remainder 0
```

Thus, the hexadecimal digits must represent 5, 11, 14, and 3; the value is $5BE3_{(16)}$.

KEY TERM

2's complement

Now, what about negative decimal numbers? Because of the simplicity with which CPU circuit operations can be designed and implemented, negative numbers are nearly always represented in what is called *2's complement* form. (We won't go into the reasons here.) In this form, a number is made negative by complementing each bit (flipping) and then adding 1. For example:

```
0010 0110 1110 1011          (hex 26EB, decimal 9963)
1101 1001 0001 0100          (after complementing each bit)
+                1          (now add 1)
_____

1101 1001 0001 0101          (hex D915, decimal -9963)
```

KEY TERM

most significant bit

One feature of this process is that if you have a reasonably small integer, all negative binary numbers have the leftmost bit or *most significant bit (MSB)* set. This has become a standard: If the MSB is set, the number is assumed to be negative. For a 16-bit integer, the largest positive number that could be expressed without using the MSB (leaving the MSB as 0) would be the following:

```
0111 1111 1111 1111          (hex 7FFF or 32,767)
```

which is the upper range limit for 16-bit integers, as you learned previously! To convert a negative binary number to a positive value, apply exactly the same rule: Flip the bits and add 1. This is a circular operation—it is applied the same for either process. If you start with a positive binary value and apply the operation twice, you will return back to the same binary value.

```
1101 1001 0001 0101          (hex D915, decimal -9963)
0010 0110 1110 1010    .      (after complementing each bit)
+                1          (now add 1)
_____

0010 0110 1110 1011          (hex 26EB, decimal 9963)
```

Don't forget to carry if the addition overflows a resulting digit. Remember, this is base-2 and the largest digit is 1. The sum of $001_{(2)}$ and $001_{(2)}$ is $010_{(2)}$. The sum of $0011_{(2)}$ and $0001_{(2)}$ is $0100_{(2)}$. Consider the following example that converts 15,048 to −15,048:

```
0011 1010 1100 1000        (hex 3AC8, decimal 15,048)
1100 0101  0011 0111       (after complementing each bit)
+                   1       (now add 1)
```
```
1100 0101 0011 1000        (hex C538, decimal -15,048)
```

CONCEPT
hexadecimal
constants

Hexadecimal integers can be expressed as constants in C++ by prefixing them with 0x. Octal constants are indicated with a leading zero. Keep in mind, however, that whatever base notation is used, the internal representation of the integer is binary or base-2. For example:

```
int y = 0x7F3C;      // 7F3C(16) or 32,572
int x = 0274;        // 274(8) or BC(16) or 188
```

y | 0111 1111 0011 1100 |

x | 0000 0000 1011 1100 |

14.1.b Low-level operators

Okay, so what? The purpose of the discussion of binary representation is to allow you to understand and use the low-level binary or bitwise operators available in C++. The first of these are the *shift* operators using the >> and << symbols. Yes, these are the same operator symbols that are used for I/O insertion and extraction. They are simply overloaded for this binary operation.

So how does the system know whether to apply an I/O operator or a shift operator when one of these symbols is encountered? If you will think back to Chapter 12, you will recognize that these two different expressions will have different signatures. Principally, if the left-side value is a stream, the signature will match an I/O operator. If the left-side argument value is an integer, a shift operator signature will be matched.

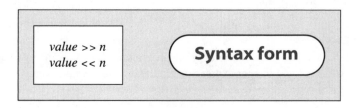

value >> n
value << n   **Syntax form**

CONCEPT

shift operators

The `>>` operator indicates a right-shift of the bits of the left-side integer value by n places. The leftmost bit (MSB) is copied or dragged to the right. The rightmost bits are simply dropped as they are shifted off the right end. The `<<` indicates a left-shift of the bits of the left-side integer value by n places. The leftmost bits are dropped as they are shifted off the left end. The bit positions left empty on the right are filled with zeros. For example:

```
int val1 = 3467;      // val1 is 0000 1101 1000 1011(2)
int val2 = 0x8123;    // val2 is 1000 0001 0010 0011(2) or -32,477
int a, b, c;
a = val1 >> 4;        // a is 0000 0000 1101 1000(2)
b = val1<< 3;         // b is 0110 1100 0101 1000(2)
c = val2 >> 2;        // c is 1110 0000 0100 1000(2)
```

Notice a couple of features about these operator results. First, left-shifting increases the value of a number, while right-shifting decreases the value. That is only natural; when you left-shift a decimal number on paper, you are multiplying by powers of 10. When you right-shift, you are dividing by powers of 10 (using integer division or truncation):

```
345
3450      equals   345 * 10
34500     equals   345 * 100
34        equals   345 / 10
3         equals   345 / 100
```

Since the internal representation of numbers is base-2 in a program, left- and right-shifts multiply or divide by powers of 2:

```
345 >> 1;      // this is 345 / 2
345 << 2;      // this is 345 * 4
345 << 4;      // this is 345 * 16
```

CONCEPT

overflow effects

Now, when you use these low-level operators, the system makes no attempt to verify that your result has not overflowed an integer variable. For example, left-shifting the value of $0000\ 1101\ 1000\ 1011_{(2)}$ by 5 would shift a 1 into the MSB or sign bit, resulting in a negative number:

```
int val1 = 0x0D8C;    // val1 is 3,467
int a;
a = val1 << 5;        // a is 1011 0001 0110 0000(2) or -20,119
```

It is simply the programmer's responsibility to ensure that a shift operation in an integer expression results in a relevant answer.

What utility do these operators have? We will see several interesting uses later. For now, you might recognize that on many computers, multiplication and division operations are quite slow with respect to shift operations. This is particularly true for machines that use emulation rather than providing specific hardware support for arithmetic multiply and divide operations. Replacing a multiply or divide using a power of 2 with a left- or right-shift might improve the efficiency of a program:

```
int x, y;

x = y * 16;        // these are equivalent, but the second may
x = y << 4;        // be faster!

x = y / 256;       // these are equivalent, but the second may
x = y >> 8;        // be faster!
```

The next set of low-level binary symbols represents the bitwise Boolean operators:

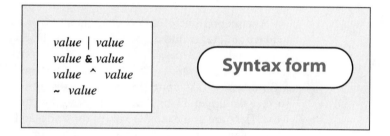

value | *value*
value **&** *value*
value ^ *value*
~ *value*

Syntax form

CONCEPT

bitwise binary operators

The | symbol represents the binary OR of two integer values. This operation is accomplished by looking at each corresponding bit pair in the two values. If *either* of these is set, the same bit position in the result will be set. The & symbol represents the binary AND of two integer values. If *both* corresponding bits in the two values are set, the same bit position in the result is set. The ^ symbol is the EXCLUSIVE OR of two integer values. If *only one* bit is set in a corresponding pair, the same bit position in the result is set. The ~ symbol represents the COMPLEMENT of a single integer value. The complement is simply the *inversion* or flipping of the bits. It is not the negative of a binary value—an additional 1 is not added to the result. Table 14.1 summarizes these operators by example.

Table 14.1 **Binary operator summary**

x	y	x | y	x & y	x ^ y	~x	~y
0110	1010	1110	0010	1100	1001	0101

These operators are most commonly used in *masking* operations. Such an operation abstracts or masks a section of an integer number for examination or use. You can easily see from Table 14.1 that ANDing any value with 1s produces the same value. ANDing with 0s produces all zeros. A mask is simply a number with 1s in positions where bits are to be copied and 0s where bits are to be eliminated.

When writing programs for data provided by others, you do not always have the luxury of defining the format of input records. For example, a common graphics file format for color images begins with a single 16-bit integer code. This code contains information regarding the version of the program used to generate the file in the top 3 bits of the number. (The rest of the bits represent other data.) The following program segment might be used to mask or abstract just these 3 bits and place them into a variable as an independent integer number:

```
int code, version;
cin >> code;                        // a 16-bit code
version = (code >> 13) & 0x7;       // value of the top 3 bits
```

The second line of this code segment is, of course, just an input operation to place an integer into the variable code. The bottom line first right-shifts this integer code by 13 bits. The result is that the upper 3 bits (out of 16) are shifted down to become the lower 3 bits. Since this may have dragged or copied the MSB down into the upper 13 bits, this value is next ANDed with $0111_{(2)}$ or 0x7 so that the upper 13 bits are set to zero, but the lower 3 bits are left as they were. Here are two example values for code and the results placed into version. Notice that, in each case, the upper 3 bits become a separate integer in the variable version:

code	code>>13	version
0110101100001111	0000000000000110	0000000000000110
1010111011011001	1111111111111101	0000000000000101

Here is another problem from the same graphics file format. An image is coded as a two-dimensional array of dots or *pixels* (picture elements). Each dot in the image is made up of three colors: red, green, and blue. This is known as RGB encoding. In this graphics file format, each color may take on 32 different values. By varying the amounts of each color, all the different colors and intensities in a picture can be produced. For example, equal amounts of all three colors produce gray. A pixel of (0, 0, 0) produces a black dot. A pixel of (31, 31, 31) produces a white dot. A pixel of (10, 10, 0) produces a yellow dot of medium intensity.

The problem is that each pixel in the file is a single 16-bit number. The MSB or leftmost bit is always 0. The amount of red is encoded into the next 5 bits, green is in the next 5 bits, and blue is the last or least-significant 5 bits. Listing 14.1 is a function that could be passed a 16-bit pixel and would then mask out and return the individual color values.

Listing 14.1

```
// colors()  Separate a 16-bit RGB pixel into individual colors
// IN: pixel is a 16-bit RGB value
// OUT: red, green, and blue are returned as individual color values

void colors (int pixel, int& red, int& green, int& blue)
{   const int FIVEBITS = 0x1F;              // lower 5 bits are 1's
    red = (pixel >> 10) & FIVEBITS;
    green = (pixel >> 5) & FIVEBITS;
    blue = pixel & FIVEBITS;
}
```

14.2 Storage qualifiers

You have already seen the declaration qualifier **const**. You remember that if this qualifier is placed in front of a declaration, the variable may not be modified by the program in later statements. The net effect is to produce a constant with a name that can be referred to throughout a program section. If the constant needs to be changed for any reason, the change only needs to be made in the declaration because the rest of the program section refers to the constant using the variable name.

CONCEPT

unsigned
qualifier

Several other declaration qualifiers are available in C++. For example, an **int** or **char** variable can be declared as representing only positive values through use of the **unsigned** qualifier:

> unsigned int *variable*;
> unsigned char *variable*;

Syntax form

When the system examines an **unsigned** variable, the MSB or sign bit is ignored. That means it is available to be used as another bit in the number. Consequently, the range of a 16-bit **unsigned int** variable is 0 to 65,535. Care must be taken when assigning regular int variables to unsigned variables if they may contain negative numbers. A negative number would simply become a very large positive value because the sign bit is now part of the number. For example:

```
int x = 12345;        // x is 0011 0000 0011 1001(2)
int y = -6789;        // y is 1110 0101 0111 1011(2)
unsigned int z;
z = x;                // z is 0011 0000 0011 1001(2) or 12345
z = y;                // y is 1110 0101 0111 1011(2) or +58,747
```

unsigned variables are very useful when using low-level operators in situations where you don't need to be concerned about representing negative integers. This qualifier can also be used to modify the data type returned by a function. For example:

```
unsigned int Factorial (unsigned int n);
```

Occasionally, you will see a shorthand notation for this qualifier in programs written by others. If the qualifier `unsigned` appears by itself, it defaults to unsigned int:

```
unsigned x;                // same as unsigned int x;
```

Two other important qualifiers are **static** and **extern**. Any variable type declaration may be qualified with **static** or **extern**.

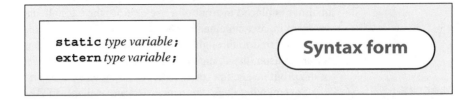

```
static type variable;
extern type variable;
```

Syntax form

Normally, variables in a function are dynamic; they are created or allocated in a function's new workspace each time a function is called. When the function returns, the workspace and the variables are deallocated. If a variable declaration is qualified with **static**, however, the variable is allocated only once. Each time the function owning this variable is called, it uses the same memory. When the function returns, the variable is still there waiting for the next function call. Listing 14.2 is a simple example of a function that could be used to assign identification numbers in sequence. Each time the function is called, it returns the next ID number not yet assigned. It doesn't need to be told (passed) the previous ID number because it remembers what it was from the previous call.

Listing 14.2

```
// AssignID ()  Returns the next ID number not yet assigned
int AssignID ()
{   static id = 0;
    return (id++);
}
```

In Listing 14.2, the initialization of the **static** variable id only occurs once because it is created only once. When dynamic variables are declared, they are initialized each time they are allocated with each function call.

The qualifier **extern** is used to allow access to global variables in another file of a project. When a global variable is declared, space is allocated and the variable is optionally initialized. (Yes, global variables are static since they are allocated only once.) In a project, however, the many files may be separately compiled. If a global variable is declared in one file, yet accessed in a second file, the compilation of this second file will cause error messages because the references cannot be matched with a declaration. If each file has a declaration for the global variable, *there will be multiple copies of the variable!*

CONCEPT

extern **qualifier**

The purpose of the **extern** *qualifier* is to allow each file in a project to contain a declaration for a global variable but have them all result in only a single copy of that global variable that all share. In other words, **extern** allows a global variable to be referenced by functions in separate files of a project.

The declaration with the **extern** qualifier does not declare a global variable; it simply allows reference to one of the same name declared in another file. To properly establish a single global variable available for functions in multiple files, the global variable should be declared (and perhaps initialized) in the normal manner *once* in *one* file. The *other* files should contain the same declaration with the **extern** qualifier (and no initialization). The original declaration allocates and initializes the variable, and the other extern declarations simply allow access to this original declaration.

```
extern float pi = 3.14159;
```

This statement is incorrect because it does not declare the variable pi. Thus, it cannot specify an initial value—that must be done with the statement that really does declare pi. The **extern** qualifier indicates that this variable is being declared in another file (and this file would like to have access).

The **extern** qualifier is also a default qualifier for function declarations. You may occasionally see function prototypes declared with the **extern** qualifier as a method of documenting that the actual function implementation is expected to be in another file.

Figure 14.1 contains a project of three files. All functions of all files are to have access to a single global **float** variable named pi. The value of variable rad is passed as a parameter in the normal fashion. The functions Area() and Circ() are to be called from the main program even though they are written in files separate from the one containing main().

It does not hurt to have an **extern** qualified prototype or declaration in addition to the original in a file. Commonly, a header file is constructed with the appropriate **extern** qualified prototypes and declarations for global access. Each file in the project simply includes this single header file to gain access to all global files and variables regardless of which files contain the original functions or declarations. Figure 14.2 shows a modified project using such a header file.

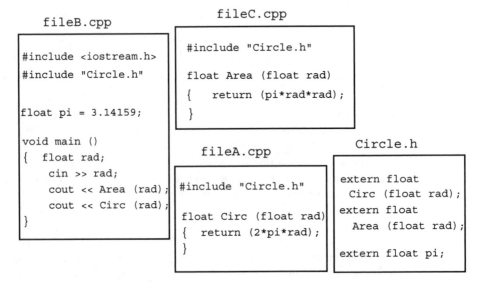

Figure 14.1 Example of an `extern` global variable declaration

Figure 14.2 Use of a header file for `extern` declarations and prototypes

There is actually another qualifier we have not discussed: **auto**. This is just the default qualifier for a dynamic local variable and is hardly ever specified explicitly. The qualifier **unsigned** and the **extern** or **static** qualifiers can, of course, be combined in a single declaration. Convention is to place the **unsigned** second:

```
static unsigned int age;
extern unsigned int cost;
```

14.3 Type casting

In Chapter 6, you learned some basic rules for the automatic conversion of primitive data types (**char**, **int**, **float**, **double**):

1. Whenever a binary operation (such as addition or multiplication) involves dissimilar data types, the *lower* data type is automatically converted to the *higher* data type. **char** is lower than **int**, which is lower than **float**, which is lower than **double**.

2. In the case of assignment, the expression value on the right side of = is first converted to the type of the target variable on the left side before assignment is made.

Converting from a lower type to a higher type (rule 1) does not change the sign or value of the original numeric value. **char** values are converted to **int** by expanding the value to the left to a full integer word (usually 16 or 32 bits). The value and sign of the ASCII value number remain the same. **int** values are converted to **float** or **double** by adding a fraction of zero. Again, the value and sign of the number remain the same.

CONCEPT
avoid using char for integers

Converting from a higher type down to a lower type (rule 2) may significantly change an original value. **float** and **double** values are converted to integer by truncation. There is rarely a good reason to assign integer values to **char** variables, but C++ allows it. Some programmers use **char** for small integer numbers in the hope of saving some memory space. This is rarely worth the effort; *use **int** variables for integer data and **char** variables for ASCII characters.* While converting **char** to **int** is not often a problem, programmers who use **char** for small integers may occasionally run into bugs that are difficult to find.

CONCEPT
lower 8 bits of int assigned to char

int is converted to **char** by selecting only the lower 8 bits for assignment. (If a **float** were to be converted to **char**, it would first be converted to integer.) As you can imagine, this can significantly change the integer value assigned to a **char** variable. This is particularly true if the leftmost or most significant bit of the lower eighth is set; it will become the sign bit of the value assigned. Consider the following:

```
char c;
int x = 4760;  // x contains 1298(16)          0001 0010 1001 1000

c = x;         // c contains 98(16) or -104 (if stored as 8 bits)

                                             C   1001 1000

x = c;         // x now contains 98(16) or -104 .

                                             X   1111 1111 1001 1000
```

In Chapter 12, you learned that automatic conversions can be extended to include newly defined classes through a constructor (for conversion *to* a class object) or by overloading the **operator** *type* **()** function (for conversion *from* a class object).

KEY TERM
casting

C++ also provides a method of explicitly converting from one data type to another known as *casting*. The idea is that a program is easier to read if automatic operators are not depended on. Actions that the programmer intends are explicitly stated.

CONCEPT

explicit casting

Casting is done simply by placing the desired type in front of the value or expression to be converted, similar to calling a function:

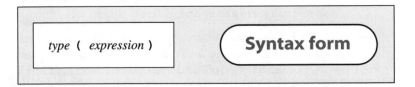

type (expression)

Syntax form

Occasionally, explicit casts can be used to prevent unwanted truncation. For example, you are aware that the division of two integers always results in an integer. If you wish the division of two integers to be a more accurate **float** value, you might cast one or both of the integers to float before the division occurs:

```
int x = 3, y = 7;
float z;
z = y / x;                   // z contains 2.0
z = float (y) / float (z) ;  // z now contains 2.33333
```

Of course, it would do no good to cast the value of the expression after the division, since truncation would have already occurred:

```
z = float (y / z);           // z contains 2.0
```

If an operator type () function has been added to a user class, explicit casts from an object of the class can also be used. If a constructor has been provided within the class with a given type argument, explicit casts to an object of the class can be used:

```
class Complex
{   public:     operator float();   // casting operator
                Complex (float a);  // constructor for float
    . . .
};

Complex value;
float z;
. . .
z = 7.5 * float (value);
value = Complex (z);
```

Just for your information, an older form of the casting operation is also recognized by C++. In this form, the type is placed within parentheses in front of the expression to be cast:

```
z = 7.5 * (float) value;
```

This older notation is somewhat inconsistent with the definition of a type as an operator and should be avoided for clarity. By not requiring the expression to be inside parentheses, it can also be less clear in allowing a reader to immediately identify what is being cast.

14.4 Pointers

You have already had a brief introduction to pointers. Here we examine the topic more fully. C++ allows the programmer to have much greater control over memory through the use of pointers.

14.4.a Pointer notation

You previously learned that when a one-dimensional array is declared, you may visualize the system creating a **const** pointer associated with the array name that points to the first cell of the array. For example:

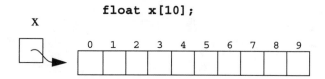

There is an alternate notation for declaring and using pointer parameters. Instead of using empty brackets, you may place * before the name. The following is an identical declaration for the function SomeFunc():

```
void SomeFunc (int *x)        same as        void SomeFunc (int x[ ])
```

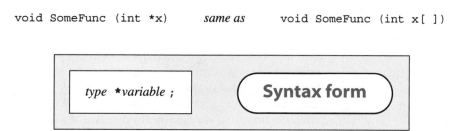

You saw this notation when referencing the owner object inside of a member function with ***this**. this is a built-in pointer to the owner. When referencing array cells with this alternate notation, the index and array pointer are added together and enclosed within an asterisk-parentheses set:

```
w = z[5];          same as        w = *(z+5);
x[n] = 21;         same as        *(x+n) = 21;
```

The asterisk in this notation means "pointed to by" and is often called the *pointer resolution operator*. So, the following example would be interpreted by the system as "assign to w the value pointed to by z plus 5 more cells":

```
w = *(z+5);
```

In other words, the value being referenced is 5 cells beyond where z is pointing. That is the same interpretation as:

```
w = z[5];
```

Here is a simple function that uses this alternate notation to sum the elements of an integer array until a negative number or zero is encountered:

```
int SumArray (int *x)
{   int sum=0, n=0;
    while (*(x+n) > 0)
    {   sum += *(x+n);
        n++;
    }
    return (sum);
}
```

14.4.b   Pointer variables

Once again, you may visualize array names as just being **const** pointers that are initialized to point to the cells requested. You may also explicitly declare pointer *variables* that are not initialized to point to one specific array:

```
int *w;
```

In this declaration, w is a pointer variable that does not point to any one specific array. Don't confuse this with the declaration of a parameter that is initialized to the corresponding argument. This w is just a local variable. A good example of this is in the declaration of array parameters. Typically, the [ ] notation is used when a pointer parameter is declared, and the * notation is used when the pointer variable is declared, but this is not standard by any means. The following are equivalent:

```
void SomeFunc (int *array);
```
same as `void SomeFunc (int array[ ]);`

The only values that should be assigned to pointer variables are pointers. Pointer values can be appropriately determined using the & operator:

&variable

Syntax form

KEY TERM
address-of operator

The & is called the *address-of operator*. Its function is to determine the correct address of a variable, which can then be used in an assignment statement and other places. For example:

```
int a=99, *b;
b = &a;
```

In this code, a contains 99 while b points to a. There are two ways to output this value of 99:

```
cout << a << endl;          // outputs 99
cout << *b << endl;         // outputs the same 99!
```

The first statement outputs the value in the cell a. The second outputs the value pointed to by b. Either a or the pointer b can be used to change the value from 99 to 100;

```
*b = 100;    same as    b[0] = 100;    same as    a = 100;
```

Array pointers can be copied without the need of the & operator, since the name of the array is also a pointer variable and has already been initialized. The following will have pointer x and pointer w point to the same array of cells. The net effect is to have two names for the same array:

```
int x[5];
int *w;
w = x;
x[3] = 77;          // sets cell 3 of array x to 77
w[3] = 77;          // also sets cell 3 of array x to 77!
```

Now, you may be thinking, "That would make a program very difficult to read if a cell or an array may be referred to by two names!" You are right, of course, but there are some situations that you will soon see where pointer variables are very useful. They can be applied with good style. At this point, the preceding segment of code simply illustrates pointer use.

There are such things as pointer constants, but unless you have a good understanding of the operating system and architecture, you will not be using them. At this point, assigning a constant to a pointer would be quite wrong:

```
int *b;
b = 100; // does not yet point to an array!
```

In the first place, the data types are different (integer vs. pointer). In the second place, you are assuming that this in some way corresponds to a memory location that is currently available. The operating system and program may not agree.

Keep in mind also that data types are still important. An `int` pointer is not the same as a `float` or `char` pointer, and these pointers should not be mixed:

```
float *p;
int a;        // 'p' should only hold the
p = &a        // address of a float!
```

14.4.c   Pointer arithmetic

It does make sense to increase or decrease pointers. In fact, we have done this already with the alternate pointer notation for arrays. For example:

```
float s[10] = {9, 3, 7, 4, 5, -1, 6, 2, 1, -3};
cout << *(s+4);                          // outputs 5, same as s[4]
```

When pointers are involved in arithmetic expressions, the system manages the result according to the type of object being pointed to. In other words, each successive pointer value represents successive cells of the appropriate type regardless of the size or number of bytes needed by a cell. Adding (or subtracting) an integer N to a pointer always results in a new pointer of the same type. This new pointer will point to a cell N beyond or N before the original pointer:

```
int x[5];
int *w, *p, *q;
w = x;
x[3] = 77;      // sets cell 3 of the array to 77
w[3] = 87;      // sets cell 3 of the array to 87
p = w+3;
*p = 97;        // sets cell 3 of the array to 97
q = &x[3];      // q also points to cell 3 of array (same as: q = x+3)
q[1] = 107;     // sets cell 4 (one beyond cell 3) of the array to 107
```

CONCEPT
pointer arithmetic
is possible

Pointer arithmetic or expressions may involve addition (increases) and subtraction (decreases). Other operations such as multiplication are not allowed. The address-of & operator and & pointer-to operator have lower precedence than the array index [] operators, equal precedence with unary operators, but higher precedence than the binary or relational operators. Make sure you understand the following examples:

```
int cost[5] = {15, 20, 25, 30, 35, 40};
cout << *cost+2;                 // outputs '17' or cost[0] + 2
cout << *(cost+2);               // outputs '25' or cost[2]
```

Special care needs to be taken with the unary operators since they have equal precedence with these pointer operators. In particular, ++ and -- evaluate from right to left, and it is always a good idea to use parentheses to ensure the precedence you intend:

```
*++cost;      // first increment pointer, then follow new pointer
(*cost)++;    // follow the pointer, then increment what it points to
```

Listing 14.3 represents a possible implementation of the library function `strlen()` intended to return the integer length of a string represented in a `char` array. Remember that this string-implementation method requires that a null character (`\0`) mark the end of the string.

Listing 14.3

```
// strlen()  Return the length of the string in the array.
// ASSUMPTION:  the string is terminated with a null char
// IN:  s is a char array containing a string
int strlen (char *s)
{   int length;
    for (length = 0; *s != '\0'; length++)
        s++;
    return (length);
}
```

As has been mentioned, the pointers associated with array names are constant and cannot be changed. Otherwise, a programmer might lose track of where the array actually resides.

```
int age[5];
age++;// pointer is constant!
```

WRONG WAY!

KEY TERM
null pointer

It generally makes little sense to compare pointers since absolute memory addresses have little meaning and may change from one execution of a program to another. One problem that occurs with pointers is detecting when a pointer variable contains a valid pointer and when it simply contains garbage. There is one special constant pointer value that can be used to indicate a pointer that is not being used. The header file `<iostream.h>` defines **NULL** as the *null pointer,* and this is often used to initialize a pointer variable or indicate that the pointer is currently not pointing to a valid memory location. Comparisons for equality with **NULL** are common:

```
int *job;
job = NULL;
...
if (job == NULL) ...
...
if (job != NULL) ...
```

The NULL pointer constant and the null character `\0` are not the same. One is a character and one is a pointer.

14.5 Dynamically allocated memory

Now that you understand pointers a bit, you are ready for their most important use. Up to this point, each array you have declared had a specific, static, nonchangeable size established when the program was written. This is especially limiting when arrays are private members of classes. Each class variable or object has the same size array. In many applications, you may wish each object to have only as many array cells as are needed. In effect, each object may need a different size of array.

C++ allows arrays to be dynamically allocated and deallocated through use of the **new** and **delete** operators, which interface with the supporting host operating system.

```
pointer = new type ;
pointer = new type [size] ;
delete pointer ;
delete [ ] pointer ;
```
Syntax form

CONCEPT
using new for
dynamic allocation

The system maintains a pool of free memory reserved for this purpose. The **new** operator returns a pointer to an area of memory from this free pool for the type specified. If the bracketed form is used, **new** returns a pointer to an array of the type and size specified. The operator may be used to initialize a pointer at declaration or to assign a pointer to a previously declared pointer variable. The type specified can be any of the primitive types *or any user-defined class or* struct. The *size* for an array allocation can be a constant *or a variable* (or expression).

```
int *ages = new int[n];      // 'ages' is an array of 'n' integer cells
float *cost = new float;      // 'cost' points to a single float cell
Complex *value;
value = new Complex;          // 'value' points to a Complex cell
Complex *many;
many = new Complex[m];        // 'many' is an array of 'm' Complex cells
```

CONCEPT
initializing
dynamic objects

When a single cell is allocated, it may be initialized within parentheses. For single or scalar class objects, the initialization is a list of arguments for a constructor that performs the actual initialization. Dynamically allocated arrays cannot be initialized.

```
char *letter = new char('a');   // initial value of 'a'
Complex *vector =
   new Complex (5.6, -8.9);     // calls matching constructor
```

Dynamically allocated space can be returned to the free pool through use of the **delete** operator. If a dynamically allocated array is to be returned to the free pool, the bracket form of the operator is used:

```
delete letter;       // delete a previously allocated char cell
delete [ ] ages;     // delete a previously allocated array of int
delete vector;       // delete a previously allocated vector cell
```

Care must be taken not to use **delete** with a pointer variable that contains garbage. This could result in sections of executable code, blocks of other variables, and who-knows-what being returned to the free pool of memory with very unpredictable results. It is okay, however, to use **delete** with a pointer variable that has been set to NULL. This has no effect and it causes no problems.

KEY TERM
dangling pointer

A pointer to memory that has been returned to the free pool is called a *dangling pointer*. After a pointer variable has been used with **delete**, the pointer is undefined and should not be referenced or used in any way. Using a dangling pointer in a reference with the pointed-to * operator is a common bug that is often difficult to locate. This is particularly true when a value is *stored* via an undefined pointer. For example:

```
Complex *vector;
...
```

WRONG WAY!

```
vector = new Complex;    // 'vector' now points to a Complex
...
delete vector;           // object pointed to by 'vector' is deleted
...
*vector = b;             // pointer is dangling!
```

CONCEPT
use of invalid pointers can create complex bugs

The system is often not able to tell the difference between garbage and a valid pointer. As you can imagine, using an invalid pointer might result in values being stored in locations you did not intend, overwriting other variables, executable code, parts of the operating system, and so on. This sort of bug may show up in a section of program far removed from the statement that actually caused the problem. The difficulties in debugging a program with pointer problems cannot be overstressed. There are more ways of shooting yourself in the foot with pointers than with any other construct in the language. The most difficult bugs to identify and localize are often associated with the misuse of pointers. As you can now see, writing off the end of an array is also an example of pointer misuse.

14.5.a Constructors and destructors

For class objects, a very common use of the **new** and **delete** operators is in the allocation of *dynamically* sized member arrays. Suppose, for example, a **Golfer** class is needed to represent players in a golf league. Each golfer has a list of scores, but some golfers have more scores than others. One approach is to have a dynamic array of scores. This is a very versatile topic, and we'll only introduce the concept here with a simple example. Consider the following initial definition for such a **Golfer** class:

```
class Golfer
{  public: Golfer(int size);              // constructor
            void AddScore(int thisscore);// add a score to the list
            int CalcAverage();            // return average score
    private: int *scores;                 // pointer to a list of scores
             int numscores;               // number of scores in list
             int maxscores;               // maximum scores poss.
};
```

When a new **Golfer** is instantiated, the programmer must indicate how many scores are to be associated with this object. Here is the constructor to create an appropriately sized array:

```
Golfer::Golfer (int size)
{   scores = new int[size];
    maxscores = size;
    numscores = 0;
}
```

KEY TERM

destructor

Thus, each **Golfer** can have a different number of scores. Now, when a **Golfer** object is no longer needed, it is still the programmer's responsibility to delete the memory for the array. For this purpose, C++ allows matching *destructor* functions for constructors. A destructor is a function automatically called when an object variable is deallocated. This occurs when the function in which the object was declared terminates (or when a delete is invoked specifically on the object). Destructors have the same name as the class (as do constructors) but are prefixed with a ~ tilde symbol:.

~classname ( ) ;   **Syntax form**

No parameters are given to a destructor, and just like a constructor, it is not explicitly called. We'll need to add a destructor to the class definition

```
class Golfer
{  public:  Golfer(int size);            // constructor
             ~Golfer ( );                 // destructor
             void AddScore(int thisscore);// add a score to the list
             int CalcAverage();           // return average score
    private: int *scores;                 // pointer to a list of scores
             int numscores;               // number of scores in list
             int maxscores;               // maximum scores poss.
};
```

and add this destructor to the implementation (`.cpp`) file:

```
Golfer::~Golfer ( )
{   delete scores;
}
```

14.5.b   Copy constructors

As long as the attribute variables of a class contain no pointers to dynamic memory arrays, you may freely assign one class object to another. The built-in capability of object assignment works just fine. It works like this: *All the attribute variables of the right-side object are copied into the corresponding left-side object.* The problem is that any dynamic memory pointed to by an attribute pointer variable isn't really inside the object; it's just pointed to by an attribute pointer. When attributes are copied, these pointers are copied, *but not the dynamic memory*! Consider the following example using the **Golfer** class:

```
Golfer Fred(5), Sam(3);
...
Fred = Sam;
```

Suppose Fred has scores {67, 69, 72, 66, 71} and Sam has scores {73, 75, 72}. What is intended is that Fred should end up with a copy of the same three scores as Sam. But two problems occur. First, the three scores of Sam are not inside this Golfer object. They are just pointed to by it. Second, what happens to the original five scores of Fred?

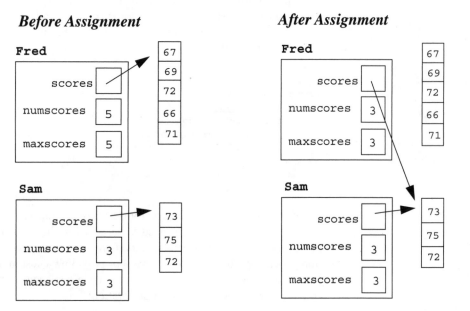

KEY TERM

shallow copy

Notice that the contents of Sam are indeed copied to become the contents of Fred. Unfortunately, that leaves the previous array Fred dangling. It also results in Fred and Sam pointing to the *same* array of scores. This is referred to as a *shallow copy*. This is what we intended:

After Assignment

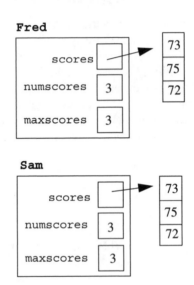

The default is always a shallow copy. If an object contains a pointer to dynamic memory, a shallow copy is not sufficient and can lead to significant problems. We solved the problem of shallow copies on assignment by overloading the = operator with *an explicit function of our own design*. Here is one possible solution:

```
void Golfer::operator= (Golfer source)
{   delete scores;                       // dispose of original array
    scores = new int [source.maxscores];  // allocate a new array
    for (n=0; n<source.maxsize; n++)      // copy over scores
        scores[n] = source.scores[n];
    numscores = source.numscores;
    maxscores = source.maxscores;
}
```

KEY TERM

deep copy

This new = operator function for **Golfer** is known as a *deep-copy* assignment. Naturally, a prototype would need to be added to the class definition as well. This same problem of shallow copy occurs if we were to use a Golfer object as a function parameter. There is also a method of providing a custom function to make deep copies for parameters. These are known as deep-copy constructors. This is just a constructor with a special parameter declaration:

$classname::classname$ (**const** $classname$&);

Syntax form

This deep-copy constructor should do the same thing as the deep-copy = operator in making a copy of the parameter into the host object. In fact, the simplest thing to do is just call the = operator function you have specially written for a deep copy. Remember, you can refer to the owner of a member function as an entire object using the `this` pointer:

```
Golfer::Golfer (const Golfer& source)
{   *this = source;
}
```

CONCEPT

when deep copy is needed

The last few pages have introduced a lot of new features to your C++ knowledge. It can be quite confusing trying to figure out when deep copy is needed, when destructors are important, and so on. A simple rule can help solve most situations: When a class contains a pointer to dynamically allocated memory, always consider implementing:

1. a default constructor to initialize the pointer to NULL

2. a destructor to release or free allocated memory

3. a deep-copy = operator for each type of supported assignment

4. a deep-copy constructor to allow objects to be used as parameters

Let's pause here and consider the impact of this new approach to dynamic arrays. It certainly is more efficient to allocate only as much space as is needed, but it is also obviously more complex to program and much more prone to bugs.

If a program is to run only with a single-program operating system such as DOS, there is often little advantage to this dynamic memory approach. All available memory can be used by the single program. Any memory not used is simply not used. A dynamic memory approach might only be justified if the programmer expects the program to at least occasionally need all of available memory. On those occasions, a dynamic approach would allow the program to store a large number of smaller strings. Other operating systems are quite different. If a program is to run with a multiprogram system such as UNIX or Windows, an efficient use of memory allows more memory resources to be used by other programs.

It's a judgment call by the programmer. Making a program more complex in order to be memory-efficient when such efficiency presents no real advantage is a poor choice. On the other hand, when efficiency can be taken advantage of by other programs, it becomes an important responsibility. Of course, an application program should probably not need to know which method is being used. Often, a class is first implemented using fixed-size arrays. After debugging, the class is modified or upgraded to use dynamically allocated memory.

14.6 Example project

In the Chapter 12 Example Project, a **Set** class was established to allow application programs to manipulate sets of integers using union, intersection, and a few other operations. Unfortunately, each **Set** object was limited to a maximum of 100 elements. Even if a **Set** object contained only a few integers, a fixed array of 100 cells was still allocated. Let's upgrade the **Set** class so that a set contains as many integer cells as needed with no limits other than those posed by available memory. In addition, we will add a few more useful functions.

We will create the header file as "adv_set.h" and the implementation as "adv_set.cpp". The important changes to the original "Set.h" header file containing the class definition will be to the private member attribute and the addition of the needed deep-copy constructor, deep-copy assignment operator, and a destructor. Instead of a fixed array of 100 cells, members becomes a pointer (Listing 14.4).

Listing 14.4

```
// adv_set.h    An improved or advanced Set class using dynamic memory
#include <iostream.h>

class Set
{   public:    Set ();                        // default constructor
               Set (const Set&);              // deep-copy constructor
               ~Set ();                       // destructor
               Set operator + (Set);          // union of sets
               Set operator + (int);          // insertion of an integer
               Set operator - (Set);          // subtraction of sets
               Set operator - (int);          // removal of an integer
               Set operator | (Set);          // intersection of sets
               int IsMember (int);            // test for membership
               void Output (ostream&);        // stream output
               Set& operator= (const Set&);   // deep-copy assignment
    private:   int *members;                  // a dynamic array
               int size;
               void Reset(void);              // private function to reinitialize a Set
};
```

The implementation will need to pay special attention to each function that changes the size of a **Set** object. Before changing the size of a **Set** object, the function must (a) deallocate the previous array and (b) allocate a new array of the appropriate size. In addition, we will now need to implement the deep-copy constructor, deep-copy assignment operator, and destructor to deallocate memory. An additional function Reset () has been added to allow a set to be cleared (Listing 14.5).

Listing 14.5

```cpp
// adv_set.cpp  Implementation file for the dynamic Set class
#include <iostream.h>
#include "adv_set.h"

Set::Set ()                               // default constructor
{  size = 0;   members = NULL;
}

Set::~Set ()                              // destructor
{  delete [ ] members;
}

Set::Set (const Set& s)                   // deep-copy constructor
{  int n;
   members = new int[s.size];             // alloc. new array of correct size
   size = s.size;
   for (n=0; n<size; n++)                 // copy set members over
       members[n] = s.members[n];
}

Set& Set::operator= (const Set& s)        // deep-copy assignment
{  int n;
   if (members == s.members)              // if a set is assigned to itself (A=A)
       return(*this);
   delete [ ] members;                    // dealloc. prev. array (if any)
   members = new int[s.size];             // alloc. new array of correct size
   size = s.size;
   for (n=0; n<size; n++)                 // copy set members over
       members[n] = s.members[n];
   return (*this);
}

// Union returns a new set containing members of both sets
Set Set::operator+ (Set s)
{  int j, pos;
   Set temp;
// first determine the new set size; the size of the owner set plus the
//   number of members of the arg. set which are not in the owner set.
   temp.size = size;
   for (j=0; j<s.size; j++)
       if (!IsMember(s.members[j]))
           temp.size++;
   temp.members = new int[temp.size];     // allocate new array
// Now copy over the owner set, then the members of the arg. set which
//   are not already in the owner set.
   for (j=0; j<size; j++)
       temp.members[j] = members[j];
```

```
        pos = size;
        for (j=0; j<s.size; j++)
            if (!IsMember(s.members[j]))
                temp.members[pos++] = s.members[j];
        return (temp);
    }


// Subtraction returns a new set containing only members of owner set
//   that do not also appear in the arg. set.
Set Set::operator- (Set s)                    // subtraction of sets
{   int j, pos;
    Set temp;
// first determine the new set size; the size of the owner set minus the
//   number of members of the arg. set which are also in the owner set.
    temp.size = size;
    for (j=0; j<s.size; j++)
        if (IsMember(s.members[j]))
            temp.size--;
    temp.members = new int[temp.size];      // allocate new array
// Now copy over the owner set, skipping the members of the arg. set which
//   are also in the owner set.
    for (j=0, pos=0; j<size; j++)
        if (!s.IsMember(members[j]))
            temp.members[pos++] = members[j];
    return (temp);
}


// Intersection returns a new set containing only members that appear in
//   both the owner set and the arg. set.
Set Set::operator | (Set s)                   // intersection of sets
{   int j, pos;
    Set temp;
// first determine the new set size; the size of the owner set minus the
//   number of members in the owner set that are not in the arg. set.
    temp.size = size;
    for (j=0; j<size; j++)
        if (!s.IsMember(members[j]))
            temp.size--;
    temp.members = new int[temp.size];      // allocate new array
// Now copy over the owner set, skipping the members not appearing in both sets.
    for (j=0, pos=0; j<size; j++)
        if (s.IsMember(members[j]))
            temp.members[pos++] = members[j];
    return (temp);
}


int Set::IsMember (int n)
 { int k;
   for (k=0; k<size; k++)
```

```
        if (n == members[k])
            return (1);
    return (0);
}

Set Set::operator- (int n)        // Subtraction of a specific integer from a set
{   int k, j=0;
    Set temp;
    if (!IsMember(n))
        return (*this);
    else
    {   temp.members = new int[size-1];
        for (k=0; k<size; k++)
            if (members[k] != n)
                temp.members[j++] = members[k];
        temp.size = j;
        return (temp);
    }
}

Set Set::operator+ (int n)        // Union of an integer into a set
{   int k;
    Set temp;
    if (IsMember(n))
        return (*this);
    else
    {   temp.members = new int[size+1];
        for (k=0; k<size; k++)
            temp.members[k] = members[k];
        temp.members[size] = n;
        temp.size = size+1;
        return (temp);
    }
}

void Set::Output(ostream& outs)        // output the members of a set
{   int n;
    for (n=0; n<size; n++)
        outs << members[n] << ',';
    outs << '\n';
}

void Set::Reset(void)        // clear all members of a set
{   if (size)
        delete[ ] members;
    size = 0;
    members = NULL;
}
```

The + union operator implementation illustrates one of the difficulties in dealing with dynamic sets. One cannot allocate a new array until the size of that array is first determined. It is not necessarily the sum of the owner and argument array sizes since some integers may be members of both sets. The only solution is to start a count with the size of the owner array and then increment this count for each member of the argument array that is not a member of the owner set. When the final count is determined, the new array can be allocated, and appropriate set members can be copied into it.

14.7 Summary

KEY TERMS   Quite a few new terms were introduced in this chapter:

1. *hexadecimal*—a positional number system with 16 digits using 0–9 and A–F.

2. *2's complement*—a form of representing negative binary numbers with the complement of the positive magnitude plus 1.

3. *most significant bit (MSB)*—the leftmost bit of a binary number.

4. *masking*—using a binary & AND operator to extract or copy certain bits from a binary number.

5. *casting*—explicitly indicating a conversion from one type to another.

6. *address-of operator*—the & operator when used in front of an object or variable.

7. *pointer resolution operator*—the * when used in front of a pointer variable.

8. *null pointer*—a special pointer value that indicates the pointer is not being used or should not be used.

9. *dangling pointer*—a pointer to an object or dynamic memory that is no longer allocated or valid.

10. *destructor*—an implicitly called function invoked when an owner object is deallocated.

11. *shallow copy*—a copy of only the internal variables within an object.

12. *deep copy*—a copy of all variables and pointers within an object and a copy of the dynamic memory pointed to by this object.

CONCEPTS   In this chapter, low-level operators for binary manipulation of integers were presented. Several new declaration qualifiers were introduced. The use of pointers to manage dynamically allocated memory was explained. Several important specific facts or rules should be remembered.

Hexadecimal constants must be preceded by 0x. Each hexadecimal digit represents a 4-bit binary number. Methods for converting decimal to hexadecimal and from hexadecimal to decimal were given. The low-level operators >> and << are used to shift the bits of a binary number right or left. There is no automatic checking for overflow or underflow of shifted values.

The low-level binary operators |, &, ^, and ~ are used to perform bitwise OR, AND, EXCLUSIVE-OR, and complement operations. These are commonly used in masking groups of bits from binary values.

The declaration qualifier **unsigned** can be used to force an integer to be interpreted strictly as a positive value. The MSB becomes available as another data bit. Magnitudes approximately twice the size of the normal **int** maximum can be expressed. The qualifier **static** forces a variable not to be deallocated when the function in which it is declared returns or exits. Upon reentry, the variable will still contain the previous value. The qualifier **extern** allows a declaration to match the declaration of the same name in another file.

When **int** values are cast to **char**, the lower 8 bits are simply extracted or masked off. A programmer can override default conversions or implicit casts by defining overloaded casting operators.

Pointers can be assigned to similarly typed pointer variables. Pointer variables can be incremented and decremented using arithmetic expressions. Pointer arithmetic is managed by the system. Each successive pointer value represents successive cells of the appropriate type, regardless of the size or number of bytes needed by a cell.

When arrays are declared, the name of the array can be treated as a **const** pointer to the array cells. Both the * pointer resolution operator and the [] array notation can be used to access an array cell.

The **new** operator can be used to allocate memory from a free-memory pool maintained by the system. **delete** is used to return memory back to the pool for later reallocation. Returning memory allocated for an array is done with **delete [ ]**.

Destructors are class member functions that are implicitly called whenever a class object is deallocated. These are commonly used to return memory acquired with the **new** operator during the life of the object.

When an object is copied as a result of an assignment operator or argument passing to a function call, the default is to copy only the exact contents of the object. Often, when objects contain pointers to dynamic memory acquired with the **new** operator, it is desirable to have a copy made of this memory being pointed to. To accomplish this, a deep-copy constructor is usually implemented.

Several hints for good programming practice and style were suggested. First, it is poor practice to use char variables as small integers. The savings over int variables are minimal while the potential for introducing bugs is significant. Second, pointer variables present a potential for serious and hard-to-find bugs. Anytime a programming bug seems difficult to find or particularly hard to explain, you should suspect the use of an invalid or dangling pointer.

When using pointer variables in classes, strongly consider implementing these member operators and functions to ensure proper deep copy and assignment:

1. a default constructor to initialize any pointers to NULL

2. a destructor to release or free allocated memory

3. a deep-copy = operator for each type of supported assignment

4. a deep-copy constructor to allow objects to be used as parameters

Table 14.2 **Example segments**

`c = a	b;`	Bitwise OR of a and b.
`c = a >> 3;`	Right-shift a by 3 bits.
`static int x;`	x is statically allocated and will remain when this function exits.
`extern float y;`	y is declared externally; access to y is allowed within this function or file scope.
`int *a, b[ ];`	a and b are pointer variables.
`Student *a = new Student;`	a now points to a newly allocated Student cell.
`T::T(const T&);`	A prototype for a copy constructor for class T.
`T::~T();`	A prototype for a destructor for class T.

14.8 Exercises

14.8.a Short-answer questions

1. Explicitly converting one data type to another is known as _____.
2. The address of a variable can be expressed by placing the _____ operator in front of the variable name.
3. The value referred to by a pointer can be expressed by placing the _____ in front of the pointer variable.
4. When the explicit contents of an object are copied into another object—but not any values or arrays pointed to outside the object—this is known as a _____ copy.
5. When the contents of an object are copied into another object—including any arrays or values pointed to outside the object — this is known as a _____copy.
6. Convert the following 2's complement 8-bit binary numbers to decimal. Remember that if the MSB is set, you must find the magnitude by taking the 2's complement of the number (remembering that the decimal value is negative).
   a. 0111 1010
   b. 0011 1111
   c. 1011 0001
   d. 1100 0111
7. Convert the preceeding 2's complement binary numbers to hexadecimal.
8. What hexadecimal value would result from the following operations?
   a. 0x0123 >>4;
   b. 0x0123 <<3;
   c. 0xFFF3 <<1;
   d. 0xFFF3 <<8;
   e. 0xFFF3 <<12;
   f. 0xF012 & 0xFF00
   g. 0x0123 | 0xF0F0
   h. 0x0123 ^ 0x0F0F

9. Convert the following 16-bit hexadecimal numbers to decimal:
   a. 0x0100
   b. 0x0007
   c. 0x7FA3
   d. 0x9010
   e. 0xFFFF
10. Suggest an expression to mask off the lower or rightmost 8 bits of `value` and assign to `result`.

    ```
    int value, result;
    cin >> value;
    result =
    ```

11. If `"fileA.cpp"` contains the global declaration **float maximum;**, what declaration should be added to `"fileB.cpp"` to allow statements access to this same global variable?
12. What is the maximum **int** value allowed in a system that utilizes 32-bit integers? What would be the maximum **unsigned int** value allowed?
13. Briefly explain the effect of qualifying a local variable declaration with **static**.
14. State whether each of the following expressions represents an integer, a pointer, or an illegal expression:

    ```
    int x[10], y, *z;
    ```

    a. x++;
    b. z;
    c. *(z+2);
    d. &y;

15. For the declaration **char *e;**, give a statement to allocate an array of 50 `char` cells to be pointed to by `e`
16. What would be the result assigned in each of the following statements?

    ```
    int a, *b, c=99, d[3] = {88, 77, 66};
    b = &c;
    ```

    a. a = *b;
    b. a = *(d+1);
    c. b = d+2;   *b = 55;
    d. c = *d;
    e. c = *(&a);

17. Give the statement that could deallocate the dynamic memory allocated in question 15.
18. Show how the filename following the name of the application program `calc` in the following command-line example could be used to open a disk file:

    ```
    c:> calc fileC.txt
    ```

19. Declare the private class variables for a class representing a `BranchOffice`. Each branch office is represented by a manager ID number, a count of employees, and an array of ID numbers (one for each employee). Branch offices may have from 2 to 30 employees. Use dynamically allocated memory so that each `BranchOffice` object contains only as many ID numbers as are needed in this array.

20. Declare the private class variables for a class representing an `Address`. Each address may have from one to five lines. Each line may require from 20 to 80 characters. Use dynamically allocated memory so that each `Address` object contains only as many address lines as are needed and each line contains only as many characters as might be needed.

14.8.b Projects

1. Develop a function to convert a string of digits into an integer. This is basically what the `Atoi()` member function of the `String` class accomplishes. You should not invoke any library functions to accomplish this result. Assume the string contains only digit characters. A single-digit character can be converted to an integer simply by subtracting the ASCII code for 0:

```
char digit = '8';
int digitvalue;
digitvalue = digit - '0';                  // contains the integer 8
```

2. A certain sound board manufacturer for PCs stores sound files with a leading 16-bit integer code. This code contains the board version (leftmost 3 bits), the board model (next 2 bits), and a number indicating the type of compression used within the file. Write a function to accept an integer code and return these three values as separate integers, as in this example:

```
int code, version, model, compression;
cin >> code;
Convert (code, version, model, compression);
cout << "version: " << version << "  model: " << model << endl;
cout << "compression: " << compression << endl;
```

3. Refer to short answer question 19. Complete the declaration of this class with the necessary member functions, constructors (for initialization), a destructor, a deep-copy constructor, a deep-copy assignment function, and an overloaded `<<` output operator. Implement these functions and verify that they work correctly with the following simple application program:

```
void main()
{   BranchOffice Head;            // an empy object
          // an office manager and 3 employees
    BranchOffice Midwest (555, 3, 66, 77, 88);
          // an office manager and 5 employees
    BranchOffice Central (999, 5, 22, 33, 44, 55, 66);
    Head = Midwest;
    cout << Head << endl;
    Head = Central;
    Central.NewEmployee (2, 35);// change employee 2's ID
    cout << Head << endl;
}
```

4. Refer to short answer question 20. Complete the declaration of this class with the necessary member functions, constructors (for initialization), a destructor, a deep-copy constructor, a deep-copy assignment function, and overloaded `<<` output and `>>` input operators. Demonstrate with an application program that `Address` objects can be assigned, input, passed to functions, and output.

5. Complete the implementation of the `Adv_String` object begun in this chapter. Demonstrate that an application program that works correctly with the `String` class also works exactly the same with this new `Adv_String` class. Verify your class with a simple demonstrating application program.

6. Develop a class for a new data type called `Polynomial`. Objects of this class should be able to represent the integer coefficients of any practical sized polynomial. Each successive coefficient would represent a successive power. For example:

$56x^4 + 21x^3 - 13x + 87$ could be stored as: 56, 21, 0, –13, 87

Allow initialization, input, output, and addition. When two dissimilarly sized polynomials are added, the smaller one should be assumed to have zeros for the missing higher-order coefficients. Verify your class with a simple demonstrating application program.

7. A simple graphics figure can be represented with a number of lines. Each line is represented with a starting position and an ending position on the display. Positions are `x,y` pairs representing horizontal (`x`) and vertical displacement (`y`). Naturally, separate figures in an image can have a different number of lines. To be efficient, one might choose to use dynamically allocated memory for figure line `x,y` pairs. You may assume a figure is limited to a maximum of 20 different lines. Implement a `Figure` class with the following member functions:

```
AddLine (int x, int y);     // add a line to the figure
AddFig (Figure z);          // add the lines of this figure
DisplayFig ();              // display the figure
```

If you have access to a graphics package on your computer, you might implement the `DisplayFig()` function by actually drawing all lines of the figure on the display. If not or if this is impractical, this function might simply list the lines as numeric values.

8. **Creative Challenge:** The manager of the Afghanistan Banana-Stand Company wishes to manage his warehouse more effectively so that banana crates are shipped to stands as fresh as possible. When a banana crate arrives from the plantation, it is assigned an ID number representing the plantation source and stored in the Miami warehouse. When a stand orders a crate, the manager wishes that the oldest bananas in the warehouse are shipped to ensure that his stock is properly rotated. Assume the warehouse can hold up to ten crates of bananas. Implement a class called `Warehouse` that allows the following operations:

a. `miami.AddCrate(id);`   // assign this ID and store the crate in the warehouse.

b. `id = miami.ShipCrate();`// return the ID of the oldest crate and remove from the warehouse.

Demonstrate this class with an application program using the following transactions to show that the crates in the Miami warehouse are shipped in the order they arrive:

```
miami.AddCrate(71);
miami.AddCrate(28);
miami.AddCrate(13);
miami.AddCrate(43);
miami.AddCrate(19);
miami.AddCrate(23);
miami.AddCrate(41);
miami.AddCrate(52);
cout << miami.ShipCrate();
cout << miami.ShipCrate();
cout << miami.ShipCrate();
cout << miami.ShipCrate();
miami.AddCrate(63);
miami.AddCrate(89);
miami.AddCrate(83);
cout << miami.ShipCrate();
cout << miami.ShipCrate();
miami.AddCrate(43);
cout << miami.ShipCrate();
cout << miami.ShipCrate();
cout << miami.ShipCrate();
cout << miami.ShipCrate();
cout << miami.ShipCrate();
cout << miami.ShipCrate();
```

9. **Creative Challenge:** The banana warehouse problem had a limit for the number of crates a warehouse could hold. Redo this problem and remove this limit. A warehouse should be able to hold as many crates as the computer memory will allow. If the application program does not have enough room for a desired number of crates, the problem should be solved by buying more memory and not by modifying the application program.

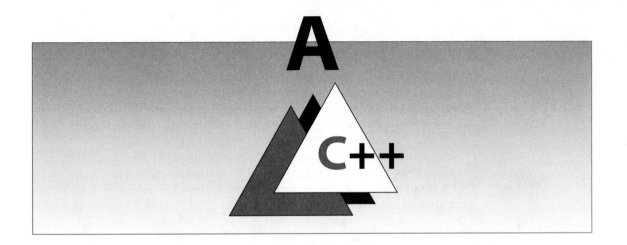

Windows
95/98/00/NT

One of the most common operating systems for personal computers is
Microsoft Windows. While there are several revisions of this popular system, they
are all used in a similar manner. Developing C++ programs on personal computers using Microsoft Windows requires at least a fundamental knowledge of using
this system.

An operating system can be thought of as the program that controls the computer
hardware on behalf of specific applications. In addition, the operating system manages disk files, printers, network connections, and so forth on behalf of the user.
There is much more detail and functionality than these two simple statements indicate, but this is a good perspective for a new student.

While much of the program writing, debugging, and execution associated
with assignments and examples in this text is done within a program development
environment (PDE) such as Microsoft Visual C++ 6.*x* or Borland C++ Builder,
several important operating system abilities can also be very useful. Rather than a
detailed tutorial on using Windows, we'll look specifically at how to accomplish
these operations.

A.1 Versions

The first commonly used windowing operating system by Microsoft was Windows 3.1. This release is quite out-of-date and is rarely seen today. For the most part, personal computers based on the Intel processor run the versatile and robust Windows 95 or later versions. We won't bother with the specific differences and enhanced capabilities of these versions and revisions.

It is important to differentiate between the Windows operating system and the Windows operating system *GUI*. A GUI is a graphical user interface. This is what the user sees and how the user uses the keyboard, mouse, and so on to indicate desired operations. As a beginning student studying this text, most of the differences you might notice between the Windows 95, 98, 00, and NT GUIs are cosmetic. The operations you will need are all accomplished in the same manner.

A.2 Basics

A couple of basic concepts are all that we need. All Windows systems and configurations have several features in common. At the bottom of the display is a bar called the Taskbar. The rest of the display is collectively called the Desktop. The Taskbar can be continuously displayed or only appear when the mouse cursor is placed at the bottom of the display. On the Desktop, additional menus and icons might be displayed. On the Taskbar, a Start button is always displayed.

An *icon* is a small picture that represents an action, file, or folder. A *folder* is a collection of related files. A *file* is a collection of related information and can be an executable program, a document, or some other type of data. There is no real standard for icon pictures (and they may in fact change from PC to PC), but the picture will often give you an idea of what the icon represents.

One important set of icons is used to represent a folder. There are several minor variations on the folder icon, but the concept is the same. Opening a folder gives you access to the related files or documents within it.

temp

Basic options and operations can all be done by manipulating the mouse. The mouse cursor is moved to the appropriate location, and the *left* mouse button is used in one of three ways:

1. click: Quickly press and release.

2. open: Quickly press and release twice or double-click.

3. drag: Press and hold the mouse button while moving the cursor to a new location and then release.

A.3 Disk files

Each disk system on a computer is assigned a letter name followed by a colon. Some disks have removable media (such as floppy disks) and others are nonremovable or *hard*. Typically, the floppy disk system is assigned **a:** while the primary hard disk is labeled **c:**, but this is not a standard. You will want to ask your lab instructor or system manager for your system's disk assignments.

Each disk contains a set of folders and files. Folders are hierarchical. In other words, a folder may contain another folder. A folder or file may be represented with an icon or with a textual *filename*. A *complete* filename lists the disk system and the folder hierarchy as well as the actual filename. Names are separated by backslash symbols. Under Windows (as opposed to C++), letter case does not matter, and a name may contain spaces. A filename (as opposed to a folder name) may also have a suffix appended after a period or dot. The suffix is an aid to indicate the type of data in the file. For example, the suffix **.exe** indicates the file is an executable program.

For example, suppose a header file Head.h resides on the a: disk in the folder MyHeaders. The complete filename is:

```
a:\myheaders\head.h
```

A.4 How do I . . .

You don't need to be an expert in Windows to study C++ programming, but a few operations are quite useful. Rather than present a detailed tutorial on using the Windows GUI, we'll focus on the operations. The following represent the GUI steps that can be used to accomplish each operation. *Keep in mind that there are usually several different ways to accomplish a given operation in Windows*—it is very versatile. Some of these different methods depend on your particular setup and configuration. The following steps were chosen as the most general and most likely to be the same regardless of setup.

The rest of this appendix is organized as a helpful index of operations. Each section presents an operation and the steps used to accomplish that operation.

A.4.a Start an installed program

There are two methods. First, many systems will have been configured to display an icon on the Desktop for the particular program that has been installed. To start this program, double-click on the associated icon. For example, the icon for Microsoft Visual C++ Version 6.x PDE is:

Second, if there is no icon for the program on the Desktop, click on the Start button to bring up the primary menu:

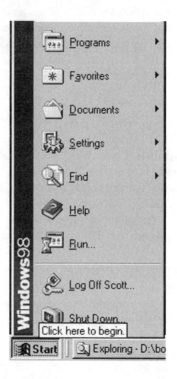

Next, click on the Programs folder to open a menu of available program files and folders. You actually don't need to click on the Programs folder. Simply leaving the mouse cursor over the folder for a moment will also bring up the Programs menu. The Programs folder icon is a variation of the folder icon in that it contains executable files or programs. Anytime you see this folder icon, you will know that there are several program choices.

The menu that now appears lists all the available programs, each with an associated icon. Some of the entries will be more program folders. Continue to click on program folders until the executable program is available. Now click on the correct program icon. For example, here are the menu choices on one particular system used to start the Microsoft Visual C++ PDE:

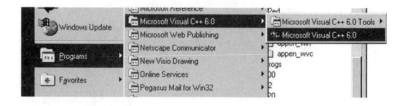

A.4.b Terminate a program

A program will typically have a menu choice in the upper left corner of the program window named File. Click on this name to bring up a file menu. One choice will always be Exit. Click here to terminate. Alternately, many programs will have a small X button in the upper right of the program window. You may also click here to terminate.

A.4.c Start a personal C++ program

When you write and build a C++ program, the program will not normally be listed in the Program menu because it hasn't been *installed*. Typically, only commercial programs are installed. Your program may still be executed by clicking on the Start button and then clicking on the Run menu choice. Enter the complete filename and click on OK to run the program. You do not need to include the .exe suffix, although it does no harm.

A.4.d Show the contents of a floppy or folder

Each Windows Desktop contains a My Computer icon. Opening this icon will present a page of icons and associated names for each disk system available (along with a few other icons we won't worry about). Opening the icon, a disk generates a page of icons and names for each folder and file on the disk.

The initial display is always a set of disk systems representing the computer system. Expanding or opening a folder or disk drive icon will expand the display in a hierarchical manner. Naturally, a floppy disk must be in the drive before Windows can show the contents of the floppy.

At the top of the My Computer window, you will see a set of menu choices. You may *backup* the My Computer display to a previous page of icons using the Back button.

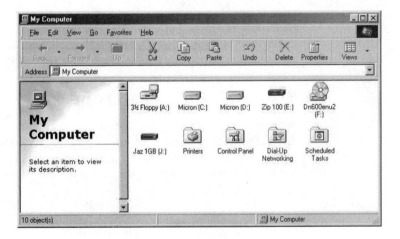

A.4.e Copy a file to a floppy

Using the My Computer icon, page down to and open the folder from which you wish to copy a file. Now click on the file icon using the right mouse button and choose the Send To option in the menu presented. This will provide a list of destinations, including the floppy drive. A copy of the file will then be created on the floppy.

A.4.f Delete a file

Using the My Computer icon, page down to and open the folder containing the file to be deleted. Click on the file icon and choose the Delete menu choice at the top of the window. The system will ask you to confirm sending this file to the Recycle Bin, which is a nice way of saying garbage can.

A.4.g Show the space available on a floppy

Open the My Computer icon and click on the floppy disk icon. The display will show the current capacity, contents, and free space on the current floppy.

A.4.h Print a file

Files are normally printed using the application that was utilized to create the file. For example, .cpp files are most easily printed using the PDE. Select the File menu at the top right of the PDE window. Within this menu, select the Print option.

A.4.i Copy a project

A PDE project is actually a folder. You can copy a project folder using the same method used earlier to copy a file. Unfortunately, a project folder may be very large and may not fit on a floppy disk. You may safely remove temporary files in a project prior to making a disk copy. These will automatically be rebuilt the next time you build your program. For example, Microsoft Visual C++ projects will contain a Debug and perhaps a Res folder which can safely be deleted. At this point, the project folder is probably small enough to be copied to a floppy.

A.4.j Format a removable disk

When a new box of removable disks is purchased, the disks may or may not be properly prepared or *formatted* for use. If you inadvertently place an unprepared new disk in a drive and attempt to use it, the system will automatically detect that it has not yet been formatted and ask if it may proceed it do so prior to continuing with the requested operation.

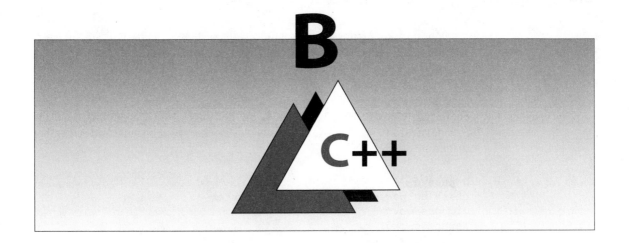

UNIX: Gnu C++, `make`, and Debugging

C++ requires the help of an underlying operating system. Appendix A covered Windows systems, and this appendix covers the use of the UNIX Gnu C++ compiler, the **make** utility, and the Gnu debugger for simple program development. Just as with the other appendixes, this is not a complete user's guide—those are readily available. Rather, the focus is on aspects of UNIX that are important to introductory C++ program development.

B.1 Logging on

One major difference between UNIX and most PC operating systems such as DOS and Windows is that computers using UNIX often allow more than one user at a time. Each user has a user name (sometimes called an account) and a password. You may not need a password the first time you use the system. Your user name and initial password (if applicable) will probably be assigned to you by the system administrator. To initiate a session under UNIX, simply enter your user name (and password if required) in response to the prompt(s). A typical interaction looks like the following:

```
logon: scott
password:
```

You will notice that the password does not display while you are entering. After initiating the session successfully, you will see important information messages followed by a prompt. Typically, the prompt is a $ or > character, but this may be different for your system. During your first session, you should specify a new (or initial) password for subsequent sessions using the **passwd** command. You will be asked to enter the old password (if applicable) and the new password twice. Choose a password of at least six characters and remember that case is significant:

```
$ passwd
changing password for scott on system
old password:
new password:
retype new password:
```

B.2 Files and directories

If you are familiar with Windows or have read Appendix A, you will notice a number of similarities between Windows and UNIX. If not, *you should first read Appendix A sections A.1 through A.3 for an introduction to files and operating systems.* The developers of Windows purposefully incorporated many of the time-proven features of the older UNIX operating system. The concepts of filenames, directories and hierarchy, wildcards, and command interpretation are very similar. While there are many significant differences, most of those differences are associated with operations beyond what you need for an introductory class doing simple file management.

Like Windows, UNIX organizes files into a hierarchy of directories. While Windows utilizes the backward slash \ to show this hierarchy and indicate the root directory, UNIX uses the forward slash /. Windows allows filenames with an optional dot and three-letter extension, whereas UNIX has very few restrictions on file or directory names. The dot is commonly used in filenames and some application programs, and development tools may assume certain filename endings, but UNIX actually treats the dot just like any other character. Windows does not consider letter case while UNIX is case sensitive. Windows assumes that executable files, source files, and so forth have appropriate endings or extensions. By so doing, they will not allow a user to print an executable file or execute a source file. UNIX makes no such assumptions. It is up to the user to keep track of the contents and purpose of files.

The top directories in a UNIX system are usually the responsibility of the system administrator. When a user name is added to a system, the administrator creates an initial home directory for that user in an appropriate place in the hierarchy. A user needs only be concerned about his or her home directory and the files and subdirectories it contains. For example, consider a possible directory structure for user scott. Here, indentation shows the hierarchy or subordination:

```
scott
   .cshrc
   .login
   accounts
       smith.data
       jones.data.2
       oldacnts
           rectify
           johnson.data.3
           white.data.old
       report_from_previous_accounts
   work
       rectify.cpp
       rectify.make
       oldacnts
           rectify
```

In this example, the home directory contains two files (.cshrc and .login) and two directories (accounts and work). The accounts directory contains four files and a subdirectory. The number of directories (or subdirectories) and their locations are under the user's control. Notice that the work directory and the accounts directory (under the root) both have subdirectories with the same name (oldacnts). These two directories also have a file of the same name (rectify).

B.3 The user interface

After initiating a UNIX session, an interface chosen for you by the system administrator will be initiated. There are many different interfaces available. They range from simple command-line interpreters or shells to sophisticated graphical windows systems. Within these interfaces, there are so many different editors in use that it would be a bit unrealistic to attempt to explain how to use each. I'll leave the explanation of the interface and the editor you will be using to your instructor. Keep in mind that the interface and editor are not UNIX; they are simply tools whereby the user can form and send requests to the underlying UNIX system to create, edit, execute, print, or otherwise manipulate files.

B.4 Gnu C++

Once a C++ source program has been stored into a file using the interface and tools of your UNIX system, you must ready the program for execution using a compiler. Even though many different user interfaces are available for UNIX systems, only a couple of C++ compilers have become common in UNIX teaching environments.

They are quite similar, and we will take a look at one: Gnu C++. This discussion assumes you are either using a simple shell interface or are running a shell interface within a graphical window.

There are two ways to prepare a program for execution: using command lines and using a make or project file. To understand how to use the latter, you must first understand the command-line method, and we'll look at that first. The compiler can be invoked using the **g++** command in a variety of formats. Here is perhaps the simplest. The **g++** is followed by a set of options and a set of source filenames:

$ **g++** *-options   sourcefiles*

While other scenarios are possible, it is best to give source files the suffix .cpp just as with all examples in the text. The most common **g++** option is used to specify the name of the file to contain the executable program. You should always use this option when the result of the command is to construct an executable file. This option uses -o followed by a filename. Most commonly, programmers do not give the executable file any suffix at all. Suppose, for example, that you have a simple program in a single file named myprog.cpp. The following would ready this program to be executed as file myprog:

```
$ g++ -o myprog myprog.cpp
```

If you forget to specify the -o option, the system will save the executable program in the file a.out. If errors were encountered during compilation, appropriate messages will be displayed and no executable file will be prepared. If no error messages are displayed, the program can now be executed simply by entering the executable filename as a command. In effect, you have actually just added a new command to your system:

```
$ myprog
```

If a program consists of several source files, they can be listed together (separated by blanks). For example, if a program consists of three source files — myprog.cpp, myfuncs1.cpp, and myfuncs2.cpp—the following command could be used to prepare myprog for execution:

```
$ g++ -o myprog myprog.cpp myfuncs1.cpp myfuncs2.cpp
```

This command would cause the Gnu system to compile each of the three source files in turn and then link them together (along with any library functions that have been referenced) into the myprog executable file.

Often, it doesn't make sense to do all this work if a change has been made to only one file. Why recompile all three if two have not changed? A useful Gnu option, specified by -c, causes files to be compiled but not linked together into an executable program. The compilation work is saved to a file with the same name as the associated source, but with the suffix .o. We call these *object* files, and they represent compiled sources that have not yet been linked into an executable file. Now, what if a program consists of only a single source? All program files must still be linked with system library functions in order to be executable. In other words, use of -c precludes use of the −o option, but you will want to use the −o option eventually to produce the executable file.

These .o files may be used in other Gnu C++ commands, however. For example, the following four commands produce the same executable myprog as the single command given earlier:

```
$ g++ -c myprog.cpp                    (produces myprog.o)
$ g++ -c myfuncs1.cpp myfuncs2.cpp    (produces myfuncs1.o,
                                                  myfuncs2.o)
$ g++ -o myprog  myprog.o myfuncs1.o myfuncs2.o
```

The last command runs quite quickly because the compilation work has previously been done, and only linking is required to produce myprog. Now suppose a change is made to myfuncs1.cpp. To recompile and rebuild myprog, the following could be used:

```
$ g++ -o myprog myprog.o myfuncs1.cpp myfuncs2.o
```

In this command, the previously compiled versions of two files are used (myprog.o and myfuncs2.o) as is the newly edited source in myfuncs1.cpp. Here the .cpp source file is compiled and then linked to the other two .o files to produce a new myprog.

Notice that header files are not usually listed in **g++** commands. The internal #include lines within source files take care of the appropriate referencing.

B.5 Make files

There is a mechanism under UNIX (comparable to the *project* files of Microsoft Visual C++ discussed in Appendix C) to enable the efficient management of programs consisting of many source files. Rather than manually deciding which Gnu C++ commands must be used and then typing these often long commands each time the executable file must be reconstructed, one can utilize the **make** command or tool. This command has the ability to *run only those g++ commands that are necessary* to rebuild an executable file.

First, a file must be created containing appropriate information concerning the components of the program project. This file is named makefile and contains segments in the following format:

destination_file: *component_files*
              command(s) to create destination_file from component_files

The first line contains the destination file (and a colon) followed by a set of component files. The following line contains the **g++** command that should be used to create the destination file from the component files. There can be as many of these segments as desired. If more than one segment is present, you may think of them as being considered from the bottom up. Each time we use the **make** command, the date associated with the last creation of the destination file (if it exists) is compared with the dates of the component files. If any component file has a more recent date, the command given on the following line is executed. In other words, if any component file has been changed since the destination file was last created, the destination file is rebuilt.

This is actually much simpler than that last paragraph makes it sound! For example, let's return to the myprog executable, which is to be constructed from myprog.cpp, myfuncs1.cpp, and myfuncs2.cpp. Let's also assume that the header file myprog.h is used in the first two source files. Suppose makefile contains the following:

```
myprog:         myprog.o myfuncs1.o  myfuncs2.o
                g++ -o myprog myprog.o myfuncs1.o myfuncs2.o

myprog.o:       myprog.cpp  myprog.h
                g++ -c myprog.cpp

myfuncs1.o:     myfuncs1.cpp myprog.h
                g++ -c myfuncs1.cpp

myfuncs2.o:     myfuncs2.cpp
                g++ -c myfuncs2.cpp
```

Now, to construct the executable file myprog, we *do a make*. Actually, this is an abbreviated phrase for "run the make command":

```
$ make
```

This command causes the following steps to occur as the four sections in the file makefile are examined from the bottom up:

1. Check the date of myfuncs2.o against myfuncs2.cpp. If myfuncs2.cpp is more recent, compile myfuncs2.cpp to create a new myfuncs2.o.

2. Check the date of myfuncs1.o against myfuncs1.cpp and myprog.h. If either component has a more recent date, compile myfuncs1.cpp to create a new myfuncs1.o.

3. Check the date of myprog.o against myprog.cpp and myprog.h. If either component is more recent, compile myprog.cpp to create a new myprog.o.

4. Check the date of myprog against myprog.o, myfuncs1.o, and myfuncs2.o. If any component has a more recent date, relink the three .o files to create a new myprog executable.

Thus, when any of the source or header files of this project are edited or modified, a single **make** command determines which **g++** commands are necessary and runs them. If all the destination files are up-to-date, the **make** has no effect.

If you think about it for just a minute, there are several variations of the preceding makefile that would also work. Consider this one with only one section:

```
myprog:  myprog.cpp myfuncs1.cpp myfuncs2.cpp myprog.h
         g++ -o myprog myprog.cpp myfuncs1.cpp myfuncs2.cpp
```

This single-step makefile will accomplish the correct result, but it isn't very efficient. If any of the components have a newer date than the executable myprog, then *all* the sources are recompiled. It's best to construct a makefile using the strategy demonstrated in the first example. From the bottom up, construct a section to build each .o file from the corresponding .cpp file. At the top, construct a section to build the executable file from the appropriate .o files.

Notice that this example makefile contains .h files as components in some sections. This is not always necessary, but it is a good idea. There are also approaches that can be used to *imply* actions to be done. It is best to avoid these approaches at this point in your career. By getting into the habit of being explicit regarding which component files must be consulted to construct the destination, you will avoid many problems. Once again, header files need not be listed in **g++** commands. The internal #include lines within the source files take care of the appropriate referencing.

What if you have two projects in the same directory? The file utilized by **make** does not actually need to be called makefile; that is just the default. If you give the file another name, such as myprog.make, you should follow the **make** command with a -f option and the file containing the make sections:

```
$ make -f myprog.make
```

There are many other uses for the make command and many other ways to accomplish this result with a makefile, and the mechanism of this simple example will serve you well.

B.6 Gnu debugging

A debugger is a utility that allows one to execute a program in steps or segments while watching what is going on inside, monitoring the values associated with variables to catch a bug as it happens. One of the more common debugger utilities used with Gnu C++ is the Gnu debugger **gdb**. This utility allows you to:

1. Specify locations where your program should pause during execution.
2. Examine (and perhaps change) variables while your program is paused.
3. Continue to the next program pause point.

Prior to using the debugger, the executable program must be compiled and linked using the g++ -g option. This causes the compiler to add important information to the executable file which will be needed by the debugger. The debugger can be invoked with the **gdb** command followed by the name of the executable program. When activated, the debugger prompt usually becomes **(gdb)**. For example, considering the example `myprog` project:

```
$ g++ -g -o myprog myprog.cpp myfuncs1.cpp myfuncs2.cpp
$ gdb myprog
(gdb)
```

There are many different commands that can be used within the debugger, and several good books are available to explain this utility extensively. Fortunately, with just a handful of commands, you can accomplish a great deal. Here are the most commonly used commands. The items within brackets indicate optional information that is not always necessary:

list [*file*:] *line1,line2*	Show source lines from line1 to line2.
break [*file*:] *function*	Set a pause point or *breakpoint* at the top of this function.
break [file:] *line*	Set a pause point at this source line number.
run	Begin execution, pausing at the first pause point.
print *expr*	Display this variable, array, or expression value while paused.
cont	Continue after pausing (to the next pause point).
next	Pause after the next line (after pausing). Step over any function calls in the line.
step	Pause after the next line (after pausing). Step into any function calls in the line.
help	Display a guide of information about commands.
quit	Exit back to UNIX.

You don't need to type an entire command. Type just enough letters so that the debugger can identify your request and differentiate it from others beginning with the same letters. For example, consider the following simple program to sum a list of five integers:

```
//sum.cpp    Sum a list of 5 integers.
#include <iostream.h>

void SumValues (int v[], int& total)
{   int n;
    total = 0;
```

```
      for (n=0; n<5; n++)
          total += v[n];
  }

  void main()
  {   int val[5], n, sum;
      cout << "enter 5 values: ";
      for (n=0; n<4; n++)
          cin >> val[n];
      SumArray (val, sum);
      cout << "sum is: " << sum << endl;
  }
```

The following is an example debug session:

```
$ gdb sum
(gdb) list 1,20
1   //sum.cpp    Sum a list of 5 integers.
2   #include <iostream.h>
3
4   void SumValues (int v[], int& total)
5   {   int n;
6       total = 0;
7       for (n=0; n<5; n++)
8           total += v[n];
9   }
10
11  void main()
12  {   int val[5], n, sum;
13      cout << "enter 5 values: ";
14      for (n=0; n<4; n++)
15          cin >> val[n];
16      SumArray (val, sum);
17      cout << "sum is: " << sum << endl;
18  }
(gdb) break 16
   breakpoint at line 16 in sum.cpp
(gdb) break 8
   breakpoint at line 8 in sum.cpp
(gdb) run
   enter 5 values: 1 2 3 4 5
breakpoint 1 at line 16 in sum.cpp
16      SumArray (val, sum);
(gdb) print n
 =4
(gdb) print val
 = { 1 2 3 4 5 }
(gdb) cont
breakpoint 2 at line 8 in sum.cpp
```

```
8                total += v[n];
(gdb) print total
 = 0
(gdb) cont
breakpoint 2 at line 8 in sum.cpp
(gdb) print total
 = 1
(gdb) cont
breakpoint 2 at line 8 in sum.cpp
(gdb) print total
 = 3
(gdb) cont
breakpoint 2 at line 8 in sum.cpp
(gdb) print total
 = 6
 . . .
```

Notice that when line 8 is reached, the value of total is zero. That is because the program has paused prior to executing this line. When allowed to continue, the debugger will execute this line and any lines that follow until the next break or pause point is reached.

Some implementations of **gdb** may have a few quirks associated with them. For example, it may seem that output does not appear immediately after the execution of a **cout** line. Rather, it appears on the screen much later. You may want to experiment with a few simple programs to become more familiar with the debugger prior to using it with a large project.

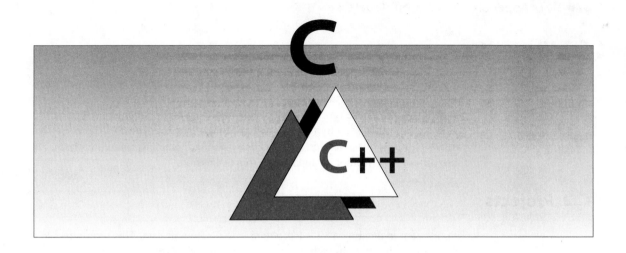

Microsoft Visual C++

The Microsoft Visual C++ program development environment is currently very popular in college computer science courses. Since there is a good chance you will be using Visual C++ (VC++) Version 6.*x*, the basics of using this system are presented here. The purpose is not to provide an exhaustive or definitive user's guide or manual, but simply to get you started. Once you have the basics, you will find you are in a better position to understand the documentation and Help manual pages provided with the system and to explore or experiment with other options and capabilities.

Before the availability of program development environments (PDEs), a student typically needed to deal with a suite of independent programs to write and debug software. An editor was used to input and correct a program source, much like writing a document with a word processor. A separate compiler translated the source into an object form or reported syntax errors. A linker then attached library functions and system resources to produce an executable file. Finally, a separate debugger was used to trace execution during program testing. A student needed to learn the commands and interfaces to each separate program.

A PDE represents the combination of all these activities and operations under a single graphical interface. The interrelation of these activities is the responsibility of the PDE and not the student. A source program can be compiled, linked, and debugged or executed with a simple sequence of mouse clicks. If a syntax error is detected, you can return to editing the source with another simple click.

C.1 Version 6.*x*

There are several popular versions of the VC++ PDE currently in use. We will focus on Version 6.*x*, which at this writing is the currently supported revision. The *x* in 6.*x* can be any digit. These represent minor upgrades that do not change the basic utilization and interface seen by the user and presented in this appendix. There are also various "editions" of a version (professional, standard, student, and enterprise), but those differences will not be apparent in this discussion.

C.2 Projects

The first step in creating a VC++ program is to create a project. This term refers to a collection of files, options, settings, and so on that define your program and how you want to work on it. Think of a project as a directory. In fact, VC++ creates a separate directory for each project. After starting VC++, select File/New from the top menu. This will bring up the New menu. The Projects tab allows you to specify the type of project to be constructed, and there are many choices! We'll start with a simple console program in this discussion (and then introduce a Windows GUI application in the next). Select Win32 Console Application, fill in the correct location, and choose a project name in the fields to the right (Figure C.1). For a simple demonstration, we'll choose a project named "square."

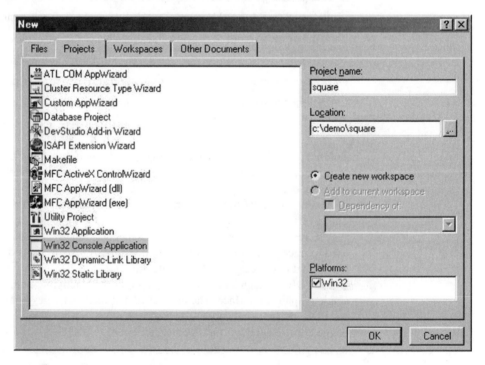

Figure C.1 VC++ project creation

When you click on OK, the VC++ project *wizard* will begin. The wizard is just a sequence of menu options that allows you to specify the type and generic nature of your project. There are several wizards available in VC++, and this one deals with the project itself. Actually, the wizard for a console application only has one menu since the choices are few. On this menu, select "An empty application" and click on Finish.

The first step in learning to use VC++ is to become comfortable with the idea that you don't need to understand it all at first! VC++ is very extensive, intended for far more than simple student programs. Even professional software developers might work years without using or needing all the libraries, tools, wizards, and other features that are available. We'll start with a simple cookbook demonstration that will give you sufficient knowledge to implement, debug, and execute all the programming projects and examples in this text.

You will notice that there are four major areas in the VC++ display (Figure C.2). The top area contains action icons in addition to the basic menus. The leftmost area is called the workspace view and is used to display either a hierarchical list of project files or project classes depending on which tab is selected at the bottom of the display. Select the FileView tab. Notice that VC++ shows three folders for your project files: Source Files, Header Files, and Resource Files. You may open a folder simply by double-clicking on the folder icon if there are any files in the folder to list.

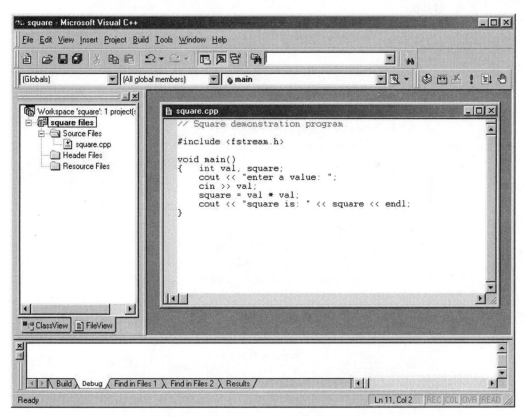

Figure C.2 Visual C++ program development environment display

The rightmost area is used for editing project files. The bottommost area is used by VC++ to display information about what is currently going on. There are five tabs or subsections to this area, but the default selection of Build is adequate for now.

VC++ has now created a number of files on your disk drive under a directory with the same name as your project. One of these files will have the same name as your project and the .dsw extension. This is known as the project workspace file. In future sessions, you may restart VC++ and open your project by double-clicking on this file.

C.3 Program files

A number of general icons are located along the top bar just under the top menu. Each of these icons is associated with a useful task in developing a program. If an icon is not appropriate at the moment, it will appear as a gray shadow.

If you place the mouse cursor over an icon and leave it there for a second, the title or purpose of the icon will be displayed. From left to right, these first seven icons allow:

- New File—create a new text file.
- Open File—open an existing text file.
- Save File—save a file to disk.
- Save Files—save all files to disk.
- Cut—cut a highlighted section of text to the Windows internal clipboard.
- Copy—copy a highlighted section of text to the Windows clipboard.
- Paste—paste the text on the Windows clipboard to the current file.

Create a new text file (using the New File icon) for your program. With the cursor in this new text file, the PDE performs much like a word processor, allowing you to insert, delete, cut, paste, and copy text to write your program. Write the following simple program to calculate the square of a number:

```
#include <fstream.h>
void main()
{   int value, square;
    cout << "enter a value: ";
    cin >> value;
    square = value * value;
    cout << "square is: " << square << endl;
}
```

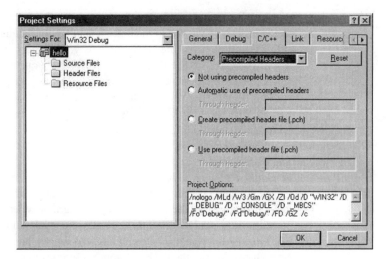

Figure C.3 Turning off the precompiled headers option

Save the file as `square.cpp` using the Save File icon. Now indicate that this is a source file for your program by adding the filename to the Source Files folder in the workspace: Right-click on the Source Files folder and select Add File to Folder. Choose the `square.cpp` file from the list of files presented. If you choose to close the `square.cpp` file, you may reopen it for editing simply by double-clicking on the file in the Source Files folder. If your program uses local header files (this example program does not), you would create these files in the same way, saving them to the Header Files folder. You may ignore the Resource Files folder for now.

The next step is important. VC++ generally uses *precompiled headers*. This allows it to build your program more efficiently, but it adds a level of complexity for you, particularly if you are going to reuse header files from another program. Turn this option off by selecting Project/Settings from the top menu. Click on the project name in the left side of the settings menu, click on the C/C++ tab, and choose Precompiled Headers under the category list. Select "Not using precompiled headers" and click OK to close the window (Figure C.3).

C.4 Building

After writing and editing the file (or files) of a project, you are ready to translate your program source files into an executable file. This step also links in any library routines referenced by the program. This is known as *building*. The following icon bar is very convenient. If this icon bar is not visible on your system, these same operations are available under the top Build menu choice. You may also add this icon bar to your top menus with Build/Customize/BuildMini_Bar.

The Build icon performs the build operation. The system status and any error messages can be viewed in the bottom segment of the display. By default, the executable file will be given the same name as your project and have the .exe extension. It will be placed in the Debug subdirectory of your project directory. The Execute icon can be used to suspend the PDE and execute your program in a separate console window. When your program has finished, the message "Press any key to continue" will appear. The next keypress will close the console window of your program and return you to the PDE.

You may also execute your program outside of the PDE, for example, using the Start/Run choice from the Windows menu. If you execute your program outside of the PDE, the console window will immediately close when termination occurs without presenting the "Press any key to continue" message. This is an important difference to recognize. Consider the earlier example program. When the user enters a number, the program will calculate the square, display the result, and terminate—causing the console window to be closed. This all happens in less than a second, and the user doesn't get a chance to read the result! If your program is to be run outside the PDE, you may wish to add a couple of lines to the bottom to allow the user time to read the result:

```
cout << "Enter 0 to continue";
cin >> value;
}
```

C.5 Debugging

What if your program does not execute according to what you had in mind? The Breakpoint icon can be used to cause your program to suspend at a specific point in execution to allow you to examine the intermediate contents of variables. Place the cursor on a line in the squares.cpp file where you would like the program execution to pause and then click this "hand" icon. The line will be marked with a dot, indicating a *breakpoint*. This time, execute your program using the Go icon instead of the Execute icon. When execution reaches a breakpoint line, the program will pause and the PDE display will change to *debug mode* (Figure C.4).

In this mode, most VC++ systems are configured to display the current source file, the debug icon bar, and a variables window as in Figure C.4. (If this is not the case, these options can be added using the Tools/Customize menu choice at the top.)

The source file shows where the program has been paused: the next line to be executed. The bottom display shows the current values of variables. In this example, note that the breakpoint occurs after the user has entered a value. The variable val contains the entered number (23) while the variable square still contains garbage. The debug icon bar that follows presents the options for further execution.

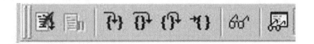

The following icons are very useful:

- Step Into—Execute the current line and pause again. This allows your program to be executed one line at a time.

- Step Over—The same as Step Into, but function calls are treated as a single instruction.

- Stop Debugging—Abandon debugging and return to program editing.

- Break Execution—Immediately pause the program. This is useful if your program enters a loop or never reaches the breakpoints you have set.

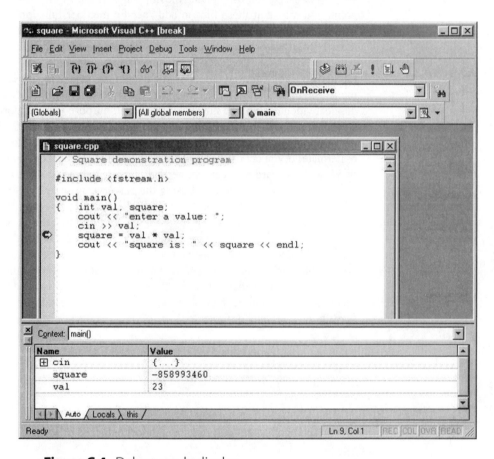

Figure C.4 Debug mode display

C.6 Class support

If your program utilizes classes, VC++ provides excellent support to help you manage your project. Naturally, a class may be added to a project simply by creating the appropriate .cpp and .h files and making them part of the project in the same manner you did for the original .cpp file. You may also use the *class wizard*. Select Insert/New_Class from the top menu. In the class wizard menu, simply choose the appropriate class type, name, and base classes (if any).

For simple programs that do not utilize windows or a GUI, the class type will generally have only one choice: Generic Class. When you click on OK to close the wizard menu, the wizard will automatically write as much of the code as is possible without knowing the purpose of your class. You will see two additional files added to your project in the workspace: a .cpp and a .h file named for your class. The .h file will contain the class definition with default constructor and destructor function shells. The .cpp file will contain the implementations of these two members. At this point, you may edit these files to add specific member functions and variables for your needs. You should also complete the default constructor and destructor if these are needed. If they are not needed, simply leave the empty function shells as they are.

You will notice that the wizard places some unexpected boilerplate code at the top and bottom of the .h file. This serves two purposes. First, it ensures that if you manage to include the .h file multiple times or recursively in other .cpp files, these duplicate includes will be ignored. The second purpose is to support the use of pre-compiled headers. Remember that we turned that option off for simplicity. Generally speaking, one just adds member variables and functions as needed and ignores the boilerplate. If you choose to leave the Precompiled Headers option enabled, it is best to allow the wizard to create all needed classes. Importing class files from another project, which were not created using the class wizard, requires the programmer to add this necessary boilerplate.

When your project includes classes, you will find that the ClassView tab on the workspace is quite helpful. Just as the FileView shows a hierarchy of files in your project, the ClassView tab displays a hierarchy of project classes and members. If you double-click on a class member function, the file containing the function implementation will be opened for editing, and the cursor will be placed at the appropriate function. Nice! Small icon symbols next to each member indicate whether the member is public, private, or protected.

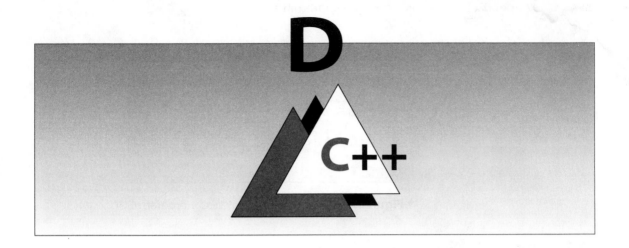

VC++ Windows Programming

The "Visual" part of Visual C++ means that it not only provides the PDE functions mentioned in Appendix C, but will actually write a significant part of your program itself if you choose to have a graphical user interface (GUI). Anytime you use a program that allows the user to operate using mouse click buttons, pull-down menus, or pop-up windows, you are using a GUI. This approach to programming has become the standard, and any competent software developer is expected to produce applications with effective GUIs.

The manual coding of GUIs for the display of buttons, pop-up windows, pull-down menus, and so on is very complex programming. VC++ addresses this problem with a GUI! Using the mouse and menus of options, VC++ (a) allows a developer to lay out an application GUI by dragging and dropping icons and then (b) constructs the code necessary to display and manage the given layout operation. As a result, most of the user interface is written by VC++, and the developer is freed to work on the application programming itself.

The complete coverage of VC++ GUI programming is beyond this text. In fact, such complete coverage may be beyond the printing industry's ability to bind such a large book. This discussion provides a cookbook demonstration of a simple type of very general GUI known as a *dialog*. Using the concepts of this demonstration, a wide variety of programming applications can be constructed.

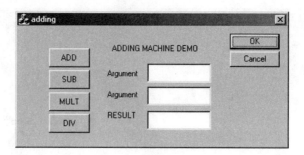

Figure D.1   Demonstration calculator program GUI

D.1 Demonstration

Consider the simple demonstration calculator program in Figure D.1. The user types a number into each of the two Argument boxes and then clicks on one of the four function buttons. The result of the indicated operation appears in the RESULT box. This simple program requires hundreds of C++ code lines, and the executable program is over 105,000 bytes in size. Using VC++, I was able to write this program in about 10 minutes and actually only provided 12 lines of code myself. The rest was added by VC++ wizards. This concept will become clearer as we continue.

Many GUIs utilize the same basic functionality: buttons for operations, labels for annotation, and display boxes where users may input values or values may be displayed. This is known as a single-window dialog GUI. Each button, label, or display box is called a *control*, which may be a poor choice of words, but the purpose will become clearer later on. While there are other types of GUIs, and many programs utilize more than one type, this is a good place to start.

D.2 Project files

The first step in creating a VC++ GUI program is to create the project. Select File/ New in the top menu to bring up the project creation menu. This will bring up a menu. For a Windows GUI program, select MFC AppWizard.exe. MFC stands for Microsoft Foundation Classes, the basic library of classes containing the functionality of GUI operations.

Next, enter a name for your project in the "Project name:" box and change the Location to reflect where on your disk you wish the project directory to be created. Click OK and the project wizard will begin.

A GUI project wizard provides many more options and selections than were seen in Appendix C for simple console programs. Each menu window has four buttons at the bottom:

You may page back and forth through the menu windows with Back and Next buttons until you have made all your choices. The Finish button is chosen last and completes the wizard menus. For this discussion, select only the following options:

- Dialog based
- 3-D controls
- MFC standard
- Yes please (I would like to generate source file comments)
- As a shared DLL (how I would like to use the MFC library)

The last option (shared DLL) may not be presented depending on which edition of VC++ you are using. In that case, the default is exactly the same. When you click on Finish, the wizard writes as much code as is possible for your program without knowing the program's purpose. As mentioned in Appendix C, this is called *boiler-plate*. While the boilerplate for a simple console application is just a few lines, the boilerplate for a Windows GUI may consist of hundreds of fairly confusing C++. Just ignore it for now.

The PDE now presents a skeleton dialog GUI containing three controls (Figure D.2). In the center is a simple label to inform you that this is where additional controls may be added. The first step is to delete this label. Click on it and press the Delete key. In the upper right are two default control buttons: OK and Cancel.

If for some reason you lose track of this dialog GUI layout display, you can always bring it to the front of the display by double-clicking on the GUI icon in the Dialog directory under the Resource tab of the workspace on the left of the PDE display.

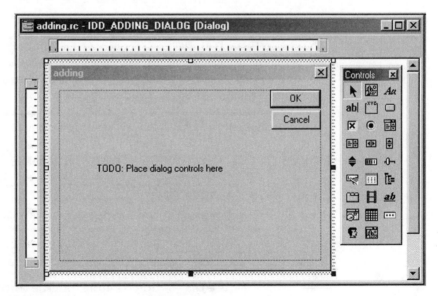

Figure D.2 Calculator program GUI layout workspace

D.3 GUI layout

Appearing now on the PDE display you will find the Controls menu. This is simply a list of currently available controls for your GUI. To lay out the calculator GUI, we simply drag controls from the menu to the skeleton dialog.

Place the cursor on a control for a moment and the name of the control will be displayed. This demo will only be using three of these controls: Static text, Button, and Edit box.

D.3.a Labels

Static text is used for annotation. Drag the Static text control to the GUI and position it at the top. Next (with this control still selected), type text for the label: ADDING MACHINE DEMO. You may resize the label and move it in the standard Windows manner by dragging the box or its edges or corners. Notice that the font does not change when you make the box bigger. In the same manner, add Static text for the two Argument labels and the RESULT label.

D.3.b Buttons

Next, add the buttons. Drag the Button icon to the GUI and size appropriately. With Button still selected, type in new text to replace the default caption so that your button indicates ADD. Now left-click on the button and select Properties to change the default ID or name (Figure D.3). The ID allows you to refer to this button in the program code. The default ID will be IDC_BUTTON1. Most of VC++ boilerplate creates names and IDs with a prefix to attempt to describe the type and use of a name; the IDC prefix stands for IDentification Control. It is generally best to leave this prefix alone. Make the name more meaningful by changing the ending to IDC_BUTTON_ADD. Repeat this same procedure for the four buttons (with similarly meaningful captions and names).

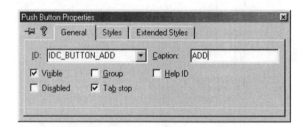

Figure D.3 Button control Properties menu

D.3.c Edit boxes

Finally, add the Edit boxes. Simply drag the Edit box control to the appropriate place and size. Again open the Properties menu for the box and give the ID a more meaningful name. In place of the default IDC_EDIT1, use IDC_EDIT_ARG1. We need to associate a variable with each Edit box. This variable will be used (by the boilerplate code written by VC++) to copy information from (or to) the box to (or from) your program. To associate a variable with an Edit box, again right-click on the control and this time choose the ClassWizard menu option (Figure D.4). Select the Member Variables tab at the top of the window and then select the Edit box ID (IDC_EDIT_ARG1). At the right of the window, choose Add Variable. A subordinate window will pop up asking for the variable's name, category, and type. Again, a prefix is suggested by the wizard for the variable name m_. Complete the name as m_arg1. The Category default should be Value. Select **int** as the Variable type. Repeat this process to associate variables with the IDC_EDIT_ARG2 and IDC_EDIT_RESULT Edit boxes.

At this point, the GUI is complete! You can (and should) build the program and execute it just to ensure that the GUI is correct. The boilerplate code written by the wizard along with the Windows 95/98/NT operating system represents a fully functional GUI with workable buttons and data-editable boxes—pressing the buttons and entering values into the boxes just won't accomplish anything. You can move your GUI around the screen as with other Windows applications. When another window is opened on top of it and then removed, it nicely restores its appearance. (We'll ignore minimizing for now.) Notice that the buttons even change shape when pressed to help the user.

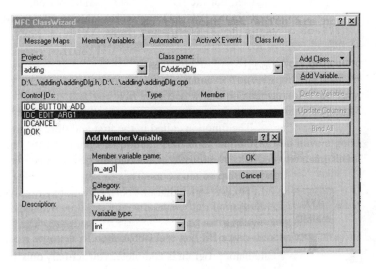

Figure D.4 Associating a variable with an Edit box.

Your program will terminate when you click on OK or CANCEL *or* when you press the Return key after entering a value into an Edit box. Remember this last feature: By default, the user should click on an Edit box to select it and then use the keyboard to enter a value. The Backspace, Del, Insert, and Arrow keys may all be used to help enter a value. After entering the value, use the mouse to select another Edit box or choose a button. The Return key should not be used for this simple demo.

D.4 Message handlers

So far, we have a fully functional GUI, and we haven't written a single line of code. The last step is to associate code with each of the four operator buttons. When writing code for a VC++ GUI, you are *adding* code to the boilerplate provided by the wizards. The simplest way to think of it is as adding functions for a `main()` program written by someone else to call. We need to add four functions with one to be invoked when the user clicks on each of the operator buttons. These functions are known as *message handlers* or *control notification handlers*. Double-clicking on a Button in the GUI layout will cause the wizard to suggest a function name (the suggested defaults are usually fine). Accept the suggested name by clicking on OK, and the wizard will write an empty function and place the cursor within that function for you to edit or complete. There will even be a helpful comment:

```
//TODO: Add your control notification handler code here
```

This is where you place the code to be executed when this Button is pressed by the user. For the IDC_BUTTON_ADD button, the code should add the values currently in the IDC_EDIT_ARG1 and IDC_EDIT_ARG2 boxes and display the value in the IDC_EDIT_RESULT box. Here it is:

```
UpdateData(TRUE);
m_result = m_arg1 + m_arg2;        // add operation
UpdateData(FALSE);
```

The function called in the first and third lines is very useful. When the parameter is the word (system defined constant) **TRUE**, the values in all the Edit boxes are copied into all their associated variables. When the parameter is the word **FALSE**, just the opposite occurs. The associated variables are displayed in their associated Edit boxes. Notice that this performs more work than we need. We only need values copied *from* the first two Argument boxes and then *into* the RESULT box. But no harm done.

Now, if you add similar code to each of the other three operator Buttons, your calculator program is complete. You actually only wrote 12 lines, and 8 of these lines were just calls to `UpdateData()`.

D.5 Windows concepts

What about understanding all the boilerplate code written by the wizard? One significant advantage of using C++ is that it allows a programmer to easily use (or reuse) code written by others without the need to understand that code completely. Don't worry about it for now. However, a couple of concepts may be interesting at this point, but not necessary. The following discussion is somewhat simplified, but a good foundation.

In a simple console application, the operating system passes control to `main()`, which subsequently controls the execution of the program. You may have noticed that there is no `main()` in the boilerplate code of the preceding example. In a sense, the Windows operating system is the `main()` program, and each application is simply added or linked into it. The basic concept of Windows applications is that the program is controlled by *events*. Some basic events are a keystroke, a mouse click on a button, or resizing a window. An event is defined by an action and the location of that action. A notification handler (or event handler) is simply a function that is to be called when the event occurs. To add an event handler, the function not only needs to be written, but the handler needs to be registered. In other words, the operating system needs to be told which handler to call for each event (or set of events).

When an event occurs, the operating system looks in a table of registered event handlers and invokes the correct one. If no handler is registered for an event, the event is ignored. For example, when your calculator program is covered by another window, the calculator GUI is overwritten on the screen. When the calculator GUI is uncovered (an event), the event handler `OnPaint()` is invoked to repaint the GUI on the screen. Notice that the boilerplate of your calculator contains such a function. If it did not, the uncover event would be ignored and your calculator would not be redisplayed.

There are literally hundreds of events that can be handled for a Windows application, giving the program a great deal of diversity and flexibility in GUI design. Some are quite standard and can be provided by the wizards, such as the `On-Paint()` handler. Others are specific to a particular application, such as your **ADD** Button handler. Writing a Windows application is a matter of writing event handlers and registering them. The detection of events and the calling of event handlers are usually standard and may not change between sets of applications. The details of this boilerplate are quite complex.

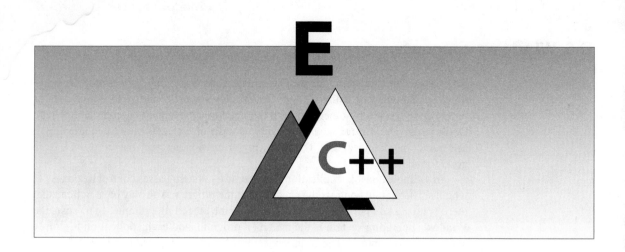

ASCII Codes

ASCII table of characters and associated codes

char.	dec.	hex.	char.	dec.	hex.	char.	dec.	hex.
NUL	0	00	+	43	2B	V	86	56
SOH	1	01	,	44	2C	W	87	57
STX	2	02	–	45	2D	X	88	58
ETX	3	03	.	46	2E	Y	89	59
EOT	4	04	/	47	2F	Z	90	5A
ENQ	5	05	0	48	30	[	91	5B
ACK	6	06	1	49	31	\	92	5C
BEL	7	07	2	50	32	]	93	5D
BS	8	08	3	51	33	^	94	5E
HT	9	09	4	52	34	_	95	5F
NL	10	0A	5	53	35	`	96	60
VT	11	0B	6	54	36	a	97	61
NP	12	0C	7	55	37	b	98	62
CR	13	0D	8	56	38	c	99	63
SO	14	0E	9	57	39	d	100	64
SI	15	0F	:	58	3A	e	101	65
DLE	16	10	;	59	3B	f	102	66
DC1	17	11	<	60	3C	g	103	67
DC2	18	12	=	61	3D	h	104	68
DC3	19	13	>	62	3E	i	105	69
DC4	20	14	?	63	3F	j	106	6A

Continued

ASCII table of characters and associated codes (continued)

char.	dec.	hex.	char.	dec.	hex.	char.	dec.	hex.
NAK	21	15	@	64	40	k	107	6B
SYN	22	16	A	65	41	l	108	6C
ETB	23	17	B	66	42	m	109	6D
CAN	24	18	C	67	43	n	110	6E
EM	25	19	D	68	44	o	111	6F
SUB	26	1A	E	69	45	p	112	70
ESC	27	1B	F	70	46	q	113	71
FS	28	1C	G	71	47	r	114	72
GS	29	1D	H	72	48	s	115	73
RS	30	1E	I	73	49	t	116	74
US	31	1F	J	74	4A	u	117	75
space	32	20	K	75	4B	v	118	76
!	33	21	L	76	4C	w	119	77
"	34	22	M	77	4D	x	120	78
#	35	23	N	78	4E	y	121	79
$	36	24	O	79	4F	z	122	7A
%	37	25	P	80	50	{	123	7B
&	38	26	Q	81	51			124	7C
'	39	27	R	82	52	}	125	7D
(	40	28	S	83	53	~	126	7E
)	41	29	T	84	54	DEL	127	7F
*	42	2A	U	85	55			

Answers to Odd-Numbered Questions

The following are possible answers to odd-numbered short answer questions 1–19 of each chapter. In some cases, there may be more than one correct answer. This is particularly true for code designs and code fragments. These answers should help you determine if you correctly understand the concepts associated with a question.

F.1 Chapter 1

1. volatile
3. declaration
5. literal
7. A syntax error represents an illegal statement. A semantic error is an error in logic. Using a variable that has not been declared is a syntax error. Dividing by 2 when you should have divided by 3 is a semantic error.
9. (a) input, (b) output, (c) input, (d) output
11. (a) `new_car_cost`, (b) `yards_gained`, (c) root of distance, (d) `ave_score`, (e) `payoff_time`

13. `x = ((a * y * y + 3) / (4 - a)) * 3.14;`

15. it doesn't matter

17. The compiler does not know your intent. The incorrect formula may be a logic error, but it nevertheless may be valid C++ statements.

19. Reserved words: `float`, `main`, `void`. Other words that should not be used for variables or other purposes are `cout`, `cin`, and `endl`.

F.2 Chapter 2

1. condition

3. definite or counted loop

5. before

7. indefinite loop

9. (a) false, (b) true, (c) true, (d) false, (e) true

11. (a) –1, (b) 999, (c) –1, (d) –9999 (assuming no bank would ever allow an account with such a negative balance!)

13. (a)
```
if (cost < 0.0)
      cout << "yes";
   else ;
```
(b)
```
if (cost > 0.0)
      if (cost <= 100.0)
          cout << "yes";
       else;
   else;
```

15.
```
count = 0.0;
sum = 0.0;
while (count < 25.0)
{  cin >> value;
   sum = sum + value;
   count = count + 1.0;
}
```

17. (a) The condition is not enclosed in parentheses.

    (b) The block of statements within the condition is not enclosed in braces.

19.
```
if (age < 100.0)
    if (age > 25.0)
        cout << "yes";
    else
        cout << "no";
else
    cout << "no";
```

F.3 Chapter 3

1. argument
3. Arguments are values or variables passed to a function. These values are represented inside the function as parameters.
5. standard library
7. `float`
9. at the top of the file prior to **main**
11. `x = sqrt(distance);`
13. The variable `cost` is a parameter—it cannot also be a simple variable.
15. `monthly_payment = Payment (52.0, 0.009);`
17. `SomeFuncB()` should come before `SomeFuncA()`
19. `#include <math.h>`

F.4 Chapter 4

1. analysis, design, coding, testing, and maintenance
3. In the analysis stage, the programmer defines the purpose and goals of the program. A budget and schedule are also defined.
5. coding
7. In the maintenance stage, features are modified, enhanced, or added to meet the evolving needs and requirements of the client.
9. (a) calculation, (b) condition, (c) counted loop, (d) counted loop, (e) indefinite loop, (f) indefinite loop
11. *get the hours and rate values from the user*
    if (hours > 40.0)
    { *calculate and output pay based on overtime formula*
    }
    else
    { *calculate and output pay based on no-overtime formula*
    }
13. *initialize the count and running sum to zero*
    prompt user and get the first number in the list
    while (number > 0.0)
        { *add number to running sum*
            add 1 to the count of numbers processed
            get the next number
        }
        calculate the average
        output the sum and average

15. *prompt the user and get the hours and rate values*
```
if (hours <= 40.0)
{    calculate pay based on standard formula
}
else
{    calculate pay based on one of two appropriate overtime formulas
}
```
output pay calculated

17. *output table heading*
```
N = 1.0;
while (N <= 5.0)
{    calculate and output powers 2, 3, 4, 5, and 6 of this value of N
     N = N + 1.0;
}
```

19. *prompt user and get number of apple boxes and cost per box*
calculate order cost
```
if (order_cost > 1000.00)
{    reduce order cost by 5%
}
```
output order cost

F.5 Chapter 5

1. arguments

3. prototype

5. An `ASSUMPTION` comment statement is placed at the top of a function indicating assumptions that must be true if the function is to perform correctly. These assumptions can be verified during execution as an aid to debugging.

7. Code reuse simplifies the development and debugging of a new program and decreases the time and cost.

9. `float GetValueBetween (float min, float max);`

11. literal, expression, and **const** identifier

13. When a function is intended to modify an argument, a reference parameter should be used. If a function only needs to examine an argument, a reference parameter should not be used.

15. Testing a program with hand-calculated data may not allow a developer to identify all program bugs because all possible sets of input data may not be tried.

17. Stubs allow a developer to test the structure and actions of the main program (or other calling function) prior to adding details of the called function. This simplifies debugging since fewer details must be tested and examined during a debugging session.

19. `fstream.h`

F.6 Chapter 6

1. `int`
3. 3.0
5. The comma is not allowed.
7. Arguments must match parameters in type and number.
9. white spaces
11. (a) 13, (b) 0, (c) 1, (d) 1
13. (a) 5.76E-6
    (b) 5.76E11
15. When multiplying or adding two large values, the result may be too large to fit into the appropriate type, and overflow will occur.
17. ```
    int y;
    y = x; // truncate the value of x to a whole number
    if (x == y) ...
    ```
19. Z, [, \,], ^, -, ', a, and b

F.7 Chapter 7

1. braces { }
3. nonzero
5. || operator
7. ten lines (for each value of *n* from 0 to 9)
9. the second (*expression₂*) and third (*expression₃*)


11. ```
    0,  0
    0,  1
    0,  2
    0,  3
    0,  4
    1,  1
    1,  2
    1,  3
    1,  4
    2,  2
    2,  3
    2,  4
    3,  3
    3,  4
    4,  4
    ```
13. (a) true, (b) false, (c) true
15. **int, char**

17. The default case is executed if no other case matches the **switch** variable.

19. (a) a++, (b) b*=2, (c) c+= (a++)

F.8 Chapter 8

1. (a) `grades.dat`, (b) `address.dat`, (c) `temp.txt`, (d) `curbal.dat`

3. `.exe`

5. file variable

7. << is the insertion operator; >> is the extraction operator

9. `precision()`

11. class

13. `fstream infile ("b:\\accounts\payroll.dat", ios::in);`
15. `fstreaminfile; infile.open ("b:\\accounts\payroll.dat", ios::in);`

17. `cout.precision(5);   cout.width(10);`

19. (a) 7777, (b) 7777 preceded by four blanks, (c) 876.5432, (d) 0.0000,
(e) 1234500000.0000

F.9 Chapter 9

1. string

3. white space

5. concatenation (the + operator)

7. dot

9. Two equal strings must be the same length and contain the same characters (of the same case).

11. (a) okay, (b) okay, (c) a string cannot be assigned an integer, (d) a string cannot be assigned a single character, (e) okay

13. `<string>` (or in some systems `<string.h>`)

15. a string of 95 characters terminated by a NULL character

17. Yes, if it is enclosed in quotes to convert it into a string of length 1 (see answer 11(d))

19. (a) okay, (b) okay—the string will be assigned this sequence of digit characters, (c) okay—the file represented by the string value will be opened.

F.10 Chapter 10

1. (a) `int x[10]`
(b) `float y[5] = {5.6, 7.8, 9.1, 2.3, 4.5};`   (the array size 5
(c) `char z[12] = "hello world";`   could be left out)
    or `char z[] = "hello world";`
    or `char z[] = {'h', 'e', 'l', 'l', 'o', ' ', 'w', 'o', 'r',`
                    `'l', 'd',   '\0'};`

3. index or subscript

5. ordinal

7. 0

9. Having an array index go out-of-bounds and forgetting that array indexes begin at 0 are two common errors.

11. `for (n=0; n<19; n++)`
`        cout << values[n];`

13. `for (n=0; n<19; n++)`
`         sum += values[n];`

15. `void SomeFunc (int x[ ]):`

17. The second is not automatically terminated with a NULL character.

19. `float percent[2][3] = {{0.13, 0.52, 0.35}, {0.26, 0.54, 0.20}};`
or `float percent[3][2] = {{0.13, 0.26}, {0.52, 0.54}, {0.35, 0.20}};`

F.11 Chapter 11

1. legal

3. Fred Jones F s

5. 5 (the index of `"Smith"` within the name)

7. `cout << sentence.length();`

9. `cout << sentence.find(' ', 0);`

11. `char x[11];`

13. The string and the automatically added NULL character are nine characters long—too long for the array of eight cells.

15. `strcpy()`

17. The `==` comparison operator does not compare the *contents* of the two `char` arrays by default.

19. `if (strcmp(word1, word2) < 0)`
`       cout << "less";`

F.12 Chapter 12

1. object-oriented programming

3. polymorphism

5. application interface

7. `person` is the object, `Getname()` is the public member function

9. The : : is most commonly used in the implementation of class member functions in the class .cpp file. Each member function name is preceded by : : to associate it with the class.

11. a semicolon

13. A constructor may not be explicitly called—it is automatically invoked when a class object is declared.

15. There are many member functions that could be included. Here are the obvious ones:

```
class Course
{public:  void AddName (string thisname);    // add a new student
          void RemoveName (string thisname);// remove a student
          int GetLocation ();                // return the location code
          void SetLocation ();               // change the location
          string GetTeacher ();              // return teacher's name
          void SetTeacher (string thisname);// change teacher's name
private:  string students[50], teacher;
          int location;
};
```

17. in the public section: `float Magnitude ();`

19. in the public section: `Complex operator= (int a);`

F.13 Chapter 13

1. At least one application of the rule toward a trivial problem must not be recursive. A recursive application of the rule should be applied toward a simpler problem.

3. call tree

5. public

7. `if-else`

9. No to both statements. However, there are problems for which one method will result in perhaps a simpler program to write and implement.

11. If this string is nonempty:

   (a) output the first character if the string parameter is passed to this function

   (b) call this same function and pass it the rest of the string

   otherwise, return

13.

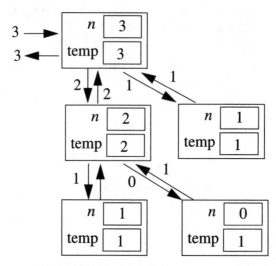

15. It would require eight comparisons—starting with 64 and dividing the number in half successively will produce a single name in eight steps.

17. Ten recursive calls can be avoided

```
int Fib (int n)
{   int temp;
    if (n <= 1)
        temp = 1;
    else if (n == 2)
        return 2;
    else if (n == 3)
        return 3;
    else
        return (Fib(n-1) + Fib(n-2);)
}
```

19.

name: Carl		name: Carl		name: Carl
first: 0	→	first: 0	→	first: 2
last: 9		last: 3		last: 3
mid: 4	←	mid: 1	←	mid: 2
found: 2	2	found: 2	2	found: 2

← 2

F.14 Chapter 14

1. casting

3. asterisk

5. deep

7. (a) 7A, (b) 3F, (c) B1, (d) C7

9. (a) 256, (b) 7, (c) 32,675, (d) –28,656, (e) –1

11. `extern float maximum;`

13. `static` variables are not automatically deallocated when the function in which they are declared exits.

15. `e = new char[50];`

17. `delete [] e;`

19. ```
class BranchOffice
{ ...
   private:int manager, count, *employees;
};
```
```

Index